Jaguar Books on Latin Ar

D0846746

Series Editors

WILLIAM H. BEEZLEY, Professor of History, University of Arizona
COLIN M. MACLACHLAN, John Christy Barr Distinguished Professor of
History, Tulane University

Volumes Published

John E. Kicza, ed., *The Indian in Latin American History: Resistance,
Resilience, and Acculturation* (1993; rev. ed., 2000).
Cloth ISBN 0-8420-2822-6 Paper ISBN 0-8420-2823-4

Susan E. Place, ed., *Tropical Rainforests: Latin American Nature and
Society in Transition* (1993). Cloth ISBN 0-8420-2423-9
Paper ISBN 0-8420-2427-1

Paul W. Drake, ed., *Money Doctors, Foreign Debts, and Economic
Reforms in Latin America from the 1890s to the Present* (1994).
Cloth ISBN 0-8420-2434-4   Paper ISBN 0-8420-2435-2

John A. Britton, ed., *Molding the Hearts and Minds: Education,
Communications, and Social Change in Latin America* (1994).
Cloth ISBN 0-8420-2489-1   Paper ISBN 0-8420-2490-5

David J. Weber and Jane M. Rausch, eds., *Where Cultures Meet: Frontiers
in Latin American History* (1994). Cloth ISBN 0-8420-2477-8
Paper ISBN 0-8420-2478-6

Gertrude M. Yeager, ed., *Confronting Change, Challenging Tradition:
Women in Latin American History* (1994). Cloth ISBN 0-8420-2479-4
Paper ISBN 0-8420-2480-8

Linda Alexander Rodríguez, ed., *Rank and Privilege: The Military and
Society in Latin America* (1994). Cloth ISBN 0-8420-2432-8
Paper ISBN 0-8420-2433-6

Darién J. Davis, ed., *Slavery and Beyond: The African Impact on Latin
America and the Caribbean* (1995). Cloth ISBN 0-8420-2484-0
Paper ISBN 0-8420-2485-9

Gilbert M. Joseph and Mark D. Szuchman, eds., *I Saw a City Invincible:
Urban Portraits of Latin America* (1996). Cloth ISBN 0-8420-2495-6
Paper ISBN 0-8420-2496-4

Roderic Ai Camp, ed., *Democracy in Latin America: Patterns and Cycles* (1996). Cloth ISBN 0-8420-2512-X   Paper ISBN 0-8420-2513-8

Oscar J. Martínez, ed., *U.S.-Mexico Borderlands: Historical and Contemporary Perspectives* (1996). Cloth ISBN 0-8420-2446-8 Paper ISBN 0-8420-2447-6

William O. Walker III, ed., *Drugs in the Western Hemisphere: An Odyssey of Cultures in Conflict* (1996). Cloth ISBN 0-8420-2422-0 Paper ISBN 0-8420-2426-3

Richard R. Cole, ed., *Communication in Latin America: Journalism, Mass Media, and Society* (1996). Cloth ISBN 0-8420-2558-8 Paper ISBN 0-8420-2559-6

David G. Gutiérrez, ed., *Between Two Worlds: Mexican Immigrants in the United States* (1996). Cloth ISBN 0-8420-2473-5 Paper ISBN 0-8420-2474-3

Lynne Phillips, ed., *The Third Wave of Modernization in Latin America: Cultural Perspectives on Neoliberalism* (1998). Cloth ISBN 0-8420-2606-1   Paper ISBN 0-8420-2608-8

Daniel Castro, ed., *Revolution and Revolutionaries: Guerrilla Movements in Latin America* (1999). Cloth ISBN 0-8420-2625-8 Paper ISBN 0-8420-2626-6

Virginia Garrard-Burnett, ed., *On Earth as It Is in Heaven: Religion in Modern Latin America* (2000). Cloth ISBN 0-8420-2584-7 Paper ISBN 0-8420-2585-5

Carlos A. Aguirre and Robert Buffington, eds., *Reconstructing Criminality in Latin America* (2000). Cloth ISBN 0-8420-2620-7 Paper ISBN 0-8420-2621-5

Christon I. Archer, ed., *The Wars of Independence in Spanish America* (2000). Cloth ISBN 0-8420-2468-9   Paper ISBN 0-8420-2469-7

John F. Schwaller, ed., *The Church in Colonial Latin America* (2000). Cloth ISBN 0-8420-2703-3   Paper ISBN 0-8420-2704-1

Ingrid E. Fey and Karen Racine, eds., *Strange Pilgrimages: Exile, Travel, and National Identity in Latin America, 1800–1990s* (2000). Cloth ISBN 0-8420-2693-2   Paper ISBN 0-8420-2694-0

Reconstructing
Criminality
in Latin America

Reconstructing Criminality in Latin America

Carlos A. Aguirre and Robert Buffington
Editors

Jaguar Books on Latin America
Number 19

A Scholarly Resources Inc. Imprint
Wilmington, Delaware

© 2000 by Scholarly Resources Inc.
All rights reserved
First published 2000
Printed and bound in the United States of America

Scholarly Resources Inc.
104 Greenhill Avenue
Wilmington, DE 19805-1897
www.scholarly.com

Library of Congress Cataloging-in-Publication Data

Reconstructing criminality in Latin America / Carlos A. Aguirre and
    Robert Buffington, editors.
        p.   cm. — (Jaguar books on Latin America ; no. 19)
    Includes bibliographical references.
        ISBN 0-8420-2620-7 (cloth : alk. paper). — ISBN 0-8420-2621-5
(pbk. : alk. paper)
        1. Crime—Latin America. 2. Criminal justice, Administration of—
Latin America. I. Aguirre, Carlos, 1958–   . II. Buffington, Robert,
1952–   . III. Series.
HV6810.5.R43   2000
364.98—dc21   99-41036
                                                                              CIP

♾ The paper used in this publication meets the minimum requirements of
the American National Standard for permanence of paper for printed library materials, Z39.48, 1984.

Acknowledgments

We gratefully acknowledge the support, enthusiasm, patience, and excellent advice of the Jaguar series general editors, William Beezley and Colin MacLachan. This volume was their idea. We also thank Donna Guy for her crucial support, especially in the planning phase of this project. And for their cheerful competence with some of the most tedious details, we thank Norma Koetter, Rachel Green, Kari Malecek, and the rest of the History Department staff at St. John's University.

About the Editors

CARLOS A. AGUIRRE is an assistant professor of Latin American history at the University of Oregon. He is the author of *Agentes de su propia libertad: Los esclavos de Lima y la desintegración de la esclavitud, 1821–1854* (1993), and co-editor, with Charles Walker, of *Bandoleros, abigeos y montoneros* (1990) and, with Ricardo Salvatore, of *The Birth of the Penitentiary in Latin America* (1996). Between 1990 and 1996, he was a MacArthur Fellow at the University of Minnesota, and has received grants from the Harry Frank Guggenheim Foundation, the American Philosophical Society, and the John Simon Guggenheim Foundation. He is currently completing a book on the history of prisons in Lima between 1860 and 1930.

ROBERT BUFFINGTON is an assistant professor of Latin American history at Bowling Green State University. He has published articles on crime, criminality, and sexual deviance in Mexico. He is the author of *Criminal and Citizen in Modern Mexico* (2000). His current research explores the "sentimental education" of Mexico's popular classes.

Contents

Introduction: Conceptualizing Criminality in Latin America

Robert Buffington

Titles are a tricky business. Too often they are chosen in haste with more than seemly attention and given a catchy phrase à la mode. Our title—chosen in the hall between sessions at a Latin American Studies Association annual meeting—was no exception. As the cognoscente probably suspect, the inspiration came directly from Martin J. Wiener's excellent *Reconstructing the Criminal: Culture, Law, and Policy in England, 1830–1914* even though we knew then that this volume would bear only a passing (if suggestive) resemblance to its namesake. To make matters worse, the choice was both hurried and uninformed since, at that time, we had only a vague notion of which essays the volume would come to include. Still, the title sounded good and so we kept it. At least for the time being.

Later—articles chosen, consciences pricked, minds focused—we reconsidered. To our surprise, the title still worked despite its undistinguished selection process. Once assembled, it turned out that all the collected essays addressed, albeit very differently, the social construction of crime, criminals, and criminality in Latin America—the way in which different Latin American societies at different times in their respective histories viewed, described, defined, and reacted to "criminal" behavior. Like Wiener, we chose "reconstruction" over "construction" to acknowledge that concerns about criminality were not voiced (or constructed) in a vacuum but developed in social, cultural, and historical context. Writing from his Fascist prison cell, Antonio Gramsci argued that political ideologies, rather than developing new ideas, rearticulate old ones; in effect pouring old wine into new bottles.[1] We would argue that the same process informs the reconstruction of criminality. For us (Wiener stops at 1914), the gerund "reconstructing" reflects the uneven, incomplete, ongoing nature of the reconstruction process—indeed, for Latin America a discernable end is not yet in sight. One slight deviation: we have preferred "criminality" in order to stress the constructed, categorical nature of "the criminal" which is present but ambiguous in Wiener's English usage (although not in the Spanish *lo criminal*).

Our title's claim to represent "Latin America" needs justification as well. With some distinguished exceptions, research on crime in Latin America is still in its infancy. Only two of these essays (Michael C. Scardaville and Alma Guillermoprieto's) have been previously published in English and only one (Pablo Piccato's) in Spanish. Under the circumstances, spotty coverage of the region is unavoidable, if regrettable. For this reason too, Mexico and Argentina are overrepresented because the bulk of the research on crime is being done by historians of these countries. In spite of this obvious limitation, we believe that the themes and trends presented in these essays have regional application. We do, however, acknowledge the dangers of facile generalization. Economic historians in the 1970s made a cottage industry out of dependency theory; the devastating impact of neoliberal economics offers them similar opportunities in the 1990s. But they suffered inevitable and often justified criticism for daring a regional analysis in the face of Latin America's undeniable diversity. Nevertheless, most scholars would agree that these attempts were and will continue to be more useful than not. We hope our attempt is equally so.

Effective regional periodization is the thorniest problem of all. Again, this is especially true for Latin America, where historical and cultural differences between Argentina, Brazil, Colombia, Peru, and Mexico are much greater than among other ex-colonial societies like Australia, Canada, and the United States (although probably not India, Zimbabwe, and Jamaica). Nevertheless, we can—like dependency theorists before us—sketch in the broad outlines of a Latin American reconstruction of criminality. In fact, the projects are directly related. As Colin MacLachlan demonstrates in *Spain's Empire in the New World*, colonial and neocolonial relationships can never be just economic but must also include the ongoing transmission of an entire cultural matrix that links economic structures to systems of political and social control.[2] Thus, understanding the Western European (and to a lesser extent North American) connection is crucial to any attempt to periodize the reconstruction of criminality in Latin America. More to the point, while the jury is still out on the historical origins, causes, and local applications of the "reconstruction" process, for Western Europe at least, there is some consensus as to general historical trends.

Most scholars agree on the broad historical context for modern attempts at social engineering: the expansion of capitalist relations of production, the consolidation of bourgeois political hegemony, the rise of modern nation-states. Historically oriented social theorists as different (even antagonistic) as Michel Foucault and Jürgen Habermas, to cite only the most influential, have argued for a profound epistemological shift in European notions of political authority and social control that began with the eighteenth century's Age of Enlightenment. For our purposes, their different approaches provide useful and complementary insights into Enlightenment-inspired social reconstruction.[3] As the essays that follow make clear, at some fundamental level the contested theoretical field mirrors the complex, confused, and even contradictory nature of the historical "reality."

With deep intellectual roots in Marxist theory, Habermas not surprisingly grounds post-Enlightenment social engineering in sociological and historical processes. "The concept of modernization," he informs us, "refers to a bundle of processes that are cumulative and mutually reinforcing: to the formation of capital and the mobilization of resources; to the development of the forces of production and the increase in the productivity of labor; to the establishment of centralized political power and the formation of national identities; to the proliferation of the rights of political participation, of urban forms of life, and of formal schooling; to the secularization of values and norms; and so on."[4] Bound up in these political, economic, and social changes was a radically new model of "bourgeois" politics that rejected established political authority—especially the symbolic person of the monarch—for an impersonal, "rational" authority mediated by private individuals operating freely in the newly developed "public sphere."[5] This decisive shift in the fundamental nature of authority demanded new forms of legitimation, which in turn required new ideologies and technologies of social control based on reconstructed notions of citizenship and criminality.

Once reconstructed, however, these notions were "naturalized" and thus removed from public contestation. In the late seventeenth- and early eighteenth-century *liberal* capitalist phase, political theorists had linked legitimation to marketplace metaphors of free exchange whether of commodities or ideas. With the *advanced* capitalist phase beginning in the late nineteenth century, a depoliticized, technocratic society gradually replaced the historically-contingent bourgeois public sphere. "The quasi-autonomous progress of science and technology," Habermas insists, "then appears as an independent variable on which the most important single system variable, namely economic growth, depends. Thus arises a perspective in which the development of the social system *seems* to be determined by the logic of scientific-technical progress . . . [and] the process of democratic decision-making about practical problems loses its function and 'must' be replaced by plebiscitary decisions about alternative sets of leaders of administrative personnel."[6] Habermas thus divides the post-Enlightenment historical field into two parts: the first characterized by public debate (at least among the bourgeoisie) about the goals and methods of social reconstruction, the second by top-down, technocratic social engineering.

Foucault's causation and periodization are similar although, as a philosopher of language, he emphasizes the discursive-imaginative aspects of the Enlightenment epistemological shift: "In the eighteenth century, the development of demographics, of urban structures, of the problem of industrial labor, had raised in biological and medical terms the question of human 'populations,' with their conditions of existence, of habitation, of nutrition, with their birth and mortality rate, with their pathological phenomena. . . . The social 'body' ceased to be a simple juridico-political metaphor . . . and became a biological reality and a field for medical intervention."[7] Not surprisingly perhaps, this medicalized discourse (and perception) encouraged and indeed shaped a general reconstruction of crime and punishment determined, as Habermas would have it, by the "logic of scientific-technical progress." In the dramatic introduction to *Discipline and Punish: The Birth of the Prison* for example, Foucault juxtaposes a shockingly graphic description of the *public* drawing and quartering of the regicide Damiens and an absurdly bland *private* prison timetable written eighty years later. He argues that the discursive-cognitive shift that occurred in the years between these two cultural artifacts reflected a redistribution of "the *entire* economy of punishment" from public spectacles that demonstrated the power of political authority (that is, the king) to an impersonal carceral system that disguised its disciplinary mechanisms (and will to power) behind a facade of "scientifico-legal" knowledge.[8] The ultimate result, he concludes, is a microphysics of power that:

> presupposes that the power exercised on the body is conceived not as property, but as a strategy, that its effects of domination are attributed not to 'appropriation', but to dispositions, manoeuvres, tactics, techniques, functionings. . . . In short, this power is exercised rather than possessed; it is not the 'privilege', acquired or preserved, of the dominant class, but the overall effect of its strategic positions. . . . Furthermore, this power is not exercised simply as an obligation or a prohibition on those who 'do not have it'; it invests them, is transmitted by them and through them; it exerts pressure upon them, just as they themselves, in their struggle against it, resist the grip it has on them.[9]

In other words, as Foucault sees it, the modern subject simultaneously perpetuates and resists the carceral system that constituted it in the first place.

So, although he might agree with Habermas about the causes and effects of the epistemological shift, there are important interpretive differences. In particular, Foucault's periodization differs from Habermas's because he evinces little interest in the brief emergence of a public sphere that is quickly if tragically overcome by the will to knowledge/power of technocratic elites. Thus his explanation examines the germination, growth, and flowering of the ideologically-charged seeds of a naturalizing social science that over the course of the nineteenth and twentieth centuries sent its deep and hidden roots into every nook and cranny of modern society (including the "individual" subject). The fundamental difference here is teleological: for Habermas, in spite of its many flaws, the Enlightenment project provides a model—the bourgeois public sphere—for liberation; for Foucault, in spite of its many merits, it produces a model—the carceral system—for repression.

But what does all this mean for the periodization of Latin American reconstructions of criminality? Quite a bit, as it turns out.

For one thing, as Benedict Anderson notes, Latin Americans were the "Creole pioneers" of modern nationalism, one of the driving forces behind post-Enlightenment social reconstruction.[10] So, although most of Latin America at independence (1810–1821 in most of Spanish America, 1824 in Brazil, 1898 in Cuba and Puerto Rico) lagged behind Western Europe and the United States in several sociological characteristics that Habermas and Foucault associate with modernization—capital formation, incipient industrialization, free wage labor, etc.—Latin American elites nevertheless participated (participate) enthusiastically in the debate it engendered and sought (seek) to reconstruct their societies in its image.

For another, the timing makes sense. In the late eighteenth century, inspired by Enlightenment efforts to rationalize human societies, Bourbon reformers in Spain sought to impose political, economic, social, and cognitive order on their Latin American colonies. "The state," MacLachlan tells us, "motivated by a goal-directed ideology, theoretically had to be an active and rigid enforcer."[11] Attempts to explain and regulate crime and criminality as potent symbols of social dysfunction (metaphoric irrationality) were logically at the forefront of this project. Sometimes these attempts worked, frequently they did not. But once begun, the process was inexorable. In metropolitan centers like Mexico City for example, social control efforts had a significant if not always decisive impact (see Michael Scardaville's essay in this volume); this was not the case in peripheral Arequipa (Sarah Chambers). Either way, the initial steps in the post-Enlightenment reconstruction of crime in Latin America had been taken by the end of the eighteenth century. The pace accelerated in the years following independence. The elite gaze focused first on lower-class men and the restoration of order to urban streets and the rural countryside (Richard Warren, Ricardo Salvatore, Pablo Piccato). As in Habermas's liberal capitalist phase, these interventions were hotly contested, at least within the bourgeois public sphere (Warren), and often resisted by their intended targets as well as local elites concerned about the usurpation of their prerogatives—traditional or newly acquired—by centralizing national governments (Salvatore).

By the end of the nineteenth century, with the gradual rise of an increasingly centralized and technocratic state, that gaze had begun to fracture and intensify as it envisioned the more specific criminalities of blacks (Thomas Holloway), women (Kristin Ruggiero), street vendors and beggars (Piccato), prostitutes (Katherine Bliss), political dissidents (Laura Kalmanowiecki), and narco-traffickers and gangs (Alma Guillermoprieto). In this "advanced capitalist" phase, as both Habermas and Foucault agree, scientifically trained specialists—criminologists, penologists, psychiatrists—dominated the discursive terrain, inhibiting if not totally closing off public debate (Ruggiero, Piccato). Modernization, while it has generally strengthened state power in Latin America, has not always resulted in more open societies.

Nevertheless, this unrequited love affair with modernization is crucial to understanding the continued obsession with post-Enlightenment social reconstruction. As Habermas rightly suggests, the promises of modernity—including the ideal of a truly democratic public sphere—represent the heart of the Enlightenment project. Following the lead of Marxist theorists like Gramsci, recent historians of Latin America have stressed the "hegemonic" character of capitalist society, especially its remarkable ability to garner legitimacy and support even from marginal social groups in postures of resistance.[12] In spite of an often classist, racist, and sexist elite discourse about criminality that by the late nineteenth century had erected a scientific facade to disguise its social Darwinist anxieties about national degeneration (Piccato, Ruggiero), many Latin Americans experienced the reconstruction of criminality as liberation rather than repression. At the most obvious level, although mediated by language (discourse) and thus unquestionably a social construct, crime was (and is) a "real" problem: murder, rape, assault, theft, fraud, etc., could (can) affect and afflict anyone regardless of class, race, or sex. Thus elite efforts to address the "crime problem" were not automatically resisted, at least not until they crossed over into obvious assaults on traditional practices (Salvatore).[13]

Even as discourse, elite social reconstruction could attract a broad clientele. The possibilities of rational "public" debate that so enthused liberal lawmakers, rather than arbitrary decree, the opportunity to escape the violent barbarities of the countryside graphically depicted by Domingo Sarmiento, the freedom from the oppressive surveillance of parish priests in Augustín Yáñez's "village of black-robed women" cannot be dismissed simply as elite propaganda.[14] These were much heralded and, more importantly, directly experienced liberations. Thus, even as it served to legitimate capitalist relations of production, centralized national governments, and expanded state power, the impersonal "rule of law" had real advantages. And the lower classes, usually on the receiving end of both crime and elite anticrime efforts, often recognized the benefits of reform projects (Scardaville), lamented their failure (Piccato, Guillermoprieto), or sought to turn them to their advantage (Bliss). Efforts to police women shared this ambiguous character, relieving and intensifying repression at the same time (Ruggiero, Bliss). Elite-driven or not, social reconstruction promised (and sometimes even delivered) benefits to all sectors of Latin American society. As Habermas reminds us, forgetting the liberatory pole of this double movement would be a huge mistake. The recent "democratization" of Latin America and especially the widely proclaimed role of nongovernmental organizations in voicing the concerns of marginal groups suggest to optimistic analysts a potential reopening of a "public sphere" after decades—some would say centuries—of often brutal repression.

This said, Foucault's pessimism provides a necessary corrective. As all the essays in this volume demonstrate, over the past two centuries the state has greatly increased the scope and intensity of its intervention into Latin American societies, sometimes with disastrous results. The process began in earnest toward the end of the nineteenth century with the widespread dissemination of positivism and social Darwinism which privileged "scientific" expertise and favored an uncontested, top-down style of social reform all in the name of "Order and Progress" (Ruggiero, Piccato). In countries like Brazil (Holloway) and Argentina (Kalmanowiecki) for example, national police forces turned (and continue to turn) the liberating potential of the Enlightenment project completely on its head by systematically and brutally repressing any "criminal" group that opposed (opposes) the status quo. In Medellín, "self-defense" groups took (and continue to take) the law into their own hands (Guillermoprieto). These cases reaffirm Foucault's contention that "power is not exercised simply as an obligation or a prohibition on those who 'do not have it'; it invests them, is transmitted by them and through them; it exerts pressure upon them, just as they themselves, in their struggle against it, resist the grip it has on them."[15] Rule of law promises liberation and social justice; institutionalized power runs the risk of obliterating both.

Put simply, the Enlightenment project both liberates and represses precisely because the liberating act itself unleashes social forces that newly constituted (liberated) elites need to control in order to ensure their own survival.[16] That the elites and their clients would define these social forces as criminal is hardly surprising. Nonetheless, the malleability of discursive reconstruction—the penchant for criminalizing any opposition to authority—is especially distressing in light of Latin America's recent past, conflicted present, and uncertain future. Many questions confront Latin America in the twenty-first century: Will the Enlightenment project finally fulfill its democratic promises? Will the painful restructuring demanded by economic modernization eventually bring social justice to Latin America? Or will widespread repression in the name of "Order and Progress" again cast its authoritarian pall over the region? Like Habermas and Foucault, the essays in this book suggest any number of possible outcomes, some hopeful, others not. "Time is forever dividing itself toward innumerable futures," the *criminal* in a Jorge Luis Borges detective story is warned, "and in one of them I am your enemy."[17]

Notes

1. See for example Chantal Mouffe, "Hegemony and Ideology in Gramsci," in Tony Bennett et al., *Culture, Ideology, and Social Process: A Reader* (London: The Open University Press, 1981), pp. 219–34.

2. Colin MacLachlan, *Spain's Empire in the New World: The Role of Ideas in Institutional and Social Change* (Berkeley: University of California Press, 1988).

3. On their philosophical differences see Jürgen Habermas, *The Philosophical Discourse of Modernity: Twelve Lectures, trans. Frederick Lawrence* (Cambridge: MIT Press, 1987), chapters 9 and 10.

4. Ibid., p. 2.

5. Jürgen Habermas, "The Public Sphere," in Chandra Mukerji and Michael Schudson, *Rethinking Popular Culture: Contemporary Perspectives in Cultural Studies* (Berkeley: University of California Press, 1991), pp. 401–2.

6. Jürgen Habermas, *Toward a Rational Society: Student Protest, Science, and Politics*, trans. Jeremy J. Shapiro (Boston: Beacon Press, 1970), p. 105. His italics.

7. Michel Foucault, "The Dangerous Individual," in Lawrence C. Kritzman, ed., *Michel Foucault: Politics, Philosophy, Culture: Interviews and Other Writings, 1977–1984* (New York: Routledge, 1988), p. 134.

8. Michel Foucault, *Discipline and Punish: The Birth of the Prison*, trans. Alan Sheridan (New York: Vintage Books, 1979), p. 7. Our italics.

9. Foucault, *Discipline and Punish*, pp. 26–27.

10. Benedict Anderson, *Imagined Communities: Reflections on the Origin and Spread of Nationalism*, rev. ed. (New York: Verso, 1991), chapter 4.

11. MacLachlan, *Spain's Empire in the New World*, p. 131.

12. See especially William H. Beezley, Cheryl E. Martin, and William E. French, eds., *Rituals of Rule, Rituals of Resistance: Public Celebrations and Popular Culture in Mexico* (Wilmington, DE: Scholarly Resources, 1994); Gilbert M. Joseph and Daniel Nugent, eds., *Everyday Forms of State Formation: Revolution and the Negotiation of Rule in Modern Mexico* (Durham: Duke University Press,

1994); and Florencia E. Mallon, *Peasant and Nation: The Making of Postcolonial Mexico and Peru* (Berkeley: University of California Press, 1995).

13. E. P. Thompson explores the hegemonic ambiguity of "rule of law" in *Whigs and Hunters: The Origin of the Black Act* (New York: Pantheon Books, 1975), pp. 258–69.

14. Domingo F. Sarmiento, *Life in Argentina in the Days of the Tyrants; or Civilization and Barbarism* (New York: Hafner Press, 1868) and Augustín Yáñez, *The Edge of the Storm/Al Filo del Agua*, trans. Ethel Brinton (Austin: University of Texas Press, 1963), p. 3.

15. Foucault, *Discipline and Punish*, pp. 26–27.

16. For an in-depth exploration of this "paradox" see Theodor W. Adorno and Max Horkheimer, *Dialectic of the Enlightenment* (New York: Continuum Publishing Co., 1975).

17. Jorge Luis Borges, "The Garden of the Forking Paths," trans. Helen Temple and Ruthven Todd, *Ficciones* (New York: Grove Press, 1962), p. 100.

1

(Hapsburg) Law and (Bourbon) Order: State Authority, Popular Unrest, and the Criminal Justice System in Bourbon Mexico City[1]

Michael C. Scardaville

The Enlightenment project that initiated the "reconstruction" of crime in Latin America began with the Spanish Bourbon monarchs, especially Charles III (1759–1788). Appalled by two centuries of haphazard, irrational Hapsburg statecraft, Bourbon reformers sought to restore the Spanish empire to its former glory with a comprehensive political, economic, and social overhaul. These reforms included efforts to expand and "rationalize" the colonial criminal justice system—courts and police in particular—especially in Mexico City, the linchpin of the American empire. Most scholars note that while political and economic reforms might have improved the imperial economy, they also tended to alienate colonial elites who were used to considerable autonomy under the less efficient Hapsburg system. That was not necessarily the case with all Bourbon social reforms.

In the following essay, Michael Scardaville, associate professor of history at the University of South Carolina, argues that "the reformed criminal justice system of Mexico City, in its dual capacity as Bourbon enforcer and Hapsburg mediator, diffused social conflict, keeping it within acceptable limits and lessening the possibility for open rebellion against colonial authorities." Scardaville's work underscores the crucial role of the criminal justice system in legitimizing political authority. He argues that to fulfill that function the legal system must mediate more or less fairly and effectively between and among social "classes." And, in Mexico City at least, it apparently did. "In spite of occasional abuses," Scardaville assures us, "the reformed lower criminal courts of Mexico City were generally effective in meeting the needs of the urban poor," thereby ensuring a loyal and, more important, passive urban underclass throughout the

difficult early years of the independence movement. That Bourbon hege-
mony required considerable accommodation to traditional Hapsburg le-
gal practices reinforces the rearticulated character of Enlightenment
"modernity."

The relative absence of riots in colonial Mexico City is an intriguing phenomenon which has attracted the recent attention of scholars interested in questions of social stability and conflict. While the Mexican countryside experienced over 130 rebellions in the eighteenth and early nineteenth centuries, the cities by comparison remained calm.[2] The most cogent explanation of urban lower-class passivity during the late colonial period has been formulated by Eric Van Young, who suggests that a number of short- and long-term social and economic forces converged to keep the cities, most notably Mexico City, relatively quiet during the wars for independence. Among those he noted were urban social service and food distribution institutions, the presence of security forces, an atomized and fluid social order, the lack of traditional communal rights to defend, and weak organizational means to focus discontent.[3]

The purpose of this essay is to explore a key but neglected reason for this urban passivity, namely the enhancement of state legitimacy and authority in the viceregal capital in the generation before the Hidalgo revolt. I believe Van Young's conjunctural and structural factors do not give enough weight to the colonial state's role in lessening the possibility of popular rebellions in Mexico City, particularly in the decades before the Hidalgo uprising.[4] I would suggest that the state's ability to maintain its authority and legitimacy in the capital at a time of demographically induced pressures, a period between the 1770s and 1810s, played a decisive role in diffusing social conflicts and in minimizing the potential for open rebellion. The nature of political authority had been a pivotal factor in the three major riots which did erupt in Mexico City in the seventeenth and early nineteenth centuries. For instance, the *tumulto* of 1692, the most extensive popular uprising in the colonial period, can be explained largely by the relative debility and ineffectiveness of government institutions which in turn afforded an opportunity for concerted action on the part of the urban poor.[5] In fact, an examination of the few colonial and early national riots in Mexico City reveals an important common denominator: they all occurred when central authority was weak. The colonial state, through a variety of mechanisms, played a critical role in undermining the possibility of popular mobilization in Mexico City. While Van Young has identified elements which may help explain the relative calm in the viceregal capital, the multifaceted nature of state authority in the colonial urban setting has not been explored sufficiently in any explanatory model.

Urban Growth and State Authority in Late Colonial Mexico City

Mexico City, fast-growing metropolis and scene of two major riots in the seventeenth century, did not experience collective violence other than occasional worker protests in the late eighteenth and early nineteenth centuries. Despite the fears of *la gente decente* (self-identified "decent people"), the masses in this city of over one hundred thousand inhabitants did not resort to open rebellion at a time when survival was becoming more precarious.[6] This does not mean, however, that the urban poor, a racially and occupationally diverse group, were content with their plight or that Mexico City was devoid of social conflict.[7] Rather, the lower classes actively responded to protracted economic social tensions in ways other than taking to the streets against the government. Whether as a result of Van Young's urban structural factors or successful co-optative and adaptive mechanisms fostered by the state, or both, collective and direct political action in the form of rebellion was an option not exercised by the working poor of Mexico City in the late colonial period.

As commentators of the era noted, the wealth and splendor of Mexico City could not hide the poverty of many of its residents.[8] A population increase of over 50 percent between 1742 and 1810 undermined any effort by the urban poor to improve their lot in an expanding colonial economy.[9] As a result of chronic labor surpluses and periodic subsistence crises, employment opportunities were reduced, prices of essential goods increased, and real wages declined. Through migration and existing economic conditions in the city the size of the marginal population swelled, and it became even more common to see beggars and the homeless canvassing the streets. From all accounts, it appears that crime and other social problems escalated as well.[10] A rapid surge in population after 1790 made life in the city even more contentious and challenging for the poor and elites alike. Yet while the masses of Mexico City experienced considerable pressures and strains in the last decades of colonial rule, the authority of the state held in the face of popular discontent.

The abiding power of the late colonial state rested on its ability to adapt to these accumulating pressures. Beginning in the 1760s, early in the cycle of sustained population growth, the colonial authorities gradually expanded social services by organizing a poor house (Hospicio de Pobres), pawn shop (Monte de Piedad), and foundling home (Casa de Expósitos), and endeavored to create employment opportunities by establishing a tobacco factory and relaxing guild restrictions.[11] In addition, the local government took steps to insure the smooth functioning of the meat and grain distribution systems.[12] Another critical though poorly understood element in the maintenance of state power in Mexico City is the reform of the municipal criminal justice system, an expanded system that enhanced the legitimacy and hence authority of the state at critical times in the decades before and during the Hidalgo revolt.

The Bourbon Reform of Criminal Justice

The legitimacy of royal government in Mexico City and elsewhere in New Spain was based on an overlay of Bourbon and Hapsburg notions of the state shared by colonial officials and the governed alike.[13] Although both the Hapsburg and Bourbon states recognized the relationship between the administration of justice and political authority, they differed philosophically in ways that affected how the judicial system would operate and function.

The Bourbon state, activist, interventionist, materialist, and centralist, made its most significant inroads in New Spain during the reign of Charles III. For the Bourbons, the rationale for governance was the promotion of economic growth and material well-being. They used a variety of well-known institutional reforms to achieve such ends, but we should note that the Bourbons also understood the need to create internal conditions, such as the maintenance of law and order, that would contribute to economic growth. In this capacity the colonial Bourbon state, particularly in Mexico City and other urban settings, played the role of enforcer. That is, a foremost objective of the state was to support elite and government interests by attempting to control the behavior of popular groups which threatened royal authority and was deemed economically counterproductive.

Essential to the preservation of order and royal authority in Mexico City was an efficiently operating police force and court system. By the mid-eighteenth century the city had outgrown its sixteenth-century law enforcement institutions. The Bourbon viceroys began making changes in the policing of Mexico City by extending the jurisdiction of the rural-based Acordada to the viceregal capital in 1756.[14] In Mexico City this police agency and tribunal focused primarily on property crimes, leaving other offenses such as homicide and aggravated assault in the hands of the overburdened and essentially reactive Sala del Crimen, the highest ranking criminal judicial institution in the city and environs.[15] In the following decades, urban military patrols supplemented the law enforcement efforts of the Acordada and Sala del Crimen.[16]

The principal Bourbon reform in the administration of justice in Mexico City was the expansion of the local police and criminal court system between 1782 and 1790. Modeled on similar changes in Madrid, the new arrangement endeavored to deliver judicial services more rationally and efficiently. Viceroy Martín de Mayorga in 1782 ordered that the city be divided into eight major administrative districts or *cuarteles mayores* headed by high ranking creoles and peninsulars, namely the officials of the Sala del Crimen, the two local *alcaldes ordinarios* (city councilmen and administrators who also serve as judges), and the *corregidor*.[17] Each magistrate, assisted by as many as twenty police officials and a legal staff, informally judged cases (*juicios verbales*) in the tribunal established in his district.[18] Viceroy Count Revillagigedo added a ninth municipal court in 1790 along with erection of a street lighting system and a separate ninety-two person police force (*guardafaroleros*) to protect and care for the expensive equipment. Entrusted to the corregidor, this tribunal judged all offenders apprehended by the night police.[19] The reform of the municipal judiciary in Mexico City removed from the Sala del Crimen the daily concerns of enforcement, although it still reviewed cases from outside the capital and processed formal cases *(causas criminales)* submitted by the lower courts of the city.[20] By the last decade of the eighteenth century, staff from the municipal tribunals in addition to the Acordada, military patrols, and officials from the two local Indian jurisdictions policed Mexico City. The late-colonial judicial reform, in which the nine newly constituted courts handled over 90 percent of the arrests and criminal cases in the city, prevented the overload of local law enforcement institutions as the city continued to grow and experienced greater unrest and social conflict.[21]

Outwardly the reformed municipal legal and police system operated in accordance with Bourbon notions, most notably the imperative to attack the vices of the populace not simply on moral grounds, but primarily for economic and utilitarian reasons. The judicial reforms replaced the inefficient pre-1782 system which, with the exception of the limited actions of the Acordada, was largely passive in its approach to law enforcement.[22] Policing after the *cuartel* plan was implemented became considerably more active and aggressive, putting officials on the streets instead of relying solely on occasional roundups or responses to formal complaints. The colonial state used this expanded police and judicial structure to enforce an increasing number of laws against various forms of criminal behavior such as vagrancy, illegal gambling, property crimes, and drink-related offenses considered to be antithetical to the economic interests of the state.[23] This proactive approach to law enforcement in Mexico City resulted in a tenfold increase in the number of arrests and trials, the vast majority involving the urban poor, between the early 1780s and late 1790s.[24]

As evidenced in municipal arrest and court records called *Libros de Reos*, many sentences handed down by local magistrates reflected the utilitarian rationale of the colonial Bourbon state. Judicial decisions in the lower tribunals were increasingly based, not on exacting punishment, but on enabling the criminal to make an economic contribution to society. For instance, in order to utilize the mass of underemployed workers for the city's improvement, the lower courts sentenced more and more lawbreakers to forced labor as a judicial penalty. Whereas in the early eighteenth century such a punishment was given for about 10 percent of all cases of public intoxication, by the end of the century eight of every ten men arrested for this offense were ordered to perform labor on one of the municipal public works projects.[25] Other court sentences such as assigning teenage boys to an artisan workshop or sending young women to a house of honor (*casa de honra*) emphasized rehabilitation and modification of behavior as, ideally, offenders were to be provided an opportunity to learn useful job and/or domestic skills under proper supervision.[26] The levying of fines, the single most frequently used judicial penalty, served an important purpose in the eyes of the materialist Bourbon state since these monies provided most of the financial resources necessary to support an active and expanded police and court system.

Along with other governmental institutions established in the late eighteenth century, the reformed criminal justice system enhanced state power and authority in the capital. This aggressive and fiscally solvent system kept crime and social conflict in the growing city within tolerable limits and devised penalties that supported the economic philosophy of the Bourbon state.

But the energetic Bourbon approach to law enforcement did not fully displace traditional Hapsburg notions of justice. Although there was a more rational delivery of judicial services and a modification of some sentences for utilitarian purposes, the local judiciary continued to operate along Hapsburg lines in certain key respects. Traditional principles and processes of the criminal justice system were not successfully challenged by the Bourbon state.

Historically, state legitimacy, rooted in the Romano-Visigothic legal tradition of the Iberian kingdoms, was based on the provision of justice and the mediation of disputes, two of the most important functions of the Castilian state since the early medieval era. As evidenced in such legal codes as the seventh-century *Fuero Juzgo* and the thirteenth-century *Siete Partidas*, the sovereign, through the judicial system, was expected to be compassionate and benevolent as well as just and lenient in dealing with his subjects. Arbitrary behavior was considered contrary to the well-being of his flock, and social harmony would be maintained not through coercive force but by accommodating conflicting interests.[27]

The monarch, then, was viewed throughout society as a regulator of contending interest groups, mediating disputes as a means of sustaining a direct link with his subjects who, in turn, were expected to bring injustices to his attention. The courts served as the arena in which conflicts would be resolved in a fair manner through compromise and concession. The judicial system therefore did not exist simply to protect the interests of the privileged. Through the arbitration of disputes it also attended to the needs of the less fortunate who in large part were the victims of social discord.[28] In practice, then, the colonial judiciary performed dual roles to maintain public order. Not only did it enforce social norms through the imposition of sanctions, it also attempted to settle disputes brought to its attention through a form of conflict resolution.

The Bourbon expansion of the police and court system in Mexico City extended this Hapsburg mediative function of the state to greater numbers of people. The creation of nine tribunals staffed by magistrates, legal assistants, and police officials made the system more accessible to the growing urban populace, a critical aspect of judicial reform since informal structures of dispute settlement common to villages were probably not as available in a more massive and impersonal urban setting. In Mexico City there was likely greater reliance on legally constituted authority as a more formal means of conflict resolution, a reliance which in turn served to enhance allegiance to the colonial state.

The Hapsburg notion of justice prevailed in several key areas of the criminal justice system. The popular acceptance of the state as legitimate arbitrator of conflict can be seen in the frequent use the working poor in Mexico City made of the local judiciary. As documented in the *Libros de Reos*, members of popular groups regularly called upon the criminal courts to resolve disputes that could not be settled in other, nonlegal ways. In spite of an active policing policy, over one-third of all arrests in eight of the nine tribunals were made at the request of an aggrieved party, most of whom were working-class in origin.[29] A majority of cases in several offenses including debt, spouse abuse, desertion, vagrancy, and theft reached the courts as a result of a formal complaint.[30] As seen in almost two thousand cases annually, the poor relied on the system in part to enforce family discipline and insure marital responsibilities, and in part to arrange agreement with creditors or compensation for stolen merchandise. In this context, the colonial state did not act in a repressive manner. Instead, through the support it extended by way of the local judiciary, it provided specific services which met critical needs.

Judicial Practice in Late Colonial Mexico City

The poor could go to the lower courts largely assured that the hearings would be fair and sentences would be appropriate and swift. Based on Roman and medieval precedents, not Enlightenment notions of penal reform, court procedures were generally impartial and predictable, even in the thousands of informal hearings conducted in the nine Bourbon-era municipal tribunals. The magistrates generally respected the defendants' rights and conducted the hearings in accordance with rules of evidence. As representatives of royal will, the judges thus fulfilled their traditional duties of dispensing justice with, as one late-eighteenth-century viceroy stated, much "prudence and precaution in order to avoid grievances and unjust mistreatment."[31] Regardless of the race or gender of the accused, the lower courts of Mexico City did not employ mental or physical torture to extract confessions or statements; magistrates routinely ordered investigations if any doubts arose over the offender's culpability or lifestyle; guilt had to be proven if the prisoner expressed innocence; and finally, if evidence to convict was insufficient, the court immediately released the prisoner and absolved him or her of all court and jail fees. In spite of the expense of this system and the elites' perception of rising threats to public order, the municipal court system adhered to due process not so much as a legal right in the Anglo-American sense, but, emerging from medieval codes and centuries of practice, as a concession from the state to maintain allegiance and authority.[32]

This practice of proceeding in a judicious manner did not compromise the efficiency of the system. The lower courts of Mexico City sentenced 90 percent of all offenders within three days of their arrest, with at least one-half receiving punishment on the day following apprehension. The state was acutely aware that, in the words of high government officials, "brevity and promptness of punishment . . . (are) the most effective means to enjoy the beneficial effects of the Laws."[33] The speed with which conflicts were to be resolved in the courts was thus essential to the reestablishment of public and private tranquility in the capital. Only the most serious offenses, which amounted to only five percent of all arrests, would be subjected to the more sluggish formal judicial system conducted by the Sala del Crimen.

Sentences handed down by local magistrates were lenient, especially in cases which resulted from complaints. One reason for this moderation was that judges routinely modified the prescribed penalties in order to fit the circumstances of the crime or to take into account requests of the aggrieved party.[34] Based on authority granted in medieval codes, the magistrates exercised a considerable degree of judicial discretion since their daily contact with the urban poor enabled them to recognize the inappropriateness of the legally prescribed sanctions in the face of the social and economic realities of city life.[35]

The temperate judicial sentences helped to legitimize the state's role as mediator. While the lower courts used certain sentences as a form of punishment, such as depósito and imprisonment, they constituted only seven percent of all sentences in informal cases. Not one case resulted in the death penalty, and corporal punishment became less frequent, rarely being employed by 1807.[36] Especially in cases of family disputes, debt, theft, and assault, the city magistrates tended to act as arbitrators of justice, not conveyors of retribution. Family related offenses, for instance, experienced high acquittal and probation rates, with the judges returning most of the rebellious children and wayward spouses of both sexes to their families.[37] Debtors and convicted thieves were not formally punished, but rather were expected to indemnify their creditors or victims, and those arrested for assault generally remained in the city jail until the victim recovered and the attacker ultimately paid the medical expenses.[38]

In their totality such judicial practices underscore the Hapsburg notion of a paternalistic and benevolent state, a government that would preserve stability and order through guidance, not merely through coercion or open force. This is not to say that the local judicial system was without abuses. Reflective of the prevailing status hierarchy, race, gender, and occupation influenced the sentences handed down by the criminal courts.[39] While judicial procedures may have been impartial, the ultimate disposition of offenders often was affected by their position within the social order. Certain court sentences such as forced labor and some monetary penalties did impose hardships on individuals and families. Moreover, the poor sometimes were subjected to abusive police and prison officials. Yet such legal inequalities and mistreatment do not call into question the legitimacy of the entire system of justice or the relationship of the poor to the state. The status hierarchy was not openly challenged; the misbehaving government officials, not the system, were held at fault; and the urban poor continued to use the police and the courts to help resolve disputes within and outside the home.[40]

In spite of a series of shortcomings in the application of the law, the poor's frequent strategic use of the legal system in Mexico City contributed to the maintenance of authority in the colonial state. As seen in judicial practice, law enforcement in the viceregal capital did not exist solely to protect the interests of the dominant, propertied class.[41] Such a view is one dimensional and inadequately attentive to the philosophical and legal contexts of the period. Paradoxically, working-class use of the courts facilitated social control in the burgeoning city by strengthening the belief in state legitimacy.

Conclusion

The reformed criminal justice system of Mexico City, in its dual capacity as Bourbon enforcer and Hapsburg mediator, diffused social conflict, keeping it within acceptable limits and lessening the possibility of open rebellion against the colonial authorities. The late-colonial judiciary in Mexico City was based on traditional Hapsburg notions of justice modified by Enlightened Bourbon rationalism. The expanded municipal police displayed a show of force necessary to apprehend those who violated the Bourbon sense of order, but the courts also provided a controlled outlet for mounting social tensions. As a result of urban pressures, growing social complexity, state policy, and greater accessibility to the criminal judiciary, the use of courts as instruments of social control and as a forum for conflict resolution increased in the late eighteenth and early nineteenth centuries.

The Bourbon state indeed strove to maintain order in Mexico City, but not at the expense of providing justice, a noteworthy accomplishment given elite apprehension that the social order was imperiled in the rapidly growing metropolis. As long as the survival of the state itself was not threatened, the police and the courts of the viceregal capital did not control or punish social conflict in an oppressive manner. Rather, as was typical of the colonial judicial experience, the subordinate urban classes learned to manipulate the legal system in order to defend themselves and further their own self-interests, whether in terms of gaining leverage or power over another, obtaining scarce resources, or simply righting a perceived wrong.[42]

When approached from the perspective of the users of the law, it is evident that the poor of Mexico City viewed the criminal courts' mediative role as a tool for allaying a range of crises in their daily lives. This working-class conception of law in Mexico City helped to buttress the legitimacy and thus the authority of the late-colonial state by fostering greater political compliance among the urban poor. Since going to court often represents the closest and most intimate contact a person might have with the government, the legal system, most notably the way in which it handles a dispute, helps shape the attitudes toward the government of those who seek its assistance.[43] In spite of occasional abuses, the reformed lower criminal courts of Mexico City were generally effective in meeting the needs of the urban poor.

Critical also in understanding the absence of lower-class insurrection in Mexico City is the fact that the colonial state remained flexible and responsive at this perilous time of sustained urbanization and deprivation. Urban judicial institutions and social services generally kept pace with the population growth of the late colonial era, thereby reducing the potential for mass mobilization.[44] Significantly, the urban reforms of the late eighteenth century such as the expansion of a more effective local judiciary and the development of various welfare institutions were already in place and operating before the period of most rapid population growth in the 1790s and early 1800s. Moreover, I would suggest that the expansion of the police forces and the court system as well as the furnishing of other social services to ameliorate living conditions in Mexico City resulted in a kind of informal and co-optative political integration which fostered a dependency that was politically valuable to the state, particularly as regional insurrections challenged the colonial regime in 1810.

As a result of fiscal solvency at the local level, albeit tenuous at times, and of political acumen which enabled public institutions to remain flexible, state authority was not weakened in the viceregal capital. The reform of the municipal criminal judiciary contributed to the maintenance of political authority in Mexico City. By providing even a modicum of judicial and social services to the urban poor, especially during the decades of demographic growth prior to 1810, the state was able to retain and reinforce their loyalty and political allegiance. This enhancement of state legitimacy in late colonial Mexico City, backed by the immediate presence of police and military force if necessary, perhaps offers some additional insight into why the urban masses, unlike their rural counterparts, did not rise up to express their grievances in increasingly difficult times. While, as Van Young notes, other social and economic factors contributed to this phenomenon, the reformed and multidimensional criminal justice system played a subtle yet important role in stifling the potential for collective violence in Mexico City in the late colonial era.

Perhaps this analysis of human and legal behavior in Mexico City has broader implications for the study of social stability and law. Perhaps, for instance, the concept of legitimacy offers another framework to examine the divergent patterns of rebellion in New Spain in the late eighteenth and early nineteenth centuries. It might be argued that indigenous communities accepted, in varying degrees, two forms of legitimacy. Using the Weberian typology, one was the traditional form that constituted political allegiance in the Indian villages and another was the rational-legal form of legitimacy that underscored support to the bureaucratic colonial state. Acceptance of colonial government as a legitimate arbitrator of peasant grievances can been seen, as William Taylor asserts, in the "flood of peasant litigants to viceregal court in Mexico City."[45] Yet recourse to state institutions did supersede intra-village means of dispute resolution. In her study of a contemporary Zapotec community, Laura Nader notes that only the most serious offenses such as homicide, as well as those that cannot be settled by indigenous officials, are taken to the state courts.[46] Increasingly throughout the late eighteenth and early nineteenth centuries, legitimacy, as manifested in communal belief systems, was fractured in those communities under pressure from outside forces, particularly since redress of grievances would come at the instigation of village institutions. Competing types of legitimacy would not exist in urban centers such as Mexico City. Political allegiance to the colonial state in these places would not likely become as diluted as in Indian villages feeling the pinch of late colonial land and population pressures.[47]

Moreover, this analysis of social control in Mexico City might begin to provide a comparative understanding of the functioning of law in the Anglo and Roman legal traditions. Scholars have long praised the uniqueness of English common law in the evolution of Western legal culture, noting in particular its contributions in the areas of equity and legal procedure. Furthermore, historians such as E. P. Thompson and Douglas Hay argue that the domestic universality of English law in the eighteenth century facilitated and reinforced the legitimacy of the English ruling class. According to Thompson, the "hegemony of the eighteenth-century gentry and aristocracy was expressed, above all, not in military force, not in the mystifications of a priesthood or of the press, not even in economic coercion, but in the rituals of the study of the Justices of the Peace, in the quarter-sessions, in the pomp of the Assizes and in the theatre of Tyburn."[48] For Hay, the issue is how England was ruled without a police force and a large army during a sustained period of economic and social pressures. The answer likewise is found in the criminal justice system: criminal law, "more than any other social institution," made it possible for England to be governed by a small ruling class which did not have formidable repressive forces at its disposal.[49]

Thompson believes that what transpired in eighteenth-century England, "the notion of the regulation and reconciliation of conflicts through the rule of law—and the elaboration of rules and procedures which, on occasion, made some approximate approach towards the ideal," was "a cultural achievement of universal significance" as a result of a pliant and uncodified English common law.[50] Such conclusions, however, seem to miss the essence of the Romano-Hispanic legal tradition as practiced in colonial Mexico and perhaps in Spain and other regions in Spanish America. In spite of divergent legal traditions, the criminal justice system played a similar role in eighteenth-century New Spain and England.

In both places, legal procedures were in place to insure the protection of rights, and in both places the accessibility and application of law helped to enhance and sustain the legitimacy of the state and ruling classes. I would suggest that the reasons for these similarities are found not in the uniqueness of English common law but rather in the distinctive roles that law can play in diverse cultural settings. The study of criminal law, as applied in colonial Mexico, affords a new perspective to understand the nature of the Hispanic legal tradition.

Notes

1. A longer version of this essay appeared in *The Americas* 50, no. 4 (April 1994): 501–25. The author wishes to thank Elaine Lacy, Joan Meznar, Kenneth Gouwens, Lawrence Glickman, and the many other participants of the Carolinas-Virginias Seminar on Colonial Latin American History for their comments on an earlier version of this essay.

2. John H. Coatsworth, "Patterns of Rural Rebellion in Latin America: Mexico in Comparative Perspective," in *Riot, Rebellion, and Revolution: Rural Social Conflict in Mexico*, ed. Friedrich Katz (Princeton: Princeton University Press, 1988), pp. 24, 57; Alan Knight, "The Peculiarities of Mexican History: Mexico Compared to Latin America, 1821–1992," *Journal of Latin American Studies* 24 (Suppl. 1992): 105, n. 31; Jaime Rodríguez O., ed., *Patterns of Contention in Mexican History* (Wilmington, DE: Scholarly Resources, 1992).

3. Eric Van Young, "Islands in the Storm: Quiet Cities and Violent Country-sides in the Mexican Independence Era," *Past & Present* 118 (1988): 130–55.

4. Van Young admittedly focuses on the period between 1810 and 1821 when the colonial authorities undertook more extensive repressive measures to contain the likelihood of lower-class insurrection in Mexico City.

5. The failure of the food distribution system and inadequacies of the police and militia forces help explain the outbreak of the 1692 riot. See Chester L. Guthrie, "Riots in Seventeenth Century Mexico City: A Study of Social and Economic Conditions," in *Greater America: Essays in Honor of Herbert Eugene Bolton* (Berkeley: University of California Press, 1945), pp. 243–58; and Rosa Feijóo, "El tumulto de 1692," *Historia Mexicana* 14 (1965): 656–79.

6. The estimated population of Mexico City ranged from 98,000 in 1742 to 150,000 in 1810. Enrique Florescano, *Precios del maíz y crisis agrícolas en México, 1708–1810* (Mexico City, 1969), p. 171.

7. I contend that, in spite of ethnic and occupational differences, the working classes of Mexico City from artisans to unskilled laborers experienced similar degrees of financial exigencies and exhibited similar behavioral patterns in the late colonial period.

8. See for instance Alexander von Humboldt, *Political Essay on the Kingdom of New Spain*, trans. John Black (4 vols., London: 1811), pp. I, 184.

9. More specifically, population surged by 53 percent between 1742 and 1810. Florescano, *Precios del maíz*, p. 171.

10. Michael C. Scardaville, "Crime and the Urban Poor: Mexico City in the Late Colonial Period" (Ph.D. diss., University of Florida, 1977), pp. 48–89; Gabriel J.

Haslip, "Crime and the Administration of Justice in Colonial Mexico City" (Ph.D. diss., Columbia University, 1980), pp. 10–74.

11. The foundling home and tobacco factory opened in the late 1760s, and the poor house and pawn shop in the mid-1770s. The Hospicio de Pobres also served as an orphanage. The government eased guild restrictions in the late 1790s.

12. See Florescano, *Precios del maíz*.

13. For a discussion of the "philosophical matrix" of the Hapsburg and Bourbon states, see Colin MacLachlan, *Spain's Empire in the New World: The Role of Ideas in Institutional and Social Change* (Berkeley: University of California Press, 1988). MacLachlan (p. 21) asserts that the crown and its subjects had similar expectations concerning the role of the state.

14. The Acordada was established in New Spain in the early eighteenth century to combat highway banditry. Initially arbitrary in its operations, the tribunal gradually assumed more standard legal procedures. The extension of its jurisdiction to Mexico City in the 1750s was in response to repeated failures to expand the more traditional law enforcement systems in the capital. Colin M. MacLachlan, *Criminal Justice in Eighteenth Century Mexico: A Study of the Tribunal of the Acordada* (Berkeley: University of California Press, 1974); Alicia Bazin Alarcón, "El Real Tribunal de la Acordada y la delincuencia en la Nueva España," *Historia Mexicana* 13 (1964): 317–45.

15. MacLachlan, *Criminal Justice in Eighteenth Century Mexico*, pp. 78–79.

16. Christon I. Archer, *The Army in Bourbon Mexico, 1760–1810* (Albuquerque: University of New Mexico Press, 1977).

17. "Ordenanzas de la división de México en Quarteles, creación de Alcaldes de Barrio, y reglas de su gobierno, con una mapa de la ciudad," Mayorga, December 4, 1782, Archivo General de la Nación (AGN), Bandos, vol. 12, fols. 101–24; Bando, Mayorga, December 7, 1782, AGN, Bandos, vol. 12, fol. 100. In early 1785, the Audiencia extended the jurisdiction of the *alcaldes de barrio* to *cuarteles menores* other than their own, thereby in effect giving each *alcalde de barrio* jurisdiction over the entire city. Archivo Judicial del Tribunal (hereafter cited as AJT), Penal, vol. 3 (1785), exp. 12.

18. Instrucción reservada que el conde de Revilla Gigedo, dio a su successor en el mando, Marqués de Branciforte (Mexico City: 1831), p. 29.

19. "Reglamento para el gobierno que ha de observar en el alumbrado de las calles de México," Revillagigedo, April 7, 1790, AGN, Bandos, vol. 15, fols. 158–60; Bando, Revillagigedo, April 1, 1790, AGN, Bandos, vol. 15, fol. 175. Although assigned responsibility for a specific set of street lamps, each *guardafarolero* exercised jurisdiction over the entire city.

20. Archivo General del Juzgado (hereafter cited as AGJ), Penal, vol. 2 (1803), exp. 29; vol. 3 (1805), exp. 11.

21. Scardaville, "Crime and the Urban Poor," pp. 12–13.

22. *Instrucciones que los vireyes de Nueva España dejaron a sus sucesores* (2 vols., Mexico: 1867–1873), I, 237. Until the 1780s police patrols were not conducted regularly. Such passive law enforcement has its roots in medieval Castilian codes and practice. As stated in the *Siete Partidas*, judicial action generally commenced with a formal complaint, although the law made provisions to instigate an arrest if a crime was committed in public view. *Las Siete Partidas del Rey Don Alfonso El Sabio* (3 vols., Madrid: Ediciones Atlas, 1972), III, book 7, title, 8, law 28.

23. For a discussion of these laws, see Scardaville, "Crime and the Urban Poor," chapters 1 and 3–6, and "Alcohol Abuse and Tavern Reform in Late Colonial Mexico City," *Hispanic American Historical Review* 60 (1980): 643–71.

24. See Scardaville, "Crime and the Urban Poor," chapters 1 and 5. The increase in arrests greatly outdistanced the ca. 15 percent population growth of the city during this period.

25. As a result of a rapidly expanding municipal public works program in the late colonial period, forced community labor became an increasingly relied upon form of punishment. The courts sent one-third of all male offenders to the public works projects. Of the men arrested for intoxication, 83.5 percent were dispatched to one of the municipal *obras públicas*. For the early eighteenth-century figure, see Haslip, "Crime and the Administration of Justice," p. 197.

26. Assignment to a *casa de honra* and artisan workshop represented 5.4 percent and 0.9 percent of all courts' sentences for females and males, respectively. Women sent to the *casas de honra* tended to be Spanish or casta, single, and under twenty years of age. Men sent to work for an artisan were exclusively in their teens, single, and often without any practicing trade *(sin oficio)*.

27. These basic principles are embodied in a political philosophy that ordained a special relationship between the king and God through which the monarch manifests divine benevolence and compassion: "(the king) will be to them as a father who brings up his children in love, and punishes them with mercy." *Siete Partidas*, 2-10-2.

28. As reflected in the *Libros de Reos*, the overwhelming number of arrests involved perpetrators and victims from roughly the same social class. The working poor, whether artisans, semi-, or unskilled laborers, generally attacked, robbed, raped, and abused others from similar groups. There is little evidence of inter-class conflict in the judicial records. Such behavior in turn affected the operation of the lower courts since the magistrates were not as overtly swayed by class biases in the handling of cases. The philosophical underpinning of justice was easier to attain in practice given the reality of most social conflict. This point is crucial in understanding court procedures and sentencing practices in the lower courts of Mexico City, as will be discussed later in this essay.

29. Most formal complaints were filed in the eight courts associated with the *cuarteles menores*. The ninth tribunal, that of the *guardafaroleros*, responded mainly to offenses against the public order, most notably intoxication and curfew violations. More precisely, 36.5 percent of all arrests in the eight tribunals were made at the request of an injured party.

30. The percentages of arrests made in certain offenses after a complaint had been filed are as follows: debt (98.9 percent); family offenses, including spouse abuse and desertion (69.0 percent); vagrancy (57.7 percent); theft (55.2 percent). Unfortunately, the *Libros de Reos* do not give detailed biographical information about the person filing the complaint other than the relationship to the defendant.

31. Bando, Bucareli, February 14, 1773, AGN, Bandos, vol. 8, fols. 49–51.

32. MacLachlan notes that "without (this) concession, the social cooperation necessary to enable the state to impose its authority could not have been elicited." *Criminal Justice in Eighteenth-Century Mexico*, p. 44. The rights of the accused were not guaranteed by law, but were accorded through a criminal procedure that had evolved since the seventh century. Such examples of de facto rights include a court appointed public defender at the beginning of the case, the court's

ability to compel testimony and obtain and examine evidence, and the practice of having accused persons personally confront those who testify against them. This de facto granting of rights is evident in both informal and formal cases prosecuted in the courts of late colonial Mexico City.

33. Bando, Sala del Crimen, February 24, 1772, AGN, Bandos, vol. 8, fol. 53v; Beleña, *Recopilación sumaria*, 1, 5th, XCII.

34. The judges occasionally tailored judicial penalties to comply with the wishes of the complainant, particularly in violent crimes, sex and family offenses, and vagrancy. See for instance, Libros de reos: alcalde de ordinario (hereafter cited as LR:AO) (1795), fols. 6v-7, 43; LR:AO (1796), fols. 47, 72v, 145v; AJT, Penal, vol. 2 (1783), exp. 55; AGJ, Penal, vol. 3 (1805), exp. 8.

35. As stated in the *Siete Partidas*, magistrates were expected to take a variety of factors into consideration such as status of the offender, gravity of the crime, and mitigating circumstances before assigning punishment: "After the judges have diligently and carefully considered all the matters aforesaid, they can increase, diminish, or dispense with punishment, as they think proper, and they should do so." *Siete Partidas* 7-21-8.

36. An unmistakable trend in the late eighteenth and early nineteenth centuries was the decreasing use of capital punishment by the Acordada and Sala del Crimen. Established in an era of waning enthusiasm for capital punishment, the lower tribunals of the capital sentenced convicted murderers to the public works projects or released them after a prolonged investigation. Even the brutal homicide of a police officer did not merit the death penalty. AGJ, Penal, vol. 1 (1802), exp. 27; vol. 2 (1803), exp. 13 and 28; vol. 3 (1805), exp. 9 and 11; AJT, Penal, vol. 12 (1809), exp. 32; LR:AO (1796), fols. 102v, 105. Greater use of public work sentences in accordance with royal and viceregal wishes lessened reliance on corporal punishment in the late colonial period. Frequency of corporal punishment dropped from 8.3 percent of all sentences in 1795 and 1796 to only 0.2 percent in 1807.

37. Gender did not make a difference in how the court handled family related offenses such as desertion and nonsupport, as both male and female offenders generally were returned to their families. The intent of the courts was to maintain the family unit, not necessarily formally punish the transgressor.

38. LR:AO (1796), fols. 112v and 141; Libros de reos: corregidor (hereafter cited as LR:C) (1796), fol. 11; Bando, Audiencia, March 29, 1784, AGN, Bandos, vol. 13, fol. 58.

39. Equality before the law was an alien concept in the administration of colonial criminal justice. Reflective of an early modern hierarchical social order, differential treatment of offenders was inherent in the law. Most laws required imposing sentences in accordance with the sex, race, and occupation of the criminal. Even in crimes for which the laws did not specify the punishment, the courts still sentenced offenders with regard to their status. For a discussion of how gender, race, and class influenced sentencing practices, see Scardaville, "Crime and the Urban Poor," pp. 304–8.

40. To rephrase Merry on this key point, "the less powerful groups . . . do not generally think that legal ordering has produced a fair and just society. More often, the law serves as a resource in struggles over control, so that disappointment with its intervention leads to disgust but not to disillusion." Sally Engle Merry, "Law as Fair, Law as Help: The Texture of Legitimacy in American Society," *New Directions in the Study of Justice, Law, and Social Control*, prepared

by the School of Justice Studies, Arizona State University (New York: Plenum Press, 1990), p. 186. In this respect, Merry is critical of the Weberian and Goldstonian notions that an authority must be "just" in order to be legitimate. Merry contends that, at least among subordinate groups, effectiveness is more critical than justice in securing allegiance to the state.

41. For instance, Haslip posits that the police and courts existed essentially to protect elite interests and that the lower classes held the municipal judicial system in contempt. See "Crime and the Administration of Justice," pp. 198–99.

42. See for instance Woodrow Borah, *Justice by Insurance: The General Indian Court of Colonial Mexico and the Legal Aides of the Half-Real* (Berkeley: University of California Press, 1983) and Steve J. Stern, *Peru's Indian Peoples and the Challenge of Spanish Conquest: Huamanga to 1640* (Madison: University of Wisconsin Press, 1983).

43. Steven Vago, *Law and Society*, 2nd ed. (Englewood Cliffs, NJ: Prentice Hall, 1988), p. 199.

44. The Goldstone model helps us define a crucial aspect of stability in Mexico City in the late eighteenth and early nineteenth centuries: the strength of the state and its institutions in the viceregal capital was related to their capacity to cope with the potential for collective action. Jack A. Goldstone, *Revolution and Rebellion in the Early Modern World* (Berkeley: University of California Press, 1991). The thrust of his argument can be found on pp. xxi-xxvii, 1–62, and 459–82, with elaborations on 63–92, 134–45, 170–96, 249–85, and 349–62.

45. Taylor, *Drinking, Homicide and Rebellion*, p. 170. Also, Tutino believes that "repeated recourse to the Spanish state suggests that they (the peasants) perceive the courts as effective mediators between interests involved." "Agrarian Social Changes and Peasant Rebellion," p. 101.

46. Laura Nader, "Styles of Court Procedure: To Make a Balance," in Laura Nader, ed., *Law in Culture and Society* (Chicago: Aldine Publishing Company, 1969), p. 72.

47. Other key differences between city and countryside have a bearing on patterns of collective behavior. The presence of the colonial state for instance varied between *ciudad* and *campo* in that law enforcement mechanisms were not as extensively developed outside of larger settlements and off major transportation routes. As a result, repressive forces were not as immediately available in most rural areas as they were in the urban centers. As Taylor notes in his study of peasant rebellions, the state usually allowed the village uprisings to run their course, calling in the "small and often ill equipped" militia after the *tumulto* had subsided. *Drinking, Homicide and Rebellion*, pp. 119–20.

48. E. P. Thompson, *Whigs and Hunters: The Origin of the Black Act* (New York: Pantheon Books, 1976), p. 262.

49. Douglas Hay, "Property, Authority and the Criminal Law," in Douglas Hay et al., eds., *Albion's Fatal Tree: Crime and Society in Eighteenth Century England* (New York: Pantheon Books, 1975), p. 56.

50. Thompson, *Whigs and Hunters*, p. 65.

2

Crime and Citizenship: Judicial Practice in Arequipa, Peru, during the Transition from Colony to Republic

Sarah C. Chambers

The difficult process of state formation initiated in Spanish America after independence included the development and consolidation of judicial institutions and practices that, in most cases, were built upon well-established colonial traditions. At the same time, the construction of the new republics required the implementation of new notions of citizenship, rights, and equality before the law that, despite the limitations in their application, opened up new terrains for contestation and resistance.

The study of penal practices and discourses in Arequipa, Peru, during the transition from colonialism to independence illuminates this complicated process. In the following essay, Sarah Chambers, assistant professor of history at the University of Minnesota, argues that concern with public order and crime increased in the years following independence and led to stiffer mechanisms of social control. This occurrence had to do with a real increase in crime and a more efficient installation of legal procedures, but also with an emphasis on the need to enforce a new republican code of virtue. However, the rhetoric of republicanism and civil rights offered plebeians the opportunity to contest the growing intrusion of republican authorities in the regulation of their public and private lives. The formation of new independent countries thus brought about intricate political and cultural changes that also resonated in the courts, prisons, and police stations.

As Michael Scardaville pointed out in the previous chapter, the legitimacy of a government, especially in the eyes of the lower classes, rests significantly upon the actions of the judicial system. Whereas he examined changes from the Hapsburg to Bourbon regimes in colonial Mexico, this essay analyzes legal practice during the political transition from a colonial monarchy to an independent republic in Peru. A study of Arequipa between 1780 and 1854 revealed significant if somewhat contradictory changes in methods of social control and legal theory. In the first place, a growing concern among civil authorities over social disorder was reflected in a dramatic increase in the number of criminal trials after independence. The initial response to this perceived instability was an attempt to reestablish control by reorganizing the criminal justice and police systems. But in the midst of this growing repression there also emerged a diffusion of liberal ideas through the new constitutions and in the speeches of politicians and military leaders. Such ideas influenced the popular classes who used them to defend themselves against charges of criminality and to claim their new rights as citizens. A review of criminal cases throughout this period reveals, therefore, that many battles over the formation and legitimation of a new state in Arequipa were fought in the courts.

With a population of about twenty-four thousand in 1792, Arequipa served as an important commercial and administrative center in Peru. Its integration into southern trade routes through the sale of wine and liquor to the mining center of Potosí in the colonial period and the export of wool to Europe during the nineteenth century gave the city a degree of autonomy from the capital of Lima and contributed to a sense of regional identity.[1] Although the city's elite owned vineyards and plantations in nearby coastal valleys, its wealth was modest in comparison with the aristocracy of Lima, and small and medium-sized property dominated the immediate countryside. Moreover, ethnic identity was ambiguous enough to allow a majority of inhabitants to claim they were "Spanish," although many were probably light-skinned mestizos and mulattoes. Such dynamics of class and ethnicity helped to mitigate social conflict in Arequipa and further strengthened regional solidarity.[2]

Colonial Social Control

In late colonial Arequipa, the church rather than the state was concerned about the "unruly" behavior of the plebe. Under the leadership of Bishop Pedro José Chaves de la Rosa, the church tried to suppress popular customs it considered immoral. One of the first efforts of this zealous bishop was to control the popular celebrations, which he considered pagan, that accompanied official Catholic holidays. Like his predecessors, Chaves also tried to reform the "indecent" clothing worn by his flock, even threatening them with excommunication. But he put the most effort into a campaign against what he called "the public sins of concubinage." The bishop preferred not to wait for God to punish such sins, so he continually asked the civil authorities to take rigorous measures to eradicate such customs. For the most part, however, his pleas went unanswered as he complained with disappointment to the viceroy.[3]

If the bishop of Arequipa could not count upon his colleagues in government for assistance in policing the morality of his flock, it was certainly in the interest of the latter to maintain general law and order. The civil authorities may have overlooked harmless carousing among the plebe, but they could not afford to let thievery and violence get out of hand. One would expect concern over social control to have been particularly high in the late colonial period, when a series of rebellions challenged the Spanish state. In the streets of Lima, moreover, authorities faced rising crime and general plebeian disorder.[4] Nevertheless, there were few indications that the dominant groups in colonial Arequipa were worried about a threat from below.

The lack of concern about disorder among the city's authorities is reflected in their ad hoc approach to law enforcement. Larger cities such as Lima and Mexico City established police forces in the late eighteenth century in response to growing concerns about crime.[5] Although Arequipa's city council had a commissioner for police, his primary responsibility was to make sure city streets were maintained in good condition and cleaned up for special occasions.[6] The lack of an institutionalized police force became evident in a 1794 petition from the mayors of Arequipa to the royal governor (intendant) in which they lamented, "All your indefatigable zeal to see that this city is to the extent possible purged and free from troublemakers, vagrants, and harmful elements; and all our desires for the greater honor to God, good service to the Sovereign, and fulfillment of our duties, all are found to be sadly frustrated." Because jail fees generated so little income, they explained, there was not enough money to pay officers to serve on patrols. The mayors asked the intendant to establish a force of four ministers with an annual salary of fifty pesos each to be paid out of other municipal funds. The town council, in supporting this request, claimed that "the lowly plebe is almost unbridled in its excesses without this assistance."[7] The intendant, believing that he did not have the authority to make such a decision, forwarded the request to the Real Audiencia (high court) of Lima. The audiencia waited over ten years to issue a ruling. When the justices did announce their approval in March 1805 it was only provisional; if the king did not ratify their decision, the council of Arequipa would have to refund any money spent on the patrols. The council appealed this condition, but it was not lifted until 1808. On the one hand, this request reflected the local authorities' concerns about maintaining public order; on the other hand, that they were willing to wait fourteen years to establish a police force reveals that law enforcement was not their first priority.

While strict regulations may have existed, enforcement was often lax. Even in prosecuting plebeians for robbery the record is uneven. There is little in the records about petty thefts; most likely these were dealt with by local officials with punishment being restitution of the goods and/or a few days in jail. Nevertheless, of the twelve surviving cases that did make it to trial between 1784 and 1824, only four reached the sentencing stage. One reason for inconclusive prosecution was the slow pace of justice; several robbery trials lasted for years. By the time these cases reached sentencing, if they did, the punishment was often less than the time the defendant had already served. Although some prisoners languished in jail—or even died—while lawyers and justices attended to higher priority and more lucrative civil suits, others had been released on bond or escaped long before their trials concluded or were discontinued.[8]

For the most part, criminals were not targets of vindictive condemnations, and pardons to commemorate civic occasions were not uncommon.[9] In fact, accused robbers suffered more from neglect in the late colonial period than from serving out actual sentences. The frequency of jailbreaks shows that they could sometimes use that neglect to their advantage.[10] Prison security was not a high priority in the late colonial period. In 1789 for example, an accused murderer left through the open front door of the jail. The jailkeeper admitted that he had invited the prisoner to his birthday party and, believing the inmate's offer to provide music was sincere, let him out to fetch the musicians.[11] On the eve of independence, security was even more lax. When three prisoners escaped in 1821, an investigation uncovered that their shackles and cell doors were defective. The jailkeeper insisted that he had tried to get the council's deputy for jails to repair them, but the official only joked that "the prisoners were not birds who could fly over such high walls," and asserted that the Spanish Constitution of 1820 had put an end to prisons.[12]

Republican Fears about Crime

If the deputy for jails in 1820 could be so moved by compassion that "he would start crying with the prisoners, and even wanted to give them his shirt,"[13] a decade later such a benevolent attitude toward criminals would be difficult to find. One year after the recognition of independence in Arequipa, notices in the local newspaper expressed increasing concern over police services: "Arequipa, which presents the most beautiful potential to be a city lovelier and cleaner than any other, we see it nevertheless turned into a trash heap: without lighting at night, causing robberies, deaths and other disorders under the shelter of darkness."[14] Bỳ the end of the decade, fears about rising crime voiced by citizens, municipal authorities, court officials, and prefects indicated that the break from Spain had threatened social peace in Arequipa. The wars of independence and subsequent civil strife led to frequent turnovers in national and local governments, increased the supply of weapons among the population, and brought soldiers from other regions and countries, some of whom remained in Arequipa. Such instability may have created an opportunity for increased delinquency, and it certainly heightened perceptions of disorder and crime.

The increase in the number of criminal trials between the late colonial and republican periods is dramatic (see Figure 1). Compared to only 184 reported cases during the last four decades of the colonial period,

Figure 1. Criminal Trials for the City of Arequipa and Its Suburbs

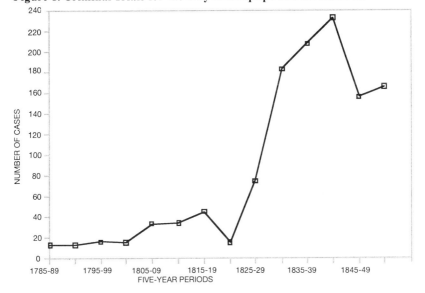

there were 1,021 criminal trials during the first thirty years after independence. The number of trials began to rise slightly near the end of Spanish rule—particularly personal injury lawsuits and disputes with authorities—reflecting perhaps an initial questioning of the legitimacy of colonial norms.[15] After independence, however, the number of crimes prosecuted really accelerated; the increase in violent crimes is particularly striking.

Several factors could account for this burgeoning of criminal trials, a twelvefold increase in the first decade after independence alone. In the first place, less reliable records for the colonial period may lead to an undercounting of crimes. Cases would have been better preserved after independence, particularly as judicial powers were consolidated under the superior court, which reviewed all cases tried by the judges of first instance. A more significant if related factor, however, is that republican courts prosecuted crimes which under the colonial system either went unheeded or were handled in oral hearings by local justices of the peace. This change in priorities is also evident in the increasing proportion of cases prosecuted at the initiative of the judge or public prosecutor (*de oficio*) as opposed to those initiated by the injured party (*de parte*). During the colonial period for example, targets of theft were responsible not only for reporting the crime to the authorities but also for presenting witnesses and formally accusing the defendant. After independence the courts were more likely to take over all aspects of the investigation and prosecution after a robbery was reported.

The crime most commonly tried in the colonial period, moreover, was also prosecuted almost exclusively *de parte*: *injurias*. Under Spanish law "injuries" could be either verbal (*de palabra*)—insults to one's honor or reputation—or physical (*de hecho*)—bodily harm inflicted either with or without weapons.[16] Judges were forbidden to prosecute verbal injuries *de oficio*, and colonial judges in Arequipa rarely tried persons for causing physical injuries.[17] After independence however, the courts increasingly prosecuted cases of physical assault—whether or not the injured party wished to press charges—under a new criminal category they called "wounds."

Finally, by looking at the striking increase in murder trials a case could be made that authorities were responding to a real rise in the crime rate.[18] From a total of six murder cases in the city between 1785 and 1824, the number jumped to ten in only the first five years after independence and forty-eight between 1830 and 1834. While some murders in the countryside may have gone undetected, it is difficult to believe that those occurring in the city would not have come to the attention of the authorities. Furthermore, there was a perception among contemporaries that crime was on the rise, especially between 1825 and 1834. As the wealthier inhabitants of the city were more likely to be the targets of theft, their concerns focused on the problems of assault and robbery. In 1829 for example, a French merchant was accused of shooting and killing a poor, drunken Spaniard; he claimed the man was trying to break into his house and presented witnesses who testified that there had been a rash of recent robberies. "The city is in a state of fear," affirmed another French merchant, "by the multitude of thieves, who attack the foreign warehouses and private homes."[19] Witnesses in other trials, when questioned why they carried weapons prohibited by law, claimed they needed them at night to protect themselves from assault.[20] Perhaps the economic disruption caused by the wars of independence increased incidents of theft and interpersonal violence. Even if most of the violent crimes occurred among plebeians, the authorities were concerned by the rise in assaults and murders, which they attributed partly to an increase in the number of knives on the market.[21]

Republican Courts

It is difficult to determine how much of the increase in criminal trials after independence was due to better record preservation, to increased vigilance by the authorities, and to a rise in the real crime rate. It is impossible to deny, however, that the problem of disorder took on a significance for the authorities of the new republic which far surpassed concerns during the last four decades of the colonial period. The judicial system had strong roots in colonial Spanish America, and served as an arbiter of disputes for diverse sectors of the population. Perhaps because of the need for trained professionals, the courts in Arequipa experienced less turnover in personnel after independence and subsequent regime changes than other branches of government.[22] The first institutional response by the new state to the problem of crime, therefore, was to build upon the stability of the criminal justice system by making its organization more rational and efficient. During the colonial period, political and judicial functions had been combined under the same officials. Mayors heard cases at the local level, the intendant—assisted by a legal adviser—was the highest judge in the department, and the Real Audiencia had final authority in appeals and oversight. In addition, members of various corporations— the Church, the military, or the merchant guilds—enjoyed special *fueros*, that is, the right to be judged in their own courts. Besides the obvious possibility for corruption, this combination of powers considerably slowed the pace of justice.[23] Proceedings were also hampered by the responsibility of the injured party to prosecute the case in many criminal as well as civil trials.

The republican form of government established after Peru's independence called for the separation of powers among executive, legislative, and judicial branches.[24] While minor disputes between neighbors would still be heard by local justices of the peace, trials for serious crimes (as well as civil litigation) were held under appointed judges of first instance. Sentences were reviewed in the second and third instances by regional superior courts, and in the final instance by the supreme court located in the capital. The Superior Court of Arequipa was established by law on

February 1, 1825, with a president, four justices (*vocales*), and a *fiscal* (similar to a public prosecutor). At the time of its installation there were already advocates who favored increasing the number of justices, and two more justices were added to the court in 1826.[25]

Clearly, the new courts in Arequipa handled a much greater volume of cases compared to those of the colonial period; in addition, a growing proportion of those cases were prosecuted by the state (*de oficio*). Whereas in the colonial period the state took on responsibility only for cases in which the injured parties did not have the means to prosecute their own cases or for crimes against the public order, republican judges in Arequipa took a more aggressive stance toward prosecution, leaving only some cases of personal injuries and sex related offenses to private plaintiffs. In spite of the heavier workload, trials generally became speedier under the new system; while robbery cases often lasted several years during the colonial period for example, it was unusual for them to take more than a few months after independence. By 1829 the court was feeling the effects of the rising crime rate not only in an increased case load, but also when one of the justices was the victim of an assault.[26] Work was piling up on the judges of first instance, causing the superior justices to fear that crimes would go unpunished: "Occupied with the immense dispatch of the civil cases they generally neglect to dedicate to the criminal cases all the attention which the good of society demands, and after long delays, it is not unusual for delinquents to find ways of escaping and thereby eluding the vigor of the laws. We should attribute to this cause the increase in criminality in this town, where robberies, which at another time were very rare, have become all too common."[27] Their request for a third judge of first instance to handle only criminal trials was approved by the central government in 1830.

The changes that took place in the organization and efficiency of the criminal justice system after independence were dramatic, and demonstrated the commitment of republican officials in Arequipa to maintaining social order and pursuing criminals. The shifts in penal philosophy, however, were more subtle. Although several constitutions were drafted during the period under study (namely 1823, 1826, 1828, 1834, and 1839), civil law was not codified under the republic until 1852, and there was no penal code until 1863.[28] Republican judges therefore were still required to base their sentences on the earlier body of Spanish law.[29] This situation created a foundation for continuity in criminal prosecution between the colonial and republican periods. Although apparent contradictions between those laws and with constitutional principles could be controversial, Spanish law gave wide discretion to judges to make the punishment fit the crime.[30]

Despite assertions by defense lawyers after independence, moreover, the Spanish criminal justice system had not been particularly punitive. Although harsh penalties such as mutilation and the desecration of bodies before or after execution existed in the written law, they were rarely applied in practice, especially by the eighteenth century.[31] Extreme punishments such as death or long prison terms were reserved for criminals considered unfit to live among other members of society.[32] Jails were for temporary detention and security only, not for punishment, although defendants were often sentenced to time already served during the trial. In practice, judges in late colonial Arequipa demonstrated both benevolence by letting off the majority of defendants accused of lesser offenses, and severity by sentencing to death criminals convicted of premeditated murder. The effect of the pardon or punishment was aimed as much at the general public as the particular defendant.

Similar practices in sentencing continued for the first half-decade after independence, although the courts began to use a wider range of punishments. But as concerns about increasing crime mounted, judges began to apply harsher penalties in an effort to stem the tide. This crackdown occurred particularly between 1830 and 1834, especially against those convicted of theft, assault, or murder. The first three constitutions called for a moderate use of the death penalty, but the Congress had not specified the types of cases in which it should or should not be applied.[33] In practice, about half of the death sentences appealed from 1825 to 1839 in Arequipa were eventually commuted to lesser penalties; the death penalty stood primarily when premeditation was clear,[34] if the victim was of higher social status than the offender,[35] or if the crime appeared particularly cruel.[36] In general, rather than condemning more convicts to the most severe penalty possible (six to ten years in prison for theft and death for murder), republican judges decreased the proportion absolved or let off with time already served and sentenced them instead to intermediate punishments of several years in public works or prison.

Republican Policing

As much as the court system was expanded and reorganized after independence, it could not handle law enforcement in Arequipa on its own. City officials needed a police force that could deliver accused criminals to the courts, patrol the streets in an effort to maintain order, and mete out fines and other penalties for minor infractions. The development of the police force however was a more gradual and uneven process than the establishment of a judicial system. Issues regarding its size, budget, structure, and jurisdiction were negotiated between civilian and military officials as well as local authorities and the central government. Never-theless, a permanent force was established as a branch of the military, and its tendency was to grow during the first decades of the republican period. The Constitution of 1839 created the position of police intendant, an official appointed by the central government who would have a corps of night watchmen under his command.[37] By the 1850s the policemen in Arequipa numbered at least fifty.

The question remains however whether the police were effective in maintaining order and deterring crime. The police squad was initially quite small, and even so had difficulty finding recruits. Occasionally delin-quents were sentenced to police duty, but it is doubtful that such con-scripts did much to improve the effectiveness or morale of the force.[38] In 1834 the police were criticized by the courts not only for being unable to prevent street fighting, but for failing to find even a suspect in the case of a boy who was killed in such a fight. "This outcome is a disgrace for a cultured town," declared the *fiscal*, "where the police should be vigilant and prepared to apprehend whoever disturbs the public order."[39] Finally, security at the jail did not improve significantly, and escapes were common.[40]

Without access to police records it is difficult to judge the effective-ness of law enforcement; minor infractions were rarely brought to trial, but instead handled on the spot through the imposition of temporary incarceration or fines.[41] Nonetheless the authorities certainly gave the impression that they were serious about enforcing local ordinances. Regu-lations governing the whereabouts of outside visitors and controlling public safety and hygiene were published in the official newspaper in 1832.[42] Soon thereafter, lists of persons fined for infractions began to appear periodically. Throughout the second half of the year over 260 resi-dents were levied between one-half real and six pesos each. The most frequent violations were failures of travelers to register or obtain pass-ports and of homeowners to light their section of the street. But the police also meted out fines for littering, raising animals in the street, drunken-ness, cockfighting, and arguing with the officers.[43] In an effort to oversee more serious crimes, the prefect ordered the superior court to submit monthly reports on the progress of all penal cases, which were also printed in the newspaper.[44] It is possible that the leveling off and then decline in the number of criminal trials in the 1840s and 1850s may have reflected the deterrent effect of increased police vigilance.[45]

Whatever the results, there was clearly a new determination by re-publican authorities to bring society under greater control. This new zeal not only responded to the perception of general disorder brought on by political instability but also represented an ideological change to republicanism. Like classical liberals elsewhere, authorities in Arequipa emphasized the importance of individual discipline. The language used to justify new regulations was striking. In ordering the closure of the cockfighting ring for example, the departmental junta argued "that cockfights clash directly with the virtue and morals that should be upheld in a Republican Government."[46] Similarly, the prefect prohibited gambling on the grounds that "it consumes the life which should be of benefit to the Nation."[47] And whereas inebriation had been considered an extenuating circumstance in criminal cases during the colonial period, republican prosecutors and judges were less inclined to accept it as an excuse and might even consider it an aggravating circumstance.[48] In contrast to their colonial predecessors, who had withheld support from Bishop Chaves, republican officials launched a campaign to reform the morality of the population.

Whereas there were no cases in the late colonial period of persons being brought to court without specific charges, republican police officers exhibited greater zeal in arresting "suspicious" characters. In 1831 for example, a man was picked up in the suburb of Yanahuara simply for being in an alley "where thieves surely meet" late at night. That same night two black men were arrested because "they are not known around here," and reports after the fact asserted that "they live closed in by day so as not to be seen."[49] Common people in Arequipa therefore found their daily lives subject to increasing regulation and harassment during the early years of the republic.

It should come as no surprise that the imposition of new controls was not accepted cheerfully by the population of Arequipa. In the first decade after independence the presence of troops in the city gave rise to clashes between soldiers and civilians. Some conflicts erupted directly out of encounters with the patrols, especially those that went out to conscript soldiers. In October 1829 for example, three soldiers apprehended an alleged deserter in Miraflores, but while they were taking him back to the barracks "they were ambushed in the plaza of San Antonio by several civilians and women, which resulted in the escape of the deserter and left the soldiers bloodied and hurt."[50] Furthermore, popular resentment of the military and police was so deeply felt that clashes also occurred when soldiers were not on duty. When police corporal Alejo Taquire was fighting with his mistress, her cries attracted two strangers who came to her defense.[51] A couple of weeks later, soldier Ramón Esquivel complained to his commanding officer that three civilians had beaten him up when he tried to buy liquor from them.[52]

Moreover, resentment of the military and police was not limited to plebeians. Shopkeepers also complained of abuses by soldiers, especially drunken ones. Andrés Bracamonte, whose wife ran a *chichería* in their house, said that he did not allow soldiers to enter the establishment.[53] Tension between civilians and soldiers was often intensified by differences in social status. Most members of the armed forces' different branches were poor conscripts, often from the countryside and of mixed race. Such social differences became dramatically clear in 1836 when a young "gentleman" died from wounds received during a run-in with a *sereno* (night watchman), Lorenzo Velasco. Velasco, who was originally from Cuzco and had only worked in Arequipa for six years, was probably an Indian or mestizo.[54] The prosecutor charged Velasco with Carbajal's death for having exceeded his duties, and called for a punishment that would serve as a warning against "the immorality and arrogance, which to society's misfortune, is the heritage of these kinds of men, who currently carry out the critical function of acting as night sentinels to conserve the public peace." Velasco's lawyer however secured his absolution; he argued that the death was accidental, and that it was necessary "to protect and assist the night watchmen to maintain their respectability and with it order."[55]

Even if this was an unusually dramatic case, judges were repeatedly confronted with the dilemma of upholding the authority of the police and military while protecting people from abuses. In a surprising number of cases the courts did not decide in favor of soldiers or policemen. In the case where a crowd had freed a "deserter" from three soldiers, the lower court charged Justo Pastor as an accomplice. But the superior court, noting that it had not even been proven that the man in question was in fact a deserter, sent the case back for further investigation.[56] Similarly, the *fiscal* saw no reason to continue investigating the incident in which the soldier Esquivel had been harmed by civilians, given that Esquivel had provoked the fight.[57] When two men were charged with attacking corporal Taquire while he was arguing with his lover, Justice of the Peace Mariano Fernández de Pascua sent a letter to the prefect in which he accused Taquire and two other soldiers of being the aggressors: "The crimes that the soldiers of the police commit . . . impels me to turn to Your Lordship as the one charged by Law with conserving order and the security of citizens."[58]

The Rights of Honorable Citizens

During the first decades after independence in Arequipa, local authorities attempted to establish control over the populace by expanding the systems of criminal justice and law enforcement. There were limits, however, to achieving a new social equilibrium solely through the use of force.

Plebeians resisted attempts by authorities to subject them to ever greater regulation, while civilian and military officials themselves did not always agree on appropriate methods of social control. The transition from monarchy to republic therefore required ideological as well as institutional changes. Although its practice was far from democratic, the new state asserted its legitimacy based upon popular sovereignty rather than divine right. In order to avoid "mob rule," republican doctrine required citizens to regulate their behavior in the interests of the common good. Such a philosophy justified an attack on popular morals, but it also provided a discourse of resistance. With the help of lawyers, victims of police repression turned in defense to the constitutions, which made all Peruvians equal before the law and established protections for basic civil rights.[59] Ideals such as liberty and equality were new to most of the population when they suddenly entered public discourse in 1824, but the notion of republican virtue did resonate with the colonial value of honor.

The early constitutions explicitly recognized every citizen's right to his honor, guaranteeing "[t]he good opinion, or reputation of the individual, as long as he is not declared a delinquent according to the laws."[60] This article was used successfully by defendants and their lawyers to win release from jail, since incarceration was considered dishonoring. When María Beltran filed charges of *injurias* against the sisters Bernarda and Juana Torres, bakers in Tiabaya, they claimed that she had been the one to come to their house, insulting them and damaging their reputation, "which according to our charter every citizen has the right to conserve as long as he is not declared a delinquent according to the laws." The *fiscal*, agreeing that jail was an "offense against honorable families," argued that not only should the women be freed but that they had the right to sue the justice of the peace for damages.[61] In 1828, Alberto Anco, a leading Indian in the parish of Santa Marta, did bring charges against the judge who jailed him during a trial instigated by his wife for adultery. The superior court censured the judge, asserting "that under no circumstances should Don Alberto Anco have been mixed in with the other criminals who occupy the jails, since his conduct and good behavior have constantly made him deserving of public acceptance and because he has been considered worthy of obtaining public offices which he has carried out fully."[62] Such decisions by the courts limited the ability of the police to maintain control by arresting "suspicious" characters. Victoriano Concha, arrested in 1829 on suspicion of being a thief, was released when the *fiscal* asserted that the evidence against him was insufficient "to have persecuted a man damaging him in his person and honor."[63]

In addition to protecting a person's reputation, the early constitutions guaranteed that "[t]he house of every Peruvian is an inviolable asylum."[64]

To be insulted in one's own home had always been considered a particularly serious affront. *Arequipeños* seized upon this constitutional guarantee to charge both officials and civilians with illegal breaking and entering.[65] In 1832 a group of youths pretending to be policemen broke into the home of a shoemaker. The judge cut the case short, but the *fiscal* protested that the crime was serious, noting, "[w]hatever the condition and wretchedness of the shoemaker Lázaro may be, and the poverty of his shack or house, it is a haven [*sagrado*] which should be considered according to the law as safe as that of the first magistrate of the Republic."[66] When José Arenaza, who claimed to be an Indian cacique, was charged with insubordination to the governor of Chiguata, he claimed that he simply had been defending the rights of a poor Indian. Turning the charges around, Arenaza had asked the governor: "Why are you coming to insult me in my house, do you not know that this is my sacred asylum . . . ?"[67]

Although working people were experiencing greater regulation and surveillance of their lives in republican Arequipa, the courts were willing to protect them—and their honor—if they were hardworking and met the norms of proper behavior. In other words, rights were made contingent upon responsibilities. In 1831, José María Madaleno, a black man from Ica, and José Torres from Sincha were picked up by a patrol as "suspicious" characters. Their claims to have "always maintained themselves with honor, and by means of their labor" were backed up by character witnesses. At the time of their arrest these men had been working for two weeks as cobblers, but they had a history of temporary jobs and general labor. Nevertheless, the judge found them to be "honest men behaving themselves with honor and without any stain on their reputations." Indignant that they had suffered because of an unjust suspicion, he ordered their release and absolved them, "restoring them to their former good reputations and fame."[68]

Sentences also reflected the new liberal work ethic.[69] Convicts had been sentenced to public works in the colonial period, but republican courts proposed it as an opportunity for rehabilitation as well as punishment, especially for juvenile delinquents. When thirteen-year-old José Benavides was sentenced to six years' service on a naval ship, his lawyer appealed, arguing that such a punishment would corrupt rather than reform the boy. The superior court apparently agreed; it reduced Benavides's sentence to three years' labor in the hospital run by the Order of San Juan de Dios "so that at the same time that he is providing this service, he shall be instructed in the art of pharmacy to which his Parents had dedicated him, according to their oral deposition." The justices further ordered the administrator of the hospital and the reverend prior to oversee the boy's conduct, not allowing him to go out onto the streets, and to instruct him daily in Christian doctrine.[70]

Justices also took the new step of assigning defendants to work for a master artisan or in an "honorable" house. In 1836 three apprentice tailors, ages twelve to fourteen, were charged with robbing their own master; two of them faced sentences of six months in jail and a year of labor in the hospital. Appealing to the justices' "enlightened" outlook, their lawyer argued that the apprentices could better be turned into useful citizens by assigning them to another master tailor known for his character and good conduct: "dedicated to their work, there will be engendered in them a love for the conservation of their good names . . . and they will be taught modesty and delicacy."[71] Once again the superior court was persuaded by such an argument; the justices reduced the boys' sentences to thirty and sixty days of public labor, after which they were to be turned over to a master tailor. The justices' belief in rehabilitation even extended to some adults. When Melchor Randes stole cloth from a petty merchant in 1831, he was originally sentenced to six years in prison. The superior court reduced his punishment to four months of public works, after which time "he shall only be able to leave jail by presenting an honorable person who will take responsibility to teach him a useful way of life, and give him an occupation." If no sponsor was found, his sentence would be increased to two years.[72]

Defense lawyers were quick to catch on to this possibility of commuting their clients' sentences, but the strategy did not always work.[73] In 1836, Pedro Morales, like Randes, was convicted of stealing a trunk of merchandise from a petty vendor in the plaza. His lawyer, arguing that he was a simple laborer with an otherwise clean record, asked that he be turned over to a master shoemaker and that his salary be docked to reimburse the plaintiff. The prosecutor countered that the crime was particularly serious precisely because "he committed the theft in spite of exercising the occupation of shoemaker, the earnings of which are sufficient to satisfy his needs." Instead of showing clemency, the superior court increased his sentence to two years, which he served out in the army.[74] Morales apparently did not fit the court's image of an honest workingman, and therefore his case stirred little sympathy.

Judges could be indignant when working people were arrested without sufficient evidence, but they believed that suspicions about the unemployed were well grounded. In 1831, Victoriano Concha was arrested a second time and charged with complicity in the case of a slave accused of stealing silver from his master. Even the *fiscal* admitted there was little evidence against Concha, but argued that merely his association with the slave combined with his unemployment was proof enough of guilt. "A man without an occupation or a known way of life," he pointed out, "will most likely transgress in all matters."[75] When Enrique Nuñes complained that he had been illegally imprisoned, Judge Pascual Francisco Suero retorted that he was a "vagrant, ne'er-do-well without an occupation, and therefore, not a citizen."[76]

Poor women, who had a hard time living up to elite notions of respectability, were least likely to receive clemency from the courts. While their behavior had probably not changed in any significant way, their sexuality was increasingly seen as a threat to public order. When María Samudio was arrested for assaulting her lover, soldier José Valdez, even the prosecutor considered the wounds so inconsequential that the charges should be dropped. He argued nevertheless that Samudio should be punished for her loose morals and that the prefect should take stern measures against women like her, because "this type of crime is repeated daily due to the toleration of the public immorality of these women, who abandoning modesty, social considerations, and family obligations, have the impudence to present themselves in public as prostituted persons."[77]

A work ethic failed to redeem women since their virtue depended upon fulfilling domestic roles. Because women who committed crimes were seen as "unnatural," officials were also less sanguine about their potential rehabilitation.[78] An editorial in the government newspaper asserted that female prisoners should work not because they would be reformed, but "so that they are not consumed by a sedentary life, so that they feel in some way the punishment of their crime, so that their passions are not encouraged believing [their crimes] forgotten, and so that the public will have proof that crimes will not increase from impunity or misunderstood compassion."[79] Such a view of women prevented Juana Pía's lawyer from winning her even a transfer from working in the jail to the hospital. The *fiscal* argued that she had become a habitual thief "due to the perversity of a corrupted heart," and would therefore "put that holy place in disorder, continuing in her habits and scandalizing the institution."[80]

Conclusion

After independence from Spain, the challenge of establishing a new state that would enjoy legitimacy was daunting. The upper classes feared that crime had gotten out of control, but the lower classes resented state intervention in their lives. The formation of the republican state therefore entailed both institutional and ideological processes.

In the midst of civil warfare and frequent changes in government personnel, the courts were a relative oasis of stability and continuity. In the absence of a new criminal code, republican judges responded to crime by applying existing Spanish laws, often more strictly than their colonial predecessors. They were assisted in this crackdown by the prefects who established a permanent police force to patrol the streets and arrest suspicious characters. Moreover, the definition of delinquency was expanded to include moral crimes that had been considered of little importance in the colonial period.

Plebeians, however, resisted this greater regulation and began to assert that they were not criminals and vagrants but honorable citizens. Defense lawyers likewise argued against those Spanish laws and penalties that conflicted with new republican principles. Recognizing that order could not be restored through force alone, authorities in Arequipa were willing to uphold the constitutional rights of workingmen who demonstrated self-discipline and a work ethic. By mid-century, republican officials appeared confident that they had reestablished order based upon this new pact. The severity of sentences began to decline and judges increasingly ordered justices of the peace to handle less serious crimes. Whether or not the popular classes thoroughly accepted the new morality, the ability of many to convince judges that they could exercise self-control allayed elite fears.

Of course the new liberal discourse did not create an egalitarian or democratic society, as poor men and especially women who could not live up to the new norms of respectability discovered. Nevertheless, the gradual process of establishing a new state during the transition following independence did allow for a debate in Arequipa over the rights of citizenship and the laws that should govern a republic, a debate that extended from clashes in the streets between plebeians and police to the courts of justice.

Notes

1. Alberto Flores Galindo, *Arequipa y el sur andino, siglos XVIII–XX* (Lima: Editorial Horizonte, 1977).

2. Sarah C. Chambers, *From Subjects to Citizens: Honor, Gender, and Politics in Arequipa, Peru, 1780–1854* (University Park: Pennsylvania State University Press, 1999).

3. Biblioteca Nacional del Perú (hereafter BNP), doc. D11643 (1801). For more examples see Chambers, *From Subjects to Citizens,* 126–136.

4. Alberto Flores Galindo, *Aristocracia y plebe: Lima, 1760–1830* (Lima: Mosca Azul Editores, 1984), and Carlos Aguirre, "Cimarronaje, bandolerismo y desintegración esclavista: Lima, 1821–1854," in Carlos Aguirre and Charles

Walker, eds., *Bandoleros, abigeos y montoneros: Criminalidad y violencia en el Perú, siglos XVIII-XX* (Lima: Instituto de Apoyo Agrario, 1990), 137–182.

5. Flores Galindo, *Aristocracia y plebe*, 153, and Gabriel James Haslip, "Crime and the Administration of Justice in Colonial Mexico City, 1696–1810" (Ph.D. dissertation, Columbia University, 1980), 97.

6. Archivo Municipal de Arequipa (hereafter AMA), Libro de Propios y Arbitrios (LPA) 3, entry dated June 21, 1792.

7. BNP doc. C1196 (1794).

8. Criminal cases are stored in the Archivo Regional de Arequipa (hereafter ARAR), filed under "Intendencia: Causas Criminales" (Int.: Crim.) for the colonial period, and "Corte Superior: Causas Criminales" (Corte Sup.: Crim.) after independence in 1824. Because the archives are not cataloged, I provide the initial date title to identify each trial as well as a brief title when pertinent. For colonial theft trials, see ARAR, Int.: Crim. (14-XII-1790), (18-VIII-1792), (3-XII-1796), (17-XI-1797), (10-IX-1799), (4-X-1800), (12-II-1801), (19-III-1806), (1-VII-1808), (21-X-1810), (27-IV-1816), (9-XII-1823).

9. See ARAR, Int.: Crim. (4-X-1800), Contra Matías Alpaca por robo, (24-XI-1803) Contra Gregorio Ramos por homicidio, and AMA, Libro de Actas de Cabildo (LAC) 26, (1-VIII-1808).

10. AMA, LPA 1 (23-II-1780 and 14-VI-1782), Libro de Expedientes (LEXP) 1, (22-IX-1803), ARAR, Int.: Crim. (15-VII-1789) Sobre la fuga de Ignacio Zegarra, and (18-I-1821) Sobre la aprehensión de Romualdo Quispe.

11. ARAR, Int.: Crim. (15-VII-1789), Sobre la fuga de Zegarra.

12. ARAR, Int.: Crim. (18-I-1821) Sobre la aprehensión de Quispe.

13. Ibid. In 1790, Deputy Juan de Dios López de Castillo similarly complained that the jailkeeper treated the prisoners badly; ARAR, Intendencia: Pedimentos (28-VII-1790).

14. "Aviso," *El Republicano* 1, 7 (January 7, 1826). See also "Policía," *El Republicano* 1, 16 (March 11, 1826), 74.

15. The decline in criminal trials between 1820 and 1824 is probably due to the disruption of the wars of independence.

16. Alamiro de Avila Martel, *Esquema del derecho penal indiano* (Santiago: Seminario de Derecho Público de la Escuela de Ciencias Jurídicas y Sociales de Santiago, 1941), 83–86.

17. The only surviving assault cases from the colonial period are ARAR, Int.: Crim. (13-VII-1810) Contra Mariano Vásquez, and (3-II-1813) Contra Manuel Rivera.

18. The number of murder trials is generally the best indication of the true crime rate; William Taylor, *Drinking, Homicide, and Rebellion in Colonial Mexican Villages* (Stanford: Stanford University Press, 1979), 73–77.

19. ARAR, Corte Sup.: Crim. (22-VI-1829), Don Santiago LeBris contra Miguel Linares. See also Archivo Histórico-Militar del Perú (hereafter AHMP [CEHMP]) Leg. 26, Num. 99, Prefect Juan Francisco Reyes to the Minister of War, July 5, 1829.

20. ARAR, Prefectura (20-II-1828), Contra Don Mariano Arróspide y Don José López por puñaladas a Marselo Arayco; and ARAR, Corte Sup.: Crim. (17-IV-1833), Contra Mateo Chávez por homicidio.

21. ARAR, Corte Sup.: Crim. (29-VI-1831) Contra Vidal Jara por homicidio. See also Arturo Villegas Romero, *Un decenio de la historia de Arequipa, 1830–1840* (Arequipa: Fundación Gloria, 1985), 314.

22. Rubén A. Bustamante Ugarte, *La Corte Superior de Justicia de Arequipa, 1825–1925* (Arequipa: Tipografía Córdova, 1925).

23. H. H. A. Cooper, "A Short History of Peruvian Criminal Procedure and Institutions," *Revista de Derecho y Ciencias Políticas* 32 (1968): 226–238.

24. Cooper, "A Short History," 215–267, and Bustamante Ugarte, *La Corte Superior*, 17.

25. Bustamante Ugarte, *La Corte Superior*, 25–27 and 57.

26. Memorandum, February 19, 1829, Archivo General de la Nación (hereafter AGN), Corte Superior de Justicia, Leg. 4.

27. Ibid., Memorandum, February 18, 1830.

28. Cooper, "A Short History," 240–249.

29. Jorge Basadre, *Historia del derecho peruano* (Lima: Editorial Antena, 1937), 219–275.

30. Ibid., 268–275, and Avila Martel, *Esquema del derecho*, 36–38.

31. Avila Martel, *Esquema del derecho*, 39–43.

32. Between 1785 and 1824, four people were sentenced to death in two trials; ARAR, Int.: Crim. (23-VI-1808), Contra Leandro Quispe y Luisa Chaves, and (14-IV-1818), Contra Romualdo Quispe y Buenaventura Roque. A study of Chile found no case in which the death penalty was applied; Avila Martel, *Esquema del derecho*, 82.

33. The 1856 Constitution outlawed capital punishment but it was reinstated in 1860. Juan F. Olivo, *Constituciones políticas del Perú, 1821–1919* (Lima: Imprenta Torres Aguirre, 1922), 57, 100, and 137; and Pedro L. Alvarez Ganoza, *Origen y trayectoria de la aplicación de la pena de muerte en la historia del derecho peruano.* (Lima: Editorial Dorhca, 1974), 15–20.

34. ARAR, Corte Sup.: Crim. (28-V-1830) Contra Gregorio Benavides, and (5-XII-1831) Contra Juan Ampuero.

35. ARAR, Corte Sup.: Crim. (30-III-1832) Contra Mariano Choqueña por el homicidio de Juana Cama [mother-in-law], (11-VII-1833) Contra Antonio Lujan por el homicidio del español Juan Hidalgo, (9-X-1833) Contra Guillermo García por el homicidio de Manuela Sedillo [sister-in-law], (9-II-1834) Contra el negro esclavo Benancio Viscarra por el homicidio de Don Francisco Pomadera; (27-VI-1834) Contra José Rodríguez por haber herido al Religioso de la Merced Fray Manuel Muñoz, and (8-I-1838) Contra Francisco Chiri por el homicidio de Mercedes Valdés [sister].

36. ARAR, Corte Sup.: Crim. (21-VIII-1832) Contra Mariano Macedo por el homicidio de Manuela Barrios [pregnant], and (20-X-1833) Contra Agustín Apaza, Fabiana Quispe y María Cayra por el homicidio de Paula Mamani.

37. Olivo, *Constituciones políticas*, 232–233, and Jorge Basadre, *Historia de la República del Perú* (Lima: Ediciones "Historia," 1961), 443.

38. ARAR, Corte Sup.: Crim. (20-X-1831) Contra Juan Galiano y Matías Bedoya, and (3-VII-1833) Contra Pablo Aguilar.

39. ARAR, Corte Sup.: Crim. (22-IX-1834) Sobre el homicidio del menor Julián Ortega.

40. During civil wars invading troops often freed prisoners, but others escaped on their own. ARAR, Corte Sup.: Crim. (5-I-1829) Contra Miguel Ramos por fuga, (7-IX-1829) Sobre un agujero en uno de los calabozos de la cárcel, (7-IV-1834) Sobre el paradero de los presos que fugaron, (24-XI-1834) Contra Mariano Villegas por estupro y fuga, (10-VI-1836) Contra Inocencio Pardo, and Prefectura (23-III-1838) Sobre la fuga de los presos.

41. Villegas Romero, *Un decenio*, 443.

42. See *El Republicano* 8, 13 (March 30, 1833), 4; 8, 30 (July 27, 1833), 1-2; 8, 32 (August 10, 1833), 7; 8, 36 (September 7, 1833), 7; 8, 48 (November 30, 1833), 7; and 8, 51 (December 21, 1833), 4–6.

43. *El Republicano* 8, 26 (June 29, 1833), 7; 8, 31 (August 3, 1833), 4; 8, 34 (August 24, 1833), 7; 8, 36 (September 7, 1833), 6–7; 8, 41 (October 12, 1833), 6–7; 8, 43 (October 26, 1833), 6; 8, 48 (November 30, 1833), 7; and 8, 50 (December 14, 1833), 7.

44. *El Republicano* 8, 39 (September 28, 1833), 5–6.

45. V. A. C. Gatrell and T. B. Hadden argue that the extension of police control has the initial effect of increasing the number of arrests, which later decreases as that example leads to deterrence; see Gatrell and Hadden, "Criminal Statistics and their Interpretation," in E. A. Wrigley, ed., *Nineteenth-Century Society: Essays on the Use of Quantitative Methods for the Study of Social Data* (London: Cambridge University Press, 1972), 353–55.

46. Quoted in Villegas Romero, *Un Decenio*, 445.

47. BNP doc. D8478 (1825).

48. See ARAR, Corte Sup.: Crim. (4-IV-1829) Contra Manuela Chalcotupa, (12-VI-1830) Contra Juan Montoya, (20-X-1831) Contra Juan Galiano y Matías Bedoya, (1-X-1832) Contra Luis Barrionuevo, (8-VII-1833) Contra Julián Martínez, (3-IX-1833) Sobre el robo y heridas inferidas al escribano Don Mariano Espinoza, (8-I-1838) Contra Francisco Chiri, and (29-IX-1841) Contra Mariano Torrico.

49. ARAR, Prefectura (21-XI-1831) Expediente criminal sobre investigarse la conducta de Ramón Llerena, José María Madaleno y José Torres. See also ARAR, Corte Sup.: Crim. (3-VII-1829) Expediente sobre el encarcelamiento de Pascual Silva sospechado de robo; (6-VII-1829) Contra Victoriano Concha por sospecharse que es ladrón; (1-VIII-1833) Contra Manuel Crispa por haberse venido de Islay a donde fue conducido para que regresase a su país; and (10-VI-1836) Contra Inocencio Pardo por haber herido a Pablo Rosado.

50. ARAR, Corte Sup.: Crim. (16-XI-1829) Contra Justo Pastor. See also ARAR, Corte Sup.: Crim. (13-III-1827) Contra Carlos Torres por haber estropeado al Comisario de Barrio de San Jerónimo y los soldados de ronda.

51. ARAR, Corte Sup.: Crim. (5-VII-1833) Contra Mariano y Pablo Blanco.

52. ARAR, Corte Sup.: Crim. (22-VII-1833) Contra Pedro José Madueño.

53. ARAR, Corte Sup.: Crim. (16-X-1825) Confesión del reo Cipriano Escobedo.

54. Carbajal's occupation was never stated, but he was always referred to as a gentleman (*caballero*).

55. ARAR, Corte Sup.: Crim. (7-V-1836) Contra Lorenzo Velasco.

56. ARAR, Corte Sup.: Crim. (16-XI-1829) Contra Justo Pastor.

57. ARAR, Corte Sup.: Crim. (22-VII-1833) Contra Pedro José Madueño. See also Corte Sup.: Crim. (29-III-1836) Contra Mariano Martín Cañoli por expresiones contra Bolivianos del Ejército.

58. ARAR, Corte Sup.: Crim. (5-VII-1833) Contra Mariano y Pablo Blanco. See also ARAR, Corte Sup.: Crim. (23-VI-1838) [mistakenly filed as 23-VII-1838] Contra Inocencio Pardo por injurias a los peones de obras públicas.

59. Olivo, *Constituciones políticas*, 39, 103, 140, 180–182, and 239.

60. Art. 193 (1823) and Art. 160 (1828); Olivo, *Constituciones políticas*, 68 and 141.

61. ARAR, Corte Sup.: Crim. (12-XII-1832) Contra Bernarda Torres, Juana Barriga y María Torres.

62. ARAR, Corte Sup.: Crim. (16-XII-1828) Don Alberto Anco apela la sentencia del Juez de Derecho que lo ha declarado adultero; the sentence was also published in *El Republicano* 4, 5 (January 31, 1829), 3.

63. ARAR, Corte Sup.: Crim. (6-VII-1829) Contra Victoriano Concha. See also Corte Sup.: Crim. (3-VII-1833) Contra Pablo Aguilar por haberle encontrado con una gorra de policía; and (2-IX-1834) Contra Don Diego Begazo y sus yernos por insubordinación a las autoridades.

64. Art. 145 (1826), Art. 155 (1828), Art. 155 (1834), and Art. 158 (1839); Olivo, *Constituciones políticas*, 103, 140, 180, 234.

65. ARAR, Corte Sup.: Crim. (4-I-1830) Contra María Escalante por falta de respeto, (12-XII-1832) Contra Bernarda Torres, (6-III-1833) Don Domingo Santayana contra el Gobernador de Uchumayo por haber allanado su casa, (17-IV-1833) Contra Mateo Chávez, (26-V-1834) Don Domingo Arias contra el Alcalde de Yanahuara, (25-VIII-1838) Juan Batista Puma y otros indígenas de Cayma quejan del mal comportamiento del Gobernador; and Prefectura (6-IV-1828) Contra el Dr. Don Francisco Paula Paez.

66. ARAR, Corte Sup.: Crim. (31-I-1833) Contra Marcelino Esquivel.

67. ARAR, Corte Sup.: Crim. (29-IX-1834) Contra Don José Arenaza.

68. ARAR, Prefectura (21-XI-1831) Contra Llerena, Madaleno y Torres.

69. Liberalism in Europe rose along with capitalism, but its application in Arequipa is not as clearly related to economic as opposed to political concerns. The regional economy did not undergo significant changes in this period, though there was probably an increase in the prevalence of waged, as opposed to forced, labor.

70. ARAR, Corte Sup.: Crim. (13-VIII-1831) Contra José Benavides.

71. ARAR, Corte Sup.: Crim. (5-X-1836) Contra Narciso Castillo, etc.

72. ARAR, Corte Sup.: Crim. (4-X-1831) Contra Melchor Randes. See also (12-VII-1831) Contra Marcelo Paredes.

73. One of the arguments used against the death penalty was that it would eliminate a person who could be useful to society. See ARAR, Corte Sup.: Crim. (11-XI-1827) Contra Miguel Ramos, (27-IV-1833) Contra Mateo Chávez, and (29-VII-1833) Contra Carlos Mamani.

74. ARAR, Corte Sup.: Crim. (28-II-1836) Contra Pedro Morales.

75. ARAR, Corte Sup.: Crim. (25-XI-1831) Contra Victoriano Concha.

76. ARAR, Corte Sup.: Crim. (2-IX-1826) Enrique Nuñes contra el Juez Dr. Don Pascual Francisco Suero por abusar su autoridad.

77. ARAR, Corte Sup.: Crim. (12-VII-1832), Contra María Samudio por heridas al soldado José Valdez. The superior court ordered that Samudio be sent back to Arica in order to end her relationship with Valdez.

78. See for example ARAR, Corte Sup.: Crim. (4-VII-1853) Contra Marta Cuadros por haber matado a su hijo Santiago Cuadros.

79. *El Republicano* 8, 34 (August 24, 1833), 6.

80. ARAR, Corte Sup.: Crim. (3-VIII-1843) Contra Juana Pía por robos de plata labrada.

3

Mass Mobilization versus Social Control: Vagrancy and Political Order in Early Republican Mexico[1]

Richard Warren

Like much of Latin America in the years following independence, Mexico was a turbulent place as liberal Federalists and conservative Centralists fought to control and define the new nation. Enlightenment notions of popular sovereignty as propagated in Europe and the United States by Masonic lodges played a major role as both sides—liberal York Rite Masons and conservative Scots Rite Masons—advanced their claims to represent the Mexican "people." Perversely, in the chaotic post-independence decades, those very "people," lower-class men in particular, represented a serious threat to public order as insurgents, inefficient workers, or criminals. Thus laws against vagrancy—perhaps the most socially-constructed crime of all—swiftly became the order of the day.

Richard Warren, assistant professor of history at St. Joseph's University, explores the politics of vagrancy in the emerging Mexican nation. He notes that "vagrancy laws were deployed in economic contexts that varied from labor scarcity to surplus; in the fight against perceived waves of criminality in growing urban areas and in declining rural ones; and to recruit cannon fodder for incessant wars." In the interstices among these different contexts, the urban poor sometimes found a voice. Nevertheless, Warren concludes that "popular discontent and intense elite factionalism . . . frightened not only the most conservative political factions but also a critical mass of 'moderates' who . . . quickly soured on the idea of mass mobilization." Thus, at this crucial juncture in Mexican (and much of Latin American) nation-building, the criminalization of the lower classes through ill-defined and unevenly enforced vagrancy laws allowed conservative and liberal elites to effectively circumvent the popular sovereignty that legitimized their competing claims to power.

Mexico City, July 24, 1845. After sitting in jail for forty-eight hours awaiting trial, Julian Guzmán, an itinerant carpenter, finally appeared before the city's vagrancy tribunal.[2] Guzmán was apprehended while hiding under a table during an after-hours raid on a billiards hall. While the defendant maintained that he had done nothing wrong that night, the vagrancy court was not interested primarily in what Guzmán was doing on July 22, but rather in how he lived his life in general. He was accused of vagrancy, which was more a crime of "being" than "doing." Mexican criminal law was still based on the Spanish colonial tradition, and while Enlightenment ideas about the control of public space and the constant demand for military recruits in late colonial and early republican Mexico had an important effect on the implementation of vagrancy laws, the fundamental definition of the vagrant did not change greatly in the late eighteenth and early nineteenth centuries.[3] In contrast to "legitimate" mendicants—invalids for example—vagrants were individuals capable of honest labor who did not perform it and who survived therefore by socially unacceptable means such as thievery and gambling. The rejection of conventional forms of work by able-bodied men was seen as a threat to public order, family structure, and the state. Vagrancy was considered the "fecund seed of so many crimes" that aggressive means were needed to impede its spread.[4]

Julian Guzmán's dilemma then was not how to convince the court that he had committed no crime. Rather, he had to convince the judges that he was a productive member of society. Like all accused vagrants in Mexico City at that time, he was given the opportunity to present character witnesses who might confirm his place in the community and steady employment record. Unfortunately for the defendant, the witnesses—the owner of the billiards hall, a police officer, another carpenter, even Guzmán's father—would only attest under oath that the accused was a gambler, an unreliable employee, and a son who would neither abide his father nor go to confession. Failing to produce evidence to the contrary, Guzmán was found guilty of vagrancy by the tribunal's judges and remanded to the district prefect for sentencing.

Many observers lamented that an "epidemic" of vagrants like Guzmán had descended on Mexico's capital in the aftermath of the independence struggle. In 1822, Joel Roberts Poinsett, who would later serve as the first United States ambassador to Mexico, commented that the city's large vagrant population "issue forth in the morning like drones to prey upon the community, to beg, to steal, or in the last resort to work."[5] Almost two decades later, Frances Calderón de la Barca, the wife of Spain's first ambassador to Mexico, described her fears of walking the city's streets after dark. As she passed the crowded *pulquerías*, she expected "every moment to be attacked" and wished to be anywhere else, "even on the silvery top of Popocatepetl," one of the volcanoes looming over the valley of Mexico.[6] Foreign observers were not alone in their concerns about the city's security. Mexican periodicals of the era were filled with articles lamenting the infestation of vagrants, which threatened to drag Mexico into anarchy. Editorialists and pamphleteers urged the leaders of successive post-independence governments to act decisively in the fight against vagrancy.

It would seem that the recently independent government responded to these clamorings. In 1828 the national congress formed a special court solely to prosecute vagrancy cases, of which Julian Guzmán's trial is but one of hundreds. Guzmán's case was unusual however, not for the circumstances of his arrest or the content of the trial's proceedings, but for its outcome: Guzmán was one of only a small number of accused vagrants found guilty during this period. Despite the many continuities in criminal law and ongoing public concerns with vagrancy, convictions in post-independence Mexico City fell dramatically compared to colonial levels (see Table 1). A review of cases prosecuted before the vagrancy tribunal between 1828 and 1850 reveals an overall conviction rate of

Table 1. Vagrancy Cases

Year	Not Guilty	Guilty	Other[1]	Total[2]
1797–98	16 (21.3%)	47 (62.7%)	12 (16.0%)	75
1812	10 (18.5%)	36 (66.7%)	8 (14.8%)	54
1828–31	66 (88.0%)	9 (12.0%)	0 (0.0%)	75
1845–46	54 (72.0%)	21 (28.0%)	0 (0.0%)	75
1865–66	46 (61.3%)	29 (38.7%)	0 (0.0%)	75

Sources: 1797–98: Archivo General de la Nación (AGN), Ramo Criminal, leg. 556, exp. 1–13; leg. 609, exp. 7–9; 12–18; leg. 675, exp. 8; leg. 462, exp. 6; 1812: AGN Criminal, leg. 8616, exps. 398–460; 1828–31: Archivo del Ex-Ayuntamiento de la Ciudad de México (AACM), vols. 4151–4153; 1845–46: AACM, vols. 4155–4156; 1865–66: AACM, vols. 4784–4788.

1. "Other" refers to persons for whom no verdict was discovered, or in the cases from the colonial period those persons deemed "useless" to the crown because of physical incapacities. These persons were released.

2. The total for 1812 was based on all available vagrancy cases for that year in the AGN, Ramo Criminal. For all other years a sample of seventy-five cases was selected from the files listed above.

less than 22 percent, with convictions in many years falling well below that average.[7] In contrast, data from two distinct periods during the twilight of colonial rule (1797–98 and 1812) reveal a conviction rate of over 60 percent:[8]

This seeming paradox between heightened distress over a society on the verge of anarchy and lower conviction rates can be solved by analyzing the broader historical context in which the "vagrancy crisis" of early republican Mexico took place, especially the ongoing battle over the meaning and practice of popular sovereignty. During the era under study in this essay, the relationship between individuals and the state, the very basis of political legitimacy, underwent a reevaluation. Each of the myriad political programs espoused during this era, including ersatz monarchism, was based somehow or other on the concept of an "elected" government. The ongoing experiment in popular sovereignty opened a political space within which the urban poor might develop a new role and gain a new voice in politics, which created increased tensions within Mexican society. The contradictory forces of early republican political mobilization versus elite fears of anarchy filtered into the general debates over vagrancy as well as the quotidian deliberations of the vagrancy tribunal. This essay will analyze the evolution of political conflict in post-independence Mexico and its relationship to perceptions of and actions against vagrancy.

The Masonic Lodges and Mass Political Mobilization in the 1820s

Mexico's post-independence political system traced its roots to the Spanish Constitution of 1812 and the first popular elections conducted during the wars of independence. Electoral procedures for Mexico City included among other things: indirect popular elections for municipal councils and legislative assemblies; the construction of large electoral units based on the city's parishes; and a vague definition of suffrage that included no specific income or property restrictions.[9] In the 1820s, the first decade after independence, two Masonic lodges (the York Rite and Scots Rite lodges) struggling for political dominance saw in these structures "a way to incorporate in a more rational political form the enormous potential force of the masses, and with this the political system was opened to a more extensive participation of basically urban . . . popular groups."[10] The York Masons in particular utilized the electoral system to their advantage. In poor neighborhoods they distributed thousands of sample ballots inscribed with their candidates' names, and on election day they gathered up large numbers of supporters to descend upon the polls en masse. In addition, they launched a populist propaganda campaign to distinguish themselves from their rivals. While the Scots Masons experimented with similar tactics, such as prefabricated ballots, they generally eschewed the connection with the masses that the York Masons embraced, opting instead to portray themselves as moderate defenders of order and property. Nonetheless, driven by these intense rivalries and organizing tactics, elections became regular occasions when thousands of the city's poor took to the streets to exercise their rights.

Early partisan debates between the two lodges took place mainly within the newspaper pages of the Yorks' *El Aguila Mexicana*, and *El Sol* controlled by the Scots. Writers for *El Sol* accused the York Masons of using politics merely as a way to secure government patronage jobs for lodge members and of promoting a malignant spirit of class conflict and anarchy. York militants responded that "we want even the most wretched citizen to be able to make use of their rights."[11] The city's popular classes kept abreast of the newspapers' political positions: at one point a mob of several hundred threatened to break *El Sol*'s presses for perceived offenses against their heroes.[12] Political ideas also circulated on the streets in songs, broadsides, and public rituals.[13]

Between the lodge's establishment in 1825 and the presidential election of 1828, the York Masons gained political control of the capital. The congressional elections of 1826 were the first of many struggles between the York and Scots' lodges, and they showed the potential power of popular mobilization. Over thirty thousand votes were cast, about twenty-three times more than the previous congressional elections in 1824. This historic high in voter turnout yielded a landslide for the York Masons. The Scots' Rite press complained that their rivals had manipulated the electoral process by paying poor folk to vote more than once, arguing that in the parish of Salto del Agua for example the number of votes cast exceeded the number of eligible voters by six times. On the other side of the aisle, the York press praised these elections as a further step toward the perfection of civil society.[14]

Events surrounding the 1826 elections were the first salvos in an ever more complex political war. Rather than consolidating firm political control, the York lodge split in 1827 when a large number of members decided that the new political culture, promoted by radicals within their own lodge, threatened national unity as political activities grew far beyond massive voter turnout controlled from above by the Masonic lodges' leaders. The electoral struggles became bound up with a general unrest among the urban poor that manifested itself in a broad array of phenomena, from increasingly tumultuous celebrations of public holidays like Independence Day to riots and other street confrontations, especially as the most radical members of the York lodge began to promote more aggressive means to drive out of Mexico the Spaniards who had remained there after independence.[15]

Many former York Masons including those who controlled *El Aguila Mexicana* joined with more conservative forces and formed a loose coalition to demand various reforms to combat "disintegration." In municipal council meetings, congressional debates, and the press, the members of this coalition presented their evidence that Mexican society was under the influence of a "scandalous effervescence" that threatened the entire social and political order.[16]

The Formation of the Vagrancy Tribunal

Anti-York political groups recommended a number of reforms, including more restrictive electoral laws, to save the country from anarchy. In addition, in the spring of 1828 the congress passed legislation to form a new court in Mexico City for the sole purpose of combating vagrancy. Authors of the legislation thought that rigorous enforcement of the law would simultaneously reduce the level of crime in the city and the number of York Mason shock troops. For its part, the Mexico city council, which counted York Masons among its numbers, also supported the law because they saw it as a way to gain a new level of control over the judicial process, since the new tribunal's judges would be appointed from the city council.[17]

While it was not difficult to convince a majority of legislators and municipal officials that the city's vagrant population posed a threat to all "decent folk," the new vagrancy tribunal failed to reduce the number of vagrants. The near universal desire of the elites to reduce the criminal element was inextricably connected to numerous other factors, including ongoing political conflicts. In addition, in the efforts to implement the new legislation one finds ample evidence of the huge gap between elite perspectives and the daily life of the city's masses.

Numerous officials charged with enforcing vagrancy legislation owned various types of bars and restaurants—*pulquerías, vinaterías, cafés*—that relied on the patronage of the legislation's targets. One municipal official charged with enforcing anti-vagrancy laws informed the government that "of my three assistants, one has a café and another a *vinatería* and one cannot expect them to denounce those who contribute to their subsistence."[18] Further, a number of officials expressed their ideological opposition to the policy of sending the guilty to serve in the army rather than training them for the job market.[19]

Lacking the cooperation of many local officials, the army was deployed in raids on the city's drinking establishments and gaming houses, which were seen as vagrant hangouts and hotbeds of political organizing. These raids produced hundreds of suspects, yet almost all were released. Pardon, as noted in the Julian Guzmán case, was based on proof that the accused was an "honorable" man, a claim established by the declarations of upstanding members of the community like employers, neighbors, municipal officials, or family members. Unlike Julian Guzmán, a preponderant majority of accused vagrants presented supportive testimony from the requisite character witnesses.

Vagrancy trials also provided an opportunity for the city's poor and its municipal leaders to exchange information about the political, social, and economic realities of the period. During their trials the accused were asked to confirm a variety of personal data, explain the circumstances of their arrest, and answer any questions that tribunal members might have. Accusations leveled against suspects often rested on several assumptions, for example that work was abundant for the ambitious and that morality expressed itself both temporally and spatially. One defendant was asked why anyone would go to a *pulquería*—drinking *pulque*, fermented cactus juice, was considered a lower-class vice—in the middle of the day when honorable men were at work. Another was asked what he was doing walking the streets at midnight, "this being an hour at which honorable men were retired in their homes and only prostitutes and vagrants walked around damaging the public [order]." A third defendant, an unemployed carpenter, was rebuffed by the tribunal, which could not believe that a truly skilled craftsman could not find work "in such a populous city."[20]

In response to these kinds of queries, the defendants and their character witnesses often declared that the accused were either short-term victims of the post-independence economic slump or perhaps guilty of a temporary moral lapse, but this did not mean they were vagrants. The vagrancy tribunal, composed of municipal council members, saw themselves not only as judges in a criminal trial but also as protectors of the city's residents, and while many times they condemned the defendants' behavior, they were reluctant to declare them guilty of vagrancy.[21] In an economic and social context in which vagrants could not be readily distinguished by appearance or behavior, in which the government contemplated distributing identification cards to municipal workers so they might have "proof" of their status as employed persons when confronted by police, and in which even policemen themselves were not immune from being pressed into military service as vagrants, it is not hard to understand why the tribunal judges would be reluctant to convict large numbers of men arrested simply for violating a vague spatial/temporal/moral equation.[22]

The Presidential Succession of 1828

The presidential succession of 1828 convinced an even broader group that the new political culture threatened all "decent folk," and that a more aggressive and integrated approach to governmental and social control was necessary. As the term of the first president of the Mexican republic, Guadalupe Victoria, approached its end, York radicals promoted the candidacy of General Vicente Guerrero, a hero of the Independence War and a leader of the lodge. Ex-York Masons and more conservative groups supported the moderate Manuel Gómez Pedraza, President Victoria's minister of war. Pro-Gómez Pedraza forces denounced Guerrero as promoting a mob mentality in politics;[23] pro-Guerrero forces countered that if the elections for president were truly popular rather than placed in the hands of the state legislatures, there was no doubt that Guerrero would win.[24] However, the state legislatures held the key to the presidency, and with the support of provincial moderates Manuel Gómez Pedraza received a majority of votes in eleven state legislatures while Guerrero won nine.[25] Even before the tally was made official, reports that Gómez Pedraza had won circulated in the press. Within days of the election, General José Antonio López de Santa Anna proclaimed against the results. Santa Anna's reasons for rebelling remain unclear, although many observers attributed the act to personal animosity between the president-elect and the Veracruz *caudillo*.[26] However, in most of the country including the capital a tense but generally quiet atmosphere prevailed in the first weeks after the election.

The first post-election disturbance of the peace in Mexico City looked like it might occur on Independence Day, September 16. On September 15 the municipal council moved into secret session to discuss the trouble they saw brewing. Although the Santa Anna rebellion had not spread to the city, the council requested extra troops to keep order because a rumor had reached them that the radicals were distributing money in a poor neighborhood, trying to recruit a crowd to disrupt the day's festivities.[27] The extra troops ensured a tranquil Independence Day, but they could not prevent the coming turmoil.

Armed revolt finally exploded in the capital at the end of November as pro-Guerrero forces rose up inside the city. As the balance of armed troops turned against Gómez Pedraza, he decided to flee the city. Now that rebels controlled the fate of the nation, they insisted that the congress install Guerrero as the "legitimate" president. Then, in the shadow of Gómez Pedraza's capitulation and motivated by the pent up resentments against their enemies, a mob sacked one of the city's most important markets, the Parián. Hundreds, perhaps several thousand, participated in the riot, which drove much of the city's elite off the streets out of fear. Sporadic looting, particularly by the military regiment deployed to restore order, continued for several days.[28]

The Parián riot became the great symbol of 1820s radical mobilization. Conservative leaders accused the radicals of offering the Parián as a "gift" to the urban poor in exchange for their support. In addition, for many this attack against property confirmed fears of the relationships among popular sovereignty, the political mobilization of the urban poor, and anarchy. In contrast, some radicals suggested that the whole event was exaggerated, while others argued that no matter what the damage, the riot was a logical response to the continued exploitation of the poor by a small elite of "sweat suckers."[29] While the absence of documentation prevents a quantitative analysis of the nature of the riot and its participants, it is important to emphasize that this uprising, the largest in Mexico City in over one hundred years, was directly related to the political climate, although the level of high poverty and social resentments clearly contributed to the course of events.[30]

Guerrero's administration did not survive the following year. While the judicial system virtually ceased to function and popular agitation accelerated, conservative forces regrouped during 1829. A wave of regional rebellions against Guerrero broke out, bringing to power Vice President Anastasio Bustamante, who took control of the government in the name of the *hombres de bien* (decent men) at the end of 1829. During the following months this coalition attempted a decisive change in the capital's political life.

"Decent Men" and the Search for Order

The *hombres de bien* were an amorphous group. Some were moderates with ties to the Scots' Rite lodge, some had personal loyalties to Bustamante, and others had an ambitious conservative agenda.[31] While the Bustamante regime still professed loyalty to the Federalist Constitution of 1824, its leaders shared a desire to centralize state power, reclaim political and social space from the poor, and overturn a number of Guerrero policies unpopular with civilian and military elites.[32] As part of their reassessment of political order, during the spring of 1830 the congress debated electoral reform for the federal district and passed a new law in July.

The 1830 electoral reform contained numerous innovations. First, the basic electoral unit changed from the parish to the *manzana* (a rough equivalent would be a city block), which increased the number of polling places from eighteen to 245.[33] Second, the new law designated that the municipal council appoint an electoral commissioner for each *manzana*. These commissioners would conduct a census and distribute ballots to all eligible voters prior to each election, the first attempt in Mexican history to assess voter eligibility before election day. Prior to the reform the York Masons had been able to organize "invasions" of the polls, with large groups descending on each polling place armed with thousands of identical prefabricated ballots carrying the names of York candidates. The new law was designed to eliminate these strategies by reducing the number of voters as well as the number of people gathering at any single polling place on election day. The 1830 law did not change the ephemeral definition of voter eligibility, but it did change the relationship between individuals and the political process. Electoral commissioners had the power to deny a ballot to anyone, and it was incumbent upon individuals to appeal a commissioner's decision and prove that they deserved a ballot.[34]

The editors of *El Sol* praised the new legislation as bringing an end to "the vices and scandalous abuses" of the 1820s, but the *hombres de bien* did not stop their renovation program at electoral reform.[35] They pursued with renewed vigor an anti-vagrancy campaign, including the assignment of "vagrant quotas" to be met each week by neighborhood officials.[36] The strategies of the *hombres de bien* were no more successful in raising the conviction rate or reducing the vagrant population than those of their predecessors, and again, the political context affords us the keys to understanding the nature of this program and its subsequent failure.

The Municipal Council versus the National Government

Beginning in 1830 the problems of vagrancy, elections, and political order increasingly were subsumed by the struggle between the municipal council, striving to maintain its institutional power, and a national government moving to further centralize state functions. In his annual report to congress in 1831, Minister of Interior and Foreign Relations Lucas Alamán denounced the municipal council for its role in "having converted Mexico City into an asylum and shield for criminals." Alamán promised that his government would be steadfast in its campaign to eliminate the criminal element despite continued resistance from city officials.[37]

Rather than rely on the uncertain support of the municipal council and its employees, the Centralist governments of the 1830s used other mechanisms in their campaign against the urban poor. Government decrees lamented the "facility with which vagrants are absolved in the tribunal, [and with which] it is said that those who have no occupation are credited [with having one]."[38] In response to this problem, in 1834 the Santa Anna government launched an aggressive campaign to identify the poor population and separate the honest working classes from vagrants and other criminals. A new law decreed that all domestic servants would have to carry an identification card stating their name, address, salary, and employer's name.[39] A similar identification card system was contemplated for municipal employees as well.[40]

This law preceded the 1834 congressional elections, seen by Centralists as an opportunity to solidify their control over the state apparatus. As those elections neared, the federal district governor exhorted the city's electoral commissioners on behalf of the president to be especially vigilant when conducting the pre-election neighborhood census, so that the city's vagrants, the "fecund seed" of crime, might be identified and punished at the same time that preparations for the election continued.[41]

While it is difficult to find precise data on the outcome of the 1834 election, one observer noted that conservative Centralists dominated the new legislature.[42] The next year a conservative newspaper exulted that, finally, the "mob does not rule."[43] Following this theme in his 1835 address to congress, the minister of justice promised that by using decisive action the central government would reverse the lamentable failures of previous governments in the war against vagrancy and social deterioration.[44] Nonetheless, Centralists still did not control the municipal council, and tensions continued between its members and the local appointee of the national government, the federal district governor.[45] Events in 1835–36 convinced conservatives that further measures would be required to consolidate their power in the face of this continued opposition.

One mechanism used to wrest more power from the city government was the establishment in 1835 of a new "police assistant," who would patrol the streets under the authority of the federal district governor independently of the municipal council. Members of the council immediately complained that the people of Mexico City could not confide in a police official who did not report to the municipal council, the popularly elected body charged with protecting the city and its inhabitants. They wrote to the president and congress, describing this officer as a loose cannon who abused his authority and violated the civil rights of the city's poor by rounding up suspected vagrants and sending them off to military service without trials. In retaliation, the federal district governor leveled criminal charges against three members of the city government. This comedy of mutual recriminations continued without resolution into the fall of 1836, as new congressional elections loomed on the horizon.[46]

Centralist Revisions

In early October of that year, the federal district governor warned the city council to choose electoral commissioners carefully.[47] However, when the governor saw the list of proposed commissioners, he felt their selection was evidence of an antigovernment conspiracy and wrote immediately to the secretary of interior and foreign relations to argue that the municipal council planned to use the elections to bring down the central government by appointing as commissioners "not a small number of persons notoriously disaffected from the present administration."[48] Five days after the governor sent this letter, the elections were suspended while a new electoral law was designed.[49] The new election law created by the Centralist government of 1836 was the most restrictive yet. The congressional committee that drafted the legislation praised the 1830 electoral reform as a step in the right direction, but insisted that Mexico, populated by a "new people" unaccustomed to representative government, had suffered from excessive factionalism and class conflict. These afflictions could be reduced, the committee members argued, by limiting suffrage to persons who had annual incomes of at least one hundred pesos.[50]

This recommendation was incorporated into the law, and in 1836 specific financial thresholds for suffrage and officeholding were established for the first time in Mexican history. Centralist governments over the next decade remained convinced that these restrictions were necessary, if insufficient, to maintain political order. In fact, in 1842 the suffrage threshold was raised to two hundred pesos per year. In addition, since the problems of political participation, vagrancy, and social control had been so closely identified with each other, conservative Centralists continued the campaign to guard social space with the same vigor with which they planned to guard political space. In 1845–46, congress expanded the definition of vagrancy to include a long list of occupations defined as illicit or unproductive, and a number of legal discovery and trial procedures were eliminated for vagrancy cases.[51] Two decades of popular sovereignty and political upheaval had merged in many minds the correlation between driving the poor from the polls and driving vagrants from the city.

Conclusion

In the early modern era, nation-states throughout Europe and the Americas employed diverse strategies in anti-vagrancy campaigns including deportation, the military levy, even forced marriage. Enlightenment thinking had placed a new focus on the vagrancy issue as political thinkers criticized the traditional concept of Christian charity as encouraging mendicity and laziness. Yet at the same time, many proposed that the state had a responsibility to create a political, social, and economic environment in which able-bodied persons could find employment and delinquents could be transformed into productive members of society. These reflections on the origins of vagrancy and its solution occurred in the midst of the fluctuating material circumstances of societies in transition to modern forms of political and economic organization. Vagrancy laws were deployed in economic contexts that varied from labor scarcity to surplus; in the fight against perceived waves of criminality in growing urban areas and declining rural districts; and to recruit cannon fodder for incessant wars. However, given the ambiguity in the definition of vagrancy and the economic realities for the majority of the urban and rural populations of the early modern era, it was always extremely difficult to distinguish vagrants from poor, but honest, workers. This was as much a reality in France and England as it was in Mexico.[52]

State-directed attempts to control public space and the labor force in Mexico during this era were complicated (and in many ways determined) by the simultaneous development of the concept of popular sovereignty and its repercussions. None of the anti-vagrancy efforts or electoral reforms discussed in this essay could guarantee stability in post-independence Mexico since they failed to address the roots of instability, which lay at other levels of the social and economic structure. Nevertheless, the above discussion highlights fundamental changes in Mexican political culture. During this era, popular discontent and intense elite factionalism dovetailed with a transformation in political discourse and the organizing strategies for political power. The early results of this volatile mix frightened not only the most conservative political factions but also a critical mass of "moderates" who, like the intellectual and statesman José María Luis Mora, quickly soured on the idea of mass mobilization. In one famous 1830 editorial, Mora suggested that Mexico's political morass stemmed fundamentally from "the scandalous profusion with which political rights have been squandered, being made extensive and common [so as to include] even the lowest classes of society."[53]

Mora's position illustrates well the connection between politics and the "social question" in Mexico after independence. The era was characterized by an ongoing experiment in state-building that included ever-changing rituals of popular sovereignty as one essential component. From time to time elite factions, unable to secure control of the state through other means, attempted to gain support from the urban poor while the poor themselves fought for a say in shaping the republic. The vocal presence of the poor in the streets and at the polls provoked strong reactions, which included not only calls for electoral reform but also campaigns against vagrancy. These programs failed to reduce the number of urban poor folk or criminality, nor did they produce stable regimes. The conflation of the very real problem of urban poverty with the political enfranchisement of the poor ultimately served only to exacerbate the painful transition from colony to nation-state in Mexico.

Notes

1. This essay is based in part on the paper, "Vagrancy and Political Order in Nineteenth Century Mexico," presented at the American Historical Association Annual Meeting, January 1994. The current essay extends the arguments made in that paper and introduces new material. My sincerest thanks to the participants in that session, and especially to Dr. Eric Van Young, who served as the panel's commentator. Financial support for this research has been provided by grants from the Fulbright Program, the American Historical Association, the University of Chicago Center for Latin American Studies, and St. Joseph's University.

2. This case is found in the Archivo del Ex-Ayuntamiento de la Ciudad de Mexico (hereafter AACM), vol. 4778, exp. 285.

3. For a discussion of vagrancy during the first centuries of Spanish colonial rule, see Norman F. Martin, *Los vagabundos en la Nueva España* (Mexico: Editorial Jus, 1957). Silvia M. Arrom has written extensively on vagrancy legislation in the eighteenth and nineteenth centuries. See Arrom, "Vagos y mendigos en la legislación mexicana, 1745–1845," in *Memoria del IV Congreso de Historia del Derecho Mexicano* (Mexico: Universidad Nacional Autónoma de México, 1988), 1: 71–87; Arrom, "Documentos para el estudio del Tribunal de Vagos, 1828–1848: Respuesta a una problemática sin solución," *Anuario Mexicano de Historia del Derecho* 1 (1989): 215–35; Arrom, "Beggars and Vagrants in Mexico City, 1774–1845," paper presented at the American Historical Association Annual Meeting, 1988. Valuable discussions of the changing relationship between the urban poor and the state during the late colonial era include Pamela Voekel, "Peeing on the Palace: Bodily Resistance to Bourbon Reforms in Mexico City," *Journal of Historical Sociology* 5, no. 2 (1992): 183–208; Anne Staples, "Policía y Buen Gobierno: Municipal Efforts to Regulate Public Behavior, 1821–1857," in William H. Beezley, Cheryl English Martin, and William E. French, eds., *Rituals of Rule, Rituals of Resistance: Public Celebrations and Popular Culture in México* (Wilmington: Scholarly Resources, 1994); and Juan Pedro Viqueira Albán, *¿Relajados o reprimidos? Diversiones públicas y vida social en la ciudad de México durante el siglo de las luces* (Mexico: Fondo de Cultura Económica, 1987).

4. AACM, vol. 4151, exp. 6, August 11, 1834.

5. Joel Roberts Poinsett, *Notes on Mexico, Made in the Autumn of 1822* (1824; reprint, New York: Frederick A. Praeger, 1969), 49.

6. Frances Calderón de la Barca, *Life in Mexico: The Letters of Fanny Calderón de la Barca* (1843; reprint, eds. Howard T. Fisher and Marion Hall Fisher, Garden City, N.Y.: Doubleday, 1966), 203.

7. Sonia Pérez Toledo, *Los hijos del trabajo: Los artesanos de la ciudad de México, 1780–1853* (Ph.D. diss., El Colegio de México, 1993), 378. Using a different method, Frederick J. Shaw, Jr., *Poverty and Politics in Mexico City, 1824–1854* (Ph.D. diss., University of Florida, 1975), 280, calculated a conviction rate of 18 percent over the course of the tribunal's history, with an additional six percent of suspects released into the custody of family or employers. My own calculations from a sample of seventy-five cases taken during the first three years of the vagrancy tribunal's existence (1828–31) indicate a conviction rate of only 12 percent during the early days of the tribunal. AACM, vols. 4151–4153.

8. For 1797–98, Archivo General de la Nación, Mexico (hereafter AGN), Ramo Criminal, leg. 556, exp. 1–13; leg. 609, exp. 7–9; 12–18; leg. 675, exp. 8; leg. 462, exp. 6. For 1812, AGN Criminal, leg. 8616, exps. 398–460.

9. See the "Constitución de la monarquía español, promulagada en Cádiz el 19 de marzo de 1812," in Juan E. Hernández y Dávalos, ed., *Colección de documentos para la historia de la guerra de independencia de México de 1808 a 1821* (1877–1882; reprint, Mexico: Instituto Nacional de Estudios Históricos de la Revolución Mexicana, 1985), 4: 50–118; "Bando del corregidor intendente de la Ciudad de México en que se convoca a los vecinos de ella para que el día 29 de noviembre designen a los electores que deberán proceder al nombramiento de alcaldes, regidores y procuradores síndicos," in Rafael de Alba, ed., *La constitución de 1812 en la Nueva España* (Mexico: Secretaría de Relaciones Exteriores, Imprenta Guerrero Hermanos, 1912–13), 1: 227. Studies of elections during the Independence War include Antonio Annino, "Prácticas criollas y liberalismo en la crisis del espacio urbano colonial: El 29 de noviembre de 1812 en la ciudad de México," *Secuencia* 24 (1992): 121–58; Virginia Guedea, "Las primeras elecciones populares en la ciudad de México, 1812–1813," *Estudios Mexicanos/Mexican Studies* 7, no. 1 (Winter 1991): 1–28; Virginia Guedea, "El pueblo de México y las elecciones de 1812," in Regina Hernández Franyuti, ed., *La ciudad de México en la primera mitad del siglo xix. Tomo II. Gobierno y política/Sociedad y cultura* (Mexico: Instituto Mora, 1994); Nettie Lee Benson, "The Contested Mexican Election of 1812," *Hispanic American Historical Review* 26, no. 3 (1946): 336–50. For a more extensive analysis of the data on electoral procedures, participation, and outcomes used in this essay, see Richard Warren, "Elections and Popular Political Participation in Mexico, 1808–1836," in Vincent C. Peloso and Barbara A. Tenenbaum, eds., *Liberals, Politics, and Power: State Formation in Nineteenth Century Latin America* (Athens: University of Georgia Press, 1996).

10. Luis Alberto de la Garza, "Hombres de bien, demagogos y revolución social en la primera república," *Historias* 15 (1986): 49.

11. *El Aguila Mexicana* 4: 110, August 18, 1826.

12. AGN, Grupo Documental Gobernación, leg. 799, caja 1, exp. 3, August 17, 1828.

13. *El Aguila Mexicana* 5: 281, October 8, 1827. For a discussion of the ways in which information circulated through popular and informal channels in Mexico City during the Independence War, see Hugh M. Hamill, "Royalist Propaganda and *la porción humilde del pueblo* During Mexican Independence," *The Americas* 36, no. 4 (1980): 423–44.

14. *El Sol* 4: 1164, 1165, 1171, August 21, 22, and 28, 1826; *La Verdad Desnuda* 2, March 1833; *El Aguila Mexicana* 4: 115, August 23, 1826; *La Voz de la Patria* 2: 15, March 15, 1830.

15. For a discussion of the split in the York lodge, see Lorenzo de Zavala, *Ensayo histórico de las revoluciones de México desde 1808 hasta 1830* (1831–32; reprint, ed. Manuel González Ramírez, Mexico: Porrúa, 1969), 317, 326; Michael P. Costeloe, *La primera república federal de México (1824–1835): Un estudio de los partidos políticos en el México independiente* (Mexico: Fondo de Cultura Económica, 1975), 81. For popular anti-Spanish agitation in January 1824, see AACM, vol. 288a, page 7. For general discussion of the role of popular agitation in the Spanish expulsion controversy of the late 1820s, see Harold Dana Sims, *The Expulsion of Mexico's Spaniards* (Pittsburgh: University of Pittsburgh Press, 1990), especially 19–31; Costeloe, *La primera república*, especially 87–113; Romeo Flores Caballero, *Counterrevolution: The Role of the Spaniards in the Independence of Mexico, 1804–1838*, trans. Jaime E. Rodríguez O. (Lincoln: University of Nebraska Press, 1974), 96.

16. See AACM, vol. 148a, August 14, 1828; *Colección de artículos selectos sobre política, sacados del águila mexicana del año de 1828* (Mexico: Imp. de Galván, 1828).

17. José Antonio Serrano O., "Levas, Tribunal de Vagos y Ayuntamiento: La ciudad de México, 1825–1836," paper presented at the Seminario Internacional, "La experiencia institucional en la ciudad de México, 1821–1929," Universidad Autónoma Metropolitana-Unidad Iztapalapa, Mexico City, October 5–6, 1995.

18. AACM, vol. 4151, exp. 5.

19. AACM, vol. 4151, exp. 4.

20. AACM, vol. 4152, exp. 80; vol. 4151, exp. 13; vol. 4151, exp. 28. In each of these three cases the accused man was excoriated for his behavior, but each was found not guilty.

21. Serrano, "Levas, Tribunal de Vagos y Ayuntamiento," 23–26; Arrom, "Beggars and Vagrants," 11–13.

22. For the government identification program, see below and AACM, vol. 4151, exp. 6. There is at least one case of a police inspector who was conscripted into the army as a vagrant. The action drove much of the city's police force off the streets for several days in protest, and out of fear. AACM, vol. 307a, July 1, 1859.

23. *Oigan las legislaturas los proyectos de Madrid* (Mexico: Imp. José Márquez, 1828).

24. *El amigo del pueblo* 6, August 6, 1828. For an analysis of the press and the elections of 1828, see Will Fowler, "The Mexican Press and the Collapse of Representative Government During the 1828 Presidential Elections," paper presented at the Latin American Studies Association XIX International Congress, Washington, D.C., 1995.

25. As Harold Sims noted, many of the legislatures voting for Gómez Pedraza had been formed in elections prior to the rise of the York lodge. Sims, *The Expulsion*, 44. N.B.: The federal district did not get a vote for president.

26. Costeloe, *La primera república*, 189.

27. AACM, vol. 148a, September 15, 1828; AACM, vol. 290a, September 15, 1828.

28. The best discussion available of the riot is Silvia M. Arrom, "Popular Politics in Mexico City: The Parián Riot, 1828," *Hispanic American Historical Review* 68, no. 2 (1988): 245–68.

29. For example, Lorenzo de Zavala, *Juicio imparcial sobre los acontecimientos de México en 1828 y 1829* (New York: C. S. Winkle, n.d.; reprint, Mexico: Imp. de Galván, n.d.) made the "exaggeration" argument. José Ignacio Paz, *Estupendo grito en la acordada . . .* (Mexico: Imp. del Correo, 1829), advocated the "legitimate revenge" argument.

30. Arrom, "Popular Politics," 250.

31. The ideological landscape of the era is examined in Will Fowler, "Dreams of Stability: Mexican Political Thought During the 'Forgotten Years.' An Analysis of the Beliefs of the Creole Intelligentsia (1821–1853)," *Bulletin of Latin American Research* 14, no. 3 (1995): 287–312; and Jaime E. Rodriguez O., "Oposición a Bustamante," *Historia Mexicana* 20, no. 2 (1970): 199–234.

32. For the economic policies of the "*hombres de bien*," see Barbara Tenenbaum, *The Politics of Penury: Debts and Taxes in Mexico, 1821–1856* (Albuquerque: University of New Mexico Press, 1986), 35–37; and Robert A. Potash, *Mexican*

Government and Industrial Development in the Early Republic: The Banco de Avío (Amherst: University of Massachusetts Press, 1983), 39–71.

33. Although the city was divided into only fourteen parishes, the largest parish, El Sagrario, was usually broken up into four districts for voting purposes.

34. "Reglas para las elecciones de diputados y de ayuntamientos del distrito y territorios de la república (12 julio 1830)," in *Legislación electoral mexicana, 1812–1977* (Mexico: Secretaría de Gobernación, 1973), 46–52.

35. *El Sol* 2: 531, December 13, 1830.

36. In October 1830 the federal district governor notified the municipal council on behalf of the executive branch that city officials would be responsible for the arrest of at least four vagrants each week. AACM, vol. 4151, exp. 19.

37. Serrano, "Levas, Tribunal de Vagos y Ayuntamiento," 29.

38. Manuel Dublán and José María Lozano, *Legislación mexicana ó colección completa de las disposiciones legislativas desde la independencia de la República* (Mexico: Imp. del Comercio, 1876), 2: 724, August 20, 1833.

39. "Circular relativa al padrón para elección de diputados y prevenciones en cuanto a vagos, casas de prostitución, de juego o escándalo, y acerca de la educación de la juventud (8 agosto 1834)," in *Legislación electoral mexicana*, 53–56.

40. AACM, vol. 4151, exp. 6.

41. Ibid.

42. José María Luis Mora, *Obras sueltas de José María Luis Mora, ciudadano mexicano* (Paris: Librería Rosa, 1837), 1: 271.

43. *El mosquito mexicano*, September 22, 1835.

44. *Memoria de ministerio de justicia y negocios eclesiásticos de la republica mexicana* (Mexico: Imp. El Aguila, 1835).

45. AGN, Ayuntamientos, vol. 16, pages 235–36, October 28 and December 31, 1834.

46. AACM, vol. 295a, pp. 9ff., January 13, 1836; *Acta del cabildo celebrado por el exmo. ayuntamiento de México en 30 de mayo de 1836, mandada imprimir por el mismo con los documentos a que se refiere* (Mexico: Imp. José Mariano F. de Lara, 1836); *Acusación que el licenciado Gabriel Sagazeta, síndico segundo del exmo. ayuntamiento de esta capital, eleva, como procurador del comúm, al soberano congreso nacional contra el señor gobernador del distrito Don José Gómez de la Cortina* (Mexico: Imp. de Galván, 1836).

47. AACM, vol. 862, exp. 27.

48. AGN, Ayuntamientos, vol. 20, p. 76 ff., November 24, 1836.

49. AACM, vol. 862, exp. 27, November 29, 1836. It is interesting to note that new conservative legislation in the 1840s created a federal office with veto power over the municipal council's commissioner selections. *Ley sobre eleccion de ayuntamiento en el departamento de Mexico* (Mexico: Imp. Vicente García Torres, 1845).

50. *Proyecto de ley sobre elecciones populares presentado al congreso general en la sesión de 17 de octubre de 1836 por la comisión respectiva, y mandado imprimir por acuerdo del mismo* (Mexico: Imp. José M. F. de Lara, 1836).

51. See Arrom, "Documentos para el estudio," document 5.

52. For France, see Colin Jones, *Charity and Bienfaisance: The Treatment of the Poor in the Montpellier Region, 1740–1815* (Cambridge: Cambridge University Press, 1982); Jack A. Goldstone, *Revolution and Rebellion in the Early Mod-*

ern World (Berkeley: University of California Press, 1991); Thomas McStay Adams, *Bureaucrats and Beggars: French Social Policy in the Age of the Enlightenment* (New York : Oxford University Press, 1990); Arlette Farge, *Subversive Words: Public Opinion in Eighteenth-Century France* (University Park: Pennsylvania State University Press, 1995). For England, see Lionel Rose, *Rogues and Vagabonds: The Vagrant Underworld in Britain, 1815–1985* (London: Routledge, 1988); Gareth Stedman Jones, *Outcast London: A Study in the Relationship Between Classes in Victorian Society* (New York: Pantheon, 1984).

53. José María Luis Mora, "Discurso sobre la necesidad de fijar el derecho de ciudadanía en la república y hacerlo afecto a la propiedad," *El Observador*, Mexico, April 14, 1830; reprinted in Mora, *Obras sueltas*, 2: 289–305.

4

The Crimes of Poor *Paysanos* in Midnineteenth-Century Buenos Aires

Ricardo D. Salvatore

In this innovative chapter, Ricardo Salvatore, professor of history at the Universidad Torcuato di Tella, Buenos Aires, uses quantitative data to deconstruct one of the most powerful myths about Argentina's past: that of the violent nature of the inhabitants of the pampas. Literary, political, and historical representations have always referred to the lower classes of Buenos Aires province as immersed in a perpetual state of political violence and property crimes, the first emanating from the particular features of the gaucho culture, the second from the expansion of the estanciero *economy and the ensuing impoverishment of the rural population.*

Analyzing previously unused statistics, Salvatore comes up with a radically different picture: first, the number of arrests in each jurisdiction was quite low, thus casting doubts about a "generalized" situation of violence and crime; second, most offenses were not against persons or property but rather against the state—including, prominently, actions of resistance against forced military recruitment. The military needs of the Rosista state forced authorities to criminalize certain acts, customs, and practices that would have been otherwise tolerated; rural crime, and in particular those acts directed against the state by the same token should be treated as a conscious attempt to resist such state policies. The analysis of rural "criminality" thus needs to incorporate an ideological and political dimension usually overlooked in studies about crime. By looking at rural crime and repression in Buenos Aires province, this article suggests, we are looking at a crucial angle of the struggles around the nature and limits of the post-independence state.

Anyone who studies the history of a social group's criminal behavior must deal with inherited constructions. Literary, political, legal, or historical representations of subaltern subjects usually contain statements that frame these subjects' possibilities of experience. It is in this context overladen by statements of alterity ("otherness") that the social historian of crime must build an understanding of the functions and meaning of crime and justice in the past.

Typically, those concerned with the representations and mentalities of a society in relation to crime have been reluctant to use statistics to validate or challenge accepted views. Overwhelmed by the task of interpreting the immense variety of texts, images, and discourses, they have left for others the processing and interpreting of quantifiable data. In this essay I will proceed against the current, using a statistical reconstruction to ponder the validity of a hegemonic discourse about violence and crime. The reconstruction of criminal statistics in midnineteenth-century Buenos Aires province, I suggest, could be used to problematize an old and established conception: the violent nature of the pampas.

The result of this exercise should not be viewed as an affirmation of positivist criteria or the countering by simple opposition of an established model. Rather, it should point to the need to explore the hidden dimensions of a given society: conflicts over authority and the legitimacy of the legal order, the social construction of subaltern subjects, the claims and arguments of those subject to imprisonment and punishment. Reconstructed statistics usually do not lend themselves to these types of inquiries. But, with our attention focused on the question of categories, power relations, and communication, statistics of crime can clear the way for posing new questions about these issues. For example, a table about the characteristics of crime in a given society allows us to address, in addition to obvious questions of criminalization, social control, and the functioning of the justice and penal system, other interesting issues related to social conflicts like the construction of the subaltern subject and the normativity of the legal order.

Until recently, historical and literary representations of the Rosas era (1829–1852) painted the Buenos Aires countryside as a place saturated with political violence and crimes against property. Political violence appeared as the corollary of a *gaucho* culture that engendered personality types submissive to authority and given to unpredictable outbursts of violence; violence that was contended and channeled by *caudillos* like Juan Manuel de Rosas. On the other hand, the prevalence of cattle rustling and other crimes against property in these representations resulted from the expansion of the *estancia* economy and its concomitant imposition of property rights: a typical proletarianization story that left the rural poor with few options other than theft and poaching.

Literary representations of the Rosas period connected—and on occasions, conflated—the "violent nature" of the populace with the terror unleashed by the dictatorship against its *unitario* enemies.[1] Founding texts of Argentine literature such as Domingo Sarmiento's *Facundo*, Esteban Echeverría's *El Matadero*, or José Mármol's *Amalia* presented this perspective. In *Facundo* the author exiles himself in order to narrate the life and works of a local caudillo, Facundo, who epitomizes the innate barbarism of the pampas. In *El Matadero* the hero crosses the city and falls prey to the vexations of the Federalist rabble working in a slaughterhouse in the Buenos Aires suburbs. *Amalia* tells the story of five *porteños* (Buenos Aires residents) of the traditional elite who plot against Rosas, are betrayed by a *mazorquero* (secret policeman) passing for a friend, and suffer all the violence of "Federalist terror." In these works, a culture of violence developed that was fed by the natural environment and stimulated by a repressive political system until it became a natural condition of sociability in the pampas.[2]

"The gaucho's violent nature," says R. González Echevarría, referring to literary constructions of the pampas, "makes him both a man of nature and a man outside the law."[3] Travel accounts and memoirs replicated this paradigm by placing violence at the core of gaucho identity.[4] Naturally, contemporary critics of the regime and their successors depicted the Rosas period as an age of terror.[5] Historians echoed these characterizations by presenting the Buenos Aires countryside as a propitious terrain for crimes of violence and passion (knife fights, wounds, murder, etc.).[6] Unchecked by an insufficient or nonexistent rural police force and the persistence of an intractable folk culture which denied any "civilizing process," gauchos were able to express their "violent nature" without limits.

Other authors found in the pre-Caseros period a total lack of security for property owners, a period when the theft of cattle and hides rose in proportion to the development of the ranching economy. Historians and literati have portrayed the fate of the rural poor as intimately connected with the choice between honest labor and theft (cattle rustling in particular).[7] Deprived of their possessions, gauchos were forced to enter the estancia economy as wage peons; otherwise they had to confront and suffer the arbitrary rule of rural justices and frontier military officers. Those who escaped this constellation of local power entered a life of marginality in which theft became synonymous with survival. When not the result of an innate "barbarian nature," the crimes of poor *paysanos* (rural residents) appeared as the result of a criminal policy that aimed at controlling their movements, channeling their labor to military purposes, and pushing them into the hands of labor-thirsty landowners. Not seen as a program of contested conceptions of morality, politics, and economic rights, the justice system remained a tool to enforce class domination and control.

Despite being central to the validity of a host of propositions concerning the society, politics, and culture of Buenos Aires during the Rosas period, the issue of crime has been insufficiently explored by historians. A few studies relying on statistics for the city of Buenos Aires have reinforced earlier views about the increasingly coercive relations between the state and poor *paysanos*.[8] These studies have emphasized the continuities between the immediate post-independence period and the Rosista regime, drawing on the similarities among types of crimes, population at risk, and the characteristics of the justice system (leniency, clientelism, arbitrary practices, etc.). None of these studies has teased out the implications of Rosista recruitment policies on the region's criminality, a question that appears central to the relationship between the state and the laboring poor.[9] This study proposes to fill this gap by means of a statistical reconstruction of criminality during the Rosas period. This essay suggests that new data on the frequency and types of crimes committed—particularly data about the mobility of poor paysanos and the prevalence of "crimes against the state"—will give new insights into the sociability of rural communities and, by extension, problematize the perspective consolidated by powerful historiographical and literary traditions about the role of violence in the lives of poor paysanos.

The Data

In this essay, I present the preliminary results of a statistical reconstruction of crime in Buenos Aires province during the period 1831–1851. This reconstruction is based on the *Partes de Novedades*, quarterly reports sent by the justices of the peace to governor Juan Manuel de Rosas informing the dictator about the people arrested during each period. In these reports, justices included cases of delinquents sent to the governor for a decision and those delivered to a nearby regiment. Generally, these felons were sentenced to service in the armed forces. Rarely included in these reports were people jailed on a short-term basis (from a few days up to two months) or punished with penalties other than military service (the stakes, public flogging, forced labor in the local church). Typically the arrested traveled on horseback, their hands and sometimes their feet in shackles, accompanied by one or two guards. Before departing they were subjected to an interrogation by the justice of the peace or local police chief. Upon their arrival in Buenos Aires (at the prison of Santos Lugares or the general headquarters in Palermo), another interrogation awaited the prisoner.

Though the reports are not complete, our data comprising 1,674 observations could be taken as a representative sample of felons transported from the countryside to Buenos Aires.[10] We estimate that the data derived from the Partes de Novedades comprise about 23 percent of the total number arrested during this period (see Table 1). Coverage for most *partidos* (judicial districts) appears sufficiently ample, ranging from 21 to 64 percent of the estimated number of felons; only in the cases of Las Flores, Chivilcoy, and San Nicolás is the sample small, ranging from 2 to 5 percent.

Table 1. Sample Size and Estimated Number of Crimes, Buenos Aires Province (1831–1851)

Partido	Months with Records	Sample Size[1]	Estimated Number of Crimes[2]	Sample Ratio[3]
Lobos	116	214	482	0.44
Arrecifes	82	100	338	0.29
Areco	156	215	373	0.58
Azul	134	81	158	0.51
Tordillo	104	41	140	0.29
Monsalvo	44	39	246	0.16
Quilmes	86	132	439	0.30
Chascomús	154	104	253	0.41
Luján	108	241	699	0.34
Baradero	96	34	144	0.24
Cañuelas	108	41	135	0.30
Dolores	48	47	414	0.11
Ensenada	132	23	109	0.21
Ranchos	180	112	175	0.64
Las Flores	6	18	840	0.02
Chivilcoy	14	19	540	0.03
Navarro	100	155	504	0.31
San Nicolás	44	58	1,082	0.05
Total	1,712	1,674	7,071	0.23

1. Number of crimes reported.
2. (Number of crimes reported/months with records) times 252 months.
3. Sample size/estimated number of crimes.

Taken at the site of arrest, our source provides better data than other studies on the incidence and nature of rural criminality during the Rosas administration.[11] But like other statistical reconstructions, this one should be taken only as an approximation because it unavoidably underestimates two sources: crimes of "correction" and "*contingentes*." Though governor

Rosas insisted on the standardization of the Partes de Novedades, the reporting of crimes varied from one *partido* to the next. Perhaps the greatest bias was the justices' tendency not to report what they considered
"crimes of correction," misdemeanors usually penalized with fines, a few
days in jail, or a simple warning; because these crimes did not require
sending the prisoner to Buenos Aires, most justices decided it was not
necessary to report them.[12]

In addition, we know that the infamous *contingentes* (people arrested
for the sole purpose of fulfilling military recruitment quotas) were only
partially registered.[13] In an 1835 *Acuerdo*, Rosas mandated that all justices of the peace send two or more men each month to man the Federalist
army. How effectively the justices complied with this order is hard to
estimate. In our reconstructed statistics there are prisoners taken in order
to fulfill the *juzgado's* (court) quota, but their number seems suspiciously
small. Moreover, on many occasions justices reported "no arrest" during
the quarter, contrary to the governor's orders. This may be an indication
of the difficulty of forcibly drafting people on a regular basis.[14]

In order to interpret the statistics produced by these reports, it is necessary to understand the double function of the justice system during the
Rosas era.[15] First, it was a mechanism for recruiting soldiers from the
working poor residing in the countryside. In addition to *levas* (forced con-
scriptions) and *contingentes*, justices found other ways to make common
delinquents pay their tribute to Rosas' war machine with their bodies.
Second, the justice system was a mechanism for restoring the "tranquility
of the countryside." This meant achieving the "moral order" imagined by
governor Rosas: respect for property and authority, compliance with the
practices of Catholicism, political conformity with the Federalist regime,
and no public display of defiance to the values of family and work. Justices of the peace were supposed to enforce the two types of justice.

In practice, the visibility of the two types of social control were different. The first, oriented towards the defense of the motherland, left more
visible marks in the official transcript. Each deserter sent to governor
Rosas traveled with a *clasificación* describing his crime; consequently,
justices took care to include deserters in their quarterly reports. The same
could be said for murderers, rapists, and thieves: they all committed crimes
that escaped the power of local justices. Hence they were regularly included in the reports. Misdemeanors related to "moral order" (drunkenness, carrying knives, playing cards, swearing) were instead handled locally
and, consequently, reported to the governor only when the arrestee was
suspected of more serious violations (or when the justice was unsure about
Rosas's instructions). The differential visibility of felonies vis-à-vis misdemeanors, while making us cautious about the propositions we can de-

rive from this evidence, should not deter us from using this data as an approximate indicator of criminality in the countryside.

A Violent Countryside?

Even after correcting our estimates to allow for underreporting, we are left with a total estimated number of felonies which seems modest for a countryside reputed for its violence and criminality. Increasing the 7,070 felonies by 40 percent to 9,900 still amounts to less than 500 arrests per year in the whole province, or between one and two prisoners sent by each *partido* each month, a number curiously close to the quota required by the governor. The low number of prisoners per month is consistent with the fact that, on many occasions, justices reported that a term had passed *sin novedad*, that is, without having taken any prisoners.[16] Reports with no new prisoners represented nine percent of extant reports for Chascomús, 12 percent of the reports from Azul, 18 percent of those from Monsalvo, 21 percent of those from Areco, 31 percent of those from Baradero, 34 percent of those from Ensenada, etc. These figures do not correspond with the image of a violent countryside or with an state decidedly committed to the repression of crime.

Information about the types of crimes repressed reinforces this suspicion (see Table 2). Felonies against persons were remarkably few; they represent less than 13 percent of all arrests. Wounds and beatings were the most frequent felonies falling under this category, followed by homicide and related offenses.[17] Reported homicides were relatively few; knife fights resulting in homicides took place quite far from the gaze of authorities (usually in private residences or in the open country) and police devoted little effort to investigating these cases. We can imagine that many deaths went unreported in this society (those of political adversaries, Indians, and *provincianos*) but we cannot ascertain the scale.

The few cases of rape reported indicate a preoccupation of state authorities in protecting (however marginally) the honor of rural women. Abducting women, an aggression that served as a substitute or complement of courtship, was also repressed.[18] The fact that these types of offenses were prosecuted at all reveals something about the role of women in this wartime economy. Soldiers' wives left behind to care for farms and households during military campaigns demanded state protection. They received free meat to complement the family diet and usually mediated for benefits or privileges for their husbands. This gave them a bargaining position useful in redressing male violence.

Crimes against public order (disturbing the peace, drunkenness, fights, gambling, carrying a knife, etc.) were not numerous. Drunkenness and

Table 2. Crimes by Type, Buenos Aires Province (1831–1851)

Type of Crime	Number of Cases	Percentage
Against property	**552**	33.1
Theft	508	
Other	44	
Against persons/honor	**219**	12.9
Wounds and beatings	96	
Homicide and related	63	
Rape, kidnapping, etc.	33	
Insults	23	
Other	4	
Against the state/government	**627**	37.6
Desertion	285	
Dodgers and "bad service"	39	
Without document	295	
Other	8	
Against public order	**225**	13.5
Vagrancy	141	
Drunkenness	13	
Fights	22	
Gambling	1	
Carrying a knife	14	
Runaways	14	
Desconocido	13	
Other	7	
Political crimes	**17**	1.0
Insurrection/conspiracy	2	
Unitarios	15	
Other crimes	**32**	1.9
Orden superior	20	
Other	12	
Total	1,669	100.0

Source: Data base Presos Remitidos, N=1674, tomado de Jueces de Paz, Partes de Novedades.

disturbing the peace, a major cause for police arrests in the decades following 1880, were in this period rather rare.[19] This could mean that the claim of the regime to have restored the "order of the countryside" was true or that these types of offenses were greatly underreported. According to the impressionistic information provided by a few trials, violence in taverns was less frequent than assumed. As paysanos knew that the combination of bad language, gambling, and drinks could lead to deadly *desafíos* (violent disagreements), they tried to avoid confrontations. The police, lax about many other regulations, were particularly demanding when it came to the collection of knives at *pulperías* (taverns). When someone, drunk or annoyed, disturbed the peace, the justice of the peace handled the issue personally. Those detained received a flogging, paid a fine, or suffered at the stake (*cepo*) for a day or two before they were released.

Vagrancy, the most prevalent crime against public order, was more a condition or characterization than an offense.[20] Charges for vagrancy were used selectively to underscore the negative valuation made by residents about a newcomer whose morality and willingness to work was in doubt. Added to the *filiación* (basic charge), "vagrancy" served as justification for the arrest or as an aggravating circumstance of another crime. Characterizing the felon as *vago y mal entretenido* (vagrant and without position), the justice of the peace could complicate the charges against the arrested.

Very few of those in custody were suspected of "political crimes," that is, of being *unitarios*. This should not surprise us, for political opponents were always a minority in Buenos Aires province which *federales* associated with the merchant and the propertied classes and particularly with urban residents.[21] *Unitarios* were by definition outside the honest and patriotic corps of rural communities. Nevertheless, it is useful to remark on the limited frequency of these offenses in contrast to cases of desertion, traveling without documents, and theft. In the countryside, paysanos took care not to express opposition to the regime, so they were rarely arrested for these types of violations.

Crimes Against the State, Crimes Against Property

The countryside that most poor paysanos knew and inhabited was not as overridden by interpersonal violence and theft as presented in the literature.[22] In fact, neither of these two types of crimes seems to have been prevalent. A third category of crimes that we may call "crimes against the state" surpassed in magnitude both crimes against property and against persons. This category refers to a series of illegalities surrounding the obligation of males to provide military service to the provincial state. Deserters, draft dodgers, people traveling without identification, and neighbors accused of providing bad service to local authorities comprised 37 percent of all arrested.

These crimes were directed not against property or particular persons but against the state. They represented a rejection by poor paysanos of their obligation to provide military or police service in the terms and time demanded by state authorities. Paysanos's defense of their own time (spent as paid labor on ranches or farms, or more commonly tending their own livestock) clashed with the requirements of the provincial state engaged in recurrent wars and campaigns. The tension between these two uses of paysano labor provided the substance of the "crimes" most systematically prosecuted by the state and more frequently committed by peons and day laborers.

Deserting the military and traveling without proper identification were the two most frequent violations in this category. Desertions were a breach of the implicit contract between paysanos and the state for the provision of military service. After a short time in the army, a sizable portion of the men drafted rejected the terms and conditions of their engagement—length of service, inadequate pay, bad treatment, unlawful "private" use of their labor—and deserted the ranks. Later, under interrogation, deserters explained that these very conditions of life in the army provided the "reasons" for their crimes.[23] Sometimes soldiers deserted one battalion only to join another where they thought conditions would be more favorable.

We cannot estimate at this point the rate of desertion in the Federalist armies. Data generated from another source (a database of 1,364 soldiers drafted between 1810 and 1860) puts registered desertions at 25 percent of those recruited.[24] The same source provides another approximation to this problem. While most assignments (*destinos*) included the obligation to serve three, four, or more years, the actual time of service was much shorter. Almost 60 percent of the recruits left the army before the first year was over, the average term of service being close to ten months.

Traveling without identification and related offenses like forging passports and changing names involved both resistance and accommodation. Clearly there were paysanos who resented the increasing "documentation" of their movements—a process connected not only with the state's need for social control but also with the expansion of property rights—as a requirement that conflicted with their independent way of life. But more generally, not carrying identification was a crime of ignorance or a product of fear. Those who knew the consequences of traveling without a passport tried to get one by legal or illegal means. Forging passports and *guías* (passes), traveling under another person's name, and stealing documents became quite common practices. Those unaware of this requirement or afraid to face the police authorities to obtain a passport, mainly *provincianos*, were apprehended on their way to Buenos Aires.

Crimes against property were important, comprising 33 percent of the registered cases. Among these crimes, theft was prevalent. Of the cases where information was recorded, the stealing of cattle and horses ranked first at 70 percent. The taking of *efectos* (clothes, riding apparel, and hides mainly) followed in 20 percent of the cases. Cases involving stolen money involved another 6 percent. At a time when the state tried to consolidate property rights in cattle by controlling the commercialization and transportation of stolen cattle, the prevalence of theft as a chief motive for arrest is to be expected. On a first reading, these crimes could be taken as a reaction by poor paysanos to state regulations that criminalized the customary appropriation of free-roaming cattle. On a closer reading, however, we notice that more was at stake.

The crime of theft most frequent in the province bore little resemblance to thievery by highwaymen or bandits described by European travelers. Most "burglaries" were committed by one or two individuals (90 percent of the cases), usually in the environs of a house, ranch, *chacra* (small farm), rural tavern, or *campo* (the countryside). The stolen object was often of little significance: one or two horses or cows, less than half a dozen hides, a few items of riding gear. Victims of these crimes were often described as male (89 percent), neighbor (42 percent), *patrón* or *hacendado* (21 percent), or *pulpero* (tavern owner) or merchant (13 percent). Thieves were usually described as having no clear attachment to the community, people such as temporary peons, newcomers (*desconocidos*), or having no resources living off the *vecinos*' (resident citizens) property. Horses were appropriated as often as cattle, an indication of the transportation needs of most felons (many of whom were deserters).

An examination of the types and circumstances of crimes against property supports our assertion that criminality centered around the relationship between the state and poor paysanos on the question of military service. Among the animals illegally appropriated, horses outnumbered cattle, supporting the view that rapid transportation to escape prosecution was more important than appropriating food (or, alternatively, that stealing cows was more tolerated by authorities and neighbors than stealing horses). A good horse and riding apparel were the main items a deserter had to steal in order to make a successful escape.

The characteristics of cattle theft are indicative of the purposes of many felons. Of the 274 documented cases: 170 felons drove the cattle or rode the horses, 50 slaughtered animals on the spot, 39 sold cattle with alien brands or made counterfeit branding, and 15 were accused of skinning the animals to make *botas de potro* (calf-skin boots) or sell the hides. Clearly the aim of ascending illegally to the status of small property owner (having their own *tropillas* of horses or herds of cattle) coexisted with the use of stolen objects to satisfy immediate needs (wearing boots, eating beef). The customary appropriation of cattle and horses, a tolerated behavior among neighbors, was a crime when committed by "outsiders."[25]

Theft statistics depict a rural society with unclear boundaries of property (despite the government's insistence on branding cattle and horses) and a moral economy quite tolerant of the direct appropriation of items necessary for transportation and food. This was not a society organized around a binary social division—small against large proprietors, poor against rich—but a society with a multiplicity of small conflicts. Some of these felonies refer to conflicts between *patrones* and *peones*, or between the *pulpero* and his customers. Others emerged instead out of conflicts over property rights between neighbors and newcomers, usually *agregados* (non-proprietary residents, generally small-scale producers and farmers), tenants, and peons living outside their native region. But thefts also show a form of resistance directed against the state. Illicit trade in cattle and horses by paysanos made a mockery of the most visible signs of property. In ways comparable to paysanos who forged passports and militia papers, cattle and horse thieves forged brands and transport papers in defiance of state regulations.

A Question of Service

Rather than being engaged in a war against property owners, poor paysanos were involved in a daily confrontation with the state over the issue of military service. The state of Buenos Aires, preoccupied with manning its armies, had criminalized the customary activities of peasants and laborers (including the direct appropriation of cattle and horses) and punished infractors with long terms in the army. The rural poor responded in kind, avoiding militia registration, shirking real military service, and, once forced into the army, deserting when conditions became intolerable. To remain out of reach of military recruiters and rural police, poor paysanos put into practice multiple "arts of deception": forging passports, permits, and release papers; hiding their uniforms; changing names; seeking refuge among relatives and friends; keeping their past to themselves; changing jobs frequently.[26]

In a period of recurrent wars and heightened "nationalism," lack of paysano cooperation with the military apparatus was remarkable. Although all males eighteen and older had to enlist the militia, many tried to avoid this obligation by moving from town to town. Seventy-one percent of the arrested (the most mobile part of the province's peon class) said they had not complied with this mandatory registration. Those who said they had were unable to prove it: only six percent of the arrested were able to produce enrollment papers at the time of their arrest. Those who were not registered *milicianos* (militiamen) could still be regular soldiers and comply with their obligations to the federation. Few actually did. When asked whether they belonged to a regiment or army unit, less than eight percent of the arrested admitted it. Fewer still were those who could prove this engagement, for less than three percent carried passports with them and less than five percent were able to produce release papers (*licencias* or *bajas*).[27]

This left the impression among military recruiters and justices of the peace that poor paysanos, particularly those unknown (*desconocidos*) to the towns, were always resisting the draft. This resistance appears all the more remarkable once we consider that rural communities as a whole did not oppose or resist the draft. Unlike French and Catalan peasant communities during the Revolution and Napoleonic Wars who defied the central state from a position of autonomy and communal work, towns of rural Buenos Aires were permeated by ideological divisions and regulated to a large extent by representatives of the "central" state.[28] Under such circumstances, resisting the draft was often an individual enterprise assisted by friends and relatives, rarely a collective struggle.

Few among the arrested (37 percent) declared they had provided military service to the federation. Among this group the opinion of what constituted "military service" differed: 48 percent of them claimed combat experience, another 16 percent had joined an army unit, a militia, or served temporarily in frontier outposts or camp drills (*destacamentos* and *cantones*) (see Table 3). The rest said they had rendered services which the army classified as "passive": driving cattle to a regiment, tending horses

Table 3. Type of Military Service Rendered by Prisoners

Type of Service	Number of Cases	Percentage
Joined an army corps	44	6.0
Joined military campaigns	356	48.7
Joined local militias	27	3.7
Did *destacamentos* and cantones	50	6.8
Tended army's horses	55	7.5
Served on police *patrullas*	26	3.5
Served the local justice	30	4.1
Served in his province	19	2.6
Participated in cattle drives	85	11.6
Carried mail	7	0.9
Participated in brandings	7	0.9
Carried firewood	6	0.8
Slaughtered cattle	3	0.4
Served the *postas*	3	0.4
Cared for state ranches	3	0.4
Other	9	1.2
Total	730	100.0

for a military *caballada* (herd), slaughtering cattle for soldiers' consumption, taking care of confiscated *unitario* ranches, or helping the justice of the peace or local police chief in occasional *partidas* (excursions) and *patrullas* (patrols).

All these services appeared to military recruiters as much less patriotic and demanding than defending the "federal cause" on the battlefield. Furthermore, none of these services exempted males from their obligation to enlist in the militia or army. Consequently, recruiters insisted that arrested paysanos who could not prove membership in the militia or regular army be given a military assignment. Paysanos on the other hand wanted these "passive services" to count as military duty.

Those who had provided no service to the federation (or had been only marginally involved in its defense) could expect a punishment proportional to their "crime": years of service in the federal army. Available information about the fate of the arrested underscores the state's use of the criminal justice system for recruitment purposes. Military service rather than imprisonment, banishment, or corporal punishment awaited most delinquents. We know the destination of 532 of the prisoners (32 percent of the Partes de Novedades data): 353 were sentenced to serve in the army, 58 were simply assigned to a nearby regiment, 4 were sent to the police department, 50 were freed and 55 pardoned, with 2 more released from service, 5 punished with extended service, 2 banished, and 3 executed.

To military recruiters, the worst crime was noncompliance. Consequently, the identification and arrest of deserters constituted a major objective of the justice system. This explains the degree of detail around the question of "service" found in the depositions about deserters and common delinquents. Those who filed reports made an effort to include something about the military record of each arrestee. Thus, we now possess information about paysano participation in different campaigns and wars that otherwise would have passed unreported (see Table 4). The information itself reveals the state's interest in the question of service. The collected responses painted a dismal scenario for military authorities: only a third of the arrested were able to give any details about their participation in the wars of the federation.

The interrogation of prisoners aimed at identifying deserters. Whether arrested for theft, fights, or vagrancy, felons were asked to tell their "histories" to the justice of the peace. As the felon recounted his past he dropped information about past campaigns and wars, which made him suspect as a possible draft dodger or deserter. Usually, having "dispersed" after a battle counted as desertion, regardless of a soldier's later efforts to rejoin his battalion. Thus, crimes against property or persons could easily

Table 4. Military Campaigns in Which Arrestees Had Participated

Military Campaign	Number of Cases	Percentage
War of Brazil (1825–1828)	19	3.4
First "Restauration" (1829)	157	28.3
Campaign to Córdoba (1830–31)	63	11.4
Second "Restauration" (1833)	49	8.8
Indian Campaign of 1833–34	41	7.4
Southern Rebellion (1839)	52	9.4
Invasion of 1840	57	10.3
Entre Ríos Campaign (1840–1842)	38	6.8
Cuyo Campaign (1841)	14	2.5
Chasing Indians	20	3.6
Other campaigns	44	7.9
Total	554	100.0

turn into crimes against the state. Only if the arrested was a *vecino* and a *buen federal* (good patriot) could his military experience be taken for granted and the interrogation concentrate on his civil wrongdoings.

That is why we should try to read our statistics in the context of the state's anxieties. The "question of service," being essential for the conduct of war, was the major preoccupation of the Rosas administration. Against this imperative, the defense of property and the moral management of rural communities took second place. From below, the issue was more ambivalent as poor paysanos included in their survival strategies the defense of custom, resistance to authority, and accommodation to the "documentary order" demanded by the Rosas regime. In their view, all "crimes" were related. Their acts of direct appropriation cannot be dissociated from their struggle against the state in order to avoid or reduce their military obligations. Besides money and cattle, thieves sought clothes, riding apparel, hides, and a few other disposable items (such as horsehair or tallow) that could be used as a means of exchange at rural taverns. For an itinerant rural worker without identification or a deserter escaping apprehension, these commodities were as good as cash; with them, they could continue defying the authority of a justice system designed to impress poor paysanos into the army.

A Criminal Class?

Who were the arrested? Were they a special segment of the rural population? Did they constitute a "criminal class?" To an extent the Rosista justice system was discriminating in terms of class. It was based on identification, description, and classification practices that attempted to separate the working poor—the so-called *clase de peón de campo*—as the target of police surveillance and main provider of military personnel. People who worked as peons for a living, who wore *chiripá* and *poncho* (the typical gaucho "diaper-style" riding pants and cloak), who were unable to read and write, and who possessed no more than a horse, a set of clothes, and simple riding apparel, were members of this "class." On their shoulders fell the burden of manning the Federalist armies. Other members of rural society like *hacendados*, *criadores* (small-scale producers), farmers, foremen, merchants, and artisans, though obliged to perform some type of service for the state, were generally exempted from active military duty. As *vecinos* they had to enroll in the local militia and render "passive services," occasional and limited duties in *destacamentos* (posts), *cantones* (barracks), or *patrullas*.

In practice however, this "class-ification"—the process of identifying and separating socioeconomic classes—was difficult to carry out. Given the egalitarianism in fashion mandated by Federalist political culture, poor paysanos looked no different from "middling" paysanos. At least in the countryside, the enforcing of class by appearance was more difficult than governor Rosas imagined. Regarding occupational status, social difference was also ambiguous to the extent that many rural residents—small-scale cattle raisers and farmers as well as peons—reported to work in *faenas de campo* (work gangs). Waged labor was not a good indicator either. *Agregados*, tenants, and laborers all had to engage in occasional work at neighboring estates.

Thus, the practical separation of a peon class rested on the issue of residence: long-term residents of a given rural town or partido tended to see delinquent tendencies in the recently-arrived and the traveler. Itinerant workers (peons and day laborers) in particular were always suspect of having violated the law in other districts. Gradually, with the growth of rural towns and subsequent consolidation of the justice and police apparatus, there developed a distinction between *vecinos* and *transeúntes* (non-residents) which profoundly affected the functioning of the justice system.

Whereas *vecinos* could be trusted to perform a multiplicity of small tasks required for the functioning of a well-ordered town (arrests, prosecutions, transporting and slaughtering cattle, road repairs, mail, etc.), the *transeúntes* were suspected of avoiding not only these services but also the more fundamental task of defending the federation. Outsiders, *desconocidos*, and youngsters without parental supervision were the first targets of press gangs or *levas*, precisely because older male residents found their manners and morals lacking compared to the ideal of order in the Federalist republic—they were prejudged as *vagos y mal entretenidos* even before they committed any crime. Their autonomy, interpreted as a challenge to the tranquility and order of the province, placed young men on the move as key suspects for interrogation and arrest. The *vecinos* and *conocidos* (well-known) of each district on the other hand had greater opportunities for escaping arrest or negotiating other penalties in exchange for military service.

Consequently, it is not surprising to find that *transeúntes*, most of them peons, suffered a disproportionate share of the burden of active military service while *vecinos* provided mostly "passive services." The data on prisoners reveals the extreme form of workers' nomadism the Rosista justice system had to deal with as well as a systemic bias against itinerant workers and fugitives (see Table 5). Over 82 percent of convicts had been born outside the district in which they were arrested. This proportion reached 100 percent in *partidos* recently settled north (Navarro, Chivilcoy)

Table 5. Mobility of the Arrested

Place Arrested	Born Outside Their Partido (in %)	Born Outside Buenos Aires Province (in %)	Total Number Arrested
Lobos	83.3	53.3	201
Arrecifes	83.9	67.7	99
Areco	72.8	42.0	212
Azul	89.4	46.9	32
Tordillo	100.0	42.9	35
Monsalvo-M. Ch.	100.0	65.2	23
Quilmes	84.1	51.7	118
Chascomús	89.8	54.2	96
Luján	76.3	55.5	238
Baradero	47.1	29.4	34
Cañuelas	93.0	30.0	40
Dolores	100.0	55.3	47
Ensenada	83.7	34.8	23
Ranchos	76.2	52.3	111
Las Flores	66.7	55.6	18
Chivilcoy	100.0	52.6	19
Navarro	100.0	39.1	115
San Nicolás	63.8	61.5	52
Total	82.2	51.8	1,513

and south (Tordillo, Monsalvo, Dolores, Mar Chiquita) of the Salado River, but was also high in older districts of the NW-SE corridor such as Arrecifes, Areco, and Quilmes. Nearly 52 percent had been born outside of Buenos Aires province—most *provincianos* coming from the northern provinces (and called for this reason *arribeños* or highlanders), but there were also Africans, Europeans, and migrants from neighboring countries.

The characteristics of a labor market that demanded seasonal and occasional labor and a justice system tied to the military forced poor paysanos to move from place to place in search of employment and security. And mobility was key to their survival strategy. Whether escaping the police or searching for a job, peons and day laborers had to travel a lot. Taking along a family would slacken their pace and probably represent an obstacle to most employers. So itinerant workers and *provincianos* tended to travel alone. As a result, most of the arrested were single (71 percent), an indication of the practices of mobility of poor paysanos and also of the bias of the justice system against workers on the move.

Occupations of the arrested run the whole spectrum of economic activities in rural society (see Table 6). The single largest group worked in agriculture, husbandry, and forestry (50 percent). Most were peons, though there were also *labradores* (manual laborers) and *criadores*, ranch fore-

Table 6. Occupations of the Arrested

Occupational Group	Number of Cases	Percentage
Artisans	29	3.2
Rural industry	23	2.5
Transportation	70	7.8
Commerce	20	2.2
Farming and husbandry	449	49.9
Estanciero/proprietor	24	2.7
Administrator/foreman	17	1.9
Labrador/criador	29	3.2
Peon	288	32.0
Special skill	48	5.3
Other country laborers	43	4.8
Armed forces	59	6.5
Other employments	6	0.7
Day laborers	166	18.5
Without occupation	77	8.5
Total	899	100.0

men and administrators, and occasionally an *estanciero* (rancher). Then followed *jornaleros* or day laborers (18 percent), then transportation workers (8 percent, mostly ox cart drivers and cattle drovers), and people classified as without occupation (8 percent).[29] Soldiers, merchants, workers in rural industry (leather work and meat-salting), and others made up the rest.

This limited information tells us something about the state's policy toward crime. The profile of the delinquent shows that the Rosista justice system weighed heaviest on the humblest portion of the rural population. Intent on pacifying, recruiting, and safeguarding property, the system arrested members of the *clase de peón de campo* more frequently than those of other social groups. The majority of the arrested were engaged in temporary, mobile, waged occupations (70 percent minimum) whereas the "middling sector" (*agregados*, farmers, and *criadores*) constituted a minority. Proprietors comprised only 10 percent of the arrested.

Racially, the arrested constituted a mixed bag not significantly different from the rural population at large: 40 percent were *trigueños* ("swarthy" mestizos), 32 percent were white, 9 percent mulatto, 8 percent black, 5 percent *aindiado* or *achinado* (mestizos with Indian or Asian features), and 3 percent Indian.[30] The Buenos Aires justice system, though not racially blind—recruiters were asked to register the skin color of all soldiers—did not seem to discriminate in terms of race. A slightly greater proportion of *trigueños* than in urban areas reflects the preponderance of the rural population among the arrested. The stigma against "people of color" probably remained as strong as in colonial times, but the freedoms and opportunities blacks, mulattoes, and mestizos had gained since independence made the implementation of racial justice very difficult. Only indigenous people appear underrepresented in this sample relative to their presence in the province's population. Clearly, this is related to the fact that most non-Christianized indigenous peoples (Christianized Indians were considered *aindiado* and on occasion could pass for *trigueños*) kept their distance from *cristiano* civilization and, by and large, *cristiano* law did not apply to non-Christian Indians. Pampa Indians who committed the most common crimes against the property and lives of *cristianos*, the *malones* (renegades or "ambushers"), were dealt with by the army and not by the justice system. They were generally subject to retribution in kind: punitive expeditions against their *toldos* (teepees or huts).

The ages of the arrested also mirrored the population at large: 43 percent were younger than 24; 78 percent were under age 34.[31] This means that 57 percent of the arrested were 25 or older. This age distribution might seem odd for a state preoccupied with producing young recruits for the army (and using the justice system for this purpose) but we know from other sources that the Federalist army was not so discriminating in terms of age. The obligation to enlist in regiments and the militia involved all males between 18 and 45. Justices of the peace who provided "delinquents" to man the Federalist armies did not usually consider the age of the arrested. Moreover, the system of extending service for another term as punishment for certain violations such as desertion, insubordination, or theft tended to raise the average age of the corps. As Domingo Sarmiento reported in his *Memorias del Ejército Grande*, in 1852 old soldiers constituted an important proportion of the dictator's core regiments.

Neither age nor race seems to have been the basis upon which the justice system identified and separated the "class" which would man the Federalist armies. It was rather the distinction between *vecinos* and *transeúntes*, overlapping with the distinction between resident producers and mobile peons which was at the root of the attempt to define a "criminal class" during this period. This type of criminalization—focusing on the most nomadic part of the population—was consistent with a particular definition of citizenship: that which equated permanent residency and property with political rights. Also important was the connection between criminality and the military needs of the state. Rather than responding to an attempt to moralize society or the necessity to inculcate property rights, the impressment and prosecution of delinquents during the Rosas era was directly connected with the personnel requirements of the military.[32]

Poor paysanos did not quietly accept this criminalization of geographical and occupational mobility. Peons and day laborers who were turned into soldiers, though uprooted from their communities by civil wars, tried to reinsert themselves socially and politically after deserting or being released from the army.[33] Though generally on the move (mainly to escape prosecution from the justice system or to find occasional employment in ranches, meat-salting plants, farms, or manufactures), ex-soldiers never relinquished the possibility of settling in a town and becoming socially accepted. Through this, they expected to become *vecinos* and thus regain the social, economic, and political rights lost at the time of arrest.

Conclusion

Our statistical reconstruction opens a space for a reconsideration of conventional wisdom regarding the relationship between the Rosista state and poor paysanos. First, the images of a countryside with predominantly violent forms of sociability must be reexamined in the light of statistics showing that crimes against persons and public order were infrequent. The Buenos Aires countryside, undergoing a traumatic period of wars and political persecution, showed a remarkable degree of stability and peaceful social interaction. Knife fights and duels existed, but not to the extent portrayed in the literature. Second, the prevalence of crimes against the state speaks of the need to reintroduce into the analysis of criminality the political and ideological dimensions of paysano illicit behavior. The issue of recruitment, according to these statistics, appears to be central to the operation of the justice system and therefore to the discussion of those paysano experiences in relationship to the provincial state. Third, we need to look more closely into the meaning of theft in these rural communities as a prerequisite for understanding the diverse sources of conflict.

By deserting, absconding, forging documents, and disguising themselves, poor paysanos fought against provincial state representatives, trying to impose their own interpretation of the fundamental political contract with the state: the obligation to serve the nation under particular circumstances and for a limited time. Similarly, the continuous resort to cattle rustling, poaching, and illegal sales of unbranded hides or cattle can be seen as a response by quite mobile paysanos to the state's efforts to demarcate property rights that criminalized customary appropriation. Crimes against property and crimes against the state were closely related. A significant portion of thefts were actually ancillary crimes in a desertion. Significantly, poor paysanos had to contest their right to directly appropriate a cow, a sheep, or a piece of hide (usually with resident small property owners) in order to continue on the move, the basic survival strategy common to deserters and itinerant peons.

The crimes of poor paysanos appear in this light as a double struggle: on the one hand a struggle against the military apparatus of the state— that is a contestation against forced recruitment, unpaid salaries, irregular provisions of uniforms and rations, abusive language, and corporal punishment—and on the other hand a struggle against the strict enforcement of property rights without concern for "necessity," that is, a defense of the customary right of direct appropriation of cattle, horses, and hides. If we are to read the crimes of poor paysanos as resistance, we should specify the values or conceptions that served as grounds for such a contestation. The crimes against the state referred to unfulfilled promises made by the post-independence state to its citizens in arms. The crimes against property pointed instead to the continued use among paysanos of rules of sociability and behavior that defied state intrusion in the ownership of and commerce in cattle, horses, and hides.

Besides, poor paysanos' illegalities point to the existence of a conflict in the formation of the post-independence state. I refer here to contradictions between the rhetoric of the leadership about the "rights and liberties of the people" and the burdens the post-independence state imposed upon the shoulders of Africans, creoles, women, and the poor. Coerced military recruitment of the poor, while proprietors could avoid active military duties, conflicted too visibly with the "abolition of privileges" proclaimed by the assembly in 1813. In the same fashion, the restrictions imposed upon the mobility of people (passport laws) contradicted the promises of personal liberty made by the revolutionary leadership.

The crimes of poor paysanos can be read as a normative and proce-dural contention with the state and the proprietor classes regarding the nature of post-independence society. The association of citizenship with residential habits—the adaptation of the colonial condition of *vecindad* to republican realities—meant in practice the segregation of itinerant work-ers, *provincianos*, Africans, and women from the body of the republic and the criminalization of the most mobile part of the rural poor. Rather than a society of rights and opportunity, this was a society of privilege where the poor could no longer claim citizenship. In this regard, it seems that poor paysanos were asserting the type of civil and economic rights de-nied them by the very historiography which construed them as defense-less victims of *hacendados* or as passional barbarians operating in an economy of violence. By hiding from the draft, deserting their battalions, forging passports and *guías*, and appropriating food, poor paysanos were enforcing in practice the rights promised to them since independence (free-dom of movement, right to income, equality under the law) and leveling the inequalities produced by Rosista recruitment policies.

Notes

1. See Adolfo Prieto, *Proyección del rosismo en la literatura argentina* (Rosario: Facultad de Filosofía y Letras, 1959); and Avelina Ibañez, *Unitarios y federales en la literatura argentina* (Buenos Aires: Imprenta López, 1933).

2. For a critical analysis of *El Matadero* see Jorge Salessi, *Médicos, maleantes y maricas* (Rosario: Beatriz Viterbo, 1995), 55–74. On *Facundo* see Roberto González Echevarría, "A Lost World Rediscovered: Sarmiento's *Facundo*," in T. Halperín Donghi et al., *Sarmiento, Author of a Nation* (Berkeley-Los Angeles: University of California Press, 1994), 220–56. On *Amalia* see Doris Sommer, *Foundational Fictions* (Berkeley-Los Angeles: University of California Press, 1991), chapter 3.

3. González Echevarría, "A Lost World Rediscovered," p. 246.

4. R. Cunninghame Graham, for example, depicted the sociability of the Ar-gentine countryside as explosive and violent. Gauchos were good conversation-alists and prudent in their words but, when offended, they quite easily became enraged and bloodthirsty. Robert Cunninghame Graham, *El Río de la Plata* (Buenos Aires: Secretaría de Cultura de la Nación, 1994), 20.

5. See for example Rafael Palumbo, ed., *De la historia. Efemérides sangrientas de la Dictadura de Juan Manuel de Rosas con un apéndice de sus robos* (Buenos Aires: Talleres Gráficos R. Palumbo, 1911). Contemporary observers such as Santiago Calzadilla reported, in different words, the same image of state-sponsored violence. *Las beldades de mi tiempo* (Buenos Aires: A. Estrada, 1944), 166–69.

6. "Were rural males more violent and lawless than other sectors of society? The answer must be yes";—state Slatta and Robinson—"they lived in a violence-prone macho subculture on the frontier." Richard W. Slatta and Karla Robinson,

"Continuities in Crime and Punishment: Buenos Aires, 1820–1850," in Lyman L. Johnson, ed., *The Problem of Order in Changing Societies: Essays on Crime and Policing in Argentina and Uruguay, 1750–1940* (Albuquerque: University of New Mexico Press, 1990), 24.

7. See for example John Lynch, *Argentine Dictator: Juan Manuel de Rosas, 1829–1852* (Oxford: Oxford University Press, 1981) and Richard W. Slatta, *Gauchos and the Vanishing Frontier* (Lincoln: University of Nebraska Press, 1983).

8. Slatta and Robinson, "Continuities in Crime and Punishment," and Mark D. Szuchman, "Disorder and Social Control in Buenos Aires, 1810–1860," *Journal of Interdisciplinary History* 15, no. 1 (Summer 1984): 83–110.

9. Rosas's recruitment policies included the obligation of all males between 18 and 45 to enlist in the provincial militias. In times of military campaigns the justices of the peace could mobilize part of these militias just by calling them to take up arms. More frequently however, military commanders had to rely on the regular army manned by delinquents such as those analyzed in this chapter. These were called *destinados*, for they were sentenced or "destined" to served in the army. Some of the regular soldiers were forcefully recruited in taverns, roads, and other public places—the *levados*. In addition, the armies recruited soldiers through contracts, offering volunteers an advanced payment of money. These were called *enganchados*. See my "Recrutamiento militar, disciplinamiento y proletarización en la era de Rosas," *Boletín del Instituto de Historia Argentina y Americana 'Dr. E. Ravignani,'* 3a. serie, no. 5 (1992): 25–47.

10. The extant *Partes de Novedades* correspond to 37 percent of the period elapsed between 1831 and 1851.

11. Slatta and Robinson based their estimates on data on prisoners held during 1822 in the city's jails and prisons, and on a second sample drawn from 657 cases taken from Trelles' summary index of police reports from 1827 to 1850. Szuchman uses data on urban arrests taken from the newspaper *El Lucero*, the only rural statistics being those of San Antonio de Areco, c. 1825.

12. The Navarro justice of the peace, one of these exceptions, included 16 out of 200 of these reported crimes. The San Nicolás justice found 44 felonies (out of 189 observations) not worthy of sending the felon to Buenos Aires. On occasion, justices made clear to governor Rosas that they were not recording those detained *por causas leves* (for petty offenses). In June–August 1839 the justice wrote: "On different occasions . . . they have arrested and imprisoned 27 individuals more for causes that merited no more than temporary detention . . . who have been released after one or two days." In May–August 1838 he wrote, "The signatory makes no reference in the present part to 29 more individuals that have been imprisoned for trivial offenses and released by this court." Juzgado de Paz de San Nicolás, *Partes de Novedades*, AGN X 21-7-1.

13. The Chascomús justice of the peace, for example, omitted in his reports those prisoners put into his custody by other authorities as well as people arrested by "superior orders" to satisfy a request for a recruitment quota. In his report for January–February 1837, the justice wrote: "Not included are the prisoners sent to Monsalvo and Dolores . . . because these [prisoners] lack their *Clasificación* and they are sent back as is required." Juzgado de Paz de Chascomús, *Partes de Novedades*, AGN X 20-10-7.

14. The number of *levados* depended on the disposition of each justice of the peace towards drafting the youngsters in his district, the community's protection of draft dodgers, and the circumstance of being at war or peace.

15. This issue is more fully developed in Ricardo Salvatore, "Autocratic State and Labor Control in the Argentine Pampas, Buenos Aires, 1829–1852," *Peasant Studies* 18, no. 4 (Summer 1991).

16. Quite likely, what justices meant by the phrase *sin novedad* was that there had been only minor offenses not worthy of reporting to the governor. Again, this reinforces our view about the bipolarity of the justice system during this period: the affairs of the local justice (the preservation of order in the countryside) need not concern the provincial government as long as the justices of the peace were able to keep that "peace and quiet."

17. Insults were a chief triggering mechanism for these *peleas* (fights) which resulted in wounds, beatings, and on occasion homicide.

18. On the "theft of women" see Carlos A. Mayo, *Estancia y sociedad en la Pampa 1740–1820* (Buenos Aires: Biblos, 1995), 179–190.

19. See Julia Kirk Blackwelder and Lyman L. Johnson, "Changing Criminal Patterns in Buenos Aires, 1890–1914," *Journal of Latin American Studies* 14, no. 2 (1982): 359–380.

20. In a context where very few of the *transeúntes* and peons had a *contrata* (certificate of employment) to show the authorities, the indictment for vagrancy could apply to almost anybody.

21. Being a *unitario* was not a reproducible type of crime: those arrested for expressing words damaging to the 'federal cause' could count on their banishment from town as well as the confiscation of their property.

22. Estimates by Slatta and Robinson taken from the police summary index for 1822–1850 show the following breakdown: crimes against persons 39 percent, crimes against property 32 percent, crimes against the social order 18 percent, gambling 6 percent, fugitives 5 percent. Slatta and Robinson, "Continuities in Crime and Punishment," 33.

23. See Ricardo Salvatore, "The Reasons of Deserters," paper presented to the Program in Agrarian Studies, Yale University, February 1994.

24. Work in progress. Estimates prepared will be included in my book manuscript "The Wandering Working Class," chapter 3.

25. In the context of a society with few or no fences and few written contracts, theft among neighbors (typically small-scale producers) was an important means of settling disputes.

26. See James C. Scott, *Domination and the Arts of Resistance: Hidden Transcripts* (New Haven: Yale University Press, 1990).

27. Though peons had the obligation to carry a *contrata* or employment paper, *less than one percent* actually did.

28. See Richard C. Cobb, *The People's Armies: The Armées Revolutionaires; Instrument of the Terror in the Departments* (New Haven-London: Yale University Press, 1987); Alan Forrest, *Conscripts and Deserters: The Army and French Society during the Revolution and Empire* (New York-Oxford: Oxford University Press, 1989); and Michel Brunet, *Le Roussillon: Une société contre l'Etat 1780–1820* (Toulouse: Association des Publications de l'Université Toulouse-Le Mirail, 1986).

29. According to Slatta and Robinson's estimates, four percent of those in prison in 1822 belonged to this category. "Continuities in Crime and Punishment," 25.

30. Contrasted with statistics collected by Slatta and Robinson for the city's prisons in 1822: *trigueño* 21 percent, white 53 percent, black 14 percent, mulatto 9 percent, Indian 2 percent, and *zambo* (black-Indian mix) less than 1 percent.

The racial composition of the arrested in rural areas shows a greater presence of *trigueños* and a smaller proportion of whites and blacks. Ibid., table 2, p. 28.

31. In the 1869 census, 74 percent of the population living in the Buenos Aires countryside was younger than 30, 83.8 percent was younger than 40. Taken from Hilda Sábato and Luis A. Romero, *Los trabajadores de Buenos Airesz: La experiencia del mercado 1850–1880* (Buenos Aires: Sudamericana, 1992), table 5, p. 293.

32. It should also be remembered that the justice system, though connected to the war machine, was not completely in its service. Violent crimes committed by middling or high-standing paysanos were repressed in order to preserve order in the countryside. As a consequence, although day laborers and peons constituted the single largest groups among the arrested, other members of rural communities also fell under the Rosista punitive system.

33. See Salvatore, "The Reasons of Deserters."

5

Punishment in Nineteenth-Century Rio de Janeiro: Judicial Action as Police Practice

Thomas H. Holloway

The development of a modern, rational state included the creation of police institutions that would respond to the "general interest" of the population; institutions that would fight crime not with the perceived arbitrariness and despotism of the absolutist colonial model, but with rule of law and the protection of individual rights. Often however, attempts to modernize police institutions were effected in societies in which political values and economic realities were antithetical to the fundamental principles of reform.

That was the case in nineteenth-century Brazil, where successive attempts at implementing a "modern" police were carried out in order to preserve a social order characterized most prominently by the maintenance of slavery and slave relations. As Thomas Holloway, professor of history at Cornell University, demonstrates for the case of Rio de Janeiro, the police force was used first and foremost to punish and control slaves; in so doing it enjoyed prerogatives that went far beyond detention and interrogation, including de facto judicial investigation and the power to sentence and punish. The discretionary power of Rio's police acquired during the nineteenth century would leave an enduring mark on its attitude toward society long after slavery was abolished and is still visible in everyday police behavior on the streets of Rio de Janeiro and other Brazilian cities. Holloway's damning portrayal of Rio police demonstrates the arbitrariness of the social construction of criminality for a society in which the criminal justice system itself is criminal. And, in such cases, the considerable legitimizing potential of modernization itself is badly compromised.

This essay traces the development of the police system as an important feature of the formation of the Brazilian state during the period from the transfer of Portuguese organizational patterns with the arrival of the Royal Court in 1808 through the maturation of national institutions in the middle of the century as well as further institutional experimentation in the last decades of the empire. It focuses on the kinds of punishments police administered as part of their standard practice on patrol, and in carrying out the judicial function delegated to them over most minor offenses. The establishment of the police as a force to control the behavior of both slaves and free people of the lower classes in the urban environment fixed practices that persisted through later times: patrolmen physically abused detainees at the point of arrest, and many state-sanctioned punishments were administered by the police system without judicial processes (trials) or the intervention of independent judges, legal counsel, or courts.

The political elite of the new nation, updating long-standing practice, delegated to police institutions the task of repressing undesirable public behavior not only through vigilance and arrest, but also punishment. Punishments that Brazilian police meted out in their day-to-day operations evolved during the nineteenth century from openly sanctioned beating and whipping at the time of arrest to a focus on short-term incarceration, although the practice of physical assaults on detainees continued as informal practice even after excessive police violence came to be considered a problem by those in charge. The behavior thus punished was sometimes in violation of laws and commonly held notions of criminal behavior, such as theft or physical injury to another person. Often however, the behavior that Rio's police punished was not formally defined as criminal or illegal, but was in the realm of victimless offenses against norms of public order or against the hierarchy of status and authority the political elite wanted to maintain. The history of police practices in nineteenth-century Rio de Janeiro thus demonstrates that both "criminality" and its punishment are culturally and historically relative, socially constructed concepts.

From Colony to Empire

Police forces as they are known today are an artifact of the modern state, dating only from the late eighteenth or early nineteenth century in Western European countries.[1] In colonial Brazil there was no institutional structure of professional, uniformed police separate from the various levels of the judicial system and military units. A central aspect of Brazil's transition from colony to nation was the establishment of a police system on a modern mold, first and most effectively in Rio de Janeiro and eventually in the capital cities of major provinces. These institutional innovations were accompanied by the concentration of judicial control over lesser crime in the hands of the new police officials, who were thus functionally similar to the lesser magistrates of the colonial regime, with the authority to judge and punish people whose relatively minor offenses fell within their jurisdiction. A major difference was that the new organization had the assistance of a full-time, professional police force and the beginnings of an administrative bureaucracy that made the exercise of police power more standardized and efficient than had been the case during the old regime.

In colonial times rudimentary vigilance was carried out by the unarmed civilian watchman (*guarda*), hired by the town council to make the rounds and keep an eye out for suspicious activity, and the neighborhood inspector (*quadrilheiro*) appointed by local judges.[2] These lowest functionaries had no more powers of arrest than any ordinary citizen; authority remained with the magistrates and administrators higher up in the system. In times of civil disturbance a judge or other official might call for a detachment of army troops from a local garrison, militia units, or reserves called *ordenanças*. The militias were made up of local residents who wore uniforms when on duty and were armed and given some training by regular army officers, but aside from sporadic exercises and ceremonial functions they were called up only in emergencies.

The Brazilian elites that supported the moves toward independence from Portugal had a clear interest in maintaining stability and social calm. They were aided in these objectives by the process of independence itself, which progressed in stages from 1808 with the transfer of the Portuguese royal family to Rio de Janeiro, to 1831 with the abdication of Pedro I. With nearly half the population enslaved, almost all economic activity beyond peasant subsistence based on slave labor, and the example of the slave uprising in St. Domingue fresh in the minds of the dominant class, it was important to avoid a political breakdown in the process of breaking from Portugal. Independence amounted to a conservative political transition involving piecemeal institutional changes, sparing the country the destruction, animosities, and chaos a major civil war might have entailed.[3]

Among the principal areas of pressure for a clear break with the colonial past during the first years of independence were basic attributes of the state the Brazilians hoped to create: criminal legislation, judicial institutions and procedures, and the exercise of police power. In a broad sense, Brazil belatedly participated in the reform movement that swept the Atlantic world during the Age of Enlightenment and revolution in the last half of the eighteenth century and first half of the nineteenth, a movement generally identified with liberal ideology. Brazilian nationalists saw the extant police and judicial procedures as antiquated relics of a bygone era and a legacy of colonial oppression. A dilemma emerged reflecting the contradictions of liberal ideology within a highly stratified society held together by political patronage, economic exploitation, and physical coercion of the bulk of the labor force. Political leaders recognized that any fundamental break in the relations of domination on which Brazil's society and economy rested could be dangerously disruptive to their own status and control. At the same time, they wanted to move out from under colonial despotism and monarchical absolutism.[4] In Gramscian terms, a hegemonic consensus about what was necessary emerged in the upper levels of the sociopolitical hierarchy, an element of which was agreement that the lower classes, both slave and free, were to be kept in line through coercive domination.[5]

The police as a separate institution had its beginnings before formal independence, as the transfer of the Portuguese court to Brazil brought the establishment of the general intendant of police of the court and the state of Brazil on May 10, 1808. This police intendancy was based on the French model, introduced into Portugal in 1760, and was responsible for public works and ensuring the provisioning of the city in addition to personal and collective security.[6] These responsibilities included public order, surveillance of the population, the investigation of crimes, and apprehension of criminals. The intendant had the power to decide what behavior was to be declared criminal, establish the punishment he thought appropriate, and then to arrest, prosecute, pass judgment, and supervise the sentence of individual perpetrators. He thus represented the authority of the absolute monarch, and consistent with colonial administrative practice the office combined legislative, executive (police), and judicial powers. The royal decree establishing the intendancy confirmed the concept of granting judicial authority over minor offenses to the police in the following terms: "As there are crimes that require no punishment other than some correction, the Intendant may in such cases arrest such persons as deserve correction, keeping them imprisoned for a time judged by the Intendant as proportional to the disorder committed, and as seems necessary for correction."[7]

In order to assist the intendant in those aspects of his varied responsibility relating to "correcting" unacceptable behavior, on June 27, 1808, the prince regent divided the city into two judicial districts and established the new position of criminal judge (*juiz do crime*) for each. Criminal judges were subordinated to the intendant and had the same combination of judicial and police functions in their districts as he had over the city as a whole.[8] Thus the concept of combining judicial and police functions at the local level, building on the principles that oriented the colonial system, dated from the founding of police institutions in Rio de Janeiro.

Another innovation following the transfer of the royal family to Brazil was the creation of a full-time police force organized along military lines and given broad authority to maintain order and pursue criminals. This was the *Guarda Real de Polícia* (Royal Police Guard), established in May 1809 with officers and men transferred from the ranks of the regular army. Like the intendancy of police to which it was subordinate, the *Guarda Real* was intended to replicate in Rio de Janeiro an institution already existing in Lisbon. The permanent mission of the new *Guarda Real* was to "maintain public tranquility . . . and many other obligations relating to civil order."[9] They were stationed at several locations in or near the downtown area to facilitate patrolling and quick response to disturbances. Members of the *Guarda Real* became notorious as the police intendant's ruthless agents. The most famous among them, celebrated or reviled by contemporaries and later historians on both sides of these issues, was Major Miguel Nunes Vidigal, who became the terror of the vagrants and idlers who might meet him coming around a corner at night or see him suddenly appear at the *batuques* that frequently took place in the outskirts of the city. These were gatherings of common people, mostly slaves, who socialized, drank sugarcane brandy, and danced to Afro-Brazilian drum music late into the night. Without even pro forma deference to judicial process, Vidigal and his soldiers, hand-picked for their size and strength, proceeded to beat any participant, miscreant, or vagrant they could capture. Instead of the usual military sword, the normal equipment of Vidigal and his grenadiers was a whip with a long heavy shaft tipped by rawhide strips used as both club and lash. Following the beating, viciously and indiscriminately administered to slave and free alike at the time of arrest, slaves were returned to their owner's custody or submitted to the intendant or his assistants, the criminal judges, for judgment of their offense. Non-slave detainees were kept in the short-term lockup, the *casa de guarda* on the palace square (now XV de Novembro), from where some of the able-bodied were selected as conscripts for the army or navy without further legal formalities, and others went to a longer term in the city jail.[10] The procedures Vidigal became famous for—administering corporal punishment during street patrols—had no legal basis beyond the informally delegated authority of the intendant.

The *Guarda Real* established patterns characteristic of Rio's front-line police force through later periods of shifting ideological winds and institutional experimentation. Rank-and-file members were drawn from the free lower classes who were important targets of police repression. They exercised wide leeway in carrying out their mission following guidelines laid down by the civilian administrators and judges who maintained overall control. And their methods mirrored the violence and brutality of life on the streets and slave society more generally. Another similarity to later patterns is that the police was organized from the first as a military institution, so that the coercive force it exercised could be controlled by discipline, channeled through hierarchy, and directed at specific targets. The underlying rationale of a military organization is to concentrate, regulate, and direct force against an enemy. The enemy for Rio de Janeiro's police was society itself—not society "as a whole," but those members of society who broke the rules of behavior established by the same political elite that created the police and directed police action. This exercise of concentrated force can be seen as defensive, protecting the people who made the rules, owned property, and controlled public institutions that needed defending. The police force can also be seen as offensive, aimed at establishing control over territory both social and geographical—the public space of the city—by subjugating slaves and restraining the free lower classes through intimidation, exclusion, or subordination as circumstances required.

Invoking military terminology and concepts to understand Rio's police is not a figurative analogy, but a description of the way the institution was conceived and operated. The police was like a standing army fighting a social war against adversaries who were all around it. Contact with the enemy came with the guerrilla actions of street gangs, such subversive acts as absenting oneself from the control of one's owner and refusing to work, and myriad small individual violations from petty theft to insolence to being on the streets after curfew. Also like a standing army, the police force was conceived as the coercive instrument of those who created, maintained, and controlled it. Unlike warfare against an external enemy on the battlefield, however, the objective was not to exterminate or eliminate the adversary. Rather, the goal was repression and subjugation, the maintenance of an acceptable level of order and calm enabling the city to function in the interest of the class that made rules and created the police to enforce them. From the standpoint of that class, Vidigal and the *Guarda Real* were a success, despite the occasional need to impose discipline and rein in the excesses of police practices. Striking terror in the hearts of idlers, vagrants, and recalcitrant slaves was just what they wanted to accomplish.

The intendant, his staff, and the *Guarda Real* that patrolled the streets in his name spent most of their time keeping slaves in line. Some police action was to apprehend thieves and break up fights, but most of it was to capture fugitive slaves, prevent groups of slaves and free blacks from gathering in the streets or acting in a way the police patrol considered suspicious, disorderly, or disrespectful, and to deprive the same category of people of any instrument that might be used as a weapon. The restrictions on weapons possession are especially indicative of how the threat was perceived. A police edict of December 1816 specified that any slave "found with a fixed blade or folding knife, or any instrument of iron or even a sharpened stick with which he might injure or kill, even without having committed such injuries, will be whipped with 300 strokes of the lash and sentenced to three months labor on public works." If such an instrument was found, or if it was determined that the culprit had thrown away a weapon to prevent its discovery in the search following arrest, the penalty was to be administered "without any further formality or legal procedure." This was no sumptuary law to prevent commoners from wearing swords as a badge of rank to which they had no right, but a draconian measure to deprive slaves of instruments of aggression and self-defense.[11]

Authoritarian Liberal Innovations

In April 1821, King João VI returned to Portugal, leaving his son Pedro as prince regent. Less than a month after assuming the regency, Pedro took the first of several steps to introduce due process into police and judicial practices. He decreed that no one could be arrested except by a judicial warrant or in flagrante, that formal charges had to be brought against all detainees within forty-eight hours of arrest, that no one could be imprisoned without being convicted through due process in open court, and that shackles, chains, and torture could not be used as punishment. Two weeks later he decreed that a similar list of protections from the liberal Portuguese constitution would be enforced in Brazil.[12] The new intendant of police continued in the policy direction Pedro established by ordering that slaves arrested for street gang activity, weapons possession, or disturbing the peace be freed without further punishment unless formal charges were brought. In November 1821, however, the military committee in charge of security in the capital, invoking the "dangerous consequences one may expect from treating such individuals leniently," urged the minister of war to do what he could to reinstate the former policy of allowing the *Guarda Real* patrols to whip such offenders on the spot, then release them to their owners. Whipping, the committee pointed out, was the only punishment "that intimidates and instills terror in those committing these physical attacks and murders."[13] In a sharply worded reply, the new intendant protested that under the old orders to whip blacks at the moment of arrest, many free blacks, who could not legally be subjected to the corporal punishment reserved for slaves, had been summarily beaten. He made ironic reference to the futility of physical punishment intended as a deterrent, saying that if whipping could resolve the problem there would be no threat from street gangs in Rio de Janeiro.[14]

Part of the transition from absolutism to the rule of law was, in António Cándido's apt assessment, "to disguise the arbitrary will of those in charge under a pretense of legality. . . . The police of an absolute sovereign are ostensive and brutal, because an absolute sovereign is not concerned with justifying his acts. But the police of a constitutional state must be more refined," because they represent the will of a group held together by delicate consensus.[15] The consensus among elite factions was tested during the decade between the promulgation of these reforms and the aftermath of Pedro's abdication, but the slaves and free rabble whom the military committee wanted to continue to terrorize were marginal to the political process. Their opinions on the matter of whipping did not count, except insofar as the risk of a brutal beating served to deter resistance to their condition. The constitutional state, the antireformers argued, need not concern itself with justifying its arbitrary acts to the people who were necessarily the objects of repression. The need to control the many superseded the liberal principles espoused by a few. Faced with no obvious alternative method for keeping slaves under subjugation in an urban environment in which many slaves were outside the direct control of their owners, those in charge began a process of regulating the scale and form of brutal punishment that made the new state complicit in terrorizing much of the population.[16]

Reducing the degree and frequency of indiscriminate police attacks on slaves and the free lower classes did not mean that whipping was quickly eliminated. It remained as the formally sanctioned coercive basis of both private and public subjugation of slaves, and the state increasingly assumed the role in the urban environment of the whip-wielding overseer on the rural estate. An edict of December 1823 confirmed the authority of the police to whip slaves in the act of arrest, and in March 1826 the intendant ordered that any slave arrested for gang activity be summarily given one hundred lashes and detention in the Calabouço slave jail, where owners could retrieve them after paying the cost of their subsistence since arrest.[17] The approach after 1821, in slave whipping and other aspects of police activity, was increasingly to refine and standardize procedures, making the instruments of repression more precise and efficient. This trend toward specificity, exerting just the force necessary to maintain an acceptable level of "order and public tranquility," was not a rejection of the authoritarian methods of earlier times. Rather, the period from 1808 to 1821 was a period of institution-building and experimentation, and the problem eventually became that of regulating a police force that had been delegated wide authority at the time of its establishment in 1808–09.

In the aftermath of the intendant's restrictions on whipping and similar arbitrary police action at the time of independence, thefts, assaults, and general disruption of life in the city seemed to increase. Even the 1823 formal reintroduction of whipping at the point of arrest did not have the desired effect, and in January 1825 a new police intendant, Francisco Alberto Teixeira de Aragão, issued a set of police regulations that became known in Rio as "Aragão's curfew" (*o toque do Aragão*). This edict authorized police patrols to make inquiries of anyone they felt disposed to stop. Any person, slave or free, who failed to submit to questioning was considered to be resisting authority and would be subject to "whatever violent methods the circumstances require."

A curfew was established—10 P.M. in the summer and 9 P.M. in winter—after which patrols were authorized to stop and search anyone for illegal weapons or instruments that might be used in a crime. To signal the curfew, the bells of the São Francisco church and São Bento monastery were to ring for a solid half hour so that no one could claim ignorance of the time of day. The order for enforcement carried the restriction that it not be abused "nor be applied to well known persons of integrity [*nem se adote para com as pessoas notoriamente conhecidas e de probidade*]." Slaves could be searched at any time of the day or night and whipped for possession of any weapon, including wooden sticks. After curfew, whistling in the streets or passing any similar signal was prohibited, and this prohibition was extended "to blacks and men of color any time after dark, even if prior to the curfew." Any slave found after curfew "in any store, tavern, bar, or gambling house" was to be sent to the Calabouço and whipped; any free person was to pay a fine of $800 for the first such offense (more than a week's wages for a free artisan) and double for the second. The owner or cashier of the offending establishment was also to pay a fine of $600, double for the second infraction, triple that and loss of his operating license for a third offense. The same penalty was to apply to businesses that permitted gatherings on their premises, "especially blacks, after their business was completed."[18] These regulations explicitly discriminated against free blacks and "men of color" in the same breath as references to slaves. On the other end of the scale, persons of "integrity" were explicitly spared the restrictions of the curfew and the indignity of being searched for weapons. More broadly, these regulations discriminated against activities that the white elite for the most part did not engage in, but which were central to the social life of poor people and slaves in Rio.

One of the main criticisms legal reformers made of the old legal and judicial system inherited from late colonial times was that it was "arbitrary," meaning that the decision to charge a person with a crime, the basis for conviction, and sentence were largely left to the whim of the arresting officer or presiding magistrate. Brought before the intendant of police or one of the criminal judges who assisted him, the case was disposed of by the same authority under which the arrest was made. There was no public or officially neutral presence at the judicial proceeding, and at the lower level for minor crime there was often no record of the case. A detainee was brought before the presiding authority; the arresting officer or a bailiff stated the charge and described the event; and the judge pronounced sentence. The culprit was immediately locked up in the city jail for punishment. When an inspection of the jail was carried out in 1833 there were 340 prisoners, for 43 of whom there were no records. No one could say why they were there, what their sentence was, or how much of it they had served.[19]

The institutional structure inherited from the late colony, which was maintained through the early independence era, suffered a serious crisis following the abdication of Emperor Pedro I in April 1831. There ensued a period of institutional transition and experimentation during the regency, culminating in a law in December 1841 which reorganized the police and judicial system of empire. In the institutional hiatus following Pedro I's abdication, soldiers of the *Guarda Real de Polícia* mutinied in July 1831 and went on a rampage through the streets of Rio. The unit was then disbanded and replaced by a new military structure known originally as the Permanent Municipal Guard Corps, which became the basis for the uniformed and militarized urban police force of today. In 1832 a newly written code of criminal procedure abolished the office of police intendant, which was replaced by a chief of police appointed by the minister of justice. The 1824 constitution had authorized the establishment of a system of locally elected justices of the peace on the British model. The first such local judges were elected in the late 1820s, and in Rio de Janeiro they were soon subordinated to the command and authority of the minister of justice. The 1832 procedural code gave justices of the peace broad responsibility for vigilance in their districts to guard against crime and investigate those that could not be prevented. As the lowest level criminal judge with jurisdiction over most minor violations, the justice of the peace followed in the functional footsteps of the intendant of police established in 1808, who also had authority to judge and punish the minor offenders he and his assistants arrested. In this regard the office of the justice of the peace, combining police and judicial attributes, maintained an old tradition.[20]

During this transitional period the authority of the new state was increasingly extended into the public space of the city, where it increasingly intersected with the private authority of master over slave. A relationship was worked out by which the state buttressed and complemented the owner's right and responsibility to control the behavior of human property. In the process the independent authority of the justices of the peace was increasingly subordinated to centralized control, and police received formal confirmation of their traditional practice of administering summary beatings for minor offenses. An exchange in 1837 illustrates the basis for this arrangement. The chief of police reported to the minister of justice that he had passed on the minister's instructions, to the effect that "justices of the peace are not to continue to order slaves whipped without first submitting them to a judicial proceeding and formal sentencing, in the presence of their owner." But the police chief asked for further clarification, because "the police also normally order slaves whipped without judicial process, either at the request of owners or because the slaves are caught with weapons or engaging in *capoeira*, so I wish to know if your instructions also extend to the police, or only to justices of the peace." The minister replied that the requirement for formal hearings for slaves only applied to justices of the peace, and that police should continue operating under existing orders which permitted "correctional" punishment without a judicial proceeding.[21] Because justices of the peace already had judicial powers, this regulation did not prevent them from ordering slaves whipped on their own authority, but did require the order to be issued in the presence of the owner. Thus both the public authority of the state and the private rights of slave owners were maintained, and soldiers of the new military police continued their traditional practice of punishment at the point of arrest as they patrolled the streets in the name of order and public tranquility.

Those streets were often a difficult environment in which to determine acceptable levels of official violence, as police soldiers were expected to deal with the general public by applying only the "necessary" force.[22] Depending on a shifting combination of circumstances, prudent application of force in one situation might be police brutality in the next. In January 1836, regent of the empire Diogo Antonio Feijó intervened in one such case, in which a police soldier on guard at the *Passeio Público* had injured an innocent passerby during an altercation. The administrator of the park, at Feijó's request, asked the military police commander to discipline the soldier in question "so that the public order is not at the mercy of any ruffian." Liberal sensibilities at the time saw such incidents as unacceptable brutality. Whatever value judgments one applies, it should be kept in mind that the military police soldier has always lived and worked in a hostile and violent world, and while he was not to behave like "any ruffian," he was expected to exert force to carry out his duty. Through the ensuing decades repeated regulations setting boundaries on the physical attacks on detainees, and occasional examples of the disciplining of police agents who exceeded those bounds, suggest that the day-to-day practices against slaves persisted as slavery waned and increasing proportions of those who fell afoul of police were free people.

Institutional Consolidation

A major overhaul of the judicial system approved on December 3, 1841, left the military police intact but replaced, the elected justices of the peace with appointed police chiefs, *delegados*, and *subdelegados*, who were formally authorized to judge and punish minor offenders. Under the 1841 reform, for violation of municipal ordinances and for all misdemeanor offenses, police officials had full authority to issue warrants for search and arrest, carry out the arrest, bring formal charges, set bail, hold summary judicial hearings, pass sentence, and supervise punishment—all without the intervention of any other authority.[23] For all but the most serious crime, the police chief or his appointed delegate down to the neighborhood level became accuser, investigator, arresting officer, and prosecutor as well as judge, jury, and jailer. As a contemporary legal scholar justified subsequent "summary correctional or repressive police procedures," the law granting judicial authority to police "is useful both to society and to the accused: minor crimes, and thus minor punishments, do not require so many guarantees, nor a trial full of formalities and delays that would involve more time and expense than the matter requires." He further explained that along with their "criminal" function, police officials had a "correctional" function which authorized them to "punish minor offenses, in order to prevent them from developing into bad habits and more serious crimes."[24]

In the jurisdiction of the national capital, extending local level judicial powers to appointed police officials was not an authoritarian innovation in violation of previous practices, as liberal critics later suggested. The intendant had been expressly granted such powers in 1808; they were transferred to the justices of the peace in the 1832 procedural code; and in 1841 passed on to the police chief and his delegates. There was considerable continuity in this regard from the enlightened despotism of the late colonial era through the interim period of institutional experimentation to the centralized bureaucracy of the consolidated state.[25]

A pattern of rivalry between military and civilian police institutions which bordered at times on hostility was also a recurring feature of Rio de Janeiro's police system. From the colonel commandant to soldiers on the street, military police repeatedly contested civilian domination in formal and informal ways, but the principle of the supreme authority vested in the civilian chief of police after 1841 was not directly or successfully challenged. Civilian authorities were able to maintain control at the top through the same discipline and hierarchy that gave the military police its internal unity. But the contradictions persisted of a militarized force existing in the midst of a society with which it was assigned an adversarial relationship. The flurries of memoranda attending inter-organizational conflicts reveal not only the rivalries themselves, but much about police practice and the broader context of repression and resistance in which these overlapping institutions operated.

An incident early in the history of post-1841 police machinery reflects several persistent themes including the treatment of slaves, race relations, attitudes of the military police toward society and vice versa, and antagonism among various branches of the system. This event and the subsequent exchange among the authorities involved show how these and related themes were intertwined—part of a web of relationships that reflected the central role of police institutions in the life of the city and the broader culture that produced and maintained them.

Around 7 P.M. on October 2, 1844, Mamede José da Silva Passos was walking down Vala Street (now Uruguaiana) in central Rio de Janeiro. As a ward inspector (the lowest level agent in the civilian police hierarchy) of Sacramento parish, he was expected to keep an eye on things. That Wednesday evening Passos was dismayed to encounter a patrol of the military police "beating without provocation any blacks that passed, and even a white man, who was wounded on a finger." When Passos asked the head of the patrol for an explanation of such unwarranted behavior, the police corporal replied with an insult. Despite the broad green and yellow sash of a ward inspector across Passos's chest, the military police said they did not recognize his authority, claiming that they had orders from the chief of police to beat the blacks. João Francisco Pereira, the injured white man, declined to lodge a complaint against the police, so that same night Passos took it upon himself to denounce the incident to his immediate superior, the *subdelegado* of Sacramento parish.[26]

Meanwhile, the military police lost no time in entering their version of the events of October 2 into the records with a memo from the corps commander to the minister of justice, demanding the dismissal of ward inspector Passos for abuse of authority and insulting the military police patrol and accusing him further of protecting from police action the slaves who gathered in taverns in his jurisdiction. The military police version of the original encounter was that a patrol, following standing orders to break up gatherings of slaves, was taken to task when a lowly ward inspector objected to their methods. But ward inspectors had no authority over military police, and Passos, at other times tolerant of misbehavior by slaves, seemed at least as concerned that a white man was injured on the finger

—an apparent accident—as with what he initially interpreted as unjustified physical abuse of slaves by the military police patrol.

More than twenty years after the altercation on Vala Street, on the night of January 7, 1865, during Epiphany observances, an incident took place that reflected the persistent tension between military police on the street and the ward inspectors, and the low regard in which the former held the latter. It also confirms that people were routinely beaten at the time of arrest. During the street celebrations that made the Festival of the Kings the nineteenth-century analog to Carnival in more recent times, Benedito Ferreira do Amaral was arrested for instigating public disorder by several military police working undercover in civilian clothes. A crowd gathered to protest the arrest, saying that another man who had escaped was the perpetrator of the disturbance, not Amaral. A ward inspector approached to look into the incident, but in the tumult could do little more than accompany the military police and their prisoner toward the police station. On the way the soldiers beat Amaral for no apparent reason, and when the ward inspector protested such treatment he was arrested as well. The military police delivered the two prisoners to the corporal on duty at the police post, and when the ward inspector requested permission to speak to someone in authority the corporal told him he "had nothing to say to any authority, that he was going to jail." The *delegado* who later investigated the incident concluded that "there seems to be much to censure in this case, both in the behavior of the plainclothes military police who arrested Amaral, and in that of the corporal" in his treatment of the ward inspector.[27]

Much of what the police did day-to-day was not intended to result in detention and judicial processing. One of the main goals in developing police institutions after 1831, following on practices the *Guarda Real* had begun under Vidigal, was the preemptive repression of unacceptable behavior rather than simply reacting after a problem had occurred. To the extent that the "ostensive and repressive" mission of the military police was successful, the results would not show up in arrest records but in reports of action on the street. In commenting on the relatively low number of crimes reported during 1838, the chief of police waxed almost philosophical on what made good policing: "Just as times of good fortune for nations are those which offer less material to the historian, so also when preventive policing is successful, the facts related to policing are fewer."[28] Squads of police soldiers were repeatedly and routinely sent to problem areas with explicit orders to prevent, by their presence, behavior that authorities considered criminal, dangerous, or merely threatening to the social order.

From 1831 onward military police were also admonished in regulations to use moderation in dealing with the public and to use their weapons only when necessary to defend themselves or bring a dangerous adversary under control. The new guidelines of 1858 for example, following a long list of conditions in which arrests were to be made, urged patrols to "use all temperate means [*meios brandos*] to prevent disorder, break up arguments, stop shouts and loud noises that threaten the public calm, and warn violators that they will be arrested if they persist." They were also to disperse gatherings of slaves in taverns or other places of business and ensure that taverns closed at the 10 o'clock curfew. For such minor but recurring public order offenses, arrest was to be used only as a last resort, to make good on threats. It was "absolutely prohibited" for patrols to "discuss or argue with any person regarding their professional conduct, insult those arrested in any way, whether through words or gestures, much less physically mistreat them. They may use only the degree of force necessary to contain resistance."[29] The repetition of such warnings over the years suggests that violations were also recurrent, confirmed by numerous documented cases of what is today called police brutality and the violation of human rights.

Such an incident occurred on the afternoon of September 14, 1849, in an isolated area near the botanical garden in the southern zone of the city, where police patrols could usually assume they were beyond the scrutiny of competing or supervising authority. Several slaves-for-hire were traveling along the road; one carried a pole with a dirty scrap of white cloth attached to the top. A military police cavalry squad stopped the group, and the ensuing confrontation was later described by a ward inspector who watched from his nearby house as the soldiers demanded that the slaves give them the "flag." The inspector thought this unnecessary, because police soldiers should have been accustomed to seeing coffee carriers and other teams of slaves with similar banners, "a very frequent sight around the city." The slaves immediately stopped when so ordered, indicating deference by asking the soldiers for their blessing, a ritual of submission that punctuated the relations between master and slave, parent and child, priest and parishioner, and by extension those in authority and those subject to it. When the slave holding the flag declined to give it up, the sergeant in charge grabbed the staff and hit the black with it so hard the pole broke in several places. Then two other soldiers in the mounted patrol charged the slaves with swords drawn, apparently for the fun of seeing the blacks cower and run. This was too much for the observing ward inspector, who approached and told the cavalrymen that their behavior was disturbing the peace instead of maintaining it and that "a soldier should never draw his weapon" except to overcome resistance to arrest. To this the sergeant declared to the inspector "in a quite insolent manner, that he was only following the orders he was required to carry out, whether it was with blacks or even with whites." The orders he referred to required police squads to break up suspicious gatherings, but the blacks being harassed were obviously not a gang bent on mischief; their dress, cargo baskets, demeanor, and even the flag, the ward inspector pointed out, clearly marked them as the sort of slaves who routinely hired their services around the city.[30]

1850 as Case Study

Such incidents left abundant documentation in their wake, but illustrative as they may be they are special cases, outside the routine of day-to-day police operations. The ledger book of Rio's central police station for the year 1850 provides a more typical look at police activity. The blotter in question is not a complete listing of all people arrested in Rio during the year. Some are known to have spent time in custody and not had their passing through recorded in that document. Others, particularly those apprehended for more serious crimes, were sometimes remanded directly to jails upon arrest without visiting the central police station. Slaves captured after escape as well as those arrested for a variety of offenses bringing immediate punishment were often taken directly to the Calabouço slave prison. Keeping in mind the limitations posed by arrests not recorded in it, the ledger is still a rich source for understanding how Rio de Janeiro was policed in the middle of the nineteenth century, who was affected by the system and in what way, and what sorts of behavior police were seeking to control.[31]

In some ways the information *not* recorded in the 1850 ledger is as revealing as the data that *are* available, frustrating though missing data may be for quantitative analysis. The most pervasive example is that for more than half the people brought in (911 out of 1,676, or 54 percent), the reason for detention was not recorded. The missing information must be attributed to a lack of concern on the part of police clerks and the chief of police to whom the ledger entries were formally addressed regarding the cause of arrest. The specific offense did not seem to matter very much to people who were not accountable to any higher or outside authority for the arrests they made for minor offenses and disciplinary purposes.

Another 128 detentions were for recorded reasons but not criminal offenses as such. Such "neutral" police actions included 66 men brought in for forced conscription into military service; 31were released, probably after it was determined that they were ineligible or unfit for service, or perhaps after the intervention of influential patrons. Another "neutral" category comprised the 39 cases of entry into custody for unspecified "investigation" (*averiguações*). Sometimes this referred to verifying the story of people who were not arrested but walked into the station to lodge a complaint and were held until the matter was resolved. Such was the case of Bernardino and Bartolomeu, slaves of Francisco de Paula Correia Saião, who escaped from their owner on December 2, 1850, and made it into the police station to report that Saião had threatened to hang them in an isolated beach area. Bartolomeu was wearing handcuffs when he entered the station. The two slaves were released the next day, but the blotter notes say no more about the case. Other "neutral" cases involved ten arrests for unspecified "suspicion," five for insanity, four for unspecified violation of municipal ordinances, three arrested on unspecified "complaint," and one on unspecified "request."

A total of 54 arrests in 1850 were for offenses applicable only to slaves (seven percent of arrests for known causes) and include 18 for escape, 15 for suspicion of escape, and 12 newly arrived Africans illegally imported after the 1831 prohibition on the transatlantic slave traffic. (After legal processing such people would be declared "free" and wards of the state.) Also, five slaves were arrested for disobedience, classified here as a slave offense even though the criminal code does not restrict its application to slaves. Finally, four people were brought into the police station for "irritating their owner" (*por descompor seu senhor*). One free man and one former slave (*forro*) were arrested for escape, and two other free men were brought in for suspicion of escape; these were probably escapees from jail rather than from enslavement.

By far the most prevalent activities for which people were arrested were the diverse "public order" offenses—behavior which in itself did not directly jeopardize other people or property but which was either illegal or merely unacceptable. The total of 499 arrests for disturbing public order (65 percent of all arrests for recorded offenses) included the following in descending order of numerical occurence: disorder (86), drunkenness (73), *capoeira* (69), insults (55), curfew violation (26), weapons possession (32), vagrancy (20), and quarreling (18). One grouping of public order arrests is directly related to the response of the people of Rio to the police in their midst or perhaps the contestatory nature of a segment of the population. To the 55 arrests specifically for insults, we might add eight for disobeying police orders, eight for indecent words, five for disrespect, five free people for disobedience, and one for resistance. Of the eighty-two people arrested for these acts of defiance that stopped short of physical aggression, 54 were free people and 28 were slaves.

Physical aggression is the determining characteristic of a third general type of offense: crimes against persons. Forty such cases were identified in the arrest ledger for 1850 (5.2 percent of the 765 detainees with recorded reasons for arrest): 13 of these were moving traffic violations, including 12 cases of running over a person with a vehicle and 1 case in which a running horse inflicted the injury. Assuming those cases were accidental or the result of negligence, there remain 27 cases of arrest for this type of offense that were probably for deliberate acts. They include twelve for beating another person; six for the crime of personal injury (defined in the criminal code as physical offense that caused pain, wounds, or cuts to any part of the human body); three cases of whipping a free person; two for serious personal injury (defined as causing permanent mutilation of the victim); two for attempted serious injury; and one each for attempted murder and attempted suicide. In the latter case a creole slave was found with a knife he had used to open two deep cuts in his own throat. Subtracting the attempted offenses, there remain just 23 known cases of arrest for deliberate physical injury to another person, or 3 percent of the 765 arrests with reason recorded.

Another general type of crime involves offenses against property. Along with physical assault, theft loomed large among the concerns of those with property to protect. But also like crimes against persons, relatively few arrests were recorded in the central police station ledger for theft or property damage. The 44 arrests that can be classified under this type make up 5.8 percent of the 765 brought in for known causes.

Keeping in mind the problems of missing information, the conclusion is still inescapable: despite the alarms of the propertied and powerful, relatively few wrongdoers were arrested for criminal offenses against people or property. Victimless public order offenses absorbed most of the energy and attention of Rio's police. Police activity was primarily devoted to disciplinary, preventive repression of behavior that authorities considered threatening, unacceptable, or which they concluded might lead to more serious offenses. The information gleaned from the 1850 police blotter confirms and specifies what appears in police operating guidelines and the record of operations on the street: most police activity was directed at controlling behavior that in itself was not injurious to other people, nor damaging to property, nor theft. It was behavior that violated arbitrary rules or disturbed calm and order whether actual or potential.

By the 1860s, Rio de Janeiro's repressive institutions had been modernized and standardized both on the streets and in the office as clerks began to be more careful about logging information on arrests and compiling the statistical record that is a hallmark of the modern bureaucratic state. Administrative control over policing the city had moved far beyond the days when Major Vidigal had free rein to terrorize the vagabonds and troublemakers of the 1810s. The agents of repression could examine the results of these changes in the burgeoning statistical and documentary record of the system's operation, and they and their supervisors in the political elite had reason to congratulate themselves on their achievements.

The place to measure those successes was not in the few court cases involving major crimes or in the relatively small populations of prisons where people serving long sentences accumulated. The success was on the streets, in the surveillance and control of people's activities in order to constrain unacceptable behavior. That control was supported closely by increasing numbers of arrests, primarily for victimless violations of acceptable norms of public order or as a preemptive measure during disturbances and dragnets to catch perpetrators of crime. In 1862 there were 7,290 detainees brought into the central police jail, a more than fourfold increase over 1850. In 1865 the corresponding number was 7,491. Table 1 shows arrests for those two years according to type of offense.[32]

Table 1. Arrests in Rio Police Jail, 1862, 1865

Type of Offense	1862		1865	
	No.	*%*	*No.*	*%*
Public order	5,538	76.0	6,765	90.3
Against person	507	7.0	279	3.7
Against property	1,137	15.6	349	4.7
Neutral	108	1.5	98	1.3
Total	7,290	100	7,491	100

Source: *Relatório do Chefe de Polícia do Rio de Janeiro*, 1862, 1865, annex to respective *Relatórios* of the minister of justice.

As for the eventual fate of the thousands of people arrested in these two years, many were released after spending a short time in the police station jail (2,233 in 1862 and 2,379 in 1865), and many more were sent on to the house of detention to serve longer sentences determined in internal police judicial decisions (4,001 in 1862 and 3,130 in 1865). In other words, of all those arrested and delivered to the jail, 86 percent in 1862 and 74 percent in 1865 were punished with detention under the judicial authority delegated to the police. Others were sent to military arsenals to be conscripted, to hospitals, and remanded to foreign consular authorities.

These arrest data stand in sharp contrast to the number of crimes reported to the police in these two years, shown in Table 2.[33] The chief of police, referring to the most numerous specific types of reported crimes, explained that personal injuries (306 in 1862 and 199 in 1865) were "for the most part very insignificant, no more than simple scratches and light bruises." As for the cases of theft (285 in 1862 and 156 in 1865), "the great majority involved small objects of almost no value," and among the reported cases of property damage (26 in 1862 and 12 in 1865) were "some caused by vehicles."[34]

Table 2. Reported Crime in Rio, 1862, 1865

	1862		1865	
Type of Offense	*No.*	*%*	*No.*	*%*
Public order	0	0.0	19	4.3
Against person	325	48.1	225	50.7
Against property	346	51.2	188	42.3
Not specified	5	0.7	12	2.7
Total	676	100	444	100

Source: *Relatório do Chefe de Polícia do Rio de Janeiro*, 1862, 1865, annex to respective *Relatórios* of the minister of justice.

While police authorities and the press talked about the few hundred reported occurrences of theft and assault in the course of a year, the police chief did what he could to downplay the importance of cases that reached his attention. In the meantime, police were rounding up thousands of people every year, primarily for victimless public order violations or unspecified "investigations." The mid-century reforms made traditional patterns of repression more effective and efficient, but police still operated with wide discretionary authority over the fate of those detained. If there was a fundamental change from earlier in the century it was in the efforts to replace beating upon arrest with incarceration, parallel with the decline of the proportional number of slaves in Rio's population and among those who ran afoul of police patrols.

New Police, Old Problems

In 1866, after a large contingent of Rio's military police had been sent with the first groups of troops to fight in the Paraguayan war, a new police institution called the Urban Guard was established. In justifying this new unit, the minister of justice said the goal was "nothing less than an imitation of the acclaimed police of the city of London, also adopted in Paris in September 1854." Invoking the English term "policeman" as the model, he hoped for the same "good results that some of the most populous cities of Europe have obtained from morally correct agents, charged with continually patrolling a specific and limited territory."[35] According to its advocates, a uniformed but nonmilitarized force of patrolmen would "help prevent many crimes, and prevent activities which, while not crimes as such, are nevertheless the preliminary steps toward criminal acts."

Accordingly, operating instructions ordered urban guards to arrest people for behavior that was neither a crime nor an infraction of ordinances, such as "individuals found carrying objects or packages which by reason of the quality or condition of such individuals makes them suspect." It was not a crime to carry a package in public, but if it appeared to a patrolling guard that a certain type of person should not be carrying a certain type of package, the "culprit" would be subject to arrest. Guards were further ordered to repress other unacceptable behavior, including shouting or excessive noise, and "singing and musical performances [*cantatas e tocatas*] by slaves in taverns or *botequins*," without making arrests if possible. Any person "standing near a door, wall, or fence in a suspicious way" was to be watched, interrogated, and arrested if suspicions were confirmed. Victimless threats against public order, whether real or potential, were to be the urban guards' main focus of attention and activity. Included in the operating instructions of the new organization were several pointed admonitions. In dealing with the public, a guard was to "show himself to be polite and courteous to all, very carefully avoiding disputes or altercations with anyone, always conducting himself with the utmost prudence even with those who are rude or provocative." While making arrests it was "absolutely prohibited for guards to mistreat prisoners in any manner, either by word or gesture, much less physically. If, however, a suspect does not obey and attempts to escape, guards will use the degree of force necessary to carry out the arrest."[36]

By 1869 the minister of justice was ready to give a pessimistic assessment of the experiment with "policemen." Reluctant to proclaim the Urban Guard a complete failure, he admitted that "there is no way to hide what is demonstrated in practice every minute of every day: since the creation of the guard some three years ago, public surveillance has not improved." He attributed the problem to a lack of discipline and regimentation, which would make the guards "essentially obedient. Otherwise I cannot conceive of the possibility of providing those in authority with the necessary instrument for the faithful execution of orders."[37] Without a rigid command structure and the unquestioning compliance with orders ingrained by military regimentation, control broke down. Urban guards more often acted like armed renegades than the tropical version of London Bobbies the political authorities had hoped for.

Excessive use of weapons was also a problem with the Urban Guard, as it had been with *pedestres* (pedestrian police) and continued to be with military police soldiers. In September 1869 for example, John Christ, an Englishman, was being brought in for public drunkenness when he tried to flee from the arresting guard, who then drew his sword and injured Christ. The minister of justice instructed the chief of police that "it is necessary to prevent the abuse, committed by members of the urban guard, of using their weapons to overcome any sort of minor resistance . . . punishing severely those who do so in clear violation of regulations." In October of that year military police soldiers reported the routine arrest of an urban guard "for beating an individual on Invalidos Street." In 1872 the chief of police resorted to mild euphemism when he admitted that its members of the guard had "become accustomed to certain rough manners and habits, absolutely incompatible with the character of the institution." Two years later the police chief stopped short of exonerating the guard while laying the blame for police brutality on the resistance they faced in the line of duty, noting, "Urban guards have been severely punished when investigations have shown the complaints of harshness and bad treatment of prisoners to be valid. It is nevertheless necessary to point out that in many cases a mitigating circumstance is the violent provocation on the part of the prisoners themselves against the guards, who do not always have the courteous manners and the appropriate integrity to disregard such excesses."[38]

Later incidents reflected the continuity of police practices more related to repression and arbitrary use of authority than regulating and protecting society. On July 4, 1880, three urban guards arrested a black man for disorderly conduct on Riachuelo Street and "started for the station with him, beating him unmercifully all the way." When passersby remonstrated them for such behavior, the head of the police squad said he was only following orders. On the same day "three urban guards with drawn swords pursued a man into the interior of a house on Senhor dos Passos Street, and when the proprietor protested they threatened him with their swords." As the newspaper report pointed out, "police authorities forget that such an invasion is a gross violation of law."[39] A more notorious case was the death of João Alves de Castro Malta in November 1884, after his arrest by urban guards on Sete de Setembro Street in downtown Rio. Malta was held for three days in police custody before he was turned over to the house of detention in such bad physical shape that he could not give his name to the clerk. He expired moments later and was quickly buried after police doctors declared the cause of death was "hepatic congestion." According to widespread word on the street and newspaper reports, the arresting urban guards had beaten Malta so severely at the time of his arrest that he died of his wounds, but after a forensic team appointed by the chief of police exhumed the body and confirmed the earlier official cause of death, the case was closed.[40]

As complaints and problems built up over the years, city leaders had increasing misgivings about the possibility of rehabilitating the Urban Guard, and it was finally abolished by new police regulations of March 7, 1885.[41] Reviewing its the troubled history, the minister of justice recalled that the neighborhood-based force had seemed like a good idea in 1866, "taking as a model similar institutions in more advanced nations." But achievements did not match expectations. "With the passage of time the urban guard lost prestige, and this fact, reflected in constant complaints about frequent aggression by and resistance to the guards, led to the decision to abolish the institution."[42]

A Functional System of Repression

After the extinction of the Urban Guard, the soldiers of the military police were again the main front-line force, and they expanded their ruthless procedures into the public space the Urban Guard had failed to control to the satisfaction of the people in charge. Much of what the residents of Rio de Janeiro considered commonplace by this time was still shocking to foreigners, even those from countries with a tradition of militarized police themselves. An Italian visitor in 1885, for example, minced no words in his assessment: "The police of Rio de Janeiro are the most despotic, the most arbitrary and brutal police in the world, made up for the most part of the lowest social stratum of the city, lax and violent at the same time, and which acts in a manner completely the opposite of guarding and protecting the life and security of the citizens."[43] The police soldier on the street was caught between the elite's need for control and the difficulty of dealing with a recalcitrant and hostile population, people who never accepted the intrusion of the state into their lives as legitimate and who resisted that imposition in many small ways. When police soldiers decided to assert themselves to dominate a situation or when provoked by insult, they invoked the authority of their uniform or slashed out with their weapons, thereby adding to the problem of public order rather than reducing it. What foreigners considered arbitrary brutality had become the norm, even as commanding officers and civilian officials continued their sporadic efforts to keep police practice within what they considered acceptable bounds.[44]

The disciplinary problems that plagued the military police in the last years of the empire illustrate the persistence of patterns developed decades before. Not long after the military police had expanded and taken over the duties of the extinct Urban Guard, the commander felt the need to issue a new general order "in view of the cases of beatings of persons arrested for crimes or infractions, which increase each day on the part of police soldiers." He laid the blame on squad commanders and corporals in charge of street patrols, who failed to enforce the repeated orders to prevent such abuses. Henceforth, those in command were to be held strictly accountable for the behavior of their subordinates, whose actions "affect the discipline and dignity of this corps."[45]

Directives reminding officers that they were responsible for the actions of their subordinates were soon put into effect. In October 1887 for example, military police corporal Luiz José Pereira, on duty as an orderly at the police substation in Glória parish, arrested a Portuguese man without cause and in the process grabbed him by the throat, beat, verbally insulted, and threatened him. Pereira was demoted to simple soldier and jailed for fifteen days in Santa Cruz fort, where he suffered the further ignominy of being assigned to a cleaning detail. The officer of the day on whose shift this incident took place—who initially tried to claim that the arrested Portuguese was drunk and that he suffered no beating—had a severe written reprimand entered into his file.[46]

In 1888 the colonel in command of the military police perceptively assessed the social context within which his unit operated in terms appropriate to the liberal principles of the modern state. The right of the citizen to protection, he noted, is one that all governments try to guarantee, "but it is a difficult problem, involving the morality, intelligence, and customs of the people, as well as the financial resources of the government." Referring to the relationship between the military police and society, he said "it does not take much to perceive that elements taken out of a whole to constitute a separate body will bring to the latter the properties of the former. It is no surprise, therefore, that a nation's police will exhibit the characteristics of the morality, customs, and intelligence of its people." In again justifying the military regimentation of the corps, he nevertheless recognized a problem that made police work different from the soldier's role in regular army operations. In the latter, a soldier needed to follow orders without question, and any independent action was detrimental to the unified chain of command. The military police, in contrast, needed to institute an "intelligent discipline, so that each police soldier would exercise his own initiative, as appropriate for the special circumstances he might encounter."[47]

Achieving a workable balance between discipline and initiative was a recurring issue for Rio's police forces. The experience of the nonmilitarized police units, especially the Urban Guard, as well as recurring problems within the military police itself led those in charge to favor discipline over independent action. The commander also recognized the difficulty of drawing a clear line between protection of arrestees from excessive physical coercion and the standing orders of the military police to bring violators into submission. As one *delegado* stated the quandary in 1888: "An arrested person has a right to be protected from the authority in whose custody he finds himself. But that does not mean that [the police] should not put into effect all due energy when respect for the law is not obtained by other means."[48] The precise definition of what would constitute "all due energy" in the heat of the moment, in action against a hostile adversary on the streets, remained elusive.

The military police corps was never the finely tuned, smoothly operating, and neutral instrument of state power that some political leaders might have liked. But failed experiments over the years showed that the military police was as good as the civilian elite was going to get. The complex and contentious web of police institutions established in Rio de Janeiro in the nineteenth century, the direct predecessors of today's civilian and military police organizations, engaged in a wide range of activities related to controlling the behavior of the population. Some of that behavior was formally outlawed; some was defined as unacceptable by police operating guidelines and informal consensus among those in authority; other police activity had the purpose of intimidating the public and ensuring "respect" for those who represented the power of the state on the streets. In carrying out the mandate delegated to them by the political elite, Rio's police continued to judge and punish many types of behavior as part of their daily practice.

Notes

1. A good point of entry into the extensive literature on the history of European and North American police systems is Clive Emsley, *Policing and its Context, 1750–1870* (New York: Schoken Books, 1984).
2. Lopes Gonçalves, "Instituições do Rio de Janeiro colonial: os quadrilheiros," in *Revista do Intituto Histórico e Geográfico Brasileiro* 205 (1949), 401–411. An excellent study of the colonial judicial system is Stuart Schwartz, *Sovereignty and Society in Colonial Brazil: The High Court of Bahia and its Judges* (Berkeley: University of California Press, 1973).
3. On the independence era, see A. J. R. Russell-Wood, ed., *From Colony to Nation: Essays on the Independence of Brazil* (Baltimore: Johns Hopkins University Press, 1975); and Roderick Barman, *Brazil: The Forging of a Nation, 1798–1852* (Stanford: Stanford University Press, 1988). A political and personal biography sympathetic to Brazil's first emperor is Neill Macaulay, *Dom Pedro: The Struggle for Liberty in Brazil and Portugal, 1798–1834* (Durham, NC: Duke University Press, 1986).
4. An informed and insightful collection of essays in which the contradictions of Brazilian liberalism is a recurring theme is Emília Viotti da Costa, *The Brazilian Empire: Myths and Histories* (Chicago: University of Chicago Press, 1985), especially pp. 53–77. On ideological debates and institutional experimentation

in the judicial realm, see Thomas Flory, *Judge and Jury in Imperial Brazil, 1808–1871* (Austin: University of Texas Press, 1981).

5. As Antonio Gramsci explained, "the supremacy of a social group is manifested in two ways: through 'domination' [*dominio*], and through 'intellectual and moral leadership' [*direzione intellettuale e morale*, usually translated as 'hegemony']. A social group which strives to 'liquidate' or to subjugate adversary groups, even by armed force, exercised domination; it exercises hegemony over similar or allied groups." *Il Risorgimento* (Turin: Ciulio Einaudi Editore, 1949), p. 70. See also Joseph Femia, *Gramsci's Political Thought* (Oxford: Clarendon Press, 1981), pp. 47–49.

6. Elysio de Araujo, *Estudo histórico sobre a polícia da capital federal* (Rio de Janeiro: n.p., 1898), pp. 10–27.

7. Quoted in Aurelino Leal, "História judiciária do Brasil," in *Diccionário Histórico Geográphico e Ethnográphico do Brasil* (Rio de Janeiro: Imprensa nacional, 1922), vol. 1, p. 1119.

8. Luiz Gonçalves dos Sanctos, *Memórias para servir à história do reino do Brazil*. 2 vols. (Rio de Janeiro: Z. Valverde, 1943), 1:73, 93–94.

9. Sanctos, *Memórias*, 1:133–34.

10. Mello Barreto Filho and Hermeto Lima, *História da polícia do Rio de Janeiro*. 3 vols. (Rio de Janeiro: A Voite, 1939–1943), 1:207–8; Araujo, *Estudo histórico*, pp. 55–56. Vidigal is immortalized in *Memórias de um sargento de milícias*, by Manuel Antônio de Almeida. This literary classic, first published in 1852–1854, has been read by generations of students as one of Brazil's first novels.

11. Aquivo Nacional do Rio de Janeiro (hereafter cited ANRJ), Códice 323, vol. 6, folha 35, cited in Leila Mezan Algranti, *O feitor ausente: Estudos sobre a escravidão urbana no Rio de Janeiro, 1808–1822* (Petropólis: Vozes, 1988), pp. 165 n. 20, and 171.

12. Astolpho Rezende, "Polícia administrativa, polícia judiciária, o código do processo de 1832, a lei de 3 de dezembro de 1841, a lei de 20 de setembro de 1871." Instituto Histórico e Geográfico Brasileiro, *Primeiro Congresso de História Nacional*, 4 vols. (Rio de Janeiro: Imprensa nacional, 1916), 3:403–407.

13. Portaria of November 29, 1821, from Comissão Militar to Carlos Frederico de Caula, minister of war, cited in Araujo, *Estudo histórico*, pp. 59–62, 90.

14. Cited in Algranti, *O feitor ausente*, pp. 170–71.

15. Antônio Cândido, *Teresina etc.* (Rio de Janeiro: Paze Terra, 1980), p. 113.

16. For a general compendium on slaves and slavery in this period see Mary Karasch, *Slave Life in Rio de Janeiro, 1808–1850* (Princeton: Princeton University Press, 1987). See also Kátia de Queirós Mattoso, *To Be a Slave in Brazil* (New Brunswick, NJ: Rutgers University Press, 1986).

17. José Alípio Goulart, *Da palmatória ao patíbulo* (Rio de Janeiro: Conquista, 1971), p. 195.

18. Araujo, *Estudo histórico*, pp. 126–131; Barreto Filho and Lima, *História da Polícia*, 1:281. The curfew was in force until September 1878.

19. ANRJ, IJ6-166, Ofícios do Chefe da Polícia da Corte, (OCP-C), April 23, 1833. Of the 68 prisoners held in the fort on Santa Barbara Island at the same time, 13 had no records; Brasil, Ministro da Justiça, *Relatório*, 1833, p. 35.

20. This sequence of institutional changes is more fully analyzed in Thomas H. Holloway, *Policing Rio de Janeiro: Repression and Resistance in a 19th-Century City* (Stanford: Stanford University Press, 1993), chapters 3 and 4.

21. ANRJ, IJ6-177, (OCP-C), June 12, 1837. *Capoeira* in this period was a deadly form of foot fighting practiced by urban gangs and was the scourge of the police. For a fuller discussion see Thomas H. Holloway, " 'A Healthy Terror': Police Repression of *Capoeiras* in Nineteenth-Century Rio de Janeiro," *Hispanic American Historical Review* 69:4 (November 1989): 637–676.

22. An examination of the contrast between the private realm and the public arena is Sandra Lauderdale Graham, *House and Street: The Domestic World of Servants and Masters in Nineteenth-Century Rio de Janeiro* (Cambridge, England: Cambridge University Press, 1988).

23. Crimes over which the police had full jurisdiction, from investigation of the incident clear through to sentencing and supervising punishment, included 1) violations of municipal ordinances which commonly included a curfew and prohibitions on vagrancy, loitering, public drunkenness, disturbing the peace, and gambling; 2) all crimes with a punishment of fines up to one hundred milréis; prison, banishment, or exile of up to six months, with fine corresponding to up to half that time or without additional fine; or three months in jail or public workshops, where such existed. Coleção das Leis do Brasil-Atos do Poder Legislativo, 1832, pp. 156–57 (Article 12 of the Procedural Code); 1841, pp. 75–76, (Articles 4 and 5 of the judicial reform law).

24. José Antonio Pimenta Bueno, *Apontamentos sobre o processo criminal brasileiro*, 2nd ed. (Rio de Janeiro: H. Garnier, 1857), pp. 4, 18–19, 186–189.

25. An excellent analysis of the political culture of the Brazilian empire is Richard Graham, *Patronage and Politics in Nineteenth-Century Brazil* (Stanford: Stanford University Press, 1990).

26. Memos on this affair, dated as in text, are in ANRJ, IJ6-202 (Ofícios do Chefe da Polícia da Corte), October 1844.

27. Arquivo Geral da Polícia Militar do Estado do Rio de Janeiro (hereafter cited as AG PMERJ)-Correspondência Recebida, January 18, 1865.

28. Relatório do Chefe Polícia do Rio de Janeiro, 1838, Annex to Brasil, Ministro da Justiça, *Relatório*, 1839, p. 27.

29. AG PMERJ-Ordens do Dia, December 17, 1858.

30. ANRJ, IJ6-212 (Ofícios do Chefe da Polícia da Corte), September 14, 1849.

31. The ledger book is filed in the Arquivo Nacional in Rio de Janeiro as Códice 398, "Prisóes no Rio, 1849–1850." It actually covers the period from December 15, 1849, to December 15, 1850, so for quantitative analysis I have taken the liberty of recording the last two weeks of 1849 as if they were in 1850 in order to make a complete calendar year. As a document internal to the police secretariat, the ledger was not originally intended for eventual deposit in the National Archive, and it probably went there at some point by chance, with other files. There is no record in the archive of similar books for other years.

32. These data are used here as a representative sample of the immense amount of data generated by Rio's police system after the 1850s, not all of which was regularly published or even preserved. Further details on these data are in Holloway, *Policing Rio de Janeiro*, pp. 210–213 and appendix table 5.

33. Relatório do Chefe da Polícia do Rio de Janeiro, 1863, p. 1; 1866, p. 2.

34. Relatório do Chefe da Polícia do Rio de Janeiro, 1863, p. 2.

35. Brasil, Ministro da Justiça, *Relatório*, 1861, p. 5; 1866, p. 28.

36. The regulations are in ANRJ, IJ6-195 (Polícia Militar-Contabilidade), January 27, 1866, and in Decree 3,609 of February 17, 1866.

37. Brasil, Ministro da Justiça, *Relatório*, 1869, pp. 1, 48.

38. ANRJ, IJ6-19 (Polícia-Avisos), September 29, 1869; AG PMERJ-Correspondência Recebida, October 8, 1869; Relatório do Chefe Polícia do Rio de Janeiro, 1872, p. 194; Relatório do Chefe Polícia do Rio de Janeiro, 1874, p. 198.

39. *The Rio News*, July 15, 1880, p. 2

40. Brasil, Ministro da Justiça, *Relatório*, 1885, pp. 5–6; Barreto Filho and Lima, *História da polícia*, 3: 128–130. Public indignation over this incident helped push the police chief to resign in December 1884 and led to the extinction of the Urban Guard three months later.

41. Erasto Miranda de Carvalho, "Criar novas polícias: repetir um velho erro?" *Revista da Polícia Militar do Rio de Janeiro* 1: 4 (October 1984): 13.

42. Brasil, Ministro da Justiça, *Relatório*, 1886, p. 184, annex pp. 95–115.

43. Alfonso Lomonaco, *Al Brasile* (Milan: Società Editrice Libraria, 1889), p. 47.

44. For a general study of policies dealing with the urban underclass in this period see June Hahner, *Poverty and Politics: The Urban Poor in Brazil, 1870–1920* (Albuquerque: University of New Mexico Press, 1986).

45. AG PMERJ-Ordens do Dia, November 3, 1886.

46. AG PMERJ-Ordens do Dia, October 19, 1886.

47. ANRJ, IJ6-264 (Oficios do Chefe da Polícia da Corte), March 24, 1888.

48. ANRJ, IJ6-264 (Oficios do Chefe da Polícia da Corte), March 27, 1888. See also the detailed new regulations of the corps issued April 5, 1889, in Brasil, Ministro da Justiça, *Relatório*, 1889, annex, pp. 41–92.

6

Urbanistas, Ambulantes, and Mendigos: The Dispute for Urban Space in Mexico City, 1890–1930[1]

Pablo Piccato

The late nineteenth century in Latin America was the heyday of liberal oligarchies and a "new" ideology: positivism. The eclectic Latin American usage mixed the progressive teleologies of Auguste Comte, Herbert Spencer, and the indispensable Charles Darwin. In this mixture, Latin American intellectuals and policymakers (often one and the same) found promising solutions to two pressing problems: First, positivist discourse stressed the evolutionary nature of human societies which both explained the failures of liberal "egalitarian" liberalism and legitimized/naturalized persistent social inequalities. Second, positivist technologies promised practical strategies—as opposed to legalistic liberal abstractions such as constitutions—for reversing regional underdevelopment ("degeneration" in the positivist lexicon) and attaining the ever-elusive holy grail of modernity. Not surprising given their obsession with the international "struggle for life," positivist social engineers had a lot to say about the desultory effects of crime. In fact, positivism played a crucial role in shifting the discussion from crime and the criminal act to criminality and the criminal state. It also provided the impetus for modern police and penitentiaries.

The "Order and Progress" regime of Porfirio Díaz (1876–1911), known to Mexicans as the Porfiriato, with its politically influential cadre (camarilla) of científicos (scientists), aspired to be the quintessential positivist technocracy. To científico eyes, lower-class uses of urban space threatened public order just as lower-class vice threatened national development; both clearly required discipline and surveillance. For all their popularist rhetoric, post-revolutionary elites shared these concerns albeit with greater stress on social reform than on outright condemnation. Pablo Piccato, assistant professor of history at Columbia University, explores the intersection of positivist discourse, public policy, and popular resistance on the streets of late nineteenth- and early twentieth-century Mexico City. He concludes that the effects of modernization itself—population growth, improved transportation, and lack of basic services—undermined elite efforts to spatially marginalize the urban underclasses that "had to silently and constantly disregard regulations in order to survive in the city."

O ur views of turn-of-the-century Mexico City are heavily influenced by the grandeur of its buildings and avenues and the elegance of *colonias* built during that period. It is easy to share the nostalgia for *los tiempos de don Porfirio*, when Mexican society seemed as peaceful and well-organized as the walkways under the shady trees of the Paseo de la Reforma and the Alameda. This essay, however, contends that such images of civilization were only the precarious result of a negotiation between the regime's urban modernization projects and the everyday practices of the majority of the urban population. As Porfirian and post-revolutionary elites tried to shape the city according to their desires and economic interests, they turned to the police to punish lower-class public behaviors which did not conform to those projects. The urban poor on the other hand developed a skeptical view of justice and order. They used the city in different ways, walking across the social boundaries between rich and marginal areas, challenging the authority of the police, and even subverting "official" dictates about street nomenclature.

Turn-of-the-century Mexico City embraced all the symbols of nationalism and many remarkable examples of colonial architecture. By the end of the first century of national life, the city was also the locus of progress and the capital of Porfirio Díaz's long-lasting regime. Railroads, tramways, paved and illuminated streets, broad avenues, parks, new residential areas, and tall buildings appeared as distinctive signs of material advancement. These material improvements involved drastic changes in the design and use of urban space, changes conceived on the understanding that the rich and poor were not to mingle. Urban design sought the rational division between the safe, beautiful areas of the modern city and the dangerous, unhealthy marginal zones. Urban design therefore also meant social reform: the state and the wealthy classes wanted to translate the physical changes of the city into a new culture for its inhabitants.

The elites' idea of urban renewal faced the challenge of a growing and untamed population. The urban lower classes, so distant from the aspirations of wealth and comfort associated with progress, used the city in their own way, defying the class-structured organization of the Porfirian capital. As tensions arose about the use of streets and other public areas, the government and elites relied on the police and penal institutions to instill appropriate conduct among the people. Criminal behavior (whether a genuine transgression of social norms or simply a breach of the many laws and regulations generated during the period) acquires a different meaning in the context of this dispute over uses of the city. Crime, however, was not the only way in which people defied the urban utopia of Porfirian rulers. A host of practices in the streets (vending, begging, drinking, or merely walking) also subverted the ideal social map.

The next pages will weave a counterpoint between the elite model of the city and its defiance by the urban poor. On one side I will examine the projects and policies aimed at building a modern capital for the benefit of a minority of its inhabitants. The first section will outline the ideal city designed by Porfirian rulers and its importance for the interpretation of modern Mexico. On the other side I will analyze the unwanted consequences of late nineteenth-century growth on the city's structure and, more importantly, on the everyday lives of the urban majorities. A second section will describe the demographic and technological changes that caused the model to fail and the city to grow at an unprecedented rhythm. Then I will probe into everyday practices and living conditions in the marginal city—the one growing around and within the Porfirian ideal city. These pages will emphasize the behaviors that authorities tried to reform because they deemed them a threat to progress. The final section will tackle the urban policies that sought to preserve the social geography of the city and the collective reactions to those policies.

In sum, I will look at the cultural articulation of demographic and spatial growth under authoritarian regimes. This description of a disputed city questions contemporary historiography in its contention that elite projects of urban renewal went unchallenged and achieved their goals. As the urban poor used the city in ways that contradicted those projects, elite perceptions of "dangerous" areas identified poverty with criminality. The consequence was, on the one hand, that officials increasingly relied on punishment to impose their social ideas while, on the other hand, the urban poor identified the police and judicial system with the interests of the wealthy. The ideal city failed to impose its strict divisions of urban space (particularly after the revolution), and the connection between the appropriation of urban space and the criminalization of lower-class uses remained a long-lasting feature of the capital.

The Ideal City

The changes that swept early-twentieth-century Mexico had begun nearly forty years earlier during Emperor Maximilian's attempt to turn Mexico into a modern European nation and accelerated in the late Porfiriato. The

ideal city of the 1910 centennial celebration of independence epitomized
the unifying myths of progress and nationhood.[2] The colonial center of
the city, around the Zócalo or Plaza Mayor, extended its stately architecture toward the west on Avenida Juárez, reached the Alameda park, and
turned southwest onto the elegant Paseo de la Reforma to end at
Chapultepec Castle, the presidential residence (see map). The Alameda
was part of the colonial design of the city but became an upper-class place
of leisure during the nineteenth century. The Paseo de la Reforma's wide
design and execution followed the aesthetic and urbanistic ideas that had

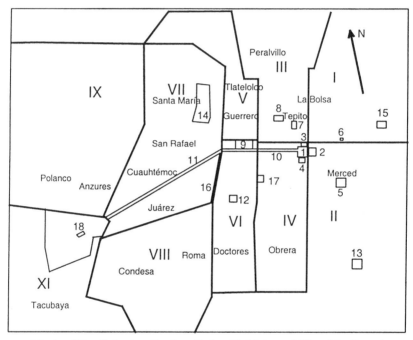

Mexico City: Colonias, Barrios, Police Districts and Sites Mentioned

References:

1 Zócalo	6 Plaza Mixcalco	11 Reforma Avenue	15 Penitentiary
2 National Palace	7 Plaza Tepito	12 Belem Jail	16 Bucareli Avenue
3 Cathedral	8 Lagunilla Market	13 Jamaica Market	17 Plaza de las Vizcaínas
4 City Council	9 Alameda	14 Central Railroad Station	18 Chapultepec Castle
5 La Merced Market	10 Juárez Avenue		

transformed Paris and other European capitals since the 1850s. Such was
the axis of a less visible modification of urban territory which resulted in
the displacement of the urban poor and Indian communities from valuable lands. Of all the cycles of change that Mexico City had experienced
after the Spanish conquest, the one which peaked during the late Porfiriato

was perhaps the most disruptive because it combined population growth, land dispossession, and heightened cultural conflict.[3]

Porfirian urban design corresponded with a drive to reorganize society within the city. Around the Paseo de la Reforma, private companies were licensed by city authorities to develop upper- and middle-class residential areas such as colonias Juárez, Cuauhtémoc, Roma, and Condesa. The word colonias designated these new neighborhoods—as if they represented the colonization of the city's wild countryside.[4] The development of colonias in a civilized, controlled environment received special attention from city authorities, who often ordered the elimination of undeserving or ill-looking buildings.[5] The designers and builders of this city had a clear idea of the social meaning of modernization: the poor had to be displaced from the elegant quarters, while city services were concentrated only in the well-kept districts.[6] Private developers believed that separating customers according to their socioeconomic status would create a stronger real estate market. This strategy meant a clear departure from the multiclass dwellings around downtown that dated back to colonial times. Porfirian investors, often closely associated with city officials, bought and partitioned lands for the wealthiest classes in privileged areas while reserving other zones for working-class homeowners. In many cases land grants caused the dispossession of community properties or the eviction of poor settlers.

The development of modern residential areas was not the only change brought by modernization. On the margins of the central city, authorities and developers had to deal with existing popular residential areas: lower-class colonias and old *barrios*. Although barrios had always existed close to the center, their poverty had preserved what Andrés Lira properly calls a "social distance" from the modern city.[7] During the Porfirian period however, these areas generated conflicts with the expected reorganization of urban society. Areas of lower-class housing, characterized by overcrowded tenements near downtown and squatters' shacks in the outskirts of the city, surrounded the center in a crescent moon that wrapped the Zócalo and Alameda on its north, east, and south sides, closer near the National Palace and further away at its extremities. The moon had its furthest points at the colonia Guerrero in the northwest and Belén Jail in the southwest. Its territory included the colonias Morelos and La Bolsa, respectively located east and northeast of the old barrio Tepito, and the colonia Obrera, none of which received adequate infrastructural investment from developers. Urbanization in these areas did not mean access to drainage, electricity, and pavement as it did for more affluent colonias. Images of neglect and poverty here contrasted with the protected environment of the central area.[8]

Life in the wealthiest colonias followed the models of privacy and autonomy enjoyed by European bourgeois households. City planners and developers shared the tacit premise that business, leisure, and production should be clearly separated, and that men and women had unmistakably different roles in public and domestic environments. The new colonias organized the living accommodations of the upper classes in single-house lots afforded with all the amenities of modern life including electricity, sewers, running water, and telephones. With these services, the inhabitants of the house did not have to rely on old-fashioned devices to satisfy their daily needs. They did not face the difficulty of manually bringing water to the household or getting rid of human waste in the street.[9]

The separation of places and activities into public and private constituted the premise for the design of buildings and streets and also guided official action regarding people's demeanor. Private behavior in public spaces had always been a concern for authorities in Mexico City. *Policía y buen gobierno* defined the authorities' greater intervention since colonial times, encompassing not only police issues but also the upkeep of streets and control of collective meetings. Just as in the seventeenth and eighteenth centuries, the Porfirian city council ordered *pulquerías* and *cantinas* concealed from the eyes of pedestrians and withdrew authorization for restaurants to place chairs and tables on the sidewalks.[10] By the end of the century the state adopted an interventionist stance on issues like pedestrian fashion traditionally outside the purview of liberal public policy. Indians (defined by their use of white trousers and shirts instead of dark suits) were forced by regulations to wear dark trousers. Repeated instances of the prohibition in the 1890s and then during Francisco I. Madero's presidency suggest the futility of the attempt.[11] The measure reflected official perceptions of "appropriate behavior" in the public space. Put simply, city authorities believed that indigenous people were not culturally prepared to use the city.

All these divisions in the use of the city were far from perfect, and the reality of urban life never accommodated itself to the Porfirian ideal. The functional divisions of urban space could not resist the erosion of everyday life because the design of the upper-class "civilized" city left outside and unplanned the very factors needed for its survival. The elegant new colonias around the Paseo de la Reforma as well as the older aristocratic homes downtown needed outside labor and supplies. The Eighth District, for example, lacked a single produce market in 1904.[12] Conversely, the urban lower and middle classes had to leave their homes to work and satisfy other everyday needs. These factors and a distinctive conception of the city on the part of the popular classes impelled the urban poor to cross the artificial borders between a modern city (where public and private functions had to be clearly separated) and another city (in their eyes, the whole city) where elite models of behavior seemed less important. The need to drink, eat, socialize, or simply earn a living through petty commerce generated strains over the use of streets. We cannot disregard the tension between the hierarchical and rigid map of the capital (imagined by the Porfirian elites) and the ambiguous, often unarticulated, horizontal view of those who lived, worked, and led their social lives on the streets. Before looking into that tension however, I will examine the factors that prevented Mexico City from becoming the model capital that its rulers envisioned.

Population, Transportation, and the Breakdown of the Model

The Porfirian regime failed to consolidate its ideal because of the constant arrival of immigrants from the rest of the country and the coeval development of new means of transportation which had been expected to facilitate progress but instead weakened social divisions and undermined the authorities' control over public spaces.

Population growth posed an unexpected problem to planners and administrators. From 1895, date of the first national census, the population of Mexico City not only grew much faster than the nation as a whole, but also faster than other cities in the country. In 1895, Mexico City had 329,774 inhabitants; by 1910, 471,066; by 1921, 615,327; and by 1930, 1,029,068. In 1895, Mexico City had 2.61 percent of the national population (12,632,427); by 1930, it had 9.17 percent (of 19,652,552). And, while Mexico City tripled in population between 1895 and 1930, state capitals doubled (from 732,047 to 1,431,007). In that period the national population increased only 50 percent.[13] As these figures indicate, rural migration to the cities began in earnest during the Porfirian era and never abated.

Despite the rural origin of most migrants, Mexico City's population was not what we can call a "traditional" society. Literacy figures, for example, suggest that the capital's population was more educated than the national average at the end of the Porfiriato and continued to be so during the following decades. While in 1900 the nation's rate of literacy was 17.9 percent, in the Federal District the percentage was 44.8. In 1930 the percentages were 38.5 and 75.1 respectively.[14] Although schooling was more accessible in the capital, many migrants came already educated. In 1895 the largest age group in Mexico City was young adults between twenty-one and thirty years old (39.22 percent of the city's total population), while the country's largest group was children ten years and under

(30.76 percent).[15] People came to the capital searching for jobs, but they did not necessarily lack education, a degree of status, or familiarity with urban life.

Other areas of the country also received immigrants during these years, but more women migrated to Mexico City. In 1895 men were 49.74 percent of the national population, while in Mexico City they made up 46.32 percent.[16] By 1930 that figure had declined to 44.86 percent.[17] In contrast, for the rapidly developing northern regions of the country the trend was in the other direction.

Mexico City offered the conditions for women to explore beyond their traditional gender roles. Census data for working women shows a sharp contrast between national figures and those of Mexico City: in 1900 women were only 16.35 percent of the national work force, in Mexico City they were 47.48 percent.[18] This did not mean however that women invaded traditionally male occupations. According to the 1895 census the trades favored by women were those of seamstress (5,505 women and no men listed by the census), cigar makers (1,709 women and no men), domestic help (25,129 women and 8,883 men), laundry workers (5,673 women and 112 men), and concierges (1,431 women and 994 men). Taken together, these categories made up 50.46 percent of the employed female population.[19] For many of these women, living in the capital meant not only leaving behind their hometowns but also the domestic environment.

In sum, turn-of-the-century Mexico City was formed by young newcomers, more educated than most Mexicans and with a strong female presence in certain areas of economic activity. Industrial jobs did not employ large numbers of people—only 1.23 percent of employed men in the city in 1895, while 10.74 percent were listed as *comerciantes* (employed in commerce) and 7.05 percent as domestic workers.[20] Moving into the capital did not necessarily translate into better living conditions, although it opened the possibility of access to better-paying jobs. Qualitative evidence suggests that while more educated and wealthier Mexicans lived in the capital, so did many people without education and with very low incomes.

Along with demographic growth, modernization brought new means of transportation. The result was the increasing ability of travelers to reach the capital and of its inhabitants to move within it. The development of railroads made it much easier for travelers to reach the capital, as one-day trips from nearby towns became possible for artisans of modest income and poor migrants. Trains developed in a countrywide network whose lines converged in Mexico City. Compared to the traditional canoes and ox carts that even in the 1880s still transported much of the foodstuff needed in the capital, trains brought more products faster and cheaper from regions beyond the valley. Soon railroads replaced canals and roads as the principal way of communicating between the city and surrounding towns.[21] The sudden ease in reaching the capital from the interior brought crowds who did not behave or dress according to "civilized" foreign models. Railroad stations bustled with outsiders visiting Mexico City in great numbers, particularly during festivities such as Cinco de Mayo and Independence Day (September 16). Different festivals brought different visitors. Observers stressed the rural demeanor of the masses of pilgrims coming for the celebration of the Virgin of Guadalupe (December 12). Regardless of origin, these visitors crowded the streets, creating a bonanza for merchants and a headache for the police.[22]

Migration meant not only geographical mobility for large groups, but also their social and spatial mobility within the city. Within the city, new means of transportation, particularly tramways, changed the way people moved. During the 1880s, private and rented coaches provided transportation for "many people, of medium and great wealth."[23] First pulled by animals, then also by electricity, *tranvías* made commuting faster and affordable, and brought the center of the city closer to the suburbs.[24] In 1903 most trams were pulled by mules, although there were electric units as well. In 1920 there were 345 kilometers of tramway lines with 370 passenger cars owned by the Compañía de Tranvías de México. Trams were cheap enough to be used by middle- and some working-class people on a daily basis, and occasionally by the poorest residents.[25] Tramways became an important element of the urban poor's everyday life. For the characters of Angel de Campo's novel *La Rumba*, the tramway was the daily means of transportation and much more. Remedios, a seamstress, went to work daily in the tramway and made it the setting for her romantic life.[26] Horse-driven cabs continued to be a common sight at the turn of the century, although drivers were usually described as "ruffians" who liked to go too fast.[27] Ox carts, mules, and hand-pulled carts were also frequent. Starting in the 1910s, automobiles added to the intricacy of transportation, with greater speed and different rules governing their movement.[28]

The impact of these new means of transportation on the popular perception of the capital was twofold. First, tramways, trains, and automobiles were commonly identified with the worst, most aggressive aspects of modernization. Walking in the middle of the street became a dangerous "rural" habit in this city. Accidents were common. Echoing public concern, the penny press called tramway drivers *mataristas* (killers) instead of *motoristas*. Due to judicial corruption, drivers enjoyed a great margin of impunity in case they ran over a pedestrian.[29] Disregard for safety by car and tramway drivers was a central consequence of urban progress from the point of view of lower-class pedestrians: a threatening environment, where victims were poor and the guilty (protected by their companies or bosses) were never punished. The world around train stations and inside coaches also offered an image of movement both attractive and dangerous. Beggars wheedled in train stations, boys peddled in tramways, theft was common, and some journalists even talked about a special kind of professional thief who targeted unaware travelers.[30]

Traffic was one of the preferred contexts of the struggle between "old" and "modern" behaviors. The use of the street for fast transportation competed with its use as a place for commerce and sociability. This created a conflict between suburban car drivers and the many residents who made their living in the streets. The city council sought to teach coach drivers to keep to their right and pedestrians to move along, reminding them "that it is forbidden to stop in the middle of the street and form groups that obstruct the circulation of vehicles and animals." The prohibition was in this case a description: vendors set up their booths in the middle of the street, blocking traffic despite the inspectors' threats.[31] Pedestrians stood in the middle of sidewalks, blocking other walkers, particularly at corners and outside theaters, and forming groups instead of lines.[32]

The second consequence of technological change was a transformed understanding of the city among the majority of its inhabitants. Modern transportation widened the perception of the urban space. Tramway lines reached as far as San Angel and made the Zócalo easily accessible. Different areas of the city were linked and it was now easier for residents to reach not only the Zócalo and Avenida Plateros but also the gambling houses in Tacubaya and other allegedly "dangerous" quarters of the city.[33] In 1882, poet Manuel Gutiérrez Nájera used the tramway as the vehicle of an imaginary exploration into passengers' lives. He already saw a different city than that of pre-tramway days: "The wagon takes me to unknown worlds and virgin regions. No, Mexico City does not start at the National Palace, nor does it end at Reforma Avenue. I give you my word that the city is much bigger. It is a great turtle that extends its dislocated legs toward the four cardinal points. Those legs are dirty and hairy. The city council, with fatherly care, paints them with mud every month."[34]

As the city expanded, society became more complex and mobile. An educated observer like Gutiérrez Nájera could travel the long legs of the turtle to reach stories and places unknown. By the same token working people became more mobile and able to reach the rich city downtown. There they engaged in "typical" activities such as peddling, drinking, begging, and even stealing that undermined the order of the Porfirian city. The impression of an ordered, stable cosmopolitan city was broken by the daily movement of its variegated population.

The Impact of Modernization on Everyday Life

What did the Porfirian design of the city mean for the urban poor? This question is at the center of any attempt to explain the relationship between modernization and crime. I will now describe the living conditions of the urban poor and examine the ways in which they coped with overcrowding, displacement, and authoritarian policies. These ways were not always in accordance with upper-class notions of "appropriate" behavior and often fell outside the law. The urban poor therefore had to cope not only with difficult material conditions but also with the disapproval of observers and authorities and the criminalization of many survival strategies.

Denouncing the bad quality of lower-class housing conditions, a 1902 report by *El Imparcial* stated a basic fact of everyday life in the city: ". . . a sizable part of the population, precisely that which does not have the best personal hygiene, live in the narrow rooms that the capital's buildings offer to the poorer classes. Those tenement houses . . . offer the most surprising spectacle of human overcrowding one could imagine. Only medieval 'Ghettos,' those typical neighborhoods in which the Jews were confined, could resemble the narrowness, slovenliness and dirtiness of these dwellings."[35] In the perspective of educated observers, overcrowding and other features of the urban poor's life made necessary their geographical and even cultural isolation. But the consequence of those conditions were an implicit challenge to elite notions of civility and undermined the class and gender divides which were supposed to structure urban life.

In the old barrios near downtown and in many of the newly developed lower-class colonias, people lived in *vecindades*—one- or two-story tenements that lacked the clear spatial autonomy of modern homes. Several families lived crammed into single- or double-room apartments with a single door that opened into a narrow hallway. Tenants shared sanitary services and the use of the hallway for cleaning or cooking.[36] In the colonia de La Bolsa for example, most tenants could not provide a warrantor. For them, rents were established on a short-term basis at relatively high rates. Landlords did not even enter vecindades, preferring to carry out their deals verbally on the street.[37] According to the *Nueva Era*, policemen did not dare enter either, because vecindades were not welcoming places: dogs were loose and aggressive, clothes hung in the middle of the hallway, and neighbors saw any government representative as an intruder. On the other hand, *vendedores ambulantes* (peddlers) entered vecindades at will, contributing to frequent thefts from tenants' apartments.[38] Commentators blamed the housing deficit for these problems. According to the 1902 *El*

Imparcial report, nothing decent could be leased for less than 50 pesos; houses renting for less than 20 pesos a month were "true troglodyte dwellings." Only the wealthy classes had improved their living conditions as a result of the building fever of recent years.[39] For the urban lower classes however, vecindades were simply their only chance for a decent dwelling.

For the less advantaged, public dormitories or inns called *mesones*, offered a roof for the night in exchange for a ticket that could be bought daily at a low cost. Thus, mesones better suited the economic circumstances of those who lacked a stable income, like ambulantes or beggars. Although ostensibly designed for travelers, mesones became the permanent address of many poor *capitalinos* who were ready to endure any inconvenience. Sleeping room on the floor (which men, women, and children shared) could become the object of bloody disputes. Felipe Toledo was arrested in 1907 because he stuck a pencil four centimeters into Amador Rodríguez's chest. Rodríguez had stepped on Toledo while seeking for some room to sleep at a mesón of the Plazuela de las Vizcaínas.[40] Conditions were less than hygienic, especially as demand grew.[41] Dormitories received large numbers of migrants during the revolution. In 1920 on an average day, 91 men, 19 women, and 8 children used the public dormitory, and in 1918 the Beneficencia Pública dormitory received 54,750 people.[42]

Elite commentators saw mesones and vecindades as the cause of the urban poor's lack of morality. Porfirian writers explained the alleged tendency among the poor to appear naked or covered by rags, or to expose the most delicate moments of their family life as a consequence of what they saw and endured in those places.[43] Observers were concerned by the mixup of inside and outside, public and private, that was a common feature of popular life. While allegations of sexual promiscuity might have been based on the imagination of observers and, at the very least, difficult to document, one clear outcome of overcrowding and lack of proper facilities was the poor's need to carry out many of the activities associated with the private in public places.

A widespread problem of popular housing, perhaps the main reason its occupants spent most of the day in the streets, was the absence of running water and sewers. Since the late colonial period, according to Marcela Dávalos, the absence of running water at home had thwarted the construction of "the modern family . . . organized by the feelings of intimacy, prudery and privacy" with the result that "inside the house the same things happened as in the street."[44] Authorities and neighbors were aware of the problems posed by the scarcity of the "precious" liquid. During the Porfiriato, water had to be brought to many areas by cumbersome means. Sanitary facilities were collective and unhealthy. Toilets in vecindades emptied into sewers or the street by open channels that ran down the middle of the hallway.[45]

The lack of water at home stimulated the development of *baños públicos* (public baths), an important institution in the lives of city inhabitants and one that further mixed intimate needs and social life. At these facilities men and women could take a shower and do laundry for a small fee. In the 1880s, baños públicos were the largest constructions of the Paseo de la Reforma, near the Alameda. Swimming pools were also crowded on hot days, especially Saint John the Baptist's day. Attendance at these facilities was high: during April 1914, 5,434 men and 5,267 women used the Baños de la Lagunilla, administered by the Beneficencia Pública.[46]

Other, less pleasing practices prompted by the lack of hygienic facilities at lower-class dwellings further offended the sensibilities of upper-class observers. Urinating and defecating in the streets was a matter-of-course for poor men and women. This problem had concerned authorities since the Bourbon period. Although public urinals were available at several sites in the city, arrests were still common in the late 1910s for "having bowel movements on the public road."[47] It was only natural to provide more urinals in the city, declared well-known physician M. Río de la Loza in 1892, for "those individuals whose occupations force them to stay outside their homes." Establishing more toilets was all the more necessary since the only available alternatives were pulquerías, where "there is the custom of having barrels or buckets used to contain the urine of any individual who wants to use them."[48] The problem became more evident on the recently paved streets near theaters and restaurants where, at night, people left "large pools of urine" and feces. For Mexican commentators, Mexico City's image compared poorly to other modern capitals, where public urinals prevented these spectacles. The city council, however, found it difficult to punish even its own employees noting, "What can the policemen do, if they have to stay eight hours in their corner, or the coach drivers, who often spend the whole day in the street, or the street merchants or, in sum, anyone who walks the city and who is far from his home, when they face an urgent need [*alguna necesidad*]?"[49] For lower-class men and particularly for women, neither their dwellings nor public facilities offered a "decent" solution to their daily bodily needs. Their only option was to ignore the dictates of urbanity and endure the shame and their repudiation by authorities and better-off residents.

Lastly, the scarcity of potable water in their homes drove people to the street in order to satiate their thirst. Men and women of all ages had to use public fountains, buy flavored water (*aguas frescas*) at booths, or patronize pulquerías. Many houses lacked wells and some were not even close to water pipes.[50] Drinking water was less of a concern for the colonias west of the center, where springs from Chapultepec provided abundant and good-quality water.[51] Pulque and thirst were commonly associated in descriptions of popular drinking. Pablo Severiano and Manuel González were so thirsty after having breakfast that they pawned a vest one of them was wearing in exchange for twenty-five cents worth of pulque. The vest turned out to be stolen, but the employee of the pulquería alleged that they were so thirsty that he could not refuse the deal.[52] In the streets, alcoholic beverages were at the center of social life. Access to pulquerías and cantinas (and thus to the worlds of prostitution and gambling which revolved around alcohol) was a powerful incentive for rural migrants to move to Mexico City. It had been so since colonial times. According to Serge Gruzinski, Indians who had left their communities were attracted by the anonymity of the city and came to enjoy the deregulated, secularized use of alcohol.[53] Alcohol and prostitution were still luring them during the Porfiriato.[54] This loss of local mechanisms to limit the use of alcohol coupled with elite concerns about the appearance of the city's population converted alcohol consumption into a central public issue during this period.

Control of alcohol in public places was not successful, as the number of commercial outlets continued to grow throughout the period. Up to 1871, the selling of pulque was officially restricted to the Calle del Aguila, two blocks north of the Alameda,[55] but by the end of the century pulquerías had surpassed any precedent in terms of quantity and extension. As the city expanded, new pulquerías emerged on the outskirts of the city with new buildings and colorful mural paintings.[56] According to official records, in 1902 there were 2,423 alcohol outlets in the capital, including cantinas, pulquerías, and smaller establishments. The greatest concentration of these was in the blocks east of the Plaza Mayor (behind the Palacio Nacional) where the number of pulquerías and cantinas was so great that it became common for authorities to deny new licenses to sell alcohol. Of the total of 924 pulquerías in the city, 170 existed inside an area around the center where they were formally prohibited.[57]

Alcohol consumption became the object of a confrontation between public policies and the "disorder" of everyday practices. City authorities sought to prevent crime and disorders by limiting hours of cantinas and pulquerías, prohibiting gambling and music at their premises, and banning the selling of alcohol during festivities.[58] Alcohol became the rationale for further official control of people's movements. Since pulque was taxed when it entered the city, even pedestrians carrying as little as two liters were arrested by the police.[59] Policemen dragged dozens of sleeping drunkards (*borrachos tirados*) from the streets to police stations. There they were summarily fined and detained overnight.[60] But in spite of these measures, Porfirian authorities never tried to fully suppress the consumption of alcohol across the city.

Finding a systematic solution to the problem of alcoholism proved difficult, in part because of strong economic interests connected to the pulque business in Mexico City. The huge demand for alcohol and increasing state supervision created quarrels between cantinas and pulquerías that had to meet municipal licensing requirements, and numerous informal outlets such as *tendajones* (small stores) and *puestos* (street booths) which sold cheap mixes of infusions and alcohol without a license, especially at night when legal outlets were forced to close.[61] The regulations of alcohol retail prompted additional tensions between the owners of small cantinas and pulquerías, and authorities—whom the former accused of giving improper advantages to the monopolistic Compañía Expendedora de Pulques and the proprietors of elegant outlets downtown. The Compañía indeed had powerful partners who were also senior public officials, such as *científico* Pablo Macedo (a high-ranking official in Díaz's government and on the city council), and made investments in real estate and railroads. The enforcement of regulations often meant revoking the licenses of the Compañía's smaller competitors. After Díaz's demise, many of the small sellers' grievances against the Compañía became public and the new governments were, at least rhetorically, more willing to act upon the fears of alcoholism as a social problem.[62] Economic interests, benefiting the same elite that condemned popular alcohol use, undermined public policies directed against the problem.

Street commerce, another ongoing source of tension between authorities and city dwellers, reinforced the street life associated with drinking alcohol. Since most city inhabitants spent their days and many nights outside, a great variety of exchanges occurred in all areas of the city. Many enterprising citizens viewed street commerce as a ready, if risky, source of income. Gaining access to a broad public was worth confronting the authorities' penchant for controlling the streets. A multitude of street services were offered. Scribes (*escribanos*, also called *evangelistas*), barbers, dentists, phonograph operators, and musicians exercised their trades on the sidewalks, with or without official authorization.[63] Women cooked and sold food (chopping beef, making tortillas, fixing tacos) in the middle of narrow streets, especially around markets like La Merced. Along with food, alcoholic beverages were sold, again without any kind of license.[64]

What these trades lacked in stability they offered in flexibility and freedom of movement. Small vegetable or candy vendors would acquire their daily stock, walk the streets or take a place on a sidewalk, and work until sunset or their merchandise was gone. They would start again the next day, using their daily earnings to renew stock. Any profit went to lodging and other needs. This practice often involved walking from La Merced market or the *embarcaderos* (docks where canoes brought in produce from the countryside across Lake Texcoco) to central streets. Forty-five-year-old María Magdalena Gutiérrez walked every day from the Jamaica market to the Fourth District to peddle vegetables. She had lived and worked (as a tortillera) in Lerma, state of Mexico, but, she informed a social worker in 1931, "after she saw that the selling of vegetables could be more profitable, she turned to such activity and moved to the capital" where she was able to earn approximately one peso a day. She spoke Nahuatl and some Spanish. Her neighbors informed the social worker about her daily routine: she woke up very early, bought the "lettuce, green peas, artichokes, etc.," sold them in the street, and returned home walking. She was arrested on the suspicion of being a beggar while more than two kilometers away from home.[65]

Peddlers like María Magdalena fought a constant battle against authorities to occupy those areas of the city where customers and money were accessible. These sellers were, since colonial times, mostly Indians who came to the capital to sell their own produce. For early nineteenth-century authorities they already represented a serious source of disorder despite their picturesque image.[66] By century's end the confrontation had become more acute as peddlers went from "natural" elements of the urban landscape to agents of social conflict, struggling for space against respectable neighbors and established merchants. The 1900 census classified only 334 persons as street peddlers, but many eyewitness accounts strongly suggest much larger numbers. In 1894, merchants of the Calle del Empedradillo near the Cathedral complained about the "plague" of ambulantes on that street. And as the city council conceded, municipal regulations could not be easily enforced due to the negligence of the police, who refused to take strong measures against ambulantes.[67]

Disputes between established merchants and ambulantes were rife. Access to space was at the root of these squabbles. Many sellers stationed themselves outside markets, offering the same products available inside which they had acquired early in the morning at lower prices.[68] The key element for economic success was to find the right spot. Food sellers outside La Merced market complained to the city council that if they were displaced to a different zone with less circulation of customers—as city authorities intended—their way of making a living would be destroyed.[69] Police agents and inspectors made peddlers' lives harder by demanding either the official permit (which most of them lacked) or a bribe.[70] The "illegality" of many street vendors became a source of additional income for policemen charged with punishing it.

Clearing the capital's central streets of ambulantes was a never-ending task. Street vendors were a traditional feature of the urban landscape. The source of tension, it could be argued, was the group of affluent merchants and urban reformers who sought to establish control over downtown streets in order to create a modern business district. In 1901 for example, neighbors and merchants of the Plaza de Santo Domingo asked the city council to remove the scribes from the colonnades of the plaza, arguing that they promoted vice and theft, and obstructed the view from the stores. The Comisión de Policía y Mercados of the city council replied that the *escritorios* had been there for more than forty years and there was enough room for everyone.[71] Tradition had established escritorios at the Plaza de Santo Domingo and peddlers should not be forced to move from that identifiable marker of their trade. Not everyone however could successfully appeal to old uses. In 1897, sellers of candy in the Zócalo asked the city council to reconsider its refusal to renew their permits. The vendors maintained that it was traditional during holidays for parents to buy candy and toys for their children in the Plaza Mayor. Banishing vendors from the plaza, they argued, would push them to the brink of "misery, with all its horrors." In this case the government was less flexible, and extended the candy peddlers' licenses for only a year. After all, the Zócalo was one of the showpieces of the ideal city, while Santo Domingo, only three blocks to the north, already belonged to the margins.[72]

Other types of exchanges challenged the social divisions of urban geography. The immediate need for cash drove people downtown to pawn their possessions. Pawnshops loaned customers amounts below the value of the objects pawned. Customers kept a ticket until they could repay the loan plus interest and recover their possessions. The principal money-lender for the poor was the Monte de Piedad, a colonial institution supervised by the city government, located across the street from the Cathedral, on the northwest corner of the Zócalo. Interest rates on loans guaranteed by property were at least 8 percent a month for amounts of less than one peso, and 6 percent for larger amounts, plus a 5 percent fee. Private pawnshops competed with the Monte de Piedad, although they extracted higher interests. The city council authorized pawnshops in other areas of the city to prevent the long lines and crowds that formed around the Monte de Piedad building, but did not allow private entrepreneurs to offer lower rates.[73]

Robbing the well-to-do was another reason poorer people entered the wealthy areas of the capital and subverted the boundaries that supposedly separated "decent" and "dangerous" territories. Accounts of pickpockets in such places as the Cathedral and elegant stores inflamed concerns about crime in general and supported the alleged need for harsh treatment for petty thieves.[74] Tramways and trains were favorite targets for petty thieves because they allowed close physical contact with watch-carrying gentlemen. Most thefts did not require violence, but exploited the open spaces of streets and public buildings. In 1911 the city council asked for special police protection for its own building, where bronze ornaments were frequently stolen.[75] It was common practice for thieves to enter a large store, grab a piece of fine silk from the counter, and try to outrun clerks and policemen.[76]

Traffic in stolen goods crossed from the respectable areas of the city to neighborhoods outside police control. Contemporaries perceived colonia de La Bolsa as an almost foreign danger zone within the city. They linked the neighborhood to the trade in stolen goods and the absence of police intervention and thus saw it as a violent place particularly dangerous for upper-class intruders.[77] The barrio of Tepito was feared as a thieves' lair. An American traveler was told that the "Thieves Market" (probably the Lagunilla market near Tepito) was the place where merchandise could be sold three months after a robbery without fear of prosecution. The visitor thought this an exaggeration, "at least nowadays under the strong hand of Díaz."[78] But robbery was an uncomfortable feature of the Porfirian capital. Even though thieves were far fewer than ambulantes, they also participated in the disruption of the capital's social geography.

Beggars were more visible than thieves in the invasion of respectable places. The fight against mendicity thus became a focus of upper-class struggles to "recover" public spaces. In 1897, influential hygienist Dr. Eduardo Liceaga proposed that beggars be sent to jail instead of the overcrowded asylum. *El Imparcial* supported the idea, arguing that it would prevent "those immoral scenes that contradict our culture."[79] Mendicants made the most of the impact of their presence near churches and around upper-class areas. In 1916, *El Universal* complained that they were a serious nuisance to pedestrians, even in downtown streets. According to the newspaper, mendicants were aggressive, showing "sickening sores, with reprehensible impudicity" and threatening to infect pedestrians. Their place was not the streets but "the farthest corner of hospitals."[80] Observers accused beggars of exaggerating or faking their afflictions in order to impress passersby. In 1917, Julio Anaya was arrested near La Merced and sent to the penitentiary for begging "and to that effect [according to the police] he pierced the skin of his neck with a needle."[81]

The location of beggars rather than their begging style dictated official intervention. Like vendors and thieves, beggars gravitated toward the central, more crowded areas of the capital. Police inspectors reported to the city council in 1895 that beggars came from outlying neighborhoods or villages, particularly during religious celebrations, although their presence was rare in suburban districts where they were quickly arrested by police.[82] The fact that mendicants occupied places associated with modernization and progress made them even more troublesome. *El Imparcial* denounced beggars roaming "in downtown streets, under the shade of the trees of the most popular avenues, in the tramway stops, where they jump at travelers."[83] In 1930, *El Universal* published a map of the zone of "greater concentration of beggars" based on a census performed by the Beneficencia Pública. The area stretched from Las Cruces to Guerrero Streets, and from Arcos de Belén Avenue to República de Panamá Street. This overlapped with the central downtown streets, the cosmopolitan zone around the Alameda and Zócalo.[84]

Peddling, stealing, begging, or drinking were certainly not the only reasons for the urban poor to appropriate the spaces of the wealthy city, but they were the most visible. Most of those who walked or took the tramway downtown sought to earn a living through more legitimate and stable means, and none relished police harassment or the possibility of jail. Working in industries, upper-class houses, government offices, or in the stores, many inhabitants of the marginal city moved daily into the central city, filling the streets with their presence. The city could not work without this movement across social boundaries. So city authorities sought to control and channel the dynamics of urban life by trying to teach the urban lower classes how to use their own city.

The Dispute for the City

For elites, crime, alcoholism, and beggary constituted the clearest violations of the boundaries of the respectable city. Thieves, drunkards, and beggars became the target of several official campaigns to "clean up" the city, when suspects were arrested and many sent to penal colonies after a cursory investigation. Perhaps the harshest campaigns took place in 1908–1910 under Porfirio Díaz's iron hand, and subsequently in 1917–1919 when Venustiano Carranza sought to consolidate revolutionary legitimacy with Porfirian methods.[85] These policies were the most aggressive example of official attitudes toward the urban lower classes. They emerged in the context of the dispute between different conceptions about the use and structure of the city. Most often however, conflicts were played out through city authorities' skewed distribution of resources which favored upper-class colonias over lower-class developments and old barrios. Issues of health, policing, and street nomenclature exemplify the confrontations between elite projects and the urban poor's use of the city. Disputed perceptions of urban space, in which certain areas were perceived as territories of crime, illustrate how the unintended consequences of modernization defeated the Porfirian model of a cosmopolitan capital.

The boundaries of Mexico City became particularly unstable during the Porfiriato. Since the early colonial period, ethnic stratification had defined an area of Spanish population around the political and religious center of the Plaza Mayor. The *traza* or outline of the central city displaced the indigenous inhabitants of Tlatelolco and Tenochtitlán to the edges of the lake that surrounded the city. According to Andrés Lira, from those early moments on, areas of Spanish and indigenous occupancy had no clear boundaries but moved and overlapped constantly. Conflicts and readjustments became a feature of urban politics, and they peaked in the second half of the nineteenth century.[86]

The external limits of the capital also lost their distinct character during this period as the capital expanded its urbanized area almost five-fold.[87] Several gates (*garitas*) had been placed at the outskirts of the city to control traffic of merchandise brought by carts. By the turn of the twentieth century however, they were rapidly becoming obsolete. Gatekeepers still collected fees on pulque and other products but the gates themselves had lost their value as markers of the city's outer limits. Moreover, their fiscal importance had been reduced by increasing railroad traffic.[88] During colonial times and until the mid-nineteenth century, city authorities had sought to monitor the influx of travelers entering through *garitas* or checking into *mesones*. Such vigilance was no longer possible during the Porfiriato.[89] The revolution further demonstrated the loss of control over the external boundaries of the city. Messengers from the Zapatista insurgency in Morelos acquired weapons, money, and information in the capital and carried them through the southern hills of the valley with relative ease, although on a small scale. The entrance of the entire Zapatista army in November 1914 was the symbolic culmination of this silent invasion.[90] Trains brought anonymous multitudes to the city. Until the 1880s the separation between recently arrived "outsiders" (*fuereños*) and city dwellers seemed clear to everyone because both groups had distinctive clothes and manners. As the city grew and its connections with the surrounding countryside intensified, fuereños were harder to discern.[91] For many capitalinos, the modernization of transportation meant a bigger urban space, but also one plagued by anonymity and danger.

Because the difference between rich and poor areas had a clear cultural dimension, upper-class colonias and lower-class developments and barrios existed in uneasy proximity. In the poorer suburbs, traditional rural ways coexisted with the newest aspects of modernization. In the suburban Seventh and Eighth Districts, unkempt open spaces challenged the goals of urbanization, prompting the city council to order the fencing of empty lots near "inhabited zones."[92] Still open to the surrounding countryside, these areas showed the unfinished transition to urban life. Dogs, horses, donkeys, pigs, cattle, and chickens were everywhere and created sanitation problems: in December 1900 the bodies of seven hundred animals were picked up and incinerated.[93] In Mixcoac, a weekend residential area south of Chapultepec, well-to-do neighbors complained about a forty-three-room tenement house they considered a focus of disease and crime, and an insult to nearby residences.[94]

Areas of older, lower-class housing near downtown presented their own problems. Many of these communities had been established in pre-Hispanic times, but others were simply the result of greater population density.[95] According to *El Imparcial*, real estate speculation, the centralization of services and commerce, and the price of tramway fares forced "our poor classes to cram like canned sardines into the small rooms available."[96] Many run-down vecindades, pulquerías, and dangerous streets were located just behind the National Palace. According to an American visitor in 1903 the proximity of the Zócalo to older barrios was verified by the fact that it "is rather the lounging-place for the lower classes, as the Alameda is for the upper."[97] After the revolution the areas close to downtown remained a world of poverty and disease. In the early 1920s, sanitary authorities considered the area north of the Plaza de la Constitución as an "endemic" zone of typhus, whose inhabitants had to be "desinsectizados" to prevent new outbreaks of the disease.[98]

Therefore, the crescent moon of the marginal city represented a threat to the security of the central city. Certain barrios and lower-class colonias were identified by *gente decente* as places of criminality and disease. An 1895 guide for visitors, suggestively entitled *México y sus alrededores. Guía para los viajeros escrita por un Mexicano. Cuidado con los rateros* (Mexico and its environs. Guide for travelers written by a Mexican. Watch out for thieves), warned that barrios such as La Merced were "famous because of the quantity of thieves who are there."[99] But La Merced market southeast of the Zócalo offered the best food prices and stock for lower- and middle-class customers. Also to the east, barrios San Lázaro, Santa Anita, La Soledad y La Palma were places of danger and disease.[100] American visitor Eaton Smith went to this "rather slummy part of the town, where the pavements were abominable, either by natural vice or from efforts to reform them, and so came to La Viga canal" on the southeastern edge of the Second District. This area connected the city with Lake Texcoco and suffered the worst effects of dusty winds and flooding.[101]

Crime and alcoholism helped to define these areas. In a 1902 survey ordered by the city council, the Second District (whose boundaries extended from the northeastern corner of the Cathedral toward the east and south and included La Merced) had the greatest number of alcohol outlets (534 of the city's 2,423). Together with the First District (north of the Second) and the Third District (neighbor to the First on the west), they had more than half the pulquerías of all the eight districts (484 of 924).[102] To the north, Tepito, La Bolsa, and Guerrero were also criminal territories. An *El Imparcial* reporter depicted colonia de La Bolsa as "the cradle of crime." He reached the colonia "as an explorer seeking the source of rivers by sailing against the stream, I followed the complex network of small streets that are the bridges sending evil from La Bolsa to invade the city." Once there "a crowd of horrible and strange figures . . . emerged before my scared eyes, beholding that dark world where people seem to come from generations of criminals."[103] El Chalequero, the famous prostitute killer first arrested in 1888, lived and committed his crimes in the colonias Peralvillo and Santa Ana, isolated areas north of the city where prostitution was rife and nobody dared to turn him in to the police.[104] To the southeast and south of the center, mainly within the Second and Fourth Districts, Belén Jail, La Merced market, and Cuauhtemoctzin street (an area of prostitution) were the foci of danger. Elite sense of the "dangerous" zones of the city derived from the perceived insecurity and lack of police in many poor areas.

Elite perception of social problems in the lower-class areas of the capital was reinforced by the authorities' biased allocation of resources to more affluent neighborhoods. The city council was in charge of making urban expansion official. It had to "receive" a colonia before granting it the benefits of urbanization. Colonias such as Roma, Condesa, Juárez, San Rafael, Santa María, Escandón, and Guerrero were the result of the development of lands that had formerly belonged to haciendas. The city council approved the official transfer of property in these areas and ensured that their developers provided all the services offered to proprietors.[105] Other areas meanwhile seemed to be ignored.[106] In 1903 for example, neighbors of colonia de La Bolsa asked for paving and street lighting, but the city council denied their request on the grounds that partitioning (or *fraccionamiento*) of the lands had not been officially approved. After a political struggle with the governor of the Federal District, the city council finally accepted the neighbors' petition, although paving was delayed. The inhabitants of colonia Obrera were involved in a similar dispute.[107]

Business needs weighed heavily in these decisions because the city council was usually elected from a group of influential citizens who had economic interests at stake.[108] Council members' social and urban reform projects had to be reconciled with the pragmatic needs of development.

The consequences were limited policies that focused, for example, on embellishment of the city.[109] Street cleaning, hygiene, and public order became targets of city government insofar as they could be addressed without great expense but with visible results in downtown and upper-class areas. Police and administrative pressures, similar to those applied against ambulantes, were used to force lower-class residents to take care of their streets and façades. In 1901 the city council forced residents to clean the façades of their buildings to offer a better image to foreign visitors attending the Pan-American Congress. The measure was all the more urgent because many quarters "not far away from the center" gave an indecorous view of dusty façades. The area of mandatory cleaning was gradually extended from Bucareli Avenue (west of the Alameda) to the doors of the Palacio Nacional, and then to all the streets leading from that central area to the railroad stations because these areas were "frequented by foreigners."[110]

Regarding street cleaning, the government's exclusive concern was for elegant streets. In 1892 a city council commission decided that a private proposal to establish a watering and cleaning service for the downtown was not worth the investment because that area was already cleaner than the rest.[111] The police were in charge of enforcing these rules, as they were often the only intermediaries between authorities and those who suffered most from lack of sanitation and urban services.

Social conflict over the uses and hierarchies of urban space also developed over public health. Official reactions oscillated between repression and neglect. In 1901 the Public Health Council indicated that a typhus epidemic had originated in the lower-class suburbs. According to the council these zones could not be sanitized unless enough policemen were available to compel their inhabitants to clean up garbage and feces. Resources, concluded the council, were insufficient to attend to both the city's suburbs and center.[112]

The poor however were aware both of danger and disease, and of the need to publicly challenge the authorities' allocation of resources. In 1901, residents of the First and Second Districts complained to the council that neglect at the Plazuela de Mixcalco was the cause of increasing mortality among them noting, "With all respect, we the subscribers inform you that we are suffering typhus, pneumonia and many other diseases whose exact name we ignore because we are ignorant of the science of medicine, . . . because of the harmful hygiene produced by the public dumpsite which the plaza known as Mixcalco located in front of our homes has become; we are invaded by a serious catastrophe of illnesses that are killing us with the electric violence of lightning . . . we thus ask to you to take the necessary measures to save us from the plague that is threatening us."[113]

Although the subscribers of the letters were only interested in street cleaning and sanitation, the city government saw the problem as one of morality. Unable to direct enough municipal resources toward the sanitation of the city's marginal areas, health authorities focused their reform attempts on changing the habits of the lower classes. Doctors denounced and prohibited practices like spitting, which they considered unhealthy. In 1902 the Public Health Council requested the city council to install spittoons in all public buildings to prevent the spread of tuberculosis, which the previous year had killed 2,013 people.[114] Inhabitants of tenement houses were advised to defecate in "portable buckets," which would be provided and collected every night by authorities. However, in 1907 the service was still not reliable in areas such as Tacubaya.[115] For authorities and observers like Julio Sesto, it was easy to blame high mortality rates on the dissipation, untidiness, and alcoholism of the urban poor.[116] Landlords were rarely mentioned as being responsible for these situations. As with the problem of alcohol consumption, it was easier to dwell on cultural explanations than to invest public resources or threaten private interests.

For city authorities, the police force was the best weapon for social reform. From their perspective, penal sanctions and police pressure could instill order and good behavior in the inhabitants of the city without changing the material conditions of their lives. A handwritten note attached to the papers concerning the discussion of traffic regulations at the city council in 1904 portrays this faith in the benefits of punishment. The author of the note, probably a council member, divided pedestrians into "cultivated persons" and "idem illiterate." The first group was to be taught about traffic rules through newspaper advertisements and signs; the second, by "insistent warnings, reprimands, constant admonishment by the police and penal sanction."[117]

Although Porfirian authorities devoted a large percentage of the city's budget to policing, it was not clear that the capital was safer by the end of the Porfiriato.[118] It was clear nevertheless that *gendarmes* (as policemen had been called since the late 1870s) were the most noticeable representatives of authority in everyday life. Police forces numbered around three thousand men and their presence was visible day and night at all downtown intersections, where police lanterns placed on the corners formed long lines and marked the areas under vigilance. Gendarmes were the key to maintaining official control of the city. They saw that pulquerías closed on time and that neighbors cleaned their streets. They were also in charge of keeping (or trying to keep) private practices out of public spaces. Among their duties, gendarmes were to prevent people from washing "clothes, dishes, buckets and other things at pipes and ditches, streets and public fountains," and to make sure that artisans did not perform their trades on the street.[119] The police also kept busy arresting couples "for having intercourse on the streets" and picking up sleeping drunkards.[120] This use of the police for "civilizing" purposes generated among the urban poor a clear sense that the "crimes" prosecuted by authorities differed according to the social background of the suspect.

One final example shows the limits of official policies in shaping the way people used the city. The debate over street nomenclature proved the reluctance of most inhabitants to passively accept urban modernization when it threatened the way in which they knew and walked the city. In 1888 the city council decided to change all street names, establishing "a nomenclature that was in harmony with the advances of the population." It was argued that the existing style (that in most cases gave one name to each block) was "irrational . . . absurd" and provoked the hilarity of foreign visitors. Observers argued that some names such as Tumbaburros, el Tomepate, and la Tecomaraña, were "ridiculous."[121] The proposed system divided the city along two axes that crossed one block east of the Alameda, identifying the streets by a number and a cardinal point. But the project soon provoked the opposition of various groups. The axes, argued critics at the city council, did not correspond with the middle of the city because of its asymmetrical growth and because "in the mind of all inhabitants" the center of the city was not a geometrical point but a "certain zone that now extends from the Alameda to the Plaza de la Constitución."[122]

When changes were enacted they provoked confusion and protests. People used both old and new street names simultaneously. In 1893, city authorities returned the signs with the old names to their places but did not eliminate the new names, which remained "official." The result was that streets had two names, in most cases the old one being used on a daily basis, the new one in official documents. Reactions to the reform varied: in the recently established colonias San Rafael, Santa María, and Guerrero the new names stuck, albeit temporarily, because people started using them. In even newer colonias like del Paseo, neighbors resisted the numeral system, preferring to use names of their own choosing. In colonias Condesa and Roma, the axis for the numbers was the Paseo de la Reforma instead of that established in 1888. According to Roberto Gayol, defender of the new system, the 1888 reform did not succeed because it lacked political support and because, in a number of new colonias, neighbors had been granted the de facto right to name streets as they pleased with no apparent intervention from city authorities.[123]

People continued to use the old names because they made more sense and corresponded with their way of viewing the city: a group of *rumbos*, or "directions" associated with important buildings or other urban markers rather than a grid. According to councilman Alberto Best, people knew the city well enough to make the numerical system unnecessary: "Each individual holds in his mind a number of streets that is enough for his business and occupations, and when he forgets or ignores one, it is easy to find it by only knowing the direction or proximity that it has with others that he still remembers." The geography of the city was learnt from infancy. In 1904 the city council recommended that the old system be reestablished, with the only reform being to unify the names of streets instead of traditional use whereby each block had its own name.[124]

City dwellers did not think of it as a centralized space but as a group of rumbos. Thus, the exchanges and movements that from the elite's perspective constituted an "invasion" of respectable areas, from the perspective of the urban poor were simply moving from one rumbo to another. Such movement in their view responded to immediate subsistence and sociability needs, and was not charged with the threat of social disorder. Nevertheless, by naming and walking the city in their own way, people undermined the model of rational order devised by Porfirian urbanists.

Judicial narratives attest to the meandering that preceded the committing of crimes. Leopoldo Villar gave police a detailed description of his movements the day he was arrested for theft: In the morning he went from his home in Malaga Street to the Hotel Regis to wait for a person who did not show up. He found his friend Emilio Vera instead, and they went to the Cine San Rafael. After the movie they walked by the Legislative Palace and, while Leopoldo was defecating near a construction site, Emilio found (he claimed) the wheel they were accused of stealing. They walked toward San Rafael Avenue, four blocks, and found some friends with whom they went to Las Artes Street, and then Leopoldo went to Mr. Arellano's house, in the sixth block of Miguel María Contreras, where he was arrested and then taken at 11:00 P.M. to the Eighth Police Inspection.[125] Since Leopoldo lacked a stable job, he had to keep moving across the city, hanging around with friends, and looking for an income. His disorderly use of the city made him a suspect. When forced to give an address, people used vague references to locate their place in the city. Nineteen percent of those arrested in the 1917–18 campaign against rateros declared no address, while others simply referred to a rumbo (for example, "la Ladrillera" for a brick-making facility).[126]

The lack of precision in the use of street names and addresses was also a way to evade authorities. The case of Josefina Ayala illustrates this tactic. She was arrested for begging in October 1930. Social workers of the Departamento de Beneficencia had to evaluate her ability to live by herself or be sustained by her family, but she gave them a false address, perhaps fearing that she or other members of her family might be further punished. She advised her son, Luis Barrios, not to use her name when visiting her in jail but to ask instead for Isabel Gómez (who was a friend of Josefina and also in prison) so he would not be detained for questioning, too.[127] Josefina had probably undergone something like the humiliating experience of Candelaria García, arrested in the same campaign: clothes burned, head shaved, sprayed with disinfectant, and forced to wear an asylum uniform.[128] Pressed by official harassment and the kind of economic hardship that forced Josefina to beg, the urban poor chose to use the city in their own way, crossing through the boundaries that were supposed to organize society and avoiding any contact with authorities.

Conclusion

Mexico City's particular brand of modernization was characterized by a permanent negotiation between the ideal city and the everyday city. Although most of the problems and policies described in this essay had antecedents in Mexico City's history (and still persist), the uniqueness of the late Porfiriato and early post-revolution resides in the clear confrontation between authoritarian regimes and a population which refused to accept elite divisions of urban space and norms of public behavior. Governments developed extensive projects to reshape urban geography and, as a consequence, the behavior of the subordinate groups. But such projects were undermined by demographic growth and technological changes. Several factors such as the development of a tramway network, the emergence of marginal colonias, and increased population density around downtown modified the lower classes' use of urban space. Besieged by unemployment, disease, and lacking water and appropriate housing, the urban poor invaded the respectable city despite the fact that the police constantly reminded them about the social divisions of the capital.

Thus, the dispute about the use of the city became a matter of crime and punishment. Many everyday practices became "criminal" in the eyes of elites and public officials. Lower-class neighborhoods were identified as zones of danger and disease. City authorities placed the police in charge of punishing the behaviors that challenged their idea of urban modernization. Other official efforts such as the extension of sanitation and control of alcohol consumption were limited by the restricted budgetary resources allotted to the marginal city and by officials' willingness to respect private interests. The profits created by real estate development and the pulque industry overrode the goals of social reform. It was easier and less costly to punish deviant behaviors and restrict the urban poor to the socially marginal areas of the capital. For the urban poor, on the other hand, justice could not be expected from above. They had to silently and constantly disregard regulations in order to survive in the city.

Abbreviations to Notes

AGN, FIM: Archivo General de la Nación, Fondo Presidente Francisco I. Madero, Mexico City

AGN, GPR: Archivo General de la Nación, Fondo Gobernación Período Revolucionario, Mexico City

AGN, PG: Archivo General de la Nación, Fondo Presidente Portes Gil, Mexico City

AGN, POC: Archivo General de la Nación, Fondo Presidentes Obregón-Calles, Mexico City

AGN, SJ: Archivo General de la Nación, Fondo Secretaría de Justicia, Mexico City

AHA: Archivo Histórico del Antiguo Ayuntamiento, Mexico City

AJ, RS: Archivo del Tribunal Superior de Justicia del Distrito Federal, Reclusorio Sur

APD: Archivo Porfirio Díaz, Universidad Iberoamericana, Mexico City

ASSA, SP: Archivo Histórico de la Secretaría de Salubridad y Asistencia, Fondo Salubridad Pública, Mexico City

Notes

1. This paper is part of my 1997 doctoral dissertation for the History Department of the University of Texas at Austin, "Criminals in Mexico City, 1900–1931: A Cultural History." I wish to thank Jonathan Brown, Ricardo Bracamonte, Fanny Cabrejo, Xóchitl Medina, Mauricio Tenorio, Pamela Voekel, and Elliott Young for their comments and corrections.

2. See Mauricio Tenorio-Trillo, "1910 Mexico City: Space and Nation in the City of the *Centenario*," *Journal of Latin American Studies* 28 (1996): 75–104; Barbara A. Tenenbaum, "Streetwise History: The Paseo de la Reforma and the Porfirian State, 1876–1910," in William H. Beezley et al., eds., *Rituals of Rule, Rituals of Resistance: Public Celebrations and Popular Culture in Mexico* (Wilmington: Scholarly Resources, 1994), 127–150 and in that same volume Tony Morgan, "Proletarians, Politicos, and Patriarchs: The Use and Abuse of Cultural Customs in the Early Industrialization of Mexico City, 1880–1910," 151–171; John Robert Lear, "Workers, *Vecinos* and Citizens: The Revolution in Mexico City, 1909–1917" (Ph.D. diss., University of California at Berkeley, 1993), chaps. 2 and 3 and a condensed version of that work in Lear, "Mexico City: Space and Class in the Porfirian Capital, 1884–1910," *Journal of Urban History* 22, no. 4 (May 1996): 444–492. A pioneering and still unmatched study of expansion is María Dolores Morales, "La expansión de la ciudad de México en el siglo XIX: el caso de los fraccionamientos," in Alejandra Moreno Toscano, ed., *Investigaciones sobre la historia de la ciudad de México* (Mexico City: INAH, 1974), 189–200; Mario Camarena, "El tranvía en época de cambio," *Historias* 27 (October–March 1992): 141–146; Estela Eguiarte Sakar, "Los jardines en México

y la idea de la ciudad decimonónica," *Historias* 27 (October–March 1992): 129–138. For a useful work on the Porfirian project of urban development applied in a state capital see Allen Wells and Gilbert M. Joseph, "Modernizing Visions, *Chilango* Blueprints, and Provincial Growing Pains: Mérida at the Turn of the Century," *Mexican Studies/Estudios Mexicanos* 8, no. 2 (Summer 1992): 167–215.

3. See Andrés Lira, *Comunidades indígenas frente a la ciudad de México: Tenochtitlán y Tlatelolco, sus pueblos y barrios, 1812–1919* (Mexico City: El Colegio de México, 1995), 262, 236, 238.

4. The name *colonia* derives from nineteenth-century colonization legislation. Jorge H. Jiménez Muñoz, *La traza del Poder: Historia de la política y los negocios urbanos en el Distrito Federal desde sus orígenes a la desaparición del Ayuntamiento (1824–1928)* (Mexico City: Codex, 1993), 9.

5. Public baths and flimsy constructions had to be destroyed to embellish and improve the entrance to colonia Roma. Report by city council member Luis E. Ruiz about the Eighth District, 19 enero 1904, AHA, Policía en general, 3644, 1691.

6. For the relationship between urban growth and social segregation among the inhabitants of the city, see María Dolores Morales, "La expansión de la ciudad de México (1858–1910)," in *Atlas de la ciudad de México* (Mexico City: Departamento del Distrito Federal-Colegio de México, 1987), 64.

7. Lira, *Comunidades indígenas*, 264.

8. See Lear, "Mexico City: Space and Class," 481–82. For the emergence of barrios out of Indian communities, see Lira, *Comunidades indígenas*, 66. On the irregular development of the colonia Obrera and its lack of sanitation, see "Informe general" by the Medical Inspector of the Fourth District, 31 diciembre 1924, ASSA, Fondo Salubridad Pública, Sección Salubridad del Distrito Federal, box 2, 28.

9. For the old uses, and the importance of water-sellers and fountains, see Antonio García Cubas, *El libro de mis recuerdos. Narraciones históricas, anecdóticas y de costumbres mexicanas anteriores al actual estado social, ilustradas con más de trescientos fotograbados* (Mexico City: Editorial Porrúa, 1986. 1st. ed., Imprenta de Arturo García Cubas, 1904), 207–214. Compare with Sandra Lauderdale-Graham, *House and Street: The Domestic World of Servants and Masters in Nineteenth-Century Rio de Janeiro* (Austin: University of Texas Press, 1992); Elizabeth Blackmar, *Manhattan for Rent, 1785–1850* (Ithaca: Cornell University Press, 1989).

10. AHA, Policía en general, 3640, 1143, 1 mayo 1896. For actions against *kioskos*, see AHA, Policía en general, 3640, 1147. See Juan Pedro Viqueira Albán, *¿Relajados o reprimidos?: Diversiones públicas y vida social en la ciudad de México durante el siglo de las luces* (Mexico City: Fondo de Cultura Económica, 1987); Pamela Voekel, "Peeing on the Palace: Bodily Resistance to Bourbon Reforms" (Ph.D dissertation, University of Texas at Austin, 1991); Jorge Nacif Mina, "Policía y seguridad pública en la ciudad de México, 1770–1848," in Regina Hernández Franyuti, comp., *La ciudad de México en la primera mitad del siglo XIX* (Mexico City: Instituto Mora, 1994), 9–50; Anne Staples, "Policía y Buen Gobierno: Municipal Efforts to Regulate Public Behavior, 1821–1910," in Beezley et al., eds., *Rituals of Rule*, 115–126.

11. *La Tribuna*, 16 octubre 1912. For a similar campaign in 1893, see Lear, "Workers, *Vecinos* and Citizens," 51, 55.

12. AHA, Policía en general, 3644, 1691.

13. *Estadísticas históricas de México*, vol. 1 (México: INEGI, 1994).

14. Ibid.

15. Ibid.; Dirección General de Estadística, *Censo general de la República Mexicana verificado el 20 de octubre de 1895* (Mexico City: Secretaría de Fomento, 1898).

16. Ibid.

17. Ibid; Departamento de la Estadística Nacional, *Censo de población, 15 de mayo de 1930* (Mexico City: Talleres Gráficos de la Nación, 1934).

18. *Estadísticas históricas de México*, 1:323.

19. *Censo general de la República Mexicana verificado el 20 de octubre de 1895.*

20. Ibid.

21. John H. Coatsworth, "El impacto económico de los ferrocarriles en una economía atrasada," in *Los orígenes del atraso. Nueve ensayos de historia económica de México en los siglos XVIII y XIX* (Mexico City: Alianza Editorial, 1990), 196–97. For an example of a short trip and a theft committed in the meanwhile, AJ-RS, 705331. For railroads replacing canoes, see Salvador Diego-Fernández, *La ciudad de Méjico a fines del siglo XIX* (Mexico City: n.e., 1937), 5.

22. Diego-Fernández, *La ciudad de Méjico*, 31.

23. Ibid., 12–13.

24. See Manuel Vidrio, "El transporte en la Ciudad de México en el siglo XIX," in *Atlas de la ciudad de México*, 68–71. The system expanded until the 1920's. Miguel Rodríguez, *Los tranviarios y el anarquismo en México (1920–1925)* (Puebla: Universidad Autónoma de Puebla, 1980), 66. For a valuable treatment of the historical role of tramways in a Latin American city, see Anton Rosenthal, "The Arrival of the Electric Streetcar and the Conflict over Progress in Early Twentieth-Century Montevideo," *Journal of Latin American Studies* 27 (1995): 319–341.

25. *El Universal*, 1 octubre 1920, p. 9. Evidence on the relative price of fares is inconclusive. In 1902 the usual expense in tramway fares for a worker was twenty-four cents and it probably included several trips. AHA, Policía en general, 3643, 1600; *El Imparcial*, 11 agosto 1902, p. 1. In 1920, according to the Compañía de Tranvías de México, the average fare was 9.5 cents, not enough according to the company, to cover costs. *El Universal*, 1 octubre 1920, p. 9. Prices increased during the late Porfiriato and the 1910s. See request of municipal employees for free tramway passes. Celadores Municipales del Ramo de Policía to the city council, 23 abril 1901, AHA, Policía en general, 3642, 1353. According to Spanish writer Julio Sesto, daily wages in the late 1900s for journeymen seamstresses or cigar factory workers was one peso. Policemen made 1.75 pesos a day. Julio Sesto, *El México de Porfirio Díaz (hombres y cosas) Estudios sobre el desenvolvimiento general de la República Mexicana. Observaciones hechas en el terreno oficial y en el particular* (2. ed., Valencia: Sempere y Compañia, 1910), 134–136.

26. Angel de Campo, *Ocios y apuntes y La rumba* (Mexico City: Porrúa, 1976), 199.

27. Eaton Smith, *Flying Visits to the City of Mexico and the Pacific Coast* (Liverpool: Henry Young and Sons, 1903), 30–34.

28. AHA, Policía en general, 3644, 1689.

29. For a case of a driver who ran over a two-year-old child and walked free after two hours with the help of court employees, see H. J. Teufer to Porfirio

Díaz, 8 febrero 1911, APD, 36, 2216-2217. See more complaints in *Gaceta de Policia*, 1:2, 19 octubre 1905, p. 3; ibid., 1:10, 24 diciembre 1905, p. 2.

30. AHA, Policía en general, 3639, 1092; Carlos Roumagnac, *Los criminales en México: Ensayo de psicología criminal. Seguido de dos casos de hermafrodismo observado por los señores doctores Ricardo Egea . . . Ignacio Ocampo* (1904; reprint, Mexico City: Tipografía El Fénix, 1912), 11, 14; *Gaceta de Policia*, 1:9, 17 diciembre 1905, p. 9.

31. *Memoria del Ayuntamiento 1901* (Mexico City: La Europea, 1902, 2 vol.), 1:505. Governor of the Federal District to city council, 22 diciembre 1898, AHA, Policía en General, 3639, 1222.

32. Enrique Ignacio Castelló to the city council, 2 agosto 1904, AHA, Policía en general, 3644, 1689.

33. See José Juan Tablada, *La feria de la vida* (1937; reprint, México: Consejo Nacional para la Cultura y las Artes, 1991).

34. Manuel Gutiérrez Nájera, "La novela del tranvía," in *La novela del tranvía y otros cuentos* (Mexico City: Secretaría de Educación Pública, 1984), 159.

35. AHA, Policía en general, 3643, 1600, clipping from *El Imparcial*, 11 agosto 1902, p. 1.

36. Sesto, *El México de Porfirio Díaz*, 245; Ramírez Plancarte, *La ciudad de México durante la revolución constitucionalista*, 426–27. For the multiple social strata among vecindad tenants in the early nineteenth century, see Jaime Rodríguez Piña, "Las vecindades en 1811: Tipología," in Alejandra Moreno Toscano et al., *Investigaciones sobre la historia de la ciudad de México (II)* (Mexico City: INAH, 1976): 68–82.

37. *El Imparcial*, 6 julio 1908, p. 4.

38. *Nueva Era*, 9 julio 1912, p. 4.

39. AHA, Policía en general, 3643, 1600, clipping from *El Imparcial*, 11 agosto 1902, p. 1. According to the Comisión Monetaria, in 1891 there were 8,883 houses in the city and by 1902 the number had increased to 11,024. José Lorenzo Cossío, "Algunas noticias sobre las colonias de esta capital," *Boletín de la Sociedad Mexicana de Geografía y Estadística* 47, no. 1 (septiembre 1937): 11.

40. For conditions in mesones see Morales Martínez, "La expansión de la ciudad de México," 68; ASSA, Beneficencia Pública, Sección Asistencial, Serie Asilados y Mendigos, 8, 8, f. 2; ibid, 9, 21; Lear, "Mexico City: Space and Class," 478–79. The case of Toledo in AJ-RS, 84, 518303. See the case of a *mesón* whose owner was fined in 1906 because of bad hygienic conditions: lack of running water, exposed and clogged sewers, common bathrooms, overcrowding, garbage that was not disposed of daily, holes in the roof and floors. ASSA, Salubridad Pública, Sección Salubridad del Distrito Federal, box. 1, 24. Many of the alleged beggars arrested in 1930 lived in *mesones*, ASSA, Beneficencia Pública, Sección Asistencial, Serie Asilados y Mendigos.

41. *Memoria del ayuntamiento de 1901*, 2:275–276.

42. Blanca Ugarte to the city council, 31 agosto 1920, ASSA, Fondo Establecimientos Asistenciales, Dormitorios Públicos, 1, 5.

43. Miguel Macedo, *La criminalidad en México: Medios de combatirla* (Mexico City: Secretaría de Fomento, 1897), 14–15; Luis Lara y Pardo, *La prostitución en México* (Mexico City: Bouret, 1908), 120–21; Pani, *La higiene en México*, 111, 221. These descriptions were not always based on direct observation.

44. Marcela Dávalos, "La salud, el agua y los habitantes de la ciudad de México. Fines del siglo XVIII y principios del XIX," in Hernández Franyuti, comp., *La*

ciudad de México en la primera mitad del siglo XIX, 300, 281. See also Ilán Semo, "La ciudad tentacular: notas sobre el centralismo en el siglo XX," in Isabel Tovar de Arechederra and Magdalena Mas, eds., *Macrópolis mexicana* (Mexico City: Universidad Iberoamericana-Consejo Nacional para la Cultura y las Artes-DDF, 1994), 48.

45. For drainage systems, ASSA, Salubridad Pública, Sección Salubridad del Distrito Federal, box. 1, 33.

46. Diego-Fernández, *La ciudad de Méjico*, 4. For a description of *baños públicos* in Lagunilla and Juárez, see vice president of the junta inspectora de la Beneficencia Pública to secretary of gobernación, 16 agosto 1913, AGN, Fondo Gobernación Período Revolucionario, 115, 77, 1. See also ASSA, Fondo Establecimientos Asistenciales, Baños y Lavaderos Públicos, 1, 15; for the regulations of the public baths of La Lagunilla, see ibid., 2, 11.

47. In October 1917, AHA, Policía Presos Penitenciaría, 3664, 1. For Bourbon official concern about these issues, see Voekel, "Peeing on the Palace"; Dávalos, "La salud, el agua y los habitantes de la ciudad de México," 292.

48. M. Río de la Loza to the city council, 27 diciembre 1892, AHA, Policía en General, 3639, 1020.

49. Report of the housing committees to the city council, 15 mayo 1901, AHA, Policía en general, 3642, 1354.

50. Report of health inspector A. Romero to Public Health Council, 10 enero 1902, ASSA, SP, SDF, box 1, 22.

51. Report by council member Luis E. Ruiz on the Eighth District, 19 abril 1904, AHA, Policía en general, 3644, 1691.

52. AJ-RS, 705331. For the linking of thirst and alcohol consumption, see *El Imparcial*, 29 enero 1906, p. 1.

53. Serge Gruzinski, *La colonización de lo imaginario: Sociedades indígenas y occidentalización en el México español, siglos XVI-XVIII* (Mexico City: Fondo de Cultura Económica, 1991), 272–275. See also Viqueira Albán, *¿Relajados o reprimidos?*, 191 and passim.

54. Roumagnac, *Los criminales en México*, 282.

55. José María Marroqui, *La ciudad de México. Contiene: El origen de los nombres de muchas de sus calles y plazas, del de varios establecimientos públicos y privados, y no pocas noticias curiosas y entretenidas* (Mexico City: La Europea, 1900), 3:189-211. For the lack of control by authorities of the spaces of collective drinking in Mexico City, see Virginia Guedea, "México en 1812: Control político y bebidas prohibidas," *Estudios de historia moderna y contemporánea de México* 8 (1980): 23–64.

56. García Cubas, *El libro de mis recuerdos*, 221–22.

57. City council to José González Parres, 7 diciembre 1907, AHA, Bebidas embriagantes, 1337, 397. The 1902 Reglamento de Bebidas Embriagantes established an area of "first category" alcohol outlets around the center of the city, where *cantinas* had to follow stricter hygienic norms and were allowed to remain open longer than those in the rest of the city, the "second category" area, AHA, Bebidas embriagantes, 1332, 115.

58. See examples of these restrictions in AHA, Bebidas embriagantes, 1332, 115.

59. Andrea Coquis to city council, 1 abril 1916, AHA, Policía en general, 3645, 1777; for seizures and arrests related to unauthorized selling of pulque, AHA, Gobernación, 1112, 120 bis y 121 bis.

60. AHA, Gobernación, 1118, 4.

61. Letter signed by "comerciantes de abarrotes y cantina," 16 junio 1909, AHA, Bebidas Embriagantes, 1338, 511; also Gervasio Suárez to city council, 24 julio 1911, AHA, Bebidas Embriagantes, 1341, 699. For the Porfirian litera-ture about alcoholism, see Pablo Piccato, " 'El Paso de Venus por el disco del Sol': Criminality and Alcoholism in the Late Porfiriato," *Mexican Studies/Estudios Mexicanos* 11, no. 2 (Summer 1995): 203–241.

62. Secretaría de gobernación to governor of the Federal District, 7 junio 1913, AHA, 1781, 1130. See Juan Felipe Leal and Mario Huacuja Rountree, *Economía y sistema de haciendas en México: La hacienda pulquera en el cambio: Siglos XVIII, XIX y XX* (Mexico City: Ediciones Era, 1982).

63. Antonio Aura to the city council, 4 abril 1899, AHA, Policía en general, 3641, 1240; for a license for a phonograph operator, AHA, Policía en general, 3639, 1060; for one to sell food, AHA, Policía en general, 3640, 1145.

64. *El Universal*, 16 febrero 1917, p. 1. *El Universal*, 13 enero 1917, p. 6. See also AHA, Sección Bebidas embriagantes.

65. ASSA, Beneficencia Pública, Sección Asistencial, Serie Asilados y Mendigos, f. 7.

66. Salvador Diego-Fernández, *La ciudad de Méjico*, 4; Marcela Dávalos, "La salud, el agua y los habitantes de la ciudad de México," 280.

67. Merchants of Empedradillo Street to city council, 23 agosto 1894, AHA, Policía en General, 3640, 1179. For the census figure, see Dirección General de Estadística, *Censo general de la Republica Mexicana verificado el 28 de octubre de 1900* (Mexico City: Secretaría de Fomento, 1901–1907).

68. See the case of *vendedores ambulantes* outside the Martínez de la Torre market, removed by order of the authority in 1901, AHA, Policía en general, 3642, 1371.

69. Tomasa Pérez and seven more women to the president of the city council, 3 julio 1915, AHA, Policía en general, 3645, 1768.

70. For merchants' resistance to inspectors in the San Lucas market, see Comisión de Mercados to the city council, 24 febrero 1899, AHA, Policía en general, 3641, 1266.

71. Neighbors and landlords of Santo Domingo to the city council, 26 julio 1901, AHA, Policía en general, 3642, 1360.

72. Santos Cisneros and thirty-three more to the city council, 11 noviembre 1897, AHA, Policía en general, 3640, 1180.

73. *Memoria del ayuntamiento de 1901*, 2:39–41.

74. *La Voz de México*, 29 enero 1890, p. 2.

75. City council to governor of the Federal District, 17 agosto 1911, AHA, Policía en general, 3644, 1699.

76. *El Imparcial*, 2 enero 1900, p. 3.

77. Ibid., 3 julio 1908, p. 1.

78. Smith, *Flying Visits*, 72–73.

79. *El Imparcial*, 1 abril 1897, p. 2.

80. *El Universal*, 24 diciembre 1916, p. 3. Carlos M. Patiño, 4 junio 1912, AHA, Policía en General, 3645, 1704; and reply by Comisión de Policía, ibid; Beneficencia Pública del Distrito Federal, *La mendicidad en México* (Mex-ico City: Departamento de Acción Educativa Eficiencia y Catastros Sociales, 1931).

81. AHA, Policía Presos Penitenciaría, 3664, 2; *Nueva Era*, 3 julio 1912, p. 4.

82. Proposal of city council member Algara to the city council, 25 febrero 1895, and reply from police inspectors, AHA, Policía en general, 3639, 1092; Inspector of the Fifth District to the city council, 7 abril 1895, ibid. See also the remarkable descriptions of social workers in 1930 in ASSA, Beneficencia Pública, Sección Asistencial, Serie Asilados y Mendigos.

83. *El Imparcial*, 18 julio 1912, p. 7.

84. *El Universal*, 3 julio 1930, p. 3a.

85. For some cases among many "campaigns" against *rateros*, see *El Imparcial*, 12 octubre 1897; *Gaceta de Policía*, 24 diciembre. 1905, p. 2; *El Universal*, 3 enero 1917, p. 5; AGN, Presidentes Obregón y Calles, 121-G-I-4.

86. Lira, *Comunidades indígenas*, 26–28, 236.

87. Morales, "La expansión de la ciudad de México," 190–91, cited by Lira, *Comunidades indígenas*, 240.

88. On the disappearance of the early-nineteenth-century markers of the outer limits of the city see García Cubas, *El libro de mis recuerdos*, 231. On the pulque *garitas*, see Guerrero, *El pulque*, 118.

89. Nacif, "Policía y seguridad pública," 33. The wider area and less precise limits of the city are clearly seen by a comparing maps of 1886 and 1906: Antonio García Cubas, *Plano topográfico de la ciudad de México formado por el ingeniero Antonio García Cubas con las nuevas calles abiertas hasta la fecha y los ferrocarriles* (Mexico City: Antigua librería de M. Murguía, 1886) and *Plano oficial de la Ciudad de México. Edición especial para el Consejo Superior de Gobierno del Distrito Federal, con motivo de la reunión del X Congreso Geológico Internacional* (n.e.: 1906).

90. *El Imparcial*, 16 julio 1912, p. 1; *La Nación*, 2 septiembre 1912, p. 1–2; *El Universal*, 21 octubre 1916, p. 3.

91. Diego-Fernández, *La ciudad de Méjico*, 5; *Gaceta de Policía*, 24 diciembre 1905, p. 2; Macedo, *La criminalidad en México*, 14–16, 4–7.

92. Comisión de Obras Públicas to the city council, 18 mayo 1900, AHA, Policía en general, 3641, 1289.

93. *El Imparcial*, 6 enero 1900, p. 2. Animals used for transportation added to the problem, as in Montevideo. Rosenthal, "The Arrival of the Electric Streetcar," 323.

94. Neighbors also complained about "la enorme cantidad de perros vagabundos que además de dar mala nota de la población y causar grandes molestidas al vecindario, constituyen un serio peligro, especialmente para los niños en la estación calurosa," Mixcoac neighbors to Public Health Council, 31 enero 1907, ASSA, Fondo Salubridad Pública, Sección Salubridad del Distrito Federal, box 1, 36.

95. Cossío, "Algunas noticias sobre las colonias," 5–9; Agustín Avila Méndez, "Mapa serie barrios de la ciudad de México 1811 y 1882," in Alejandra Moreno Toscano et al., *Investigaciones sobre la historia de la ciudad de México (I)* (Mexico City: INAH, 1974), 155–181. For the complex history of the relationship between the Indian *barrios* of the capital and the central city, see Lira, *Comunidades indígenas*.

96. AHA, Policía en general, 3643, 1600, clipping of *El Imparcial*, 11 agosto 1902, p. 1.

97. Smith, *Flying visits*, 28–29.

98. ASSA, SP, Epidemias, 32, 12.

99. *México y sus alrededores. Guía para los viajeros escrita por un Mexicano. Cuidado con los rateros* (Mexico City: Tip. Luis B. Casa, 1895), 15.

100. The quote from *El Universal*, 16 febrero 1917, p. 1. Antonio Padilla Arroyo, *Criminalidad, cárceles y sistema penitenciario en México, 1876–1910* (Ph.D. dissertation, El Colegio de México, 1995), 86–87.

101. Smith, *Flying Visits*, 41–42, 26.

102. AHA, Bebidas embriagantes, 1331, 41, f. 1.

103. *El Imparcial*, 3 julio 1908, p. 1; AGN, Fondo Secretaría de Justicia, vol. 893, exp. 4337.

104. Roumagnac, *Crímenes sexuales y pasionales: Estudios de psicología morbosa*, vol. 1, *Crímenes sexuales* (Mexico City: Librería de Bouret, 1906), 91.

105. Diego-Fernández, *La ciudad de Méjico*, 4; Cossío, "Algunas noticias sobre las colonias," 26–29; Lear, "Workers, *Vecinos* and Citizens," 56–58.

106. See Jiménez, *La traza del poder*, 191–92.

107. Cossío, "Algunas noticias sobre las colonias," 23, 31.

108. Ariel Rodríguez Kuri, *La experiencia olvidada. El ayuntamiento de México: Política y administración, 1876–1912* (Mexico City: El Colegio de México, 1996); Jiménez, *La traza*, 19, 88n.

109. See García Cubas, *El libro de mis recuerdos*, 146. For the 1903 reform and its consequences, see AHA, Policía en general, 3645, 1701. The city council's authority was greatly reduced by legal reforms in 1903 and disappeared in 1929. The institution also had to negotiate many important decisions with the governor of the Federal District, appointed by the president. See Rodríguez, *La experiencia olvidada*.

110. AHA, Policía en general, 3642, 1427.

111. Miguel Vega y Vera to the city council, 24 febrero 1892, AHA, Policía en general, 3639, 1014. Several frustrated contracts up to 1889 show the reluctance of the city council to take street cleaning under its direct responsibility, AHA, Policía en general, 3639, 1028; ibid., 3639, 1071; ibid, 3640, 1193. In 1898, prisoners swept the streets of the city, although lacking enough tools, AHA, Policía en general, 3639, 1231.

112. Public Health Council to the city council, 27 septiembre 1901, AHA, Policía en general, 3642, 1368.

113. Twenty-seven signatures to Public Health Council, 13 abril 1901, AHA, Policía en general, 3642, 1420.

114. Public Health Council to city council, 5 junio 1902, AHA, Policía en general, 3643, 1534.

115. ASSA, Salubridad Pública, Sección Salubridad del Distrito Federal, box 1, 35.

116. Sesto, *El México de Porfirio Díaz*, 231–234.

117. AHA, Policía en general, 3644, 1689.

118. That is the conclusion of Laurence John Rohlfes, "Police and Penal Correction in Mexico City, 1876–1911: A Study of Order and Progress in Porfirian Mexico" (Ph.D. dissertation, Tulane University, 1983). Published statistics of crime, however, suggest otherwise. For police budgets, see Manuel González de Cosío, *Memoria que presenta al Congreso de la Unión el General . . . Secretario de Estado y del Despacho de Gobernación* (México: Imprenta del Gobierno Federal, 1900), appendix, 804–811.

119. "Reglamento de las obligaciones del gendarme," [1897], González de Cosío, *Memoria que presenta*, appendix, 767. The use of policemen for these

purposes dates back to the role of *"celadores"* and *"vigilantes"* in the late colonial era, Nacif, "Policía y seguridad pública," 14.

120. AHA, Policía Presos Penitenciaría, 3664, 3 and 4.

121. *México y sus alrededores*, 5, 13–14.

122. *Documentos relativos a la nomenclatura de calles y numeración de casas de la ciudad de México* (Mexico City: La Europea, 1904), 35–36.

123. Ibid., 28, 32, 38, 48–49.

124. Ibid., 102–03, 25, 80–82.

125. AJ-RS, 1067901, 2.

126. AHA, Vagos y rateros, 4157 to 4160. On the meaning of walking the city, Michel de Certeau, *The Practice of Everyday Life*, trans. Steven Rendall (Berkeley: University of California Press, 1984).

127. Josefina was finally released after four months in prison, ASSA, Fondo Beneficencia Pública, Sección Asistencia, 6, 3. For a similar case of an address that did not exist, ibid., 6, 29.

128. Candelaria García to Josefa Castro, 14 octubre 1930, ASSA, Fondo Beneficencia Pública, Sección Asistencia, 7, 7.

7

Not Guilty: Abortion and Infanticide in Nineteenth-Century Argentina

Kristin Ruggiero

As in Mexico, the late nineteenth century in Argentina was the heyday of order and progress. But the elite obsession with order and progress did not always mean the same thing for women as it did for men. Kristin Ruggiero, associate professor of history at the University of Wisconsin at Milwaukee, examines social and legal reactions to two typically female crimes in late-nineteenth-century Argentina: abortion and infanticide. This was a period during which new legal and medical discourses (positivist criminology, for instance) merged with traditional views of morality, honor, and gender "nature" and roles.

Ruggiero finds that a notion such as female "honor" superseded other criteria—such as the defense of human life or the sacredness of the law— in the definition of culpability in cases of abortion and infanticide. Perpetrators of those crimes could find echo among judges to their claim that they had committed them in defense of their honor. Why was this the case? Why would a society choose not to punish—or punish leniently— women culpable of these crimes? By considering them "not guilty," Ruggiero argues, Argentine justice tried to reinforce a view that rewarded the defense of female honor and emphasized society's obligation to "protect" it: the supreme goal was not social and moral restitution or vengeance, but instead the defense of the moral order needed to guarantee social stability and progress. In that sense, the protection of women's "honor" was a special gendered case that superseded more general concerns about criminality.

The stakes for the accused in Argentine criminal trials of abortion and infanticide were usually high—not so much in their final sentences, but rather in their ability to confirm or deny honor. The discourse in these trials led to discussions and qualifications of social morality, specifically women's sexual honor, and of all circumstances surrounding reproduction. The cases show that the principle of honor was highly respected, sometimes even at the expense of life. Legislators, jurists, and forensic medical doctors, when faced with a woman's struggle to avoid her "social death" and "civil excommunication" through her loss of honor, had to choose whether to sacrifice the law to public opinion or public opinion to the law.

In the eyes of morality, the woman committing abortion or infanticide was guilty. But moral law was considered a higher law, an inappropriate standard for social law. The state represented reason and progress; and, said one lawyer, rational science demanded that social law take into account the woman's "position, her interior struggles, the motives that made her commit the crime, the culpability itself of her sex."[1] The courts heard the cases of many domestic servants and women of all classes who were unmarried, fearful of losing their jobs and/or reputations, and who were generally considered weak, impressionable, and driven by the irrationality of their "maternal organs." Not only did the woman's position have to be taken into account in sentencing, but also that of the fetus and child. The evil of the sentence, Jeremy Bentham, the nineteenth-century English jurist and philosopher wrote, had to be compared to that of the crime. "The *crime*, that is, the death of a child who ceased to exist before having known existence, could only cause feelings of commiseration for the person who, out of shame and compassion, did not want the child to grow up under such sad auspices. The *sentence*, on the other hand, was a barbarous and offensive torture imposed on an unfortunate mother blinded by desperation, who [had] harmed almost no one except herself."[2]

There remained a strong sentiment to protect infanticidal women from the harsher punishments incurred by the classification of a crime as homicide. But at the same time the idea grew that these women, at least (or especially) the reincidents, were organically degenerate. These ideas were being developed in the wider scientific world to which Argentina belonged as a newly sovereign, developing state. It was a world committed to the separation of medical and legal principles from theological and philosophical ones, and to controlling and improving society by means of new sciences such as hygiene, public medicine, and criminology. The incomplete mother and illegitimate family failed to provide a solid basis for the state and had the potential to infect and contaminate it. Qualifying and mitigating a woman's guilt, making her in a sense "not guilty," based on a respect for honor, maternity, and scientific innovations, was thus a large part of the legal and medical professionals' task of tutelage over the state's human capital, whose morality was so important to the stability and progress of society.

Abortion: The Case of the Criminal Midwife

It looked like Antonia Schoeller had gotten away with it. When she was quickly and quietly buried in 1882 in the Protestant cemetery of Buenos Aires (where her body did not need a coroner's certificate as it would have in the Catholic cemetery), her German fiancé, family, and midwife, María Baby, felt confident that the criminal abortion she had chosen, which had accidentally ended her life, would not be discovered.[3] But an anonymous neighbor disguised in a heavy veil reported it to a newspaper office, and the editor told the police, who arrested them all. Antonia had done what contemporary practice recommended in order to abort without having to resort to more dangerous mechanical means. She had taken footbaths, quinine, and drastics, but they were ineffective. She had also considered having the child in the campo, then Palermo or Belgrano, and giving it to her married sister to raise as her own, as well as depositing the child at the foundling home. However, because of her shame and because she could not bear to see her pregnancy through to term, she rejected both these alternatives. The first midwife Antonia visited refused to perform the abortion, telling her that "the sweetness and beauty of motherhood would surely console her for all the punishments she would suffer and for the scorn of her family," and that perhaps her fiancé would marry her when he saw his child. But Antonia's fiancé had already made it known that he could not marry her until his economic situation improved, and rather than the "sweetness of maternity" without a husband, she preferred suicide. So she and her fiancé allegedly hired a midwife for about 2000 pesos to provoke an abortion with a probe (the most secure method), which caused inflammation and hemorrhage, and ended in death.[4]

Criminal abortion was a hard crime to detect. Antonia, while alive, was examined by four doctors and two midwives; and after death, two autopsies were performed on her corpse. But there was still not a consensus of opinion about whether she had experienced a birth or an abortion, and thus no agreement about whether her death had been caused by post-birth illness or complications from a provoked abortion. The first autopsy doctor found evidence of dilation of the uterus and lesions, pointing to the possibility of a provoked abortion. Insecure about his findings though, the doctor requested that a second examination be done, this time by the president of the Council of Public Hygiene.[5] The second doctor was convinced that the abortion had been performed with a probe or similar instrument, and that death was due to the inflammation it produced. Since one of his public hygiene goals was to professionalize and "moralize" the profession of midwifery in Buenos Aires, perhaps it is not surprising that he denounced the midwife María Baby as the author of the abortion.

Forensic doctors lamented modern gynecology's discovery of the probe, the abortive par excellence, he said, because it allowed midwives to actually "own" the agent of their "immoral commerce."[6] Thus did María Baby fall victim to his campaign.

Suspicion about midwives' practices, motives, and professionalism was widespread among doctors, hygienists, jurists, and police. It was assumed that midwives regularly traded in illegitimate births and abortions, thus helping to cover up patients' and their lovers' "mistakes." It was also assumed that midwives, for an added fee, would personally take charge of depositing an illegitimate child in the foundling home. Midwives were also known to keep jars of preserved fetuses to use in cases where confirmation of a dead birth was needed. While we have evidence that all this is true, it only represents part of the function of midwives. Midwives also provided expert help to women for the many problems associated with menstruation, pregnancy, birth, and illnesses of the genital organs. Women generally believed that midwives were more skilled than doctors in treating female conditions, and also that, for the sake of modesty, they were more appropriate than male doctors. Besides, Antonia's experience aside, women did not necessarily have to resort to midwives for help in aborting. The same remedies that "lowered the flow" when menstruation was suspended were also efficacious in bringing about contractions and an abortion.[7]

Society's general suspicion of midwives was seen in the abortion law. Doctors, surgeons, and pharmacists, along with midwives, could be prosecuted under this law, but in reality only midwives were charged. As María Baby's lawyer pointed out, the Council of Public Hygiene had not accused the doctors in the case, who were also in some sense culpable of malpractice, though they did not actually perform the abortion. Punishment for professionals was three to six years' penitentiary and disqualification from practicing for double the time. The sentence was less for nonprofessional accomplices, which meant that accused women often attempted to deny that they practiced midwifery professionally. In María Baby's case this would have been impossible as she had a plaque on her door. The sentence for the aborting woman herself was one to three years in prison, which was reduced to one year if she had the excuse of dishonor and had provoked the abortion herself or agreed to it. The penalty for accomplices was reduced if the woman had given her consent, but this seemed to be used only to attenuate the guilt of relatives, neighbors, or lovers and not that of the midwife.[8] When a patient died as a result of the abortion—technically indicating her lack of consent—the maximum of six years was imposed on the midwife, which was María Baby's sentence.

As for Antonia, the court in effect posthumously tried her and established that she had procured an abortion to hide her dishonor.

The concept of honor was an essential element in many judicial cases, especially abortion and infanticide, calumny, dueling, and adultery, and in much juridical writing in the nineteenth century. Generally, honor referred to the good reputation that followed from virtue; and in women, to the honesty and modesty and the good opinion that they gained with these virtues. Both upper and lower classes could have honor, but often it was assumed that the sentiment was more developed in "superior" classes because of its abstract nature and complexity.[9] Dishonor, that is, the loss of honor and reputation, was described as a type of "civil excommunication." To invoke the "privilege" of the motive of honor, a woman had to demonstrate that she in fact had honor to lose—in the words of court cases "that she was honest or taken as such and that the necessity of hiding her dishonor be credible." This was translated in infanticide cases to mean that if the accused woman had previously had an illegitimate child, she had lost the right to invoke the honor clause.[10]

Why did this concept of dishonor have so much power to mitigate and excuse? In Antonia's case she was young and unmarried with an illegitimate pregnancy. Her lover of four years could not or would not marry her at the time, though he would pay for an abortion. She earned a living as a seamstress in private homes, probably for people who had contracted to do piecework for larger workshops. As her pregnancy advanced, her shame would have become obvious and she would have had to quit work. She could have chosen to see her pregnancy through by wearing loose dresses and tight corsets, and simulated "suspended menstruation" if questioned about her growing size; she could have given birth in secret and taken the child to the foundling home. Although women successfully simulated nonpregnancy, they considered it risky to use the foundling home because they might be seen. In any case, many women felt that the foundling home was a wretched place where children frequently died on the *torno* (turntable), the supposedly anonymous delivery system, before they even encountered the home's internal unhealthiness.[11] And, the legal code's "dishonor" clause recognized society's sentence of "social death" for women faced with giving birth to an illegitimate child.

There were no extenuating circumstances, however, for midwives. The courts allowed doctors, pharmacists, phlebotomists (professional bloodletters), and so on, to claim extenuating circumstances for malpractice— such as misinformation given to them by a patient, the lack of cleanliness in a patient's home, or concern for a patient's modesty—but midwives' appeals based on the same excuses were discounted as if they were not professionals, as if they were somehow more culpable. Yet when it came to sentencing, midwives were considered equal to other professionals. As midwives were pressed to become more professional in the nineteenth century, they increasingly voiced anger at their treatment. A midwife, newly-arrived in Córdoba, Argentina, from Switzerland, with diplomas from Switzerland and Uruguay and a recertification in Argentina, trying to build her reputation, was arrested for countermanding a doctor's prescription for leeches for his married female patient.[12] The doctor's diagnosis was that she was suffering from a hemorrhaging uterus, and he had ordered eight leeches to be applied to the woman's groin to relieve her "congestion" by bleeding. He had marked the location for the leeches in ink and had called for a midwife to apply them, out of modesty he said, though the midwife claimed that he had already "offended the laws of modesty" and should have merely designated the selected anatomical area to her verbally.

The midwife, convinced that the patient was pregnant and suffering from an imminent abortion, suggested to the woman's family that the leech treatment be suspended and instead recommended baths to produce "looseness in the tissues and muscles in order to facilitate the emission of the coagulated blood." "This blood doesn't serve life," she explained, "and if it remains there, it not only brings about its own corruption, but also that of the fetus, with serious problems for the mother." If the doctor had actually given her a written prescription, she told the judge, she would have followed his instructions and applied the leeches, knowing that she would be absolved of responsibility if anything happened to the patient. Moreover, the midwife argued, it was common practice for phlebotomists, pharmacists, and obstetricians, when in doubt, to suspend a doctor's prescribed treatment or remedy. She concluded, "I am a victim of the doctor's wounded vanity in a branch of science to which he perhaps hasn't dedicated much study. I was just joking when I told the women at the house that we women know more in certain cases than the doctors themselves. Women in all countries say this. I wasn't being criminal. But I'll bet I'm the only person who has had these words twisted into a crime." Her incarceration in a house of correction, where she was treated "like an infamous [perpetrator of] infanticide," had "defamed" her, and she demanded that the judge vindicate her honor, which had been "cruelly stained." He allowed her to leave the correctional and spend the rest of the trial in a private house before finally absolving her a year later.

This midwife held three certificates; she came from Europe, regarded as being considerably more medically advanced than Argentina; and she was undoubtedly one of the few certified midwives that Córdoba could boast of at this time. But she was quite obviously vulnerable nervertheless, in spite of her professionalism. It seems that even with the closer integration of midwives into the state system of medical training and controls, they continued to experience their profession's traditional suspicion and scorn. That is, their "reward" for joining the ranks of certified health care professionals, for getting a certificate and registering with the Council of Public Hygiene, seemed to be principally their subjection to greater surveillance and thus possible punishment. María Baby, Antonia Schoeller' midwife, was part of the system, too, well-trained and certified in France. But the judge sentenced her to six years' penitentiary, the maximum penalty; permanent disqualification as a midwife and disqualification for nine years from performing public charges; civil interdiction for six years; and payment of all court costs.

Prosecution of criminal abortion provides a good example of the incursion of male-directed science into a female-directed and "prescientific" traditional practice. Often the harsh treatment of midwives is explained by doctors closing ranks in order to eliminate traditional practices from "modern" medicine. Or perhaps harsh treatment also answered society's need to compensate for all that was not understood and mysterious in times when new medical knowledge was presenting the justice system with difficult questions, often without answers. If the unknowns and mysteries could be attributed to the midwife's immorality and lack of skill, so much the better.

In addition to this scientific and professional argument, there was the less elevated one of the long-standing suspicion of collusion between midwives and their female clients to deceive male society. This was part of a more fundamental contrast that was made between female and male delinquency. Man—by his nature, by his need to earn a living, by the "energy of his passions," and by his "robust physiological organization" —committed crimes of blood or against property. Women were constituted in another way. When a woman's moral sense was not sufficiently developed she committed crimes against "honesty" by "delivering her body to prostitution," or, "when her sexual passions were quenched, by serving strange passions, or performing analogous acts such as abortions and infanticides." This was her "natural and characteristic delinquency."[13] Now we have a picture of the midwife as nonprofessional, nonscientific, in league with her female patients to undermine the reproductive capabilities of society, and susceptible to certain types of criminality. As such, midwives were often made the more subtle means than outright condemnation through which to attack social immorality.

This was part of the larger commitment made in the national constitution to a person's right to "life, liberty, and honor."[14] The intent of the new law codes was not to unnecessarily endanger personal honor. Thus, the justice system was not to intervene in questions of morality except when the criminal was successful, that is, when a material act existed that could be judged. "Mistaken signs and indecorous investigations, such as happen with abortion" should not then be allowed to come to light easily.[15] This helps explain the abolition of defaming penalties in the new codes. It also puts into context the protests against men who made their wives' and daughters' moral offenses public. The public's speculation and scrutiny of these women, the court doctors' "shameful and indecent" examinations of them, and the judge's incarceration of them in houses of correction were all defaming. Not only personal honor but also national honor was protected by downplaying general immorality and deflecting it onto specific figures such as the midwife. At a time when Argentina was seeking acceptance in the group of "civilized" nations, allowing any broad depravity to come to light would have been an indication of national "degeneration."

By the end of the case against María Baby, the focus had been shifted away from the crime to the criminal. The criminal, María Baby, was described as evil, but not because of the crime she had done, which jurists defined as relatively minor. Rather, it was because the law did not recognize any extenuating circumstances for her as it did for the implicit "real" author of the act, namely Antonia, the pregnant woman. By punishing the midwife, society did get to judge social morality. And what society concluded was that the pregnant woman Antonia, since she had shown a sense of shame, fit into the correct moral order, and thus had redeemed herself. Not so her midwife.

Infanticide: The Case of the Dishonorable Mother

From his dais in a Córdoba courtroom in 1893, the judge heard Ramona Funes's confession of her crime of infanticide:

> I am a servant. The reason I am in prison is because I had a baby girl during the night and killed it, strangling it with some clothes, and when dawn came, I removed the dead baby from my room. Two years ago, I gave birth to a boy in the same house and I strangled it with my hands. I pressed on its neck. When dawn came, I buried it. My employer and his family were at home [both times], but no one knew I was pregnant. I killed the babies for fear of being punished. They were born alive, but the first one was born half strangled [commonly by the umbilical cord]. I think this is because my *patrones* punished me a little while before I got sick [that is, gave birth].[16]

Ramona's is a "textbook case" of an infanticidal mother: she was single, young (possibly even a minor), a servant, with an illegitimate pregnancy. But her confession deprived her of the extenuating circumstance she needed to be tried under the infanticide article of the penal code. She stated that she had committed the two infanticides, not to hide her dishonor but rather because she feared punishment from her employers. Her lawyer tried to make up for her error by arguing that Ramona had previously been rebuked and as a consequence "had conceived a sentiment of dignity" in which she found it too dishonoring to claim dishonor. All her actions, he stressed, showed that she did in fact have a sense of dishonor. If Ramona had not, she would have admitted her pregnancy and the birth and kept the child in her bed.

More serious than abortion was infanticide, and most legal codes distinguished between them. Infanticide was unique because its goal was not only to eliminate the material existence of the newborn, but also and mainly to destroy for the eyes of the world its name and the fact of its birth.[17] The aborted fetus was a "seed," a "hope," and not a juridical being, while the victim of infanticide was an animated being who had "impressed itself on the senses." Thus, the moral issues in infanticide were harder to understand than those of abortion, because people believed that a woman's sight of her own child had to produce in her a natural sentiment of maternity. It took more "perversity" to destroy a newborn than to "annihilate a being who no one had seen and whose existence in the world was no more than a hope."[18] Infanticide had sometimes, in the distant past and in other countries, been punished more severely than other types of homicides precisely because of its perceived perversity. The French penal code of 1810 imposed the death penalty. In nineteenth-century Argentina however, the situation was exactly the reverse, and a woman with an extenuating circumstance received a sentence of between three and six years' penitentiary.[19] Infanticide was reported much more frequently than abortion, and understandably so since it involved more visible signs: a seven to nine months' pregnancy and all the physical changes that this entailed in a woman, as well as the body of the newborn.

With some slight variations, nearly all infanticide laws of Western Europe and the Americas at this time contained two defining characteristics: the child had to be a newborn, and the crime had to have been carried out by the mother to hide her dishonor.[20] These criteria distinguished infanticide from more serious homicide. In Argentina, homicide carried a sentence of fifteen years, compared to infanticide with the norm of four-and-one-half-years' prison. As with abortion, medical experts first had to agree on a definition of the victim. For how long could a child be considered a newborn? Until the umbilical cord fell off, four to eight days after birth, or until the child was of an age to be registered and/or baptized, three days after, were possibilities used in other codes. Argentine law used the standard of three days, though this did not prevent courts from occasionally judging cases in which the children were considerably older, two to four months, under the infanticide law, because of the extenuating circumstance of the mother's dishonor.[21] In this and other ways, dishonor was the most important criterion and even took precedence over what could really be termed "its" victim.

Infanticide was the crime par excellence for the difficulties it presented to forensic medical experts. In the early part of the century a well-known Spanish codifier complained with reason that there was not enough written about infanticide in the Spanish language, but by the second half of the century, when many more works had been translated and when forensic medical procedures had advanced, this had changed. To establish the crime, medical examinations had to show that the child had been born alive, to term, and viable; that the accused had recently given birth; that the time of birth matched with the state of the cadaver; that the child belonged to the accused; and that any lesions and fractures were due to intentional violence and not occasioned by the birth itself. Autopsies of the child were difficult. Sometimes the cadaver was too putrefied to examine or too mutilated. Bodies that had been stuffed down toilets, up drain pipes, in sewers, animal pens, and trash bins challenged doctors' abilities. Even when the lungs were in a condition to be examined, they might not prove anything because the fetus might have breathed before birth and died after, since cases were reported of "moaning" fetuses. Such evidence could increase the likelihood of a woman's being accused of infanticide, as could any artificial respiration that she might give her child. Long births could produce violent contractions that could push the head of the child against the mother's pelvic bones, compress the umbilical cord and placenta, and cause a stroke in the child or inflict contusions and fractures. The child could also be strangled by the umbilical cord. All this could add to suspicion of the mother. Death could also come about from omission of care for the child once it was born; from not tying off the umbilical cord and from natural asphyxiation by inhaling expelled birth material. Accidents could produce the child's death: it could suffer a fracture from a fall, especially in a surprise birth, or suffer a dislocation of the cervical vertebrae. Sometimes the separation of the head from the body occurred in a difficult birth or due to an unskilled assistant.

Some wounds though were considered secure indicators of infanticide. These were cranial fractures (unless it could be proved that the child had fallen as it was being born); lesions made with cutting instruments; punctures made with piercing instruments such as a needle inserted into the brain through the nose, ears, temples, spinal cord, heart, anus, or vagina; asphyxiation caused by matter such as straw being inserted into oral and nasal cavities; and suffocation caused by submersion, usually in a toilet, the water closet being the most common location of clandestine births.

After a long discussion of the confusion attendant on infanticide, the Spanish codifier concluded that what used to be certain in the early nineteenth century about life and death was certain no longer, and that this made it more difficult to judge infanticide. Critics complained that the medicine of the courts ensured the impunity of women committing infanticide, but others responded that legal medicine was attempting to separate the certain from the uncertain, and that "if sometimes it succeeded in hiding the crime under its aegis, more often it protected innocence."[22]

Dishonor had its own set of extenuating circumstances too in the sense that a difficult birth and post-birth period could exacerbate a woman's sense of dishonor to the point where it turned into a criminal act. Slash wounds, cranial fractures, beheadings, and quarterings could reflect not only an intense sense of dishonor but also post-puerperal illness. Picture a young woman, suggested a doctor, obsessed for months by the fear of dishonor, who had kept her pregnancy a secret and continued to work until the day of giving birth, who had been unable to make any preparations for assistance, who in the moment of birth had to stifle her cries —and then the child came. If it cried, it meant her dishonor. Her hand covered its mouth.[23] The convergence of such dishonor with the difficulties of giving birth and post-puerperal trauma could easily explain an infanticide.

Court doctors were attuned to the dictates of modern medicine which held that the physical and mental states observed in pregnancy and birth could strongly affect behavior. Changes in the uterus could cause cerebral alterations, which in turn produced excitations of the nervous system. In the reproductive process, women could experience "maniacal explosions, a perversion of their reason, and a change in their morality and affections." Sometimes the change was merely one of temperament, and a woman might become "contemptuous and insulting." Such alterations alone were not enough to explain an infanticide, but they might well be the preliminaries of a disturbance in the brain produced by the nervous excitation of birth. The "violence" done by the uterus could impel women to commit atrocious crimes.[24] As one lawyer put it, this was a period when "animal birth smothered the dictates of reason." Not only was a woman's reason affected, but also her maternal sensitivity.[25] When it was proved that a woman had committed infanticide while in the "madness" of a postpuerperal state, she usually received the minimum sentence or was acquitted. Similar to their attitudes toward horrendous killings, judges often showed compassion to infanticidal mothers, believing that no wickedness or perversity could possibly exist that could break the strong and sustained links between mother and child.

This is why the courts showed sympathy to women who chose particularly brutal methods of killing their newborns. This seeming inconsistency was actually very rational when viewed in terms of dishonor. To a judge, the extreme barbarity of a crime indicated that the woman's sense of dishonor must have been even greater than normal to make her commit such a horrendous act. In cases from 1899 and 1903 from Buenos Aires, dishonor mitigated the savage infanticidal method of decapitation; the women received the average penalty of four-and-one-half years each. In an 1875 case from Córdoba, a woman who mutilated the genitals of her newborn received a sentence of three years, and a hanging in Córdoba in 1880 was acquitted. In contrast, a woman in Buenos Aires in 1871 who killed her newborn in a more "normal" and less barbarous way, by suffocation, but who was not able to claim dishonor successfully, received a sentence of fifteen years' prison.[26] Thus the expected correlation between brutality of the crime and severity of the sentence was inverted by dishonor, demonstrating just how important the concept was. The greater "perversity" was the act of killing *without* the manifestation at some point of maternal sentiment. In fact, a lack of maternal feeling during pregnancy, it was held, could even produce deformed, monstrous births. Lawyers thus went to great lengths to find some demonstration of maternal sentiment in a woman's past or present such as preparing clothes for the baby, getting help with the birth, or cutting the umbilical cord, all of which of course might well have also threatened to reveal the woman's secret.[27]

Because of the "unnaturalness" of infanticide, the act indicated to many people an absence of free will, especially seen in brutal killings. Since women were viewed as maternal "by nature"—not "by choice," when they committed infanticide, it had to be that free will was absent along with responsibility for their behavior, either because they feared dishonor or suffered from mental and physical disturbances. And when they did not employ the "obligatory" knowledge that all women purportedly had by nature to avoid the death of a newborn—as in protecting their child from suffocation or tying off its umbilical cord, they were also seen as lacking free will. The issue of free will, then as now, played a crucial role in people's judgment of guilt and innocence. Also, then as now, there was little agreement. The positivist school of criminology maintained that the idea that people had free will was scientifically unsustainable. For others, free will was encompassed in the very notion of being a human being rather than a beast, it was degrading to think otherwise, and loss of free will was too much to bear coming on top of Darwin's "association of mankind and monkeys." To still others, free will was of no concern: healthy or sick, responsible or not, from a metaphysical perspective delinquents should be separated out from the rest of society. Although all these theories were influential in judges' decisions, the more widely-accepted view was that birth influenced tremendously a woman's intellectual faculties, dishonor exacerbated the situation, and responsibility was thus diminished since in such cases her will was not free. As one lawyer described it, "At the moment of birth, she only fears; she has no will. There is no crime; just faintheartedness."[28]

The previous arguments did not, however, help Ramona. After almost a year of trial, the judge in Ramona's case prefaced his decision with these words:

> It's a tough job for a magistrate when he has to accept in cases like the present one that there are human beings capable of causing death to the child of their body for the simple fear of being punished, and who repeat their crime with the same plan two years later. It's enough to read the confession that Ramona makes . . . to be convinced that the infanticide law . . . is not relevant to this case. As two of our most distinguished commentators maintain, it is necessary that "hiding dishonor" be present for the blame to be attributed to it. The [social] class, life, and customs of a mother have to convince the judge that her intention was the same one that inspired the infanticide law. It has to be proved or be able to be rationally presumed that dishonor existed. But Ramona did not confess it; it has not been proven in the proceedings; and it cannot be assumed given the particular circumstances of the class of person she is from. Since the death penalty has been abolished for women, we have to assign her penitentiary for an undetermined time.[29]

The case went to an appeal. "At first sight," admitted Ramona's lawyer to the appeals court:

> this case points to a high level of human cruelty. Such criminal accounts, written on cold, silent paper, judged before cold, tranquil reason, in front of the dry, rigid text of the law, produce spasms of anger and protests of indignation against those beings of anti-human nature and of a heart that is physiologically empty. Terror moves the heartstrings upon seeing a mother heartlessly disposing of . . . the existence that had recently begun of the child who came from within her. The indignation that arises from such a crime makes it seem as if *all* the sentences of the penal code put together would lack the force and efficaciousness to punish such evil.

Ramona's lawyer went on to object however that the "circle of physical, moral, social, and physiological forces that had precipitated her fall" had not been aired in court and thus her sentence was "unjust and anti-human." He also objected to using her original statement against her, saying that people of her class were ignorant of the "weapons" that the law itself gave her for her own defense. The lawyer's description of how to deal with such people is medically poignant. With people like Ramona, he said, one has to "penetrate their brain, surprise their thought, and take the words out of their mouths that favor them and that they don't show. They have the *feeling* of shame, of honor, but they lack the *notion* of it." The lawyer's final argument was that to believe that Ramona killed her children for fear of being punished was to believe that she was either an "irresponsible imbecile" or a "prostitute"; in positivist terms, either a person who lacked free will because of being mentally deranged, or a "born criminal." Ramona was neither, said her lawyer. The dilemma, in these terms, was that if the maximum penalty was applied to Ramona, there would be no appropriate sentence for the prostitute. The crime might be the same, but not the criminals. The court, however, disagreed, and confirmed the original sentence against Ramona and sent her to the penitentiary for an undetermined time. The absence of a credible sentiment of dishonor had spread over the case a dark, sinister cloak of cold-blooded criminal intent.

Conclusion

Our focus has been on the Argentine courtroom, an inclusive space—of protagonists and professionals, juridical and medical theories, and commonly held beliefs about the nature of human normality and transgression—where individuals' lives intersected with professionals' views on how to organize and control families and society. The courtroom's theater-like staging of the vicissitudes of modern life shows an important part of the process of building the moral system necessary for modernity. What was really going on in this microcosm of individual-state relationships was the search for ways to avoid or eliminate the evils of the time—degeneration, infection, contagion—that undermined the road to "civilization." The link was clear in the minds of Argentine statesmen. Argentina was in the process of seeking its own unique identity; but at the same time its progress was linked to international perceptions. Antisocial aberrations such as abortion and infanticide were "symptoms of morbid states," "eruptions on the skin of the social body," "an index of serious illness."[30]

The issues raised in the prosecution of such crimes took doctors, lawyers, and jurists deep into discussions of the most crucial problems of contemporary society. Maternity was at the core. At the same moment that an expectant woman was described as "God himself transformed into a woman," as the most sublime creature imaginable, she was also inescapably "physically and morally under the absolute dependence of her reproductive functions," which could result in crime. The juridical "facts" proved it.[31] That something as good as maternity could turn into something so evil baffled people. Perhaps that is why the figure of the abortionist and the infanticidal woman attracted so much attention and polemic, and why they were often used as a measure of the most extreme criminality. Circling around maternity were questions of the influence of physiological states on mental states; the relationship between culpability and free will; the distinction between genuine and simulated emotions; and the valorization of life at its various stages.

Crucial was the issue of honor, which we might assume has been resolved. To be a single mother today in Argentina is no longer a social drama. In spite of this, though, Argentine legislation has maintained the motive of honor as a juridical good which is still important in the scale of values. "To hide dishonor" has been a constant theme, not only in Argentina but also in many other Latin American countries, since the promulgation of the earliest national law codes. It is not unusual, either in Latin America or in the United States, to find support for the benignness that Jeremy Bentham sought in the nineteenth century.[32]

Notes

[AGN refers to the Archivo General de la Nación in Buenos Aires, and CC to the Archivo Historico de la Provincia de Córdoba in Córdoba.]

1. CC, 1897, 6, 10, Ramona Funes's lawyer quoting Vasile Boerescu.

2. Ibid., Ramona Funes's lawyer quoting Jeremy Bentham (1748–1832), English legal philosopher who became well known in Latin America, where he hoped his theories would have an effect. He had known Bernardino Rivadavia (Argentine president, 1826–27) since 1818 and had corresponded with Simón Bolívar (Colombian president, 1821–30). He was admired by Rivadavia and Francisco de Paula Santander (Colombian vice president, 1821–28), but Bolívar turned against Bentham because of his liberalism. In Latin America, Benthamism provided a secular and modernizing ideology for liberals to use as legitimization in their conflict with conservatism and Catholicism.

3. AGN, TC, 2, B, 19, 1882, María Baby. For the law on abortion see *Código Penal de la República Argentina* (Buenos Aires: Sud América, 1887), lib. 2, sec. 1, tit. 1, cap. 3, arts. 102–106.

4. J. C. Llames Massini, *La Partera de Buenos Aires y la Escuela de Parteras* (Buenos Aires: Flaiban y Camilloni, 1915), 186. This was the going rate, and also the cost for recertification of foreign midwives in Argentina. María Baby was French. In 1895 there were reportedly 65 Argentine and 223 foreign midwives in Buenos Aires. Juan Ramón Fernández, "Reforma Universitaria," *Revista de Derecho, Historia y Letras* 1, 2 (Buenos Aires: Peuser, 1898) 113; hereafter cited as *DHL*.

5. The doctor giving the report was Dr. Julian M. Fernández, first doctor of the courts in the Cuerpo Médico Forense, established in 1882. He categorized the means of abortion into four groups. Mineral substances included arsenic, chromium acid of potassium, sulfate of copper, and sulfate of iron. Sometimes these

just produced a toxic action though, without necessarily affecting the fetus. A second group of substances that provoked uterine congestion and like drastic diuretics or purgatives included aloes, and especially savin and rue. A third group, ecbolics, worked directly on the uterus to expel the fetus. Drugs such as ergot that increased uterine contractions were the most effective, especially rye, although they often produced a poisoning rather than an abortion. Finally, mechanical means were the most reliable, using instruments such as stylets or knitting needles, or even a finger, preceded by two or three treatments to dilate the vagina using sponges and irrigations.

6. The doctor was Pedro Antonio Pardo, who held the chair of Obstetrics and Illnesses of Women and Children at the University of Buenos Aires' Faculty of Medicine, and was president of the Council of Public Hygiene, which later became the National Department of Hygiene. His regulations on midwifery became effective in 1882. It was even suggested that an extra year of training be required for midwives in "medical morality." (Llames Massini, *La Partera de Buenos Aires*, 175–190, 198.)

7. Suspended menstruation was a fairly common and serious illness; treatments were well-known and pharmaceuticals easily purchased—drastics like aloes, emmenagogues like rue and salina, purgatives, caustics, and lancets or leeches for bleedings of the feet. In addition, women could perform abortions on themselves by mechanical means—a finger, probe, or stalk of parsley—using a speculum and mirror. On the advantages of bleeding for suspended menstruation see D. J. G. de J. Perez, *Nueva Medicina Domestica* (Buenos Aires: Revista, 1854) 201–02, and on the advantages of purgatives used during pregnancy see Mr. Leroy, *La medicina curativa, ó la purga dirigida contra la causa de las enfermedades probada y analizada en esta obra*, 10th ed. (Buenos Aires: Expósitos, 1824), 138–39. On contemporary abortives in Argentina see Kristin Ruggiero, *And Here the World Ends: The Life of an Argentine Village* (Stanford: Stanford University Press, 1988), 106–07, 198.

8. Juan H. Sproviero, *El aborto: Concepción criminalista del aborto* (Buenos Aires: Centro de Publicaciones Jurídicas Sociales, 1985) 39–41.

9. Miguel F. Rodríguez, "El adulterio. Contribución al estudio de nuestra legislación penal," *DHL* 3, 7 (Buenos Aires: Peuser, 1900), 237.

10. Joaquín Escriche (y Martín), *Diccionario razonado de legislación y jurisprudencia*, vol. 3 (Madrid: Cuesta, 1874), *voce* "Infamia" and "Honor." Escriche's work, with the commentators' additions to the later editions, was one of the principal sources of jurisprudence in Argentina. Under the *voce* "Infamante pena," Escriche discusses the removal of honor through a defaming penalty such as the *horca* (a hanging machine), public shaming, or whipping. In contrast, penalties such as fines, confinement, and exile did not remove a person's honor. The commentators add at the end of Escriche's discussion that the Spanish penal code of 1870 had eliminated defaming penalties, though it still left that of "degradation." The Argentine penal code of 1887 did not contain this category of penalty, though earlier in the century public shaming was sometimes called for in infanticide cases. For example, the judge in a case from Córdoba in 1860 called for a penalty of death by garrote (an iron collar that was tightened with a screw) with the cadaver to be suspended for six hours for public viewing. This was reduced to nine years' reclusion in a house of correction. The requirement that a woman had to be honest, or at least taken as such, is discussed in Rodolfo Juan Nemesio Rivarola, *Exposición critica del Código penal de la República Argentina* (Buenos Aires:

Lajouane, 1890), vol. 2, 56, and seems to lend support to situations in which a woman's honesty could be simulated rather than genuine, and yet credible. Examples of cases where women were said not to have honor because they had already had children are CC, 1874, 349, 15, Sabastiana Martinez; CC, 1880, 422, 6, Higinia Pereyra; and CC, 1900, 3, 6, Benedicta Salguero.

11. The total population of the Casa de Expósitos in 1885 was 1,740. Out of this total, 446 children left the Casa in the following ways: 267 died in the Casa and the *torno* (this also includes children deposited dead on the *torno*), 18 were returned to their parents, 81 were hired out, 17 were reclaimed, and 63 were passed to other *asilos*. (AGN, SB, leg. 100, Casa de Expósitos, 1883–1888, 194).

12. CC, 1873, 342, 17, María Bolazzini. Even the first midwife "imported" from Europe, a French woman, was arrested in Buenos Aires in 1828. Responding to an emergency situation of a birth where the child's head was oversized, actually hydrocephalic, she used forceps, which were reserved only for the use of doctors. The child died and she was charged with malpractice. The judge acquitted her, but a group of irate medical students opposed the decision and wished her, in print, perpetual disgrace and dishonor. Llames Massini, *La Partera de Buenos Aires*, 64–65.

13. Rodríguez, "El adulterio," 393–94.

14. Article 18 of the Argentine constitution of 1853.

15. Escriche, *Diccionario razonado*, vol. 1, *voce* "Aborto." This principle was rejected by some contemporary European legal codes.

16. CC, 1897, 6, 10, Ramona Funes.

17. Ernesto García Maañón, *Aborto e infanticidio: aspectos jurídicos y médico-legales* (Buenos Aires: Universidad, 1990), 35, quoting Francesco Carrara, an important nineteenth-century Italian criminologist.

18. See Escriche, *Diccionario razonado*, vol. 1, *voce* "Aborto"; Juan José Caride, "El aborto criminal," *Anales de la Sociedad Argentina de Criminología* 3 (1937) (Buenos Aires, 1938): 121–38; and, García Maañón, *Aborto e infanticidio*, quoting the nineteenth-century Spanish criminologist Joaquin Francisco Pacheco.

19. In Argentina, if a woman had a sense of dishonor, she was punished with two years' prison in the Tejedor Code, which was in effect for much of the nineteenth century; with three to six years' penitentiary in the first national penal code, of 1887; and with reclusion for up to three years, or prison of six months to two years, in the 1921 penal code.

20. *Código penal de la República Argentina* (Buenos Aires: Sud América, 1887), lib. 2, sec. 1, tit. 1, cap. 2, arts. 100 and 101. Argentine law also included the parents of the mother as able to be charged with infanticide.

21. I have found two cases in which the child was several months old: AGN, TC, 1, I , 2, 1873, María Iguerra and Pedro Danglá. See Kristin Ruggiero, "Honor, Maternity, and the Disciplining of Women: Infanticide in Late Nineteenth-Century Buenos Aires," *Hispanic American Historical Review* 72, no. 3 (1992): 353–73, for a discussion of this case, and CC, 1878, 397, 6, Petrona Oreliana.

22. Escriche, *Diccionario razonado*, vol. 3 (1875), *voce* "Infanticidio."

23. Paul Camille Hippolyte Brouardel, *L'Infanticide* (Paris: Baillière, 1897), as cited in Juan José Caride, "El delito de infanticidio," *Anales de la Sociedad Argentina de Criminología* 12 (Buenos Aires, 1948): 148.

24. On the connection of uterine disturbances and hysterical conditions, see Sander L. Gilman et al., *Hysteria Beyond Freud* (Berkeley: University of California Press, 1993).

25. CC, 1850, 223, 14, Marquosa Solares.

26. The archival references to these cases are, in order, AGN, TC, 2, D, 57, 1899, Teresa De Michelli; AGN, TC, 2, A, 55, 1903, Felipa Arce; CC, 1875, 363, 5, Micaela Barrera and Rufina Farías; CC, 1880, 422, 6, Higinia Pereyra; AGN, TC, 1, L, 2, 1871, Juana Larramendia (see Ruggiero, "Honor, Maternity, and Disciplining," for a discussion of this last case). Brutality continued. In the mid-twentieth century, in the Buenos Aires morgue's permanent exhibit, were three victims of infanticide preserved in jars. Two had been decapitated by their mothers with sharp instruments and the third one's throat had been slashed with shears. Juan B. Bafico, "Morgue judicial de la ciudad de Buenos Aires," *Anales de la Sociedad Argentina de Criminología* 6 (1940): 65–88.

27. Ruggiero, "Honor, Maternity, and Disciplining," 358–361. The case where a lack of maternal feeling was said to have produced a deformed baby is CC, 1875, 363, 5, Micaela Barrera and Rufina Farías.

28. For the debate on free will, see Luis María Drago, *Los Hombres de presa* (Buenos Aires: Cultura Argentina, 1921), 66, who supported the positivist position that man lacked free will, and Enrique B. Prack, "Escuela Antropológica Criminal," *Revista Jurídica* 8 (1891): 109–13, 254–64, 298–306, who opposed that position. Cases where women were analyzed as not having had free will are CC, 1890, 3, 2, Delfina Moyano, and CC, 1875, 366, 6, Carmen Astudio. Sentence number 39 in Augusto Carette's *Diccionario de la jurisprudencia argentina* (Buenos Aires: Lajouane, 1907–1912), vol. 2, *voce* "Infanticidio-Filicidio," 429, directly addresses infanticide by omission of care: "Infanticide is always voluntary when the mother does not take the necessary precautions to avoid the death of the child." This is a sentence from the Cámara de Apelaciones en lo Comercial, Criminal y Correccional de la Capital Federal, vol. 8, 557.

29. The judge cited Rodolfo Juan Nemesio Rivarola (1857–1942) and Joaquin Francisco Pacheco (1808–1865), both famous jurists, the first Argentine and the second Spanish. Interestingly, decisions from courts in the federal capital in 1947 and Entre Ríos in 1953 maintained that "even if a woman did not invoke the cause of honor, it did not prohibit the court from admitting the excuse." (*Digesto jurídico. Jurisprudencia, Bibliografía*, vol. 6: *Derecho penal* (Buenos Aires: Ley, 1968), "Infanticidio," 825–828.

30. Lucas Ayarragaray, *La imaginación y las pasiones como causas de enfermedades* (Buenos Aires, 1887), 16.

31. G. Morache, "La responsabilidad criminal de la mujer diferente de la del hombre," *DHL* 4, no. 11 (Buenos Aires: Peuser, 1901), 461; 601–02.

32. García Maañón, *Aborto e infanticidio*, 44–45.

8

"Guided by an Imperious, Moral Need": Prostitutes, Motherhood, and Nationalism in Revolutionary Mexico

Katherine Elaine Bliss

At least discursively, Mexico's decade-long social revolution (1910–1920) had a significant impact on official attitudes toward crime and criminality. The progressive 1917 constitution in particular committed post-revolutionary regimes to workers' rights, land reform, and secular education. To be sure, Mexico would still be modernized and the downtrodden lower classes redeemed from poverty, alcoholism, and criminality. Only in contrast to the "criminal" Porfirian ancien régime, the post-revolutionary state would acknowledge its responsibilities and provide the resources and tutelage necessary to achieve true social progress. This redemptive process would culminate in the progressive, corporatist regime of Lázaro Cárdenas (1934–1940) and the estado papá.

Pablo Piccato's essay (chapter 6) noted lower-class resistance to científico *social engineering. This resistance had been generally haphazard and individualistic. However, Katherine Bliss, assistant professor of history at the University of Massachusetts-Amherst, argues that the more inclusive ideology of the Mexican post-revolutionary state created intriguing new possibilities for organized resistance even among criminalized groups such as prostitutes. "In Mexico City," she tells us, "prostitutes themselves joined the issues of sexual commerce and the promises of the Mexican Revolution in their written and organized protest of public policies." But participation came with a price. Collective action required a collective identity that merged motherhood, nationalism, and criminality. For prostitutes in post-revolutionary Mexico, empowerment meant acquiescing in their own criminalization. In the end they had little to show for their efforts except perhaps the not inconsiderable experience of political mobilization.*

In September 1926, five Mexico City prostitutes who identified themselves as the "women without homes" wrote Mexican president Plutarco
Elías Calles to complain about the abuses they suffered as patients at the
municipal syphilis treatment facility, the Hospital Morelos. The women
began their letter saying that they were "guided by an imperious, moral
need" in their quest to seek justice in their interaction with local health
authorities and with physicians at the hospital.[1] Only six months after the
federal government had inaugurated a series of new "rules regarding the
exercise of prostitution," Josefina Salazar, María Reyes, Amalia Domínguez, Ana Rosas, and Irma Vázquez protested that new policies governing their activities in the capital city as well as their internment in the
syphilis hospital were prejudicial to prostitutes and their interests.[2]

In the text of their three-page complaint, these women protested the
fact that hospital administrators required them to work with the janitorial
staff while they were still in convalescence. They argued, for instance,
that it was unfair for the health authorities to require three or more women
to share a bed, especially when cot partners often suffered from oozing
lesions not to mention highly infectious skin diseases. And they decried
the beatings and verbal abuse they experienced at the hands of the sanitary police who oversaw the weekly gynecological exams that placed dis-
eased prostitutes in the hospital in the first place.[3]

More notably, these women complained bitterly about a new set of
decrees which prohibited them from bringing their children to the hospital as they underwent lengthy medical treatment for such sexually transmitted diseases as syphilis, gonorrhea, and urinary tract infections. In
their letter to the president, Salazar, Domínguez, Rosas, Reyes, and
Vázquez invoked both their knowledge of the street and their concerns as
mothers, pointing out that leaving their children alone or with friends
while they recovered in the hospital set their offspring on the road to ruin.[4]

These self-proclaimed prostitutes also raised their service to society,
their love of liberty, and their respect for the principles of the Mexican
revolution as reasons that public authorities should take their complaints
seriously. In the text of their letter to President Calles, the prostitutes
warned that "if as women of the '*vida galante*' we are judged, we want to
remind you and all of Society that we are the guarantee of the home."
Articulating a series of concerns regarding the Mexican state's success in
providing social assistance to the needy, they suggested that they understood social welfare's role in the revolutionary project to "secularize" and
"modernize" Mexican social life. The women told the president that "only
you can resolve this issue, which is that we are prohibited from having
our children enter in our company into the so-called Hospital Morelos, a
fact which forces us to abandon them, turning them over to charity work-

ers or people of confidence. It is impossible for us to continue tolerating this. In all countries, even those which are backward, concern for innocent sufferers exists above and beyond the order of piety, conscience, culture and education; in the present case, however, the cultivation of such principles does not exist and suggests that we have receded from the liberties of the Revolution."[5]

In this letter—and in numerous others like it that prostitutes directed to public health authorities, corrections officials, city councillors, and presidents in Mexico between 1918 and 1940—women identified themselves as members of a social group widely regarded as deviant and quasi-criminal in order to demand government assistance and to protest official conceptualizations of their work as immoral and antirevolutionary. Calling themselves "daughters of disgrace," these women articulated their interpretations of the Mexican revolution's promises and stated how they expected to benefit from its goals to assist marginal social groups, promote collective benefits over individual interests, and foment youth protection policies.[6] As letter-writers, strikers, and protesters, they worked collectively to share their moral vision with a revolutionary regime that sought to limit their visibility and public presence in a rapidly growing metropolis.[7]

The Mexican state's interest in the sexual activities of the population had been established long before the revolution.[8] As early as 1538, Isabel of Portugal had granted the *ayuntamiento*, or city council, a monopoly on brothel administration. Toward the end of the colonial period, publicly administered correctional institutions counted sexual deviants among their inmates. In 1851, police officials in Mexico City had discussed opening a reformatory dedicated specifically to "repentant" prostitutes. Thus, when French imperial administrators proclaimed the *Reglamento para el Ejercicio de la Prostitución* in 1865, the relationship between supervised sexual commerce and issues of public health and public security was well established. And when the French abandoned Mexico in 1867, Liberal bureaucrats adopted the *Reglamento*, modifying it only slightly betwen 1876 and 1898.[9]

Between 1918 and 1940, moreover, the Mexican state's interest in prostitution coincided with international concern over such social phenomena as the "white slave" trade, the rising incidence of sexually transmitted diseases, and the implementation of eugenic public policies regarding family formation and reproduction.[10] However, in a context of revolutionary nationalism, anticlericalism, and social assistance, state interest in the reform of such cultural practices as brothel attendance gained new prominence as public officials and organized social groups alike began to work to reduce prostitution's visibility, if not its appeal, in accordance with stated revolutionary principles regarding freedom from exploitation, work, economic progress, and women's rights.[11]

This essay examines the ways in which prostitutes themselves perceived this attack on their means of earning a living and wrote public officials with remarkable frankness about their lives, related their work to the revolution, and pressured the state with respect to its intervention in sexual commerce. It is organized around the following themes: First, I explore prostitutes' career paths, noting that the decision to enter sexual commerce was often an individual one, mediated as much by social and economic circumstances as by human agents in a woman's life. In the second section, I question how prostitutes came to articulate common interests and see themselves as a collectivity, given the individuality of their trade. Third, I analyze the collective identities prostitutes assumed in approaching public officials as mothers, nationalists, and revolutionaries, examining their strategies for defending their lifestyle and their means of survival as they contested post-revolutionary public policies that threatened their well-being.

"The End of the Road": From Village to Vice Den

"The End of the Road" was the title of an anti-venereal disease film that public health officials screened in such downtown movie theaters as the Cine Isabel or Progreso Mundial in the mid-1920s.[12] Before the main attraction, audiences were shocked with graphic images of untreated venereal disease infection acquired over a lifetime of bodily abuse and vices. Authorities' purpose in showing the film was to impress moviegoers with the idea that a painful and degenerative death was the "end of the road" for prostitutes and those men who had sexual relations with them. But what was the typical "road" that a prostitute traveled over a lifetime? What social circumstances, economic crises, occupational worlds, and gender relations mediated this highway to poor health for women who started down its torturous path?

Popular conceptualizations of prostitutes' lives posited Mexico's warm climate, her people's friendliness, and a general disinclination to work as reasons prostitution occupied so many women in the capital. Newspapers invoked "tropical temperament" when describing why women went into prostitution.[13] Crime tabloids such as *Detectives: El Mejor Semanario de México* called prostitutes "women with hair on their chests," "the feminine battalion of death," and "vendors of cheap love," and portrayed them as luxury-seeking drug users.[14] School manuals warned children to stay away from those "friendly girls" who were likely to become prostitutes because of their easy nature.[15] Social workers often cited a girl's "great affection for the male sex" as the reason she had entered the sex trade.[16] Feminists cited poverty and abusive male relatives or acquaintances as causal factors.[17] And criminologists pointed to a physical malady called hyper-ovarian function, claiming prostitutes had unusually high levels of female hormones, which explained their tendency toward sexual commerce.[18] Amid this bewildering array of explanations for the prevalence of prostitution in revolutionary Mexico City, public officials estimated that in 1928 there were some 20,000 prostitutes in a metropolitan area of only 1,229,576 inhabitants.[19]

When social workers or public officials questioned prostitutes themselves about their careers and how they had come to exchange sexual intercourse for money or food, the women stressed that their road to the brothel was an often indirect path designed by the low level of female education in Mexico, plotted out by the limited work opportunities for women in the urban labor force, and paved by family difficulties and unequal power relations between women and the men with whom they lived. Prostitutes, many of whom were migrants from the countryside, cited their poor education, lack of vocational skills, and itinerant work as street vendors, domestic servants, or factory apprentices as factors in their eventual decisions to sell sexual favors as a means of earning a living.[20] In interviews for example, prostitutes often said their work was due to their "lack of preparation" and explained that they had "never found a way to resolve the categorical imperative of having to attend to their most basic necessities and in many cases those of their families."[21] The girls that social workers interviewed also reported having fewer than two years of education. Many prostitutes were from rural areas where there was no school, but even in urban centers where educational opportunities were more numerous many parents kept daughters at home to perform domestic chores.[22] Even so, women's education in general was not as widespread as educators often hoped; thus, when women did turn to prostitution there were often other mediating factors that included a desire for independence, family prejudices, and male exploitation.

For some women, prostitution was a more appealing choice than other occupations open to women who had no family support system in the capital. Certainly sexual commerce offered more work, financial gain, and independence than other jobs available to unskilled workers such as domestic service and factory apprenticeship. Domestic service often meant an abusive work situation in a home in which a woman received little compensation for her efforts—maybe twelve pesos a month—and her occupational mobility was limited.[23] Factory work for women in Mexico City—usually in textiles, ceramics, confections, or packing—was temporary, paid less than a peso a day, and could involve the unsolicited sexual advances of male co-workers.[24] In such a new and often hostile residential and occupational setting, prostitution emerged as a more lucrative and potentially more independent employment option than manufacturing or service. But besides greater financial gain and freedom, two additional issues influenced a woman's transition into sexual commerce: complicated emotional relationships and the transient nature of prostitution itself.

Most women in Mexico who eventually became prostitutes did not initiate their sexual experiences in that capacity. Rather, sexual commerce fit into an equation in which finances and work experiences compounded already complicated male-female relations, family dynamics, and sexual activities. Many young women started down the path to prostitution in the aftermath of a failed juvenile romance, for example. Over the course of the revolutionary armed struggle, the transition to prostitution found general support in a militarized society in which soldiers passing through rural areas seduced village girls, brought them to Mexico City, and after the "*entrevista íntima*" (intimate interview) abandoned them or dropped them off at the front door of a *casa de asignación* (brothel), collected a five to ten peso "finder's fee," and returned to collect part of her earnings on a regular basis.[25] For those women from the Federal District or for migrants who did find work there, participating in vending, service, and factory work gave them the time and money to spend in such activities as attending public dances, movies, and inexpensive theatrical presentations such as *carpas*, where they met soldiers and laborers passing through town, accompanied them to hotel rooms afterwards to have sexual relations, and spent the night together.[26]

The story of Concepción Garza, a sixteen-year-old migrant from Puebla who found herself alone in the capital after running away from her mother's home, is typical. After moving in with her friend Inés, Garza began attending the twice-weekly dances at the Baile Lux, where she met a worker named Pedro. Not long after they met, Pedro invited Garza to the movies and then took her to a house to "have amorous relations," buying her a dress and some shoes the next morning before disappearing from Garza's life. Hopeful that she would see Pedro again or perhaps meet another interesting young man, Garza became a regular at the dances, spending the money she earned as an apprentice at a local ceramics factory to purchase dresses and entrance tickets for the events. When questioned about her social life, Garza admitted that she did meet men at the public dances and went to local hotels to have sexual relations after the event was over. When she spoke with a social worker Garza indicated that she had sex with her dance partners and sometimes accepted "gifts" from them in the hope that they would fall in love with her and come back to rescue her from her life on the streets.[27]

Family relations and parental or spousal attitudes with respect to female sexuality also influenced a woman's decision to enter prostitution. Although social reformers such as psychiatrist and head of the Mexico City juvenile court Mathilde Rodríguez Cabo often lamented the links between capitalism, unemployment, and sexual promiscuity that led working-class women to prostitution, it was ironically often paternal prejudices that propelled a daughter who had engaged in premarital sexual activities toward a trade she might not otherwise have chosen. Parents who refused to acknowledge their daughters or receive them back into the home after they had run away, engaged in premarital sexual intercourse, or become pregnant, for example, frequently saw their daughters turn to explicit prostitution as one of the more lucrative means of earning a living on their own.[28] Although fathers were often involved in this scenario, other family members were implicated as well. In Mexico City, for example, one girl's sister-guardian had thrown her ward out of the house after learning that she had sexual relations with her boyfriend at a hotel. Living on the street, the girl eventually turned to prostitution.[29] Many girls eventually apprehended for engaging in underage sexual commerce reported that they feared returning home because their fathers would beat them once they knew they had "dishonored" the family.[30] But even in a context of low education and family rejection, the shift to prostitution was gradual, and these young women frequently started down the path to prostitution by accepting breakfast or a pair of shoes after sexual relations, as Garza had, before eventually charging money from their multiple sexual partners.[31] Radical 1930s cabaret dancer Virginia Fernández emphasized the transitory and transitional nature of sexual commerce in the capital when she spoke about one prostitute's history, saying, "The history of that girl is the history of almost all of them. The boyfriend satisfies himself at the altar of a false love that tramples the flower of innocence; the parents, instead of pardoning the girl, throw her out of the house, and then life in all its cruelty appears. She looks for work but is offered caresses; hunger looms and uncertainty and after that social deprecation; little by little the loss of scruples induces them to live as they must, without worrying about anything but getting bread to the child who has stayed home alone in the bed or watched by a charitable neighbor who lives in the same sordid tenement house."[32]

If parental prejudices were factors in this story of seduction, solitude, and sexual commerce, family obligations could make a woman's transition to prostitution a quicker one. As Fernández's statement—as well as that of the women "guided by an imperious moral need"—indicates, many prostitutes had children who depended on them for food and shelter. Sometimes child-rearing responsibilities, as Fernández indicated, were the reasons unemployed or underemployed women entered prostitution; sometimes children resulted from a life of sexual commerce in which contraception was rarely available, abortion was illegal and dangerous, and a mother did not always know the father or feel comfortable asking him for financial assistance.[33]

Although pregnancy sometimes provoked a prostitute to petition to be erased from the register, more often it kept her in a trade in order to sustain her dependents. Some women stayed in prostitution for some seven to eight years before leaving to live with someone, reporting that this was the upper limit to the number of years a woman could use her body's attractiveness to lure clientele.[34] In the 1930s for example, María Millán, a veteran cabaret worker and prostitute, told a group of fellow prostitutes that ten years was almost the maximum a body could take of repeated exposure to sexually transmitted disease, physical abuse, and a poor financial situation. Millán said that after a decade of cabaret work her physique no longer helped her attract clientele. When she addressed a group of public health officials, *cabareteras* (barmaids), and prostitutes, she proclaimed "this life is tragic, the cabaret chews out our guts. And afterwards? When we are no longer attractive, it spits us out."[35] Millán questioned how she was to bring food to her children after she was no longer desirable enough to find someone to take care of her.[36]

As Millán suggested to the assembly of prostitutes, women who left sexual commerce often did so to be with men who had committed to their financial maintenance and who were perhaps willing to accept a prostitute and her children with different fathers into his home. Thus, despite its commercial nature, the Mexico City sex trade did foster some bonds of emotional attachment between prostitutes and their customers. Occasionally, husbands or lovers encouraged women to enter or return to prostitution as a means of supplementing the household income, pushing their wives or partners in and out of the work according to the family's economic situation.[37] This was certainly the experience of María Luisa González. After meeting José Rivera in 1931 for example, González left her eight-year-old son with her mother, moved in with Rivera, and helped him vend fruit for several months before he forced her to register as a prostitute. At that time, González began working in brothels and out of local hotels on nearby Manzanares Street. Every morning González turned a portion of her earnings over to Rivera, who assured her that he was sharing it with her mother and son. But when Rivera began beating González, demanding more than a peso a day—a peso González claimed he used for entertainment purposes—she returned to the house, threw his clothes out, dragged him to the local police station, and accused him of being a pimp. However, a few weeks after the court began investigating González's claim, she returned to the police station, said that she wanted to rescind her charges, and contended that she held no grudge against Rivera. González confirmed that it was true that she had been a prostitute and had given Rivera money in the past. However, she denied that he was truly a pimp. She had accused him, she said, because she was angry, but now she was willing to forgive him and return to life by his side.[38]

Although the extent to which couples such as Rivera and González were involved in sexual commerce was frequent, parental or family organized prostitution was apparently less so. For prostitutes in Mexico City, parental exploitation most frequently affected younger women whose families lived nearby. In one case, a fourteen-year-old's father from the southern colonia Portales had placed her in a downtown brothel and collected a peso a day from the girl.[39] Another prostitute complained that her Xochimilco-based father periodically and unexpectedly showed up at the brothel where she worked to collect her meager earnings.[40] In general, prostitution outside a brothel setting was more likely to be a couple-based enterprise than an intergenerational strategy.

Given the variety of circumstances and settings in which prostitution was practiced, the lines between being a prostitute, a courtesan, an exploiting woman, or an exploited girl were often blurred. The "rules governing the exercise of prostitution" defined a prostitute as any woman who earned money from sexual relations, but in practice, any woman who suffered a sexually-transmitted disease, had more than one sexual partner, or frequented inexpensive hotels could risk acquiring the label.[41] This reflected the transitory nature of the occupation as well. Some women managed by arranging partial financial support from a favorite client who passed on a daily allowance but nevertheless did not demand exclusivity. For example, Cristina Morales worked out of a number of brothels in the area north of the city center but received money from a policeman, who gave her a peso-and-a-half each day. Morales told social workers that the policeman had a family, which was why he could not support her completely. Instead he gave her money when he could. They had an arrangement by which she went out at night to search for clientele in different hotels or at the Cabaret Eden. He visited her at a mutually convenient time.[42]

Within sexual commerce, women moved in and out of different occupational situations as their circumstances required. As with the move to enter prostitution, women in the sex trade underwent these transitions individually, but the changes themselves were mediated by financial and personal circumstances. Prostitutes moved both laterally and vertically within sexual commerce. As domestic servants, waitresses, or cabaret workers, they entered and left prostitution according to their needs. Although the *Reglamento* anticipated that prostitutes would pertain to one of three categories: *aisladas* (working alone), *en comunidad* (in community), or *clandestinas* (without a license), the fact was that prostitutes were highly mobile and moved through their occupation in a variety of different capacities.[43] Working in bars or theaters or dance halls, they encouraged men to drink by flirting and promising an after-hours sexual rendezvous to facilitate alcohol sales.[44] In fact, prostitutes rarely stayed long at any given place. For example, Elvira Castillo left the brothel on Calle Netzahualcoyotl to work as an *aislada* on Libertad after only forty-five days. Castillo complained that her former employer, Adela N., refused to pay her and owed her some shoes as well as a dress.[45] This dispute reflects the acrimonious relations between madams and *pupilas*, as women who worked in brothels were called, but it also reflects the reality that women in brothels did not make much money, were often forced to walk around without clothes during the day to prevent their flight, and rarely made enough money to climb out of debt to the *matrona* or others.[46]

Although it was rare, some women moved into brothel management as opposed to factory work or male dependence when they left sexual commerce. In theory, madams mediated between prostitutes and the state. Many women who became madams were over age thirty, and sanitary legislation did not require brothel administrators over that age to register as prostitutes, perhaps because clients, as Millán indicated, did not frequently request women over that age. Nevertheless, it seems clear that most madams had worked as prostitutes before moving into administration. In addition, although they were not expected to be sexually desirable, madams themselves moved in and out of prostitution as their economic and personal circumstances dictated. They opened and closed establishments in accordance with their needs, upgrading or downgrading their brothel registration status, or closing their establishments altogether and turning to individual work when they could no longer afford or no longer wished to run a brothel, which required considerable financial investments from licensing fees to beds, tables, and chairs; a piano, musicians, and refreshments; to sanitary requirements. In addition, the responsibilities could get tiresome. For example, Ana Sánchez, who opened a third class brothel on the Calle Ave María in February 1918, wrote the city council that "since my house is not set up to be a brothel, nor is it my desire to keep watch over a group of women, I am abandoning that project and need to work as an *aislada*, instead."[47]

But although madams such as Sánchez addressed public officials in their capacity as independent businesswomen, those who were successful often counted on the help of political contacts to circumvent stiff licensing requirements or avoid penalties for rules infractions. Agustina de la Vega was one such administrator who relied on official support. During the years of armed struggle in Mexico, Vega had managed a brothel in the Mexico City center.[48] By 1926 she had moved to the Calle de Medellín in the colonia Roma, where she occupied two apartments on a block somewhat west of and outside the designated "vice" district. When Inspección de Sanidad agents threatened to shut her down for being outside the tolerated zone, Vega apparently called in a political favor, and inspectors reported that "a high official used his influences on her behalf."[49] Forewarned of an impending sanitary police raid, Vega surreptitiously closed her establishment and secretly moved her operation to the Calle del Sol, in the colonia Guerrero, moving later to Nonoalco to the west and even later to Calle Zarco.[50]

Women such as Sánchez, Vega, the famous American madam Ruth who ran a veritable pleasure palace on the Calle Orizaba on the posh Plaza Rio de Janeiro, and Monterrey socialite Consuelo la Garza who ran a brothel full of young girls in the colonia Del Valle, captured the popular imagination in revolutionary Mexico City, where publications such as *Detectives, Mujeres y Deportes* and daily newspapers highlighted the "scandalous" activities that took place in their brothels. Not all women who exploited prostitutes did so as formally, however. Older, unmarried women such as Ofelia Pérez, who were not registered as madams or prostitutes, nevertheless occasionally exploited girls they met on the street or in factory work.[51] The experience of someone such as Pérez was more closely related to that of the general prostitute population, as the world of sexual commerce was by and large a transitional one.[52] For most women the "end of the road" was a return to petty commerce and services, treatment for disease, and working to establish a household with a suitor or former client.

Patients, Inmates, and Streetwalkers

If prostitution was an individual and transitional trade in the revolutionary capital, how did groups such as the "imperious ones" and the "daughters of disgrace" come to work collectively to defend their interests? In contexts of armed conflict and the development of social movements and legal reform, the revolution emerges as a turning point in prostitutes' self-conceptualization as a group of people with similar concerns and priorities vis-à-vis the state. At the turn of the century at least, women who registered and had their photographs taken for the sanitary inspection dressed to suggest that they were not prostitutes. Many invoked their shame and referred to themselves as "repentant" when they requested to be dropped from the registers.[53] However, by the 1920s, women who dedicated themselves to sexual commerce expressed their concerns in public and as a group. They articulated common goals and interests in the context of formal and informal networks that they discovered in public institutions and in their life on the capital city streets. They met each other and articulated their common concerns in revolutionary-era military, labor, and community activities; internment in such institutions as the Hospital Morelos and the Consejo Tutelar para Menores Infractores; and informal street occupational networks and social gatherings.

Participation in military activity, in labor organizing, and in community-based consumption protests over the revolutionary period gave women who became involved in prostitution ways to know each other and see their interests as related. In 1926, some years after revolutionary armed struggle had subsided, the group of women who identified themselves as the "daughters of disgrace" wrote to President Calles, complaining: "Mr. President, we don't know what to do; they have closed down the factories and the work in the countryside has been suspended. We think some 70 percent of us do this out of economic necessity and only 30 percent because of vice."[54] While this passage suggests that prostitutes understood official conceptualizations of their work as semi-criminal, insofar as they pointed out that only 30 percent of their coworkers were involved in the sex trade "because of vice," it also suggests that women who became involved in prostitution in the Federal District had a history of rural and industrial work.

One way that women with rural origins might have found common ground in the capital is through participation in revolutionary activity. Certainly it is possible that *soldaderas* or camp followers of rural origin found their way to Mexico City after the armies disbanded and the units returned to their villages. Camp followers—women who provided services for the armies such as cooking and cleaning—were rarely even considered eligible for wartime pensions, but *soldaderas* often had their promised pensions revoked at the last minute as well.[55] Having few marketable skills in an urban setting, some may have turned to prostitution. One woman's account of her experiences during the revolution suggests that this was common enough. After President Venustiano Carranza denied her a widow's pension on the grounds that she was young and could easily marry again, she found work as a domestic servant and then worked in a box factory before moving to the Barrio Latino, where she ran into Constitutionalist Army acquaintances and eventually found work dancing professionally and managing a local nightclub.[56] As revolutionary-era food shortages exacerbated the difficulties of poverty and unemployment, women who were family heads at a time when many men were absent from the city joined in protest over consumption issues. As women who were often involved in such trades as textiles and tobacco work, prostitutes also found common ground in the labor organization that characterized the revolutionary years in Mexico City in the context of inhospitable work conditions or factory layoffs, as the "daughters of disgrace" suggested.[57]

These examples reflect the importance of prior contacts among women who eventually became prostitutes in the 1920s. Informal street networks provided young women who worked alone in Mexico City with social lives, occupational connections, and eventually protest companions. They also help explain why women articulated their problems as members of a historically marginalized group and how women who were still children during revolutionary activity became prostitutes and activists in the 1920s and 1930s. Migrants and young girls who worked in the city as domestic servants or factory apprentices made friends and spent their free time at dances such as the Baile Lux and the Goya as well as in movies, circuses, cabarets, and bars. In these venues they socialized with men, danced and drank with them, and sometimes accompanied them afterward to such inexpensive spots as the Hotel del Perú, the Hotel Santo Domingo, or the Hotel Peralvillo to have sexual relations. In the city these activities were often an individual woman's initiation into the world of sexual commerce, but they also provided her with a way to identify social contacts. Many women met also in transient hotels and advised each other about prostitution, shared information about likely spots for recruiting clientele, and helped girls who were not eighteen avoid the Inspección de Sanidad.[58] Hotel maids, for example, advised single female guests on the relative advantages of sexual commerce, pointing out that prostitution was a better way to make money than service occupations and offered a certain degree of independence besides. A woman at the Hotel Santo Domingo told a girl who had been abandoned by her intended in the capital after she had run away from home to be with him, to throw herself into the street "for in that life she would always have money."[59] Groups of women who met at *casas de citas* (appointment houses) or in hotels moved as a group through brothels, such as those on the northerly Calle San Jerónimo, as well.[60]

Prostitutes also had a collective interest in brothel closings. The city council's effort to generate revenue by raising the fees for brothels of all categories, as well as for playing piano or drums, forced many Mexico City establishments to shut their doors between 1918 and 1928, as Ana Sánchez's petition to exchange her license for her deposit suggests.[61] Between 1925 and 1928 the *Boletín de Salubridad Pública* reported that the number of spaces registered for sexual commerce had fallen from some

300 to 190.[62] Madams who requested to close their establishments blamed a poor market for their problems. Blanca García, who ran a brothel at Cuauhtemoctzín 81, reported that "because of the losses her business had suffered because of the lack of clientele" she was shutting her doors.[63] A group of madams protested the city council's actions, writing that "insofar as there is not sufficient clientele for prostitution at this point, it is not anything like the lucrative trade it was in years past."[64] Surveys showed that brothels often employed between eight and twelve women at a time, and it may be that when the women became unemployed, those prostitutes who could not find work at other community establishments turned to each other for help and support.[65] Given the often acrimonious relations between madams and *pupilas*, it seems unlikely that brothel managers would try to find other jobs for their employees in the event of bankruptcy. Women who found themselves unemployed may have banded together to find work at the next available location.

Prostitutes' internment as patients and inmates in public institutions also facilitated their identification and articulation of common interests. Their stays in these hospitals and reformatories brought them together in venues where they met women from a variety of levels of sexual commerce, shared a living space, and underwent similar experiences and activities. Two institutions in particular filled this role: the Hospital Morelos, and the juvenile reformatory Escuela de Orientación. These institutions were in large, dormitory-style buildings where women and girls spent time together in cafeterias, classrooms, and sleeping areas.[66] In older buildings renovated in the early 1920s in accordance with revolutionary emphasis on regeneration and readaptation of marginal social groups instead of their punishment, the new agencies which focused on educating, training, and rehabilitating prostitutes inadvertently emphasized their identification as members of a deviant social group.[67]

As an institution oriented principally to curing syphilis and other sexually transmitted diseases, the Hospital Morelos counted prostitutes among the majority of its patients. Although it had served this population since the nineteenth century, post-revolutionary internal policies facilitated prostitutes' identification as such by providing formal and informal means for the women to communicate and articulate common goals. First, public health administrators had redesigned the Hospital Morelos in the early 1920s, and in addition to revamping operating rooms and redesigning the common wards to provide more light, they had added a school and workshops in order to "awaken a love for work" among the prostitute population.[68] Convalescent women studied reading and writing as well as such "feminine" crafts as weaving, leather work, and sewing.[69] Second, within the hospital itself, feminists and Catholic charity visitors, not to mention *matronas*, waged a battle for prostitutes' souls.[70] If *matronas* entered to recruit recovering young girls and veteran prostitutes alike to continue down the road to ruin, the feminists and *damas católicas* reinforced the sense of dishonor of the women interned there by questioning them about their career paths and encouraging them to continue their vocational training or praying for their "lost souls."

The hospital's policy of segregating first-class prostitutes and "honorable" women from the common patient population also fostered a sense of solidarity among the majority of prostitutes who passed through the institution. These paying women spent the length of their treatment in an area known as the *gabinete especial* where they had privacy, did not have to mingle with the common prostitutes and their babies, and could receive suitors and gifts.[71] In the common wards where, as the "women without homes" pointed out, they often had to share a cot with other patients, prostitutes formed friendships and shared work experiences and strategies as well as asked acquaintances to look after their children once they were out of the hospital. In rejecting the women "guided by an imperious, moral need" and their petition to bring their children with them, head of the Inspección de Sanidad, Dr. Siphieu, complained that prostitutes spent most of their waking hours in constant chatter about their work, friends, and lifestyle. He pointed out that the institution was "an unhealthy medium in which even in the most obscure corners of this Hospital, the adventures of the patients [are] the only point of conversation among them, their vices, their degenerations, and everything appropriate to that amoral vocation. . . ."[72] In this context, women who had practiced prostitution only clandestinely prior to being a patient at the hospital often joined friends in more formal sexual commerce venues when they got out.[73]

Like the Hospital Morelos, the correctional school for girls was a public institution that ultimately proved to be a place where young women could develop a "deviant" identity. Located in the suburb of Coyoacán in the south of the Federal District, the reformatory, which pertained to the district's *tribunal para menores*, was further from the city center and, unlike the hospital, too distant for madams or friends to visit with any regularity. The girls lived in common dormitories and studied reading, arithmetic, and civics as well as played sports and undertook training in such vocations as sewing and cooking. As at the syphilis hospital, prostitutes were the major group of inmates, but they were also occasionally segregated in order to attend special lectures on sexuality and sexually transmitted diseases, such as the infamous "End of the Road."[74]

The school's emphasis on communal living through open dormitories and classroom learning fostered an environment in which girl prostitutes, like the hospital patients, formed close friendships and even organized group escapes, after which these groups dedicated themselves to brothel work.[75] Here as in the Hospital Morelos, revolutionary policies designed to reduce the incidence of prostitution sometimes had precisely the opposite effect. In private and public settings alike, individual prostitutes became acquainted with women involved in similar work, shared common problems, and formulated strategies to protest official abuses on one hand and policies designed to limit their trade and livelihood on the other.

Reinterpreting the Revolution: Prostitutes, Mothers, and Nationalists

The women who wrote President Calles that they were "guided by an imperious, moral need" invoked their sense of nationalism, their position as mothers, and their understanding of the revolution's promises to assist such marginal social groups as poor women and children in their written protest against unfair treatment in a public institution. Noting that leaving their children behind as they spent time in the hospital for medical treatment facilitated juvenile delinquency, they observed that they had joined in letter-writing out of common interests as hospital patients and suggested that they understood the pathways of crime in the post-revolutionary metropolis. These women indicated that they understood that their work was not necessarily the most desirable. However, they also invoked their social service in safeguarding the home against more serious vices in a manner that echoed some of the colonial administrations' justifications of prostitution as a means of controlling "human needs."[76] But if, in 1926, these prostitutes invoked contradictory reasons for their collective action, the identities they espoused were relatively straight-forward—they were mothers, nationalists, and revolutionaries who had found common interests in their experiences in public life and in social assistance agencies.

Prostitutes expressed a vision of their trade and their role in national life that clashed with administrative and community protest discourses centered around conceptualizations of family and work. These women identified themselves as family-oriented, rejecting official positions that the prostitute's sexuality was infertile and at odds with motherhood. In doing so they contested the administration's attitude, embodied in an advertisement the Department of Public Health (DSP) placed on the back page of journals such as *Mujer*. In the announcement, a family is in tears, devastated by the father's extramarital affair with a syphilis-infected prostitute. The father, on crutches to display his physical deterioration as a result of the disease, stands behind the mother with his eyes downcast.

She sits with crying children on her lap. The ad placed by the DSP reads as follows: "All women, out of personal interest, are obligated to cooperate with the Department of Public Health. Syphilis in the father causes the ruin of the home. The health certificate guarantees the health of the WIFE and that of the children. A kiss, a caress, these are the frequent vehicles of syphilis contagion. Syphilis is the principal cause of miscarriages and why many children are born dead. Syphilis is not a secret sickness. If you don't confess it, your children will show it."[77] As protesters, the prostitutes rejected this notion that they were anti-family, citing their motherly obligations as responsibilities that compelled them to become involved in sexual commerce in the first place. To be sure, they acknowledged the deviant or quasi-criminal nature of their work, but they suggested that their maternal qualities counteracted any social ills they might propagate as practitioners of sexual commerce.

A 1937 meeting convened by public health officials and prostitutes to discuss policies concerning sexual commerce provided a forum for the collective expression of this sentiment. In describing her reasons for becoming a prostitute, María Millán told public health officials that she had worked in a cabaret and as a *mujer pública* to provide food and shelter for her children. Nevertheless, she said, her lifestyle was a great source of personal shame; she said she spoke for all the women in the room in claiming that her greatest desire was for her children to see her as an honorable mother, the moral, upstanding head of a family like any other. In fact, Millán painted public institutions themselves as immoral for hindering her effort to provide food for her children. Complaining about the DSP's policies, Millán said, "*Sanidad* is completely shameless. What do they know of those of us who work in the cabarets? What do they know if we go without sleeping or eating, if we suffer without food because we are sick? At the same time we have to ensure that our children remain ignorant of what we really are. It would be a matter of pride and satisfaction to take them the money we have earned working at a machine, and they said to us 'Mother, you are honorable!' " Suggesting the widespread nature of this feeling, the entire group of assembled prostitutes shouted, "yes!"[78]

Prostitutes such as Millán also invoked their faith in the revolution's economic and social policies as they undertook petitions and protests to better their living and working situations. Raising the revolution's promise to "redeem" marginal social groups, they portrayed themselves as victims of a poorly organized economy. Specifically, they questioned the industrial and agricultural policies that had characterized the Porfiriato, and espoused reform. Moreover, they questioned the assumed link between deviance and biology, articulating instead their conviction of the link between scandal and the economy, and the reckless capitalism and foreign investment that had characterized the Porfiriato. A group who wrote the DSP contested official claims that these women fomented immorality and scandal by dressing provocatively, saying that "since we have no money, we have to sell even our clothes, so as to acquire the money we lack, and almost nude, we have to go out into public."[79] Questioning the economic organization of the country, they repeated that "we have only misery and pain as companions, and disgrace for happiness," complained about the "domination of money," and decried the demands of "money, which buys all happiness."[80] They pointed to ongoing foreign control of the economy, and especially Europeans' involvement in sexual commerce as a contributing factor in the capital's low level of morality. Police reports had suggested that European men who dedicated themselves to the international white slave trade as well as to exploiting Mexican women had become entrenched in the capital in the later years of the Porfiriato, and an informal survey in 1926 had suggested that these French, Spanish, Polish, and Russian men who brought prostitutes over from Europe to the Americas still maintained a foothold in the metropolitan sex trade despite a decade of revolution.[81] At this time, several practicing prostitutes wrote to inform President Calles and the DSP that a Spaniard named Ceballos planned to open several rooms on the Callejón Pajaritos for the purposes of prostitution that would become "a center of scandalous vices and a refuge for perverse men from around the world."[82] Questioning, "Is this nationalism or betrayal?" the women furthermore complained that Sr. Ceballos would force a hapless Mexican woman to pretend to be the manager of the establishment to confuse the authorities and foster a climate in which foreign men would not only exploit Mexican labor but would also subject Mexican women to their foreign sexual proclivities.[83]

Administration officials saw prostitutes as a deviant group best separated from society through institutions and policies designed to restrict their geographic mobility. The women however embraced this identity as they challenged public policy with their own interpretations of the revolution's promises with respect to family, labor, social assistance, and economic policies. They shared their own moral vision with the president and included themselves among the revolutionary family as mothers and nationalists.[84]

"A Right to Live as *Gente Decente*"

In the 1930s, prostitutes faced two challenges from authorities and organized collectively in response to these issues: the question of female labor in cabarets between 1935 and 1937, and the dismantling of the zone of tolerance in 1938. These affronts to the practice of prostitution represented steps toward the abolition of the sex trade's regulation and formed part of larger cultural reform efforts to rid society of the social vices associated with Porfiriato corruption and inequality. Under attack, these women formed protest groups, physically resisted policies, and threatened police and authorities with fomenting scandal if they failed to respect their wishes.

As part of the larger effort to eliminate *cantinas* and reduce alcoholism in Mexico, public officials had long worried about the presence of women in bars.[85] Prohibition reached its height under President Portes Gil between 1928 and 1929, and at the federal level, legislators and congressional delegates worked to prevent women's presence in liquor-serving establishments for several reasons: first, they argued that women incited men to drink more; second, they argued that working in bars made women drink more, providing a bad example for their children; and third, they worried that it encouraged female alcoholism, and led to prostitution and the spread of sexually transmitted disease. [86]

Bars in Mexico City and especially cabarets employed waitresses who mingled with clientele, encouraged them to drink, and were paid according to the number of drinks ordered. In the 1930s, for every beer a woman sold, the proprietor paid an average of fifty centavos, and for a rum or anise upwards of a peso-and-a-half.[87] The *cabareteras*, as they came to be called, danced with cabaret patrons and urged them to drink more, hiking cabaret revenues. As flirting and promising sexual favors after-hours often sold more drinks, working in a cabaret was frequently a way for a woman to make the transition to more formal work in sexual commerce.

To prevent the mixture of sexual and alcoholic commerce in an effort to control unruly and drunken brothel clientele, sanitary legislation had prohibited the sale of liquor in brothels since the nineteenth century; but in the spring of 1931 the Department of the Federal District (DDF) passed an ordinance preventing women from working in any establishment selling alcohol. Under this legislation a woman could enter a bar only in the company of a man.[88] According to newspaper reports this effort was intended to "moralize these centers" and halt the "continuous immorality and scandal that those nasty cabarets foster."[89] But in the four years between 1931 and 1935, *El Universal* reported, the campaign to suppress cabarets had not been especially successful, and in the Federal District at least the number of cabarets only decreased from 31 to 24. By 1937, cabarets had freed themselves from restrictive legislation and stayed open until 6 A.M. But in the fall of that year the DSP under Dr. José Siurob initiated another campaign to displace women from the cabarets, "where, it is well known, they serve only to ensure that clientele drink more, and since their income depends on the number of drinks they sell, little by little these women become alcoholics, with all the bad consequences that accompany that vice."[90]

Labor leaders and cabaret workers alike conjectured that some five to six thousand women would be out of work if the policies were actually implemented. And others estimated that if the cabarets shut as a consequence, some 24,000 people would be at a loss including four hundred musicians, six hundred waiters, and five thousand women, with 18,000 family dependents.[91] Even so, labor activists such as Efraín Hurtado applauded the measure because of its purpose to strengthen the male-headed working-class family by reducing the temptations toward alcohol consumption, reckless spending, infidelity, and the spread of sexually transmitted diseases.[92]

The DSP called the initiative to oust women from cabarets "revolutionary" and invoked the right of all Mexicans to enjoy freedom from exploitative labor situations as the reason why. An advertisement the department placed in city newspapers called the women antirevolutionary and lamented that the *cabareteras* did not understand that the revolution was trying to help them by phasing out their kind of work. Reviewing the struggle between the cabarets and the department over the month of October, it reported "the first lesson we learned from those women was bitter. We were guided by our sense of revolutionary democracy, which tries to abolish the hateful classes in which a poorly organized society is divided, and we arrived, offering them our comradely hand but received in response a hostile demonstration of their inferiority complex which is exactly what keeps them in that absurd vocation of being *cabareteras*."[93] The DSP advocated that the women unionize, register with the office, and fight against abusive cabaret owners, who were perhaps the real targets of the campaign.

Prostitutes were suspicious of the DSP's initiative for two reasons: first, they worried that they would be exposed to greater dangers in their work without the surveillance of the Inspección de Sanidad. But a second reason struck at the heart of the matter: the women worried that unionization would brand them as prostitutes forever. As one woman told a reporter for *El Nacional*, "I'll keep dancing and drinking, but maybe then the work will be more dangerous, as we won't have the protection and constant vigilance of the inspectors."[94] However, she rejected the DSP's proposal that cabaret workers unionize, precisely because she did not want to remain a prostitute indefinitely. She further observed that "we have not all become what we wanted to become, but the fact is that we are workers, the worst class of workers, but we have a right to live as '*gente decente*' [decent people]."[95] Part of this right meant the privilege of deciding when to define themselves as prostitutes and when to decide to get out of the trade.[96] Instead of forming their own association then, *cabareteras* petitioned the DSP to provide them with the funds to form a clothes manufacturing cooperative as proof of its intent to help them separate definitively from their trade.[97] They also affiliated with radical political groups such as the Confederación Nacional de Veteranos de la Revolución or the Theater Workers' Association to press their demands against such foreign-owned cabarets at the Cabaret Pierrot and the Waikiki.[98] Women organized along lines of common interests, but ironically the prostitutes' movement was clearly based on an identity formulated around a common desire to move away from their trade; they did not wish to suffer discrimination, but neither did they want their status as prostitutes to be permanent. Rather, these women saw their work as a transitional phase from which they hoped to advance.

The 1938 DDF decision to dismantle the zone of tolerance sparked a more bitter protest. The location and fact of the zone had been a point of controversy among neighborhood groups, city officials, and the public health department since 1911 and had stimulated written protests from community groups, unions, and industrialists again in the late 1920s, when urban planners worked to designate a vice district on the southern periphery of the *centro*. In 1938 the DDF decided to dismantle the zone completely under the auspices of neighborhood development and in anticipation of abolition policies which would go into effect in 1940. But while neighborhood protesters had long invoked their aspirations to social mobility as a reason not to designate their barrio a tolerance zone, prostitutes adopted this language in their protests of the decree. The new zoning legislation conceptualized prostitutes as free to move throughout the city looking for work, but the women complained about the Cárdenas administration's blatant disregard for their problems by writing the president directly. As Gloria Mendoza Valdéz complained to Cárdenas, she and her associates in prostitution did not understand the DSP's closure of the zone or the constant abuses they suffered from police following the order.[99] As active protesters, the women articulated their demands in terms of motherhood and the revolution.

In October 1938 the Supreme Court's *sala penal* had sided with the DDF and the community, decreeing that the city could forcibly evict the "women of ill repute" from their homes on Cuauhtemoctzín and the surrounding streets. Although the French *matrona* Pauline Duplan had organized an appeal, the court's reasons for dismantling the zone echoed the earlier neighborhood protests in emphasizing work, youth, morality, and the visibility of vice. The opinion stated that "in that zone there are a number of factories and schools where workers and children are subjected to the relaxation of morality when they see these women and the scandals they caused."[100]

Prostitutes organized to offer a competing social vision and centered their protest demands around their own interpretations of revolutionary morality and justice. At 11 o'clock in the morning on March 18 the DSP closed down the zone with some 150 police officers. As police evicted female residents of some 250 *accesorias* (out buildings), the women gathered in the street and begged the head of the operation, officer Miguel Orrico de los Llanos, to treat the matter with the morality and justice mothers and revolutionaries deserved. As one woman cried, "Sir, this is terrible, it seems like Judgment Day. What will we do? What about our children? Many of us maintain the children the ungrateful men have abandoned. . . ."[101] Another prostitute protested, "This is not a demand of generosity but of justice" and pointed out that the women had not received prior notification and that the zone was functioning according to legal dispositions. Others threatened to foment public scandals, and as one woman observed, "If you evict us from this zone, we will have no other remedy than to invade the most central streets of the city, the hotels, cabarets, tenement houses. If you see us as a 'social ill,' with these measures we do nothing else than contaminate the rest of society, insofar as our activities will not be circumscribed in a fixed zone, under Department vigilance. Instead, we will have to find our survival as we can, however we can, wherever we can."[102]

Finally, the prostitutes directly challenged the revolutionary convictions of the government and its bureaucrats. Invoking the revolution's commitment to social welfare, they noted, "Finally, Dr. Almazán, we think that the measures that guide your department might be inspired by a quest for social welfare, we won't discuss the principles; however, we will discuss the procedures, in that in moments in which the nation suffers and in which the fight for survival is every day more difficult, and prostitution grows because of general misery, it strikes us as absurd that low level functionaries use methods abolished by the revolution to create problems for the government and the long suffering city."[103]

Once it was clear that the DSP would not budge on the matter, the women gathered on the DSP's patio at the intersection of Lieja and Paseo de la Reforma with an enormous poster that read, "Where shall we go?"[104] But it was too late. By 1940, under abolition legislation, the state viewed the practice of prostitution as a police matter as opposed to a health concern. Prostitution continued to flourish, but the state no longer regulated its practice. A woman was free to choose what road she wished, but the state was no longer involved and did not concern itself with her destination.

Conclusion

The prostitutes' protest movement emerged out of the growth of the population of impoverished urban women who dedicated themselves to sexual commerce in the 1920s and 1930s, the development of social movements in a period of armed conflict, and the spread of progressive ideologies regarding labor, social class, family, and women's rights between 1910 and 1940. In Mexico City, prostitutes themselves joined the issues of sexual commerce and the promises of the Mexican revolution in their written and organized protest of public policies that threatened their livelihoods. Although they wrote public officials to defend their work, they articulated a collective identity as mothers, nationalists—and criminals—to do so. Prostitutes saw their work as an unfortunate response to a difficult economic situation, but not one that should preclude their participation in revolutionary society. The state ultimately rejected their protests in the name of "higher" revolutionary goals, but through their protest efforts prostitutes nevertheless secured themselves a space in the "revolutionary family" as lobbyists for a more inclusive revolutionary morality than the state offered.

Notes

1. Mexico. Archivo Histórico de la Secretaría de Salubridad y Asistencia (AHSSA). Salubridad Pública (SP). Inspección Anti-Venérea (IAV). Box: 3. File: 4.

2. Ibid. See also "Reglamento para el ejercicio de la prostitución," *Boletín de Salubridad Pública*, nos. 1–2 (1926): 162–187.

3. Prostitutes suffered from syphilis, gonorrhea, lymphogranuloma—also known as Nicolas y Farve disease (sarcoidosis)—and common bacterial infections of the genital region and vaginal tract. Gastelum, "La persecución de la sifilis desde el punto de vista de la garantía social," *Boletín de Salubridad*, no. 4, 1926, 5–25. See also "Hospital Morelos," in *Memoria de los Trabajos del Departamento de Salubridad Pública, 1925–1928*, 2 vols. (México: Ediciones del Departamento de Salubridad Pública, 1928).

4. Mexico. AHSSA. SP. IAV. Box: 3. File: 4.

5. Ibid.

6. Mexico. AHSSA. Letter from Ami Aguallo, Julia Andrade, Margarita Martínez, Eufrasia Paramo, Manuela Domenzaín, and Dolores Analla to Plutarco Elías Calles, 1927, SP. SJ. Unclassified. When I reviewed this document in 1988, the archive had not yet classified the material.

7. Mexico. AHSSA. Telegram from Leonor de la Torre and Marina Martínez to Plutarco Elías Calles, 1926. SP. IAV. Box: 3. File: 3; AHSSA. Letter from "humildes servidoras" Josefina Domenzaín, Angela de los Monteros, Emma Saldívar, to Plutarco Elías Calles, 1927, SP. IAV. Box: 3. File: 7. See also, Archivo

Histórico del Ex-Ayuntamiento de la Ciudad de México (AHCM). Sanidad. Volume: 3891. Files: 5, 22, 28, 30, 44, 47 bis, 74 and Volume: 3892. Files: 182, 185.

8. See, for example, Jean Franco, *Plotting Women: Gender and Representation in Mexico* (New York: Columbia University Press, 1988); William E. French, "Prostitutes and Guardian Angels: Women, Work and the Family in Porfirian Mexico," *Hispanic American Historical Review* 72 (1992); Guadalupe Ríos de la Torre and Marcela Suárez Escobar, "Prostitutas y Reglamentarismo," in *Espacios de Mestizaje Cultural*; on the colonial period, see Steve J. Stern, *The Secret History of Gender: Women, Men, and Power in Late Colonial Mexico* (Chapel Hill: University of North Carolina Press, 1995); Ana María Atondo, *El amor venal y la condición femenina en el México colonial* (México: INAH, 1992); Josefina Muriel, *Los recogimientos de mujeres: Respuesta a una problemática novohispana social*. (México: UNAM, 1974).

9. Ricardo Franco Guzmán, "El régimen jurídico de la prostitución en México," *Revista de la Facultad de Derecho en México* 22, nos. 85–86 (1972): 84–134.

10. Alain Corbin, *Women of the Night: Prostitution and Sexuality in France from 1850* (Boston: Belknap Press of Harvard University Press, 1990); Judith Walkowitz, *Prostitution and Victorian Society: Women, Class and the State* (Cambridge: Cambridge University Press, 1980); Donna J. Guy, *Sex and Danger in Buenos Aires: Prostitution, Family, and Nation in Argentina* (Lincoln: University of Nebraska Press, 1991); Nancy Leys Stepan, *The "Hour of Eugenics": Race, Gender and Nation in Latin America* (Ithaca: Cornell University Press, 1991); Sheldon Garon, "The World's Oldest Debate? Prostitution and the State in Imperial Japan, 1900–1945," *American Historical Review* 98, no. 3 (1993): 710–732; Magali Engel, *Meretrices e doutores: prostitução no Rio de Janeiro* (São Paulo: Editora Brasilense, 1988); Asunción Lavrín, *Women, Feminism and Social Change in Uruguay, Chile and Argentina, 1870–1940* (Lincoln: University of Nebraska Press, 1995); David McCreery, " 'This Life of Misery and Shame': Prostitution in Guatemala City, 1880–1920," *Journal of Latin American Studies* 18 (1987): 333–353.

11. Katherine Elaine Bliss, "Prostitution, Revolution and Social Reform in Mexico City, 1918–1940" (Ph.D. dissertation, University of Chicago, 1996).

12. "Sección de Propaganda e Educación Higiénica," *Memoria de los Trabajos Realizados por el Departamento de Salubridad Pública, 1925–1928,* 2 vols. (México: Ediciones del Departamento de Salubridad Pública, 1928).

13. "Admonotorias: Flora y fauna del cabaret," *La Prensa,* October 28, 1937, 11.

14. "El batallón femenino de la muerte," *Detectives* 1, no. 30 (April 25, 1932): 2; "La capitana," ibid., 1, no. 40 (May 15, 1933): 2.

15. Juan Soto, *La educación sexual en la escuela mexicana: libro para los padres y los maestros* (México: Ediciones Patria, 1933), 152.

16. Mexico. Archivo General de la Nación (AGN). Consejo Tutelar para Menores Infractores (CTMI). Box: 29. File: 8213. See also, Box: 31. File: 8992, Box: 31. File: 19064.

17. Mathilde Rodríguez Cabo, "El problema sexual de las menores mujeres," *Criminalia* 6, no. 10 (June 1940): 543–44; Isabel Cosío, "The Woman in Mexico," speech presented to the Society of the Friends of Mexico, June 6, 1940, p. 7.

18. Armando Raggi Ageo, "La mujer y el delito," *Criminalia* 7, no. 7 (March 1, 1941).

19. *Quinto Censo de Población, 15 de Mayo de 1930: Resumen General* (México: Secretaría de la Economía Nacional/Talleres Gráficos de la Nación, 1934).

20. Mexico. AGN. CTMI. Boxes 1–33, 1926–1940.

21. "Las Cabareteras vs. Salubridad," *La Prensa*, October 16, 1937, p. 11.

22. Mexico. AGN. Secretaría de Fomento. Censo de 1921, Distrito Federal. Occupations by city district. Unclassified. For example, in District IV, which contained parts of the "Barrio Latino," out of nearly 4,000 children between the ages of five and ten, only 1,200 attended school. Mexico. AHSSA. SP. Servicio Jurídico (SJ). Box: 22. File: 9.

23. See, for example, Mexico. AGN. CTMI. Box: 2. File: 1806. Box: 3. File: 5103. Box: 3. File: 5366. Box: 3. File: 5707. File: 5813. Box: 4. File: 6539. Box: 24. File: 7236. Box: 24. File: 7348. Box: 29. File: 8213. Box: 29. File: 8319. Box: 30. File: 8652. Box: 30. File: 8736. Box: 30. File: 8739. Box: 31. File: 8929. Box: 31. File: 8976. Box: 31. File: 8992. Box: 33. File: 9451. Box: 33. File: 9595. Box: 34. File: 9829. Box: 34. File: 9830. Box: 35. File: 10257. Box: 38. File: 11024.

24. Mexico. AGN. CTMI. Box: 2. File: 1806. Box: 2. File: 1807. Box: 2. File: 1841. Box: 2. File: 1885. Box: 4. File: 6853. Box: 31. File: 8929. Box: 31. File: 8975. Box: 32. File: 9172. Box: 32. File: 9466. Box: 33. File: 9451. Box: 34. File: 9869.

25. AGN. CTMI. Box. 2. File: 4020. Box: 3. File: 5212. Box: 3. File: 5366. Box: 4. File: 7213. Box: 30. File: 8707. Box: 32. File: 9229.

26. AGN. CTMI. Box. 4. File: 6562. Box: 4. File: 6754. Box: 4. File: 6957. Box: 30. File: 8848.

27. AGN. CTMI. Box. 2. File: 1806.

28. Walkowitz, *Prostitution and Victorian Society*, 9. On issues of prostitution, labor, and independence, see also Luise White, *The Comforts of Home: Prostitution in Colonial Nairobi* (Chicago: University of Chicago Press, 1990), 1–28.

29. Mexico. AGN. CTMI. Box: 31. File: 8975. See also Box: 33. File: 9560.

30. Mexico. AGN. CTMI. Box: 32. File: 9300. Box: 31. File: 9106.

31. Mexico. AGN. CTMI. Box: 31. File: 8929. Box: 2. File: 1806

32. "La situación de las cabareteras: las mariposas nocturnas pugnan porque se las deje seguir trabajando," *La Prensa*, October 11, 1937, p. 11.

33. For women in this kind of situation, illegal and dangerous abortion or infanticide emerged as alternatives to keeping the child. Mexico. Archivo Histórico del Reclusorio del Sur del Distrito Federal. Quinta corte penal. Infanticidio. File: 1367/38.

34. *Reglamento para el ejercicio de la prostitución en el Distrito Federal* (México: Impresiones del Gobierno Federal, 1914), ch. 3, art. 14. Also, in 1908, Lara y Pardo had observed that most prostitutes were between the ages of fifteen and thirty. Lara y Pardo, *La prostitución en México*, 21. Women who testified at the DSP hearings about cabaret work complained that after some ten years of work in "the life," they had trouble finding work. "Lamentable situación de las cabareteras." *El Universal*.

35. "La vida miserable y trágica de las cabareteras revelada ante varios funcionarios oficiales," *El Gráfico*, October 19, 1937, p. 12.

36. Ibid.

37. Mexico. AGN. CTMI. Box: 3. File: 5211. Box: 25. File: 7392.

38. Mexico. AGN. Departamento de Prevención y Readaptación Social (DPRS). Lenocinio. Volume: 1278. File: 8-421.81-02.

39. Mexico. AGN. CTMI. Box: 3. File: 5707.

40. Mexico. AGN. CTMI. Box: 24. File: 7333. Other cases of parental procuring include Box: 29. File: 8319 and Box: 38. File: 11024.

41. Mexico. AHSSA. SP. IAV. Box: 3. File: 4.

42. Mexico. AGN. CTMI. Box: 33. File: 9596.

43. Mexico. AHSSA. SP. SJ. Box: 17. File: 19.

44. Mexico. AHCM. Diversiones Públicas—Bailes. Volume: 823. File: 4.

45. Mexico. AHCM. Sanidad. Volume: 3981. File: 5.

46. Mexico. AGN. CTMI. Box: 32. File: 9177.

47. Mexico. AHCM. Sanidad. Volume: 3891. File: 47, bis.

48. Mexico. AHCM. Sanidad. Volume: 3891. File: 49.

49. Mexico. AHSSA. SP. IAV. Box: 3. File: 8.

50. Ibid.

51. Mexico. AGN. DPRS. Lenocinio. Volume: 1278. File: 8-421-81.01

52. Ivette Blanchard, "Traficando con mujeres," *Detectives* 1, no. 30 (March 6, 1933): 3.

53. Sergio González Rodríguez, "Cuerpo, control y mercancia: La fotografía prostibularia," *Luna Córnea*, 1994, pp. 72, 74, 75. Also, Mexico. AHSSA. SP. IAV. Box: 2. File: 22.

54. Mexico. Letter from "daughters of disgrace" to Plutarco Elías Calles, 1926. AHSSA. SP. SJ. When I reviewed this document in 1988, the archive had not yet classified the material.

55. Elizabeth Salas, "The *Soldadera* in the Mexican Revolution: War and Men's Illusions," in Mary Kay Vaughan and Heather Fowler Salamini, eds., *Creating Spaces, Shaping Transitions: Women of the Mexican Countryside, 1856–1990* (Tucson: University of Arizona Press, 1994).

56. Elena Poniatowska, *Hasta no verte, Jesús mío* (México: Ediciones Era, 1969), 134–215.

57. John Lear, "Women, Work and Urban Mobilization during the Mexican Revolution," paper presented at the Latin American Studies Association International Congress, Atlanta, GA, 1994, pp. 1–2. According to Lara y Pardo's 1904–1906 survey of work that employed large numbers of women in the Federal District, the textile and tobacco industries were ones in which many prostitutes reported having experience. Luis Lara y Pardo, *La prostitución en México* (Mexico and Paris: Librería de la Vda. de Ch. Bouret, 1908), 35–40.

58. Mexico. AGN. CTMI. Box: 2. File: 4020. Box: 33. File: 9650. Box: 24. File: 7325. Box: 30. File: 8736. Box: 31. File: 8928. Box: 31. File: 8974. Box: 31. File: 9106. Box: 33. File: 9595.

59. Mexico. AGN. CTMI. Box: 2. File: 4020.

60. Mexico. AGN. CTMI. Box: 4. File: 6853. Box: 4. File: 6884. Box: 4. File: 6885.

61. Mexico. AHCM. Sanidad. Volume: 3891. Files: 47 bis, 19, 30, 44.

62. Ibid.

63. Mexico. AHCM. Sanidad. Volume: 3891. File: 30.

64. Mexico. AHCM. Sanidad. Volume: 3982. File: 196.

65. Mexico. AHCM. Sanidad. Volume: 3981. File: 50.

66. "Los dependencias del Departamento: Datos históricos acerca del hoy 'Hospital Morelos,' " *Boletín de Sanidad* (1925): 36–37, 39.

67. Bliss, "Prostitution, Revolution and Social Reform," 104–145.

68. Mexico. AHSSA. SP. SJ. Box: 15. File: 1. Also "Hospital Morelos," *Memoria de los trabajos realizados por el Departamento de Salubridad Pública*, 139–40.

69. Ibid.

70. Bliss, "Prostitution, Revolution and Social Reform," 146–180. On *matronas* recruiting women, see Mexico. AGN. CTMI. Box: 3. File: 5212.

71. "Hospital Morelos," *Memoria de los trabajos realizados por el Departamento de Salubridad Pública*, 133.

72. Mexico. AHSSA. SP. IAV. Box: 3. File: 4.

73. Mexico. AGN. CTMI. Box: 2. File: 2049.

74. Mexico. AHSSA. SP. IAV. Box: 2. File: 34.

75. Mexico. AGN. CTMI. Box: 3. File: 5813. Box: 2. File: 2049.

76. Mexico. AHSSA. SP. IAV. Box: 3. File: 3.

77. Advertisement, *Mujer: Para la Elevación Moral e Intelectual de la Mujer Mexicana* 1, no. 3 (March 1, 1927): back page.

78. "La vida miserable y trágica de las cabareteras revelada ante varios funcionarios oficiales," *El Gráfico*, October 19, 1937, p. 12. Prostitutes also aspired to being treated with respect. The women frequently complained about *Inspección de Sanidad* agents who requested bribes or sexual favors in exchange for not taking prostitutes in to the *delegación*. Mexico. AHSSA. SP. IAV. Box: 3. File: 2 and AHSSA. SP. SJ. Box: 13. File: 2, clipping of article, "Abominables excesos de miembros de policía," *El Sol*, February 12, 1927.

79. Mexico. AHSSA. SP. IAV. Box: 3. File: 2.

80. Ibid.

81. "En México no hay apaches, sólo existen souteneurs," *Revista de Policía*, May 1926; League of Nations, *Report of the Special Body of Experts on the Traffic in Women and Children*, 119–121.

82. Mexico. AHSSA. SP. IAV. Box: 3. File: 2.

83. Ibid.

84. Ibid.

85. See for example Pablo Piccato, "To Explain and Classify: The Discourse About Alcoholism and Criminality in Mexico, 1890–1912," paper presented at the Latin American Association International Congress, Atlanta, GA, 1994.

86. Ordinary session, *Diario de los debates de la XXVII Legislatura* 2, 53 (November 12, 1919).

87. AGN. CTMI. Box: 30. File: 8848. Box: 33. File: 9644.

88. Mexico. AHSSA. SP. SJ. Box: 1. File: 1.

89. "Se trata sólo de moralizar los cabarets," *Excelsior*, March 1, 1932, p. 10.

90. "No más mujeres en los cabarets," *El Universal*, October 8, 1937.

91. "Cerca de 30,000 cesantes al cerrar los cabarets," *La Prensa*, October 23, 1937, p. 11.

92. "El problema de la mujer que trabaja en cabarets," *El Nacional*, October 15, 1937, p. 8.

93. "La campaña de salubridad en los cabarets," *El Nacional*, October 25, 1937, p. 8.

94. Ibid.

95. Ibid.

96. "Las cabareteras no creen conveniente el sindicalizarse," *La Prensa*, October 30, 1937, p. 11.

97. "Las cabareteras formarán una sociedad cooperativa," *La Prensa*, October 28, 1937.

98. "Son denunciadas las maniobras de un llamado 'Sindicato Rojo' que trata de hacer huelgas ilícitas," *Excelsior*, December 6, 1937, p. 10.

99. Mexico. AGN. APR. Presidentes-Lázaro Cárdenas. File: 525.3/1.

100. "Serán expulsadas de Cuauhtemoctzín," *Excelsior*, October 16, 1938; Cuauhtemoctzín no será foco de inmoralidades: La corte niega un amparo pedido por varias vendedoras de amor," *Excelsior*, March 18, 1939.

101. "Supresión de las zonas de tolerancia: Fueron clausuradas las accesorias a todas sus habitantes en los barrios más populosas y tradicionales de la ciudad de México," *El Nacional*, May 19, 1939.

102. "Solamente se pide justicia al Sr. Dr. Leonides Andreu Almazán por la clausura de la zona de tolerancia," *El Universal*, May 19, 1939.

103. Ibid.

104. Ibid.

9

Police, Politics, and Repression in Modern Argentina

Laura Kalmanowiecki[1]

One of the darkest periods in the modern political history of Latin America is the 1976–1983 military dictatorship in Argentina. Tortures, disappearances, and illegal detentions were routine practices during those years of "dirty war." The police, together with the army, were the executors of a state design to guarantee "social order" by all means possible, regardless of their legality. More than ten years later, events in Argentina (now under a democratic regime) demonstrate that the police continue to resort to illegal procedures and, more important, still enjoy virtual impunity from any type of legal and civil mechanism of control.

This stubborn continuity led Laura Kalmanowiecki, assistant professor of sociology at Rowan University, to investigate the historical origins of such a pattern of police action. Kalmanowiecki argues that the development of Argentine police as a "reserved domain" was a process initiated long before 1976; in fact, its origins can be traced back to the turn of the century. Substantial changes effected after 1930 and especially during the Peronist regime (1946–1955) further consolidated the role of the police as an appendage of the state's political power, a process associated with the fact that Argentina's primary social evil was considered to be political and social subversion rather than "common crime." This pattern has left a legacy of despotism and arbitrariness that, in turn, has become one of the most difficult obstacles in the construction of a democratic society in Argentina.

On February 20, 1996, Buenos Aires police forces arrested 237 people near the Plaza Rocha in the city of La Plata during a student gathering in opposition to a new education law.[2] The police did not scrimp in the use of their ample repertoire of repressive practices perfected during the military dictatorship of 1976. Many members of the Buenos Aires police operated in plainclothes using unmarked cars; some even had their faces covered.[3] There is testimony to the use of lists with names of people targeted for arrest; and to the use of rubber bullets against students, passersby, and the media. But unlike 1976, many of the illegal practices employed that day, including physical attacks on reporters, appeared on prime-time television.

For some of those illegally arrested at the Infantry building—used as a detention center during the military regime—the dramatic events revived personal and collective "blood" memories. "Perhaps it was the place where my parents were tortured, perhaps by the same people," said one person. "The same is going to happen to you as to your parents . . ." members of *Hijos* (children of former detainees-disappeared) were told after being seized by the police.[4] "You should remain quiet, so your mother does not come here wearing a white scarf," threatened a policeman after a mother of the Plaza de Mayo managed to communicate with a detainee.[5] Despite the claims of some politicians that the police were preempting the actions of "leftist activists" and "infiltrators," these incidents were not isolated events.[6]

Torture and abuse are standard practice among contemporary Argentine police forces.[7] Extrajudicial killings of poor people are customary and have increased by sixty percent over the last year.[8] In fact, increased police violence touches a broadening spectrum of people being defined as targets—university students, teenagers, neighbors, workers—underscoring why the problem has become a touchstone for Argentinians who fear for their safety.

Ironically, the drama of mounting police abuses is staged in the context of the twentieth anniversary of the 1976 military coup which perpetrated clandestine terror against civil society. Twenty years ago the creation and implementation of systematic terror caused unprecedented levels of personal insecurity among citizens. Violence and fear became generalized and permeated society as a whole. Ever since democracy was restored in 1983, heightened police violence and behavior outside the rule of law recalls the past, prevents (and forbids) forgetting, and renews civil society's efforts to seek truth and justice. The "blood" memory and unspeakable horrors of the past reappear as a recurring obsession—even among those who want to heal society's wounds through reconciliation and selective memory by "looking toward the future."[9]

The human rights movement's slogan "*nunca más* (never again)" addressed the challenge, and the promise of the newly established democracy was full state control over the forces of coercion so the military would never again assume power and the police could never again abuse suspects.[10] Argentina pioneered the wave of democratization in the Southern

Cone with free elections in 1983. A pluralist party system materialized under which the Radicals held power until 1989, when the Peronist party under Carlos Menem gained a majority. However, the newly established regimes have fallen short as guarantors of civil liberties. In effect, democracy still stops at the door of the police station.[11] This is further compounded by the enormous discretionary power of police on the beat. The police inhabit a "reserved domain" outside the rule of law, and civil institutions are excluded from control and punishment of contemporary police abuses.[12]

Is police violence a simple holdover from the military regime of 1976–1983? Do Argentine forms of policing vary according to the democratic or authoritarian character of the state? Or do the police have an autonomous birthright that can be traced historically? Argentine literature refers to the police primarily as an extension of the military in repression or as specialists in the control of crime and public space, but as alien to politics.[13] Little is known about what the police look like institutionally and what they do.

A close look at the development of the Argentine police forces will trace the creation of the police as the political instrument of incumbent governments and their diversion to extralegal action against putative enemies of the regime. Despite several attempts at police reform and acceptance of democratic practices during the government of presidents Hipólito Yrigoyen and Marcelo T. Alvear, civil violence rather than crime was defined as the major threat to public order. Thus, political policing came to dominate police activities in Argentina, and this need was believed to stem from the contentious nature of Argentina which was rooted in the foreign origins of its population. In the politicization process, the police formulated an autonomous logic with a strong corporate identity that made them unaccountable to the rule of law. Paradoxically, their political operation led to their autonomization to such a degree that it is sometimes difficult to distinguish some police members from "unaffiliated" bandits.[14] A civilianized police force—one that concentrates on crime and the protection of citizens—is a prerequisite of democracy; the repressive capacity developed by the Argentinian police and lack of societal controls threatens Argentina's fragile democracy.

Development of the Argentine Police Forces

We can trace the antecedents of the evolving process of modernization and centralization of law enforcement in Argentina as far back as the late colonial period, when efforts were made to enforce the law through rural constabularies and urban night patrols. During the nineteenth century policing was understood very broadly, connoting both the protection of the security of the state ("high police" in the French sense, that is, the political police, secret police, or simply state police) as well as the welfare of the inhabitants ("low police").[15] Thus, throughout the nineteenth century the same public officials were in charge of broadly defined tasks such as the apprehension of common criminals, surveillance of political suspects, and inspection of commercial establishments. Even so, the criminal police served as the government's eyes and ears and were ready to alert it to any local circumstances that could affect general domestic security. The fact that state security was a central priority led in practice to the militarization of the embryonic police forces as a regular practice at moments of political or social upheaval.

Mark Szuchman has demonstrated in his work on the imposition of law and order in Buenos Aires between independence and the 1860s that the establishment of public order meant the establishment of forms of social control over what were perceived as the "dangerous classes."[16] The courts and police were used between 1820 and 1850 to protect and promote the interests of the propertied classes.[17] During the Argentine modernization process and the growth of its export economy, each stage in the process of transformation was accompanied by the use of the coercive powers of police and courts to protect property, maintain public order, and provide a disciplined work force.[18]

The Capital Police

Only after the supremacy of the national state was established in 1880 did a modern police department develop in Argentina.[19] In that year the city of Buenos Aires was federalized and made the national capital, effectively consolidating the monopoly of legitimate violence in the hands of the federal army and the police.[20] The Buenos Aires city police thus became the Federal Capital Police (*Policía de la Capital*), directly subordinate to the president through the minister of the interior. After 1880 the police acquired its definitive organization, and its range of activities was increasingly specified and narrowed. By this time Argentina had become a dynamic capitalist society organized around a dependent export sector. Further, the ethnic composition of the country had been remade through European immigration; on the eve of World War I almost one-third of the population had been born abroad.[21] Thus, economic growth, state-building, and more vigorous central governments brought about a need to adjust the police forces to the new and normalized order.

Although the jurisdiction of the Capital Police was formally limited to the territory of the federal capital (the city of Buenos Aires), it was by its very nature a state police. That is, since it depended on the federal government, it was entrusted in turn with the security of the state and became in that sense a national police. Even though a federal police was not formally created until 1943–44, the Capital Police had the capacity and technical means to carry out certain intelligence gathering activities and take coercive measures throughout Argentina. Once a situation was defined as menacing—politically or socially—the Capital Police provided the means (rudimentary at that point) to intervene throughout the territory of the newly consolidated nation-state.[22]

In the years that followed the capitalization of the force, police chiefs endeavored to restructure and professionalize the institution. However, functional criterion prevailed in the establishment of successive police sections and specialized organizations; ad hoc sections were created according to functional needs in a disorderly fashion. Thus, disparate agencies were initiated and named according to function but without a unified principle.[23] In practice this led to the formation of horizontal dependencies with overlapping functions that lacked a pyramidal command structure.

This changed when Colonel Ramón L. Falcón was appointed chief of police in 1906. He laid the foundations of the current basic police organization, following a scheme that ran: chief of police—Comisaría de Ordenes—Divisiones.[24] In effect, Falcón understood that only a vertical, hierarchical structure could provide the police with centralized discipline and control over the means of coercion. This logic entailed a unified central authority—the chief of police—linked to different police branches through an intermediate agency, the Comisaría de Ordenes.[25]

As a military officer, Falcón's experiences on the battlefield had taught him that armies were easily defeated if no administrative division existed between infantry, cavalry, and artillery. Therefore, he encouraged a division of labor among the main police activities, centrally coordinated at the top. Centralization, in the sense of decisions radiating from the center of power outward, would provide the police chief authoritative and binding rule-making power over a differentiated set of institutions and personnel.[26] According to a logic of hierarchical functional differentiation, Falcón reorganized preexisting sections as formal police divisions: seguridad (security), investigaciones (investigative); judicial (judicial); administrativa (administrative), sanidad (health in 1908), and bomberos (firefighters).[27] Different sections and bodies were attached to each of these divisions. The Comisaría de Ordenes was entrusted with supervising the other divisions, replacing the chief of police in his absence, and in practice operating as a subchief of police. Although these police divisions and sections were often renamed, with their personnel reallocated to new, more broadly defined sections and more specialized branches created, this basic structure varied little until the creation of the Federal Police in 1943.[28]

Furthering this process of professionalization, Colonel Falcón attempted to upgrade recruitment and training of police personnel by creating the *Escuela de Cadetes* (Cadets' School) in 1907. Nonetheless, the low educational level and high turnover of the rank and file were persistent problems. Low wages were (and remain) a main problem hindering a proper selection of police recruits. For instance, in 1898, twenty percent of police agents were illiterate; they had to memorize police ordinances and manuals. Police reformers complained that the rank and file needed the help of citizens to write reports for situations in which they intervened.[29]

The expansion and reorganization of the police forces in Argentina did not become a reality until the elites became threatened by the growth of industrial conflict, the expansion of anarchism, and the struggle of the middle classes for incorporation in the political arena. Thus, in the thick of the growth and restructuring of the Capital Police lay the perception of Buenos Aires as a citadel under permanent threat by the "dangerous classes." This fear proved prescient; in 1909, Colonel Falcón and his aide Alberto Lartigau were murdered by an anarchist.[30]

Fear of social unrest and anarchist resistance led to a considerable increase in police personnel during the parades organized to celebrate the Centenario. A 1910 reform placed under the Investigative Division the sections responsible for Public Order (political affairs), Social Order (overseeing anarchist, communist, socialist, mob, and labor activities), and Personal Custody of the President. A further reform in 1912 changed the names of these sections somewhat, but their functions varied little, although within the Investigative Division fact-finding tasks properly speaking were differentiated from technical matters.[31]

The development of the police in the first decades of the twentieth century was facilitated by two legislative measures. The 1902 Residency Law (*Ley de Residencia*) gave the executive branch the authority to restrict anarchist and labor agitation through the expulsion of any foreigner whose conduct threatened national security or disturbed public order. The 1910 Social Defense Law (*Ley de Defensa Social*) was enacted as a more comprehensive tool that, among other measures, prohibited the entrance of anarchists into the country.[32] Both laws broadened the scope of police action. The police were the crucial enforcers of these repressive measures, although the national government would also call on the army and navy when police were unable to contain strikes or when strikes spread throughout the republic.

Colonel Falcón shared with propertied elites a common perception of threat and pressed to expand available legislation in order to crush any source of labor unrest, public demonstrations, or anarchism. As early as 1907 he had urged the minister of the interior to extend the scope of anarchist surveillance to other important cities of the interior. Although the capital police collaborated with provincial police forces and alerted them to future disturbances, not much could be done unless some sort of nationalization of police forces ensued. At least, Falcón believed, it was necessary to "awaken among the other provincial police a vigilant zeal that would ensure continuous surveillance of anarchists."[33] Public order and tranquility were the overriding priorities.

It should also be noted that another view coalesced, complementing and often contradicting the repressive response to the "dangerous classes": the belief that despite legislation that expanded executive powers of repression, anarchist propaganda would be impossible to curb unless the economic and social origins of political unrest were addressed. Only enlightened legislation could curtail the spread of anarchism since it was necessary to protect labor against capitalist "greediness," which demanded inhuman efforts from the working classes.[34] In fact, from the beginning of this century it is possible to find chiefs of police such as Beazley, Rosendo Fraga, and even Falcón at the scene of strikes trying to promote negotiations between capital and labor. Nonetheless, coercive measures towards the labor movement prevailed until the corporatist institutionalization of the working classes from above under Peronism.

Some voices openly contested Falcón's police reform as leading to the militarization of the police, but these were dismissed as irresponsible and lacking an understanding of the need for social order.[35] They allegedly failed to understand that security took precedence over legal norms. In any case, these voices were too isolated and ineffective in the face of a pact of domination in which only powerful elites had a say in the country's policymaking.

Therefore, during the oligarchic pact that dominated Argentine politics until 1916, the mainstays of police structure and practices were to be grounded in protecting the interests of the landed elites: if assent to government domination was missing, obedience to the rulers was to be promoted by preventive police vigilance and sheer force. Falcón masterminded the restructuring of the police in accordance with these principles.

The Police during *Radicalismo*

Social progress brought political demands and pressure for democratization. Electoral reform put an end to the monopoly of power held by the landed classes. The 1916 elections were won by the Unión Cívica Radical, a new party standing for the defense of middle-class political rights and led by a popular figure, Hipólito Yrigoyen. Yet in spite of Yrigoyen's commitment to reform, the democratically elected Radical government responded to labor unrest with large-scale repression.[36]

In the following decades the basic structure of police organizations varied little. Nonetheless the process of specialization and professionalization was furthered. Police officers increasingly came to think of their job as a profession and of themselves as professionals. A career structure was created with the establishment of a seniority scale that regulated promotions within the institution and tried to prevent patronage (at least formally) from interfering in criminal justice careers. Also, the education of police personnel was extended and became more "scientific."

The refurbishing of the police with the notion that the institution should be modern and democratic was an idea shared by Buenos Aires law enforcement reformers during the governments of Yrigoyen and his successor, Marcelo T. Alvear. These reformers expressed hopes for the professionalization of the force in line with a new ethos that recognized that modern police were not only authorized defenders of the existing state structure but also the ever-ready helper and protector of the people.[37] Yrigoyen declared his aspiration to eradicate "militarism" from the police force and make it a completely civil organization.[38] The chief of police attempted to reshape police mentality and instill a new democratic ideal based on professionalism, technological proficiency, popular respect, and an understanding of the plight of the working classes.

Efforts were made to change the inclination of police officers to act as if in enemy territory. Democratic and pluralistic values were imparted among the rank and file through instruction manuals and speeches. Uniforms were changed with the twofold purpose of making them less military and therefore more palatable to the public while at the same time diminishing the strict distinctions that had divided the upper reaches of police hierarchy from the rank and file.

However, Yrigoyen's attempt was doomed, in part by his failure to gain the loyalty of the military. During the Tragic Week (a January 1919 attack by police and paramilitary groups on striking workers and the Jewish community) and in 1921–22 (when repressive military operations were carried out by army troops), the army acquired a more dominant role than before.[39] However, Yrigoyen's repression was not the result of an official anti-labor position but rather a reflection of the weakness of his government.[40] The escalation of social conflict and the persistence among police administrators of ideas about the "ungovernability" of the country due to its ethnic composition frustrated these attempts. In effect, police leaders shared a nativist outlook grounded in the belief that a country like Argentina, with a large foreign population, could be mobilized by subversive ideas. For example the ultranationalist writer Leopoldo Lugones—who would later become an apologist of the military regime—thought that "peoples with an immigrant makeup, like ours, are . . . the most susceptible to anarchy."[41] Therefore, police tendencies to act *manu militari*, which had prevailed since its inception, and beliefs in the need for military discipline and training of police recruits intermingled with and eclipsed efforts to civilize police forces.[42]

The Police and the 1930 Military Coup d'Etat

As mentioned above, a major police restructuring was undertaken following the 1930 military coup that put an end to the initial democratization of politics and policing in Argentina. The military men who seized the upper echelons of the police hierarchy recreated the force under a system of prefectures with the claim that the decentralization of the institution was imperative. The chief of police was now called the police prefect, and subprefectures were established.

Although the division into prefectures was of short duration, the procedures devised by the police following the oligarchic restoration, and especially by Chief of Police Luis J. García after Agustín Justo was elected president in 1932, initiated important features that left an imprint on the organization and its practices.[43] In any case, the oligarchic restoration that followed the 1930 seizure of power by the military constituted a watershed in policing. The acquisition of new weapons, modern vehicles, an up-to-date communications system, and a police broadcasting network meant that Buenos Aires became a more heavily policed society.[44] But other features that led Buenos Aires to be a more policed society than ever before were also connected to the assault upon the public and private spheres by a state whose interventionist capabilities had been greatly extended.

Police reform was curtailed after figures alien to the institution were appointed to important positions through clientism and patronage. For example, Leopoldo Lugones Jr., a former director of a reformatory, who had previously been dismissed and accused of torture of minors, was appointed as chief of the political order division in 1931. He was nominated after his father had an interview with President José Francisco Uriburu.[45] After his appointment, conservative nationalists said "*se acabó la joda*" (the time for screwing around is over).[46] And indeed, thanks to Lugones, torture became a daily routine in police precincts.

A network of espionage and surveillance was established with such a broad scope of activities at both the local and national level that it made Joseph Fouché's police system for Napoleonic France seem modest by

comparison. The objects of police repression were extended to new targets labeled as posing a threat to state security, including communists
and Radicals who had been expelled from power after 1930. Since the
previous police branches seemed to be overwhelmed by the enlarged range
of activities, the police structure was refurbished to accomplish its new
tasks. A Special Section to combat communism was created and put to
work in a expeditious fashion. Special Branch tactics included surveillance, arrests, illegal searches, and torture. They also collaborated with
provincial police forces and helped them "modernize" the monitoring of
the opposition and create local branches entrusted with the repression of
communism.[47]

Even though the Special Section has historically epitomized in Argentina the abuses of state power after 1930, less is known about the complexity of Justo's intelligence network which involved other state agencies
as well. An efficient network of surveillance and infiltration was established to confront the threat of Radical insurrection. Undercover policing
by the Political Order Branch, posing for instance as postal workers, became customary. Telephone taps (including those on the Government
House) and phonographic records of speeches by Radical politicians became part of the repressive repertoire.[48] Secret dossiers of conspiracy leaders were kept by Political Order. Indeed, since the military coup the Bureau
of Posts and Telegraphs had been headed by an active officer.[49] Likewise,
the president's secretary sent regular reports with copies and transcrip-
tions of intercepted letters. From 1931 on, intelligence gatherers succeeded
in unveiling the identity of their victims and targets within the opposition
movement and doomed the Radicals' struggle from its inception. Social
Order also collaborated at times in the surveillance of subversive activities within civilian society and the army.[50] The fetishism for collecting
information for its own sake was underway.

Likewise, secret army intelligence services were used to unravel possible plots against Justo. The navy, local police departments, and the army
collaborated in the repression of radical conspirators. For instance, lacking resources to infiltrate the activities of the exiles, the commander of
the Third Army Division, General Russo, suggested national involvement
through agents of the Investigative Division of the Capital Police.[51]

Military intelligence operations and collaboration with the police was
carried out until the end of Justo's presidency. Often the stimulus for these
intelligence operations were conditions around the country, when for example the military decided that the governor of a province or national
territory was untrustworthy. Military and police reports substantiated the
top-down knowledge and control of military action (from President Justo
to the minister of war), and their collaboration in the repression of Radi-

cals and communists. For example, Yrigoyenista governor Amadeo Sabattini, who had won elections in the province of Cordoba in 1935, was a target of police and army surveillance. By the same token his government was burdened with deceitful informants pushing for federal intervention. Likewise, a presidential secret service, which appears to be an outgrowth of the Political Order Branch of the police but which also exchanged information with army intelligence services, was at the heart of undercover operations.[52]

In sum, after the 1930 military coup and especially under the direction of Luis Jorge García, even though the basic organization of the police remained formally the same, its structure enlarged its capabilities for vigilance, surveillance, and repression. At the same time, the autonomy of the police organization was heightened. The police and military apparatus constructed at that time has remained conspicuously immune to any form of public accountability or democratic control, although many pieces of Argentina's enormous domestic intelligence apparatus are still missing. In any case, this apparatus acquired an autonomous logic, perhaps unforeseen by those who contributed to its development.

The Federal Police

The foundations established by Falcón remained basically unchanged until 1943–44, with the core of the police structure in four sections (*direcciones*): security, investigative, judicial, and administrative. The process of police centralization initiated during Falcón's tenure was further expanded after the creation of the Federal Police in 1943–44, and especially after Perón's rapid ascent to power when the police became instrumental in checking the power of the military.

Juan Domingo Perón's rise to power was set up by his involvement in the 1943 military coup. Colonel Perón set in motion the political operation that would lead to his inclusion of the labor movement within the state, but at the expense of labor autonomy. Police action was instrumental in contributing to Perón's rise to power and in maintaining it, and the police institution was redefined in the new regime that Peronism brought about. First, the incorporation of the labor movement promoted by Perón took the labor question out of the hands of the police and the army by institutionalizing mechanisms for solving labor disputes.[53] Second, with Perón, the police became the "pueblo," determined if necessary to fight even against the armed forces to defend the "well-being" of the masses against the selfishness of the Argentine oligarchy. During Peronism the police became another corporation. Corporative gains promoted by Perón for the police meant that the police had much to lose if anti-Peronist rivals took power. And, they had much to gain by stepping in and supporting Perón directly.

The situation of the Special Branch Division is especially bewildering since we have information on its practices only for the period 1931–1936 (previously discussed) and again after 1948 under Perón, with the same functions and known personnel, now incarnated by the sinister personalities of Lombilla and his aide Amoresano who continued to exercise their "trade" and train new recruits. Cipriano Lombilla and Amoresano initiated their "careers" under the command of Leopoldo Lugones Jr. According to lawyers such as Santiago Nudelman, who denounced the practice of torture in Buenos Aires police precincts, not less that twenty people had been tortured by Lombilla and his aide in the 1950s.[54] In the account of a doctor tortured by Lombilla in 1948, *Sección Especial* was located in the same building as police precinct No. 8. Undocumented arrests and "scientific" torture were regularly used against dissidents.[55] Lombilla's right-hand man Amoresano yielded information about the occasional death of prisoners who were being tortured: their deaths were portrayed as accidental, and any complaints about them were dismissed without further investigation. Although the Special Branch continued to operate under the jurisdiction of the Investigative Division, directed by Luis Serrao, it was accountable only to Perón.[56] Thus, secrecy and impunity were the trademarks of the Special Branch.[57]

The Federal Police gave the Capital Police jurisdiction over the whole territory of the country. The police was now structured along the lines of the Capital Police with the Interior Division entrusted with judicial and security tasks in matters pertaining to federal jurisdiction.[58] During Perón's government the entire police force was "Peronized" and became instrumental in support of Perón's efforts to reconcile labor and capital. When deemed necessary, repression was used against political opposition and any attempt at labor autonomy.[59]

It is my hypothesis that the statute of the Federal Police only legitimized—by presidential decree—a long-existing practice of metropolitan police intervention in municipal and local provincial matters. In fact, before the Federal Police was formally instituted, secret and political police forces were collaborating and operating on a national level, albeit in a rudimentary fashion. In any case, interventions by the Investigative Division had a local character de jure but not de facto. As the evidence during the Justo presidency reveals, not only was cooperation between the armed forces and police widespread, but in fact the Capital Police had also operated nationally in the previous decade(s).[60]

The nationalization of the Capital Police was a shared aspiration of police administrators.[61] Perhaps as far back as the first decades of the century, policymakers and police administrators had complained that the federal government lacked its own police force. As previously noted, in Falcón's view it was impossible to crush anarchism unless all the provinces adopted the same rules and procedures.[62] In the view of police administrators, only through the creation of a federal police on the model of the United States FBI, Chilean and Italian *carabinieris*, or French *gendarmerie* could illegal activities be eradicated. After the military coup of 1943, the idea of a federal police was finally put into practice. It was alleged that the prospects for the end of the war, the intensification of labor disputes, and the rationalization of public administration fostered this process.[63]

Significantly, with the enactment of the Statute of the Federal Police, for the first time police personnel were provided with a differentiated status—a police status (*estado policial*) with respect to the rest of the general administration.[64] Likewise a Police Code was proclaimed, giving police officers special legal status. From now on they were accountable only to the police regime, and no external forces could interfere. In a speech to the Federal Council of Security in 1952, Perón claimed that although the Police Code did not profess arbitrariness and prepotency, according to police privilege (*fuero*) only the police could punish the police.[65] Consequently, law enforcement personnel were removed from civilian jurisdiction, thus promoting police impunity.[66]

Under Peronism, the Investigative Division maintained its original structure but targeted the newly defined enemies of the state. Social Order was charged with the surveillance of "culture," meaning students and intellectuals, and a new section, *Orden Gremial*, inherited Social Order's principal target, the labor movement. In 1944 a new agency, the Federal Coordination Division, was initially entrusted with international espionage, but eventually preempted some tasks of the Investigative Division.

In sum, centralization and specialization were fostered in some areas of police activities, and the establishment of a Federal Police structure created the conditions for a more systematic coordination of policing. Now the Investigative Division integrated its procedures with the newly created bodies, the Interior Division and Federal Coordination. This process was furthered in 1951 with the creation of the Federal Security Council (*Consejo Federal de Seguridad*) in the Ministry of the Interior, which coordinated the Federal Police with other national agencies such as the National Constabulary and the Naval Prefecture. In 1953, mounting opposition to Perón led to further Peronist indoctrination of the police agency and more extensively coordinated surveillance. As a means to that end two bodies were created, respectively the Technical Advisory Board and the Commands.[67]

Policing in the Aftermath of the "Liberating Revolution" of 1955

Political changes after Perón's 1955 overthrow brought about the reorganization of the Federal Police. Among the changes introduced were the suppression of the Technical Advisory Board and the Police Code.[68] Although according to Adolfo Enrique Rodríguez's official account the structure of commands was eliminated, their activities continued after 1956—according to police memoirs and secret police dossiers—but were redistributed to the Federal Coordination Division. Changes introduced by the Peronist government in the police structure coexisted with previous tasks that had been reassigned during the Perón era. For example, Social Order was now handed the control of communism (was the Special Branch eliminated?) and the *Sección Gremial* was now put to work against the Peronist labor movement. Political dossiers created against the anti-Peronist opposition were relocated to the Identification branch but not destroyed.

For the first time since it was created, there was a general military takeover of the police organization. The appointment of police chiefs from outside the career structure was a well-rooted habit, and the installment of career police officers had always been the exception rather than the rule (that is, during Radical governments). From 1880, when the Capital Police was created, until September 1955 when Peronism was ousted, 30 of 47 chiefs of police had been military men, most of them still on active duty.[69] Thus, 64 percent of the chiefs of police had belonged to the armed forces. The democratic governments of Yrigoyen and Alvear appointed almost all career police officers and lawyers; that is, out of nine career police officers, seven lawyers and a public official, twelve were appointed by those governments.

What was peculiar to the 1955 realignment was the takeover by military men of the upper echelons of the hierarchy in the capital and in the federal districts (*delegaciones*) in the interior. This military takeover of the institution had no precedent in the 1930 coup. It seems that the "Peronization" of the police as an agency of the state had been so widespread that a military takeover was conceived as the only means to dismantle "the totalitarian structures" of the Peronist era. Nevertheless, previous changes in the police structure remained in place and, although the specific subjects of police attention and its methods were redirected to other targets, the post-1955 organization was not an ad hoc creation but founded on preexisting patterns of policing. Still, after Perón's overthrow the number of detainees rose as well as the incidents of police torture. Human rights violations increased in scope and severity again following the 1966 coup that brought General Juan Carlos Ongania to power.[70]

While the Peronist police had been a mainstay of the Peronist government, they had no choice but to join the winning side after Perón was deposed. In any case by then the police had become an autonomous agency, unlikely to put all its stakes on the losing side and ready to defend its own corporate interests. An internal dynamic of surveillance not answerable to the rule of law was the police domain par excellence, and this could be put to work for any government. In effect they were following their "professional" interest to maintain order.

Conclusion

In contrast to the English consensual model of law enforcement, policemen in Argentina were rarely considered to be at the service of the people, nor did they have qualms over constitutional "nuances." More attuned to the French statist model, military values and practices were considered crucial since the police were deployed as an instrument of the central government.[71] The development of police professionalization in Argentina can be seen in the light of a gradual movement toward increased corporate power and freedom from external review. Police accountability for misbehavior—either through internal proceedings within the police department or through the judiciary—have not been subject to a clear set of written rules (those that were written were disregarded in any case) but has been guided by double standards in which political criteria sometimes played a central role. Police lack of accountability and insulation from society were ingrained in the everyday world view of the Capital Police—and later on the Federal Police. In their struggle against subversion—defined and redefined following political changes—the military and the police intermingled, each perfecting its hold on domestic political policing. Despite attempts at reform and acceptance of democratic practices inculcated during Radical governments, a view that stressed the need of a militarized police because of the contentious nature of Argentina's immigrant population prevailed. Top priority was given to the repression of social and political disorder, since civil violence rather than crime was considered the major threat to public order.

In effect, political policing increasingly came to dominate the ideas of the forces' officers about their role in society. Conversely, "deviant behavior" was increasingly defined in political terms as subversive of the social order.[72] With a Manichaean view of the world, city police persecuted those who seemed to pose a danger to the lives of "decent" people, ranging from political subversives to those who defied the cultural, moral, and legal order. In the words of Col. Juan F. Velazco, chief of police under Perón, whoever rebelled against police authority was the "blackmailer . . . substance abuser . . . man of low life . . . shameless woman without prejudices . . . pamphleteer and bomb thrower."[73] This view assumed that political dissidents, crazy people, and criminals sprang from the same causes and required the same treatment: repression, social control, and reeducation. These ideas of the enemy within and the police engaged in a "war against crime" or in a "war against subversion" were constructed long before 1976. However, after 1976 the police increasingly became "willing executioners" of those deemed beyond reeducation.

The history of Argentine policing illustrates how the creation of police forces and techniques to protect lives and property and its diversion to combat public evils undermined the conditions for democracy. Police power was diverted to extralegal action against putative enemies of the regime. Since the federalization of Buenos Aires and especially during the tenure of Col. Falcón, state agents spread the means of repression, coordination, and repression throughout the nation. Despite the hopes raised by Yrigoyen's police reform, the structure that the police organization had achieved during the oligarchic regime changed very little. After the 1930 military coup, political policing became the central police function. The police was put to work for Justo's omniscient surveillance network. Changes in regimes brought about changes in police personnel through clientelistic appointments and purges; these demonstrated the vulnerability of the police to political changes. However, vulnerability to actions of the executive did not mean blind subordination. The unfolding of police codes of conduct crystallized in a strong corporate identity which would enable the police to align with Peronism as if they were just another trade union. The police continued to serve the regime while attacking newly defined enemies of the state; now the police became the "*pueblo* (people)."

Shifts in the balance of power influenced the police, and police survival depended on loyalty to the regime. Thus when Perón was ousted, the police were unlikely to stake everything on the losing side in order to defend their own interests. By now an autonomous agency not accountable to the rule of law, the police could be put to work for any government. Furthermore, this shift could be justified and legitimized by professional necessity.

In sum, the Argentine police became effective agents of political control. They became even more subordinate to whatever regime came to power than the military, and played their part in repression more covertly than the military—which ironically made them more dangerous under the authoritarian regimes that followed Perón. Their unfolding as a "reserved domain" of policy alien to the rules of contestation and accountability has hindered the consolidation of democracy in Argentina.

Notes

1. I am indebted to Juan Corradi and Eric Hobsbawm for their insightful discussions with me on earlier versions of this project; to Charles Tilly and Luis Fleischman for their thoughtful comments on this article; and to the Social Science Research Council MacArthur Foundation for their support of this research.

2 . The city of La Plata, located thirty-five miles south of Buenos Aires, was laid out as the new capital of Buenos Aires province after that city was named the national capital in 1880. The students of the University of La Plata—concentrated in compact communities—are pivotal to the life of the city.

3. *Página 12*, February 24, 1996, p. 3. *Página 12* and *Clarín* of February and March 1996 are the main sources of information in this narrative. Although these events are still under investigation, they were not isolated excesses by some "deranged" or tough policemen; police personnel followed orders. For example, the chief of Unidad Regional VI of La Plata, Comisario Mayor Basilio Holos, gave order number 054/96 on February 16 to police precincts from Berisso, Ensenada, and La Plata to "use unmarked cars." *Página 12*, March 8, 1996, p. 4, and *Clarín*, March 8, 1996, p. 10.

4. *Página 12*, February 25, 1996., pp. 8–9.

5. Ibid. Formed in 1977 by mothers whose children had been "disappeared" by the military, Madres de la Plaza de Mayo is the best-known Argentine human rights organization. The mothers protest by marching around the Plaza de Mayo in Buenos Aires, wearing white scarves and carrying poster-sized photographs of the disappeared. See Allyson Brysk, *The Politics of Human Rights in Argentina: Protest, Change and Democratization* (Stanford, CA: Stanford University Press, 1994) and Marguerite Guzman Bouvard, *Revolutionizing Motherhood: The Mothers of the Plaza de Mayo* (Wilmington, DE: Scholarly Resources, 1994).

6. In effect, according to Pedro Klodczyk, police chief of Buenos Aires province, these events were triggered by the "infiltration among students, of people following illicit ends." *Página 12*, February 24, p. 3, and 25, p. 5, 1996. Klodczyk's euphemism masks accusations against Quebracho, a leftist organization, and the presence of Hebe de Bonafini of Mothers of the Plaza de Mayo during the events. Furthermore, Hebe de Bonafini was among the injured. For the use of euphemism in the public transcript as a way of "sanitizing" and obscuring coercion see James Scott, *Domination and the Arts of Resistance* (New Haven: Yale University Press, 1990), chap. 3.

7. Over many years the Centro de Estudios Legales y Sociales (Center for Legal and Social Studies) has reported the problem of abuse of deadly force by clipping news stories of police killings. Whereas in 1994, 124 civilians and 19 policemen died in the Federal Capital and Gran Buenos Aires; in 1995, 195 civilians and 29 policemen died, allegedly in police shootouts. *Clarín*, March 17, 1996, p. 6, and *Página 12*, March 12, 1996, p. 2. The level of official violence is dismaying. See Paul Chevigny, *Edge of the Knife: Police Violence in the Americas* (New York: New Press, 1995).

8. *Página 12*, February 24, 1996, p. 4. Since I wrote this article, the situation has dramatically deteriorated. See *La inseguridad political: Violencia de las fuerzas de seguridad en la Argentina* (Buenos Aires: CELS, Human Rights Watch, Eudeba, 1998).

9. On fear see Juan Corradi et al., *Fear at the Edge: State Terror and Resistance in Latin America* (Berkeley: University of California Press, 1992). For an analysis of the construction of memory see Elizabeth Jelín, "The Politics of Memory: The Human Rights and the Construction of Democracy in Argentina," *Latin American Perspectives* 21, no. 2 (Spring 1994): 38–58. See also Carina Perelli, "Settling Accounts with Blood Memory: The Case of Argentina," *Social Research* 59, no. 2 (Summer 1992): 415–51.

10. Here, I follow Brysk, *Politics of Human Rights in Argentina*, 16.

11. Although democracy was restored in 1983, the rules of contestation and accountability were not fully applied to the military and the police. During the Raúl Alfonsin government, military uprisings and lack of discipline hampered the democratization process. Menem's pragmatic implementation of irreversible reforms—the amnesty of military officers charged with crimes against human rights—at the same time have curtailed the military and preempted its ability to stage a coup. Menem's government has halved military spending, dramatically reduced the armed forces, abolished mandatory service, and sold military enterprises. See Juan Corradi, "Menem's Argentina, Act II," *Current History* 94 (February 1995): 76.

12. Guillermo O'Donnell talks about obstacles to the consolidation of democracy presented by "reserved domains" of policy from which democratic governments are excluded in "Transitions, Continuities, and Paradoxes," *Issues in Democratic Consolidation*, ed. Scott Mainwaring et al. (Notre Dame: University of Notre Dame Press, 1992). Also see Guillermo O'Donnell, "Delegative Democracy," *Journal of Democracy* 5, no. 1 (1994): 56–59.

13. See Laura Kalmanowiecki, "Military Power and Policing in Argentina" (Ph.D. diss., New School for Social Research, 1996).

14. The bombing of the Jewish headquarters (AMIA) on July 18, 1994, and the indictment of members of the Buenos Aires provincial police in connection with this terrorist attack illustrate this problem. In this vein see Laura Kalmanowiecki, "Police, People, and Preemption in Argentina," in Martha Huggins, ed., *Vigilantism and the State in Modern Latin America: Essays on Extralegal Violence* (New York: Praeger, 1991). On the AMIA bombing see Luis Fleischman, "The Case of the Jewish Headquarters of Buenos Aires (AMIA): A Structural Approach," *MACLAS* 12 (1999): 119–34; and Laura Kalmanowiecki, "A Policed Democracy: Police and the People in Modern Argentina after the AMIA Bombing," paper presented at the conference, "The Contested Terrains of Law, Justice, and Repression in Latin American History," Yale University, 1997.

15. On police development and redefinition of its tasks see Hsi-huey Liang, *The Rise of the Modern Police and the European State System from Metternich to the Second World War* (New York: Cambridge University Press, 1992).

16. Mark D. Szuchman, "Continuity and Conflict in Buenos Aires: Comments on the Historical City," in Stanley R. Ross and Thomas F. McGann, eds., *Buenos Aires—400 Years* (Austin: University of Texas Press, 1982), 53–63 and "Disorder and Social Control in Buenos Aires, 1810–1860," *Journal of Interdisciplinary History* 15, no. 1 (Summer 1984): 83–110.

17. Richard W. Slatta and Karla Robinson, "Continuities in Crime and Punishment: Buenos Aires, 1820–1850," in Lyman L. Johnson, ed., *The Problem of Order in Changing Societies: Essays on Crime and Policing in Argentina and Uruguay, 1750–1940* (Albuquerque: University of New Mexico Press, 1990).

18. Lyman L. Johnson, preface in Johnson, *The Problem of Order in Changing Societies*, xiv.

19. When referring to a "modern police force," I define the police as the "bureaucratic and hierarchical bodies employed by the state to maintain order and to prevent and detect crime." Clive Emsley, *The English Police: A Political and Social History* (New York: St. Martin's Press, 1991), 1. I borrow here from Emsley's broad definition of a state police employed by the state police whether under national, county, or municipal authority. In this sense the modern bureaucratic policeman is not private but is an instrument of the state.

20. Alain Rouquié, *Poder militar y sociedad en la Argentina* (Buenos Aires: Emecé Editores, 1981), 70.

21. Gino Germani, *Política y sociedad en una época de transición: De la sociedad tradicional a la sociedad de masas* (Buenos Aires: Editorial Paidos, 1962), 197.

22. These provisions were delineated in Article 3 of the Reglamento of 1885, which gave Capital Police the power to intervene in matters that allegedly threatened the security of the state.

23. Among the branches created at that time are the Comisaría de Pesquisas (1886), antecedent of the Investigative Division; an Anthropometric Office that implemented the Bertillon system of personal identification (1889); and a Mutual Aid Society in 1890 (Caja de Socorros, later on the Dirección de Obra Social). In 1893 the feared Escuadrón de Seguridad (Security Squadron, currently the Mounted Police Corps) was organized on the basis of the existing Cavalry Unit. In Leopoldo C. López, *Reseña Histórica de la Policía de Buenos Aires, 1778–1911* (Buenos Aires: Imprenta y Encuadernación de la Policía, 1911), 238–41; and Adolfo Enrique Rodríguez, *Cuatrocientos Años de Policía en Buenos Aires* (Buenos Aires: Biblioteca Policial, 1981).

24. Enrique Fentanes, *Compendio de ciencias de policía* (Buenos Aires: Editorial Policial, 1979), 166.

25. The Comisaría de Ordenes replaced the preexisting secretariat and came just under the chief of police in the hierarchy. The secretary was an intermediary between the chief of police and the various sections.

26. Here I borrow from state theory the idea of the state as a territorially centralized form of organization in which a set of administrative, policing, and military organizations are headed and coordinated by an executive authority. See Theda Skocpol, *States and Social Revolutions: A Comparative Analysis* (New York: Cambridge University Press, 1979); Charles Tilly, *As Sociology Meets History* (New York: Academic Press, 1981); and Michael Mann, *States, War, and Capitalism: Studies in Political Sociology* (New York: Blackwell, 1988). In this sense it could be said that the police, as an institution that monopolizes coercion within a territorially demarcated area, needs to assert such monopoly of coercion within its own administrative domain as well.

27. The main component of the Security Division was uniformed police on street patrol distributed along the different police precincts of the capital and charged with maintaining public order, broadly defined. The Investigative Division consisted chiefly of political and criminal police (also called judicial police

or the detective force), operating in plain clothes. The work of the Administrative Division included the routine administrative tasks of the police apparatus, espcially the management of personnel and internal finances. Finally, the Judicial Division served as the liaison between police and judiciary. Branches such as those in charge of prisons, reformatories, and minor asylums also belonged to the Judicial Division. The firefighters and health divisions (the latter in charge of the health of the police personnel) were later subsumed under the other divisions.

28. The reorganization of the police into prefectures upon the establishment of the military dictatorship in 1930 should be considered as an exception of short duration since in 1933 the previous structure was reestablished, although with a radically different degree of centralization.

29. See Amleto Donadio, *Noticioso Policial* (Buenos Aires: Ediciones Anaconda, 1943); Ramón Falcón, *Memorias de la Policía de la Capital* (Buenos Aires: Imprenta y Encuadernación de la Policía, 1906–9), 4-279; Julia Blackwelder, "Urbanization, Crime and Policing: Buenos Aires, 1880–1914," in Johnson, *The Problem of Order in Changing Societies*; Laurentino Mejías, *La policía . . . por dentro* (Barcelona: Imprenta Viuda de Luis Tasso, 1913).

30. For a comparative case of the punitive crushing of political opposition in accordance with a "citadel practice" mentality, see Alf Ludtke's analysis of the Prussian police in *Police and the State in Prussia, 1815–1850* (New York: Cambridge University Press, 1989). On police expansion see also Julia Blackwelder, "Urbanization, Crime and Policing: Buenos Aires, 1880–1914," in Johnson, *The Problem of Order in Changing Societies*.

31. I do not want to confuse the reader with the innumerable police sections that were successively created. It may be more useful for present purposes to stress that the structure of four main divisions was maintained until the 1930 coup.

32. Richard Walter, *The Socialist Party of Argentina, 1880–1930* (Austin: University of Texas Press, 1977), 45–47.

33. Falcón, *Memorias*, 1906–9, p. 152 and Archivo Ministerio del Interior, 1908, file 2054.

34. José Rossi, *Policía de la Capital Federal, Memoria de la Comisaria de Investigaciones* (Buenos Aires: Imprenta y Encuadernación de la Policía, 1905), 3–22.

35. For example, *La Razón* and *El Nacional* complained that with the creation of the Escuela de Agentes in 1907, Falcón attempted to "establish a factory of police officers." For them "it would be better for him [Falcón] to go follow his military vocation in the Chaco and be replaced by a civilian who understood the police as a civil institution." Quoted in Adolfo Enrique Rodríguez, *Historia de la Policía Federal Argentina* (Buenos Aires: Policía Federal Argentina, 1975), 318. See also "El Coronel Ramón L. Falcón y la Militarización de la Policía," *Mundo Policial* (1975): 26–57. However, the young cadets were not always criticized. Some celebrated them in the tango "La Yunta Brava." Popular verses were also written in their honor such as, "They're the police cadets, captained by Falcón; they always proceed energetically, and they go serenely all the way to the top." *Revista de Policía y Criminalística* (1939–40): 15.

36. The escalation of labor conflict and the conservative reaction to it led to the "Semana Trágica" (Tragic Week) of 1919, when a paramilitary organization and police attacked striking workers and the Jewish community. In 1921–22, hun-

dreds of rural workers were massacred in Patagonia when military operations were carried out by army troops determined to crush any outburst of spontaneous violence. David Rock, *El Radicalismo Argentino* (Buenos Aires: Amorrortu, 1975); Sandra McGee Deutsch, *Counterrevolution in Argentina, 1900–1932: The Argentine Patriotic League* (Lincoln: University of Nebraska Press, 1986).

37. These ideas were in line with those expressed at the 1926 Great Police Exhibition in Berlin. On police reform during the Weimar period see Richard Bessel, "Policing, Professionalisation and Politics in Weimar Germany," in Clive Emsley and Barbara Weinberger, eds., *Policing Western Europe: Politics, Professionalism, and Public Order, 1850–1940* (Westport, CT: Greenwood Press, 1991).

38. Adolfo Enrique Rodríguez, Tomo VII, vol. 262 (Buenos Aires: Editorial Policial, 1978), 14.

39. The expansion of the army's influence in politics also can be traced to Yrigoyen's use of favoritism in making promotions and removing provincial governments, which were at the root of Argentine officers' growing disaffection. Robert Potash, *El Ejército y la Política en la Argentina, 1928–1945* (Buenos Aires: Editorial Sudamericana, 1981), 55–59; Elizabeth White, *German Influence in the Argentine Army, 1900 to 1945* (New York: Garland Publishing, 1991), 6, 86. The Logia General San Martin, a secret society created with the aim of eradicating politics from within the army, tried to influence the military policy of President-elect Marcelo T. de Alvear, who received a visit from Lieut. Col. García (chief of police, 1932–1935), Enrique Pilotto (chief of police, 1932), and Abraham Quiroga. They presented Alvear with a memorandum that listed a series of demands on his future presidency. Alvear complied with this *planteo*. Juan V. Orona, *La logia militar que derrocó a Hipólito Yrigoyen* (Buenos Aires, 1966), 17. The Logia's first president, Col. Luis Jorge García, was appointed chief of police during Alvear's presidency.

40. In Waisman's view, the use of force by Yrigoyen's party was "more a reflection of panic and a lack of capability for riot control than a systematic policy of persecuting the labor movement." Carlos Waisman, "Argentina: Autarkic Industrialization and Illegitimacy," in L. Diamond et al. *Democracy in Developing Countries* (Boulder: Lynne Rienner, 1989), 66. A good analysis of the radical government can be found in Luis Fleischman, "Civil Society and the State in Argentina: A Study of System Integration" (Ph.D diss., New School for Social Research, 1995).

41. Carlos H. Waisman, *Reversal of Development in Argentina: Postwar Counterrevolutionary Policies and Their Structural Consequences* (Princeton: Princeton University Press, 1987), 240.

42. This view prevailed in the ideas of police reformers such as José Carracedo Núñez. See his *Contribución al estudio y mejoramiento institucional de la policía de la Capital* (Buenos Aires: Talleres Gráficos de la Penitenciaría Nacional, 1928).

43. It is worth remarking that the basic structure of the police established by Falcón, and later on by Luis Dellepiane, remained substantially similar. The police organization consisted of a chief of police at the top who controlled the Judicial and Administrative divisions, Legal Advice, and Health. The general secretary was in charge of police personnel, dispatches, and archives. Dependent on the subchief of police were a garage section and the Investigative and Security Divisions, with new branches such as the Special Section in the Investigative

Division and the refurbished cavalry and infantry units in the Security Division. Likewise, there was a reduction of the centrality of the firefighters division, which was demilitarized and its functions narrowed to more specific tasks.

44. It should be noted that police coordinated fund raising and procured funds from citizens to modernize the institution.

45. Osvaldo Bayer, *Severino Di Giovanni, el idealista de la violencia* (Buenos Aires: Legasa, 1989), 286 and Rodríguez, *Cuatrocientos Años de Policía*, 207–8.

46. Bayer, *Severino Di Giovanni*, 286.

47. For example, in 1933 a secret commission was sent to Córdoba, a continual focus of Special Branch vigilance as well as of the Fourth Army Division. In the eyes of the "intelligence community," the large concentration of students in the province predisposed its population to communism, Archivo Justo, box 54, document 12, October 18, 1933, pp. 25–50. Confusion about the origins of Political Order and the Special Section divisions arises from the routine and surreptitious police practice of renaming branches without public notice, and this is why some authors see the Special Branch as a rebaptized Political Order and Political Order as a byproduct of the military coup. Rouquié, *Poder military sociedad*, 224, and Ricardo E. Rodríguez Molas, *Historia de la tortura y el orden represivo en la Argentina* (Buenos Aires: Editorial Universitaria de Buenos Aires, 1984), 94, 100. In fact, the Political Order Division had its origins in the Public Order Division in 1910, and was originally entrusted with the surveillance of political parties and threats to the security of the state. According to police dossiers, by 1915–16 it was still called the Public Order Division. In 1918 the Public Order Division was already referred to as the Political Order Division under the command of Luis Paullier. No explicit mention was made of this rebaptism of the police body. In any case, the mainstay of its activity remained the surveillance of political parties and political ideas. Socialism, anarchism, and the labor movement were entrusted to the other pivotal branch of the Investigative Division, Social Order. See *Memorias de Sección Investigaciones* from 1915 to 1919.

48. Archivo Justo, box 48, document 123 and document 84, 1934.

49. White, *German Influence in the Argentine Army*, 68, Boffi, 1933: 260.

50. Archivo Justo, box 98, document 112.

51. Archivo Justo, box 98, document 33.

52. Archivo Justo, box 99, document 9; Félix Luna, *Alvear: Las luchas populares en la década del 30* (Buenos Aires: Schapire Editor, 1972), 148–49. On the secret service see Kalmanowiecki, "Military Power and Policing in Argentina," chap. 4; and Rosendo Fraga, *El General Justo* (Buenos Aires: Emecé Editoriales, 1993).

53. Ruth Berins Collier and David Collier, *Shaping the Political Arena: Critical Junctures, the Labor Movement, and Regime Dynamics in Latin America* (Princeton: Princeton University Press, 1991).

54. In Rodríguez Molas, *Historia de la tortura*, 119.

55. Santiago Nudelman, *El Régimen Totalitario* (Buenos Aires, 1960), 3–115; Brysk, *Politics of Human Rights in Argentina*, 29–31.

56. This direct communication between Lombilla and Perón was further confirmed to me by Pedro Gamboa, chief of police from 1952 until Perón was ousted from power. In any case, for Gamboa, Lombilla was a "good guy," and much worse was the treatment that he received during his own imprisonment after 1955. Personal interviews with Gamboa, July 1994.

57. Without forcing the historical evidence, one can inquire about the extent to which the practices inaugurated then can be traced down to the most recent military dictatorship (1976–1983). In my dissertation, I suggest that to overcome the veil of secrecy surrounding the internal practice of the police apparatus, and confusion originating from the changing classification of police data, an analysis of police reports and administrative movement could be very useful. He also organized the Federal Coordination Directorate of the Federal Police and extended his power to other information apparatuses across the country. Verbitsky, 1985: 31. When Perón arrived from exile in 1973, Osinde organized a force of more than three thousand armed men, staged a shootout, and alleged that Trotskyist infiltrators had been planning an attack on Perón. The ensuing massacre fortified the right wing, which asserted that it had "saved" Perón from the left. Martin Edwin Anderson, *Dossier secreto: Argentina's Desaparecidos and the Myth of the "Dirty War"* (Boulder: Westview Press, 1993), 84–87 and Horacio Verbitsky, *Ezeiza* (Buenos Aires: Editorial Contrapunto, 1985), 31, 115.

58. When the Federal Police was created in December 1943, its commander was also the commander of the Capital Police. The Capital Police was converted into the Federal Police, and the Interior Division was created and placed in charge of the provinces. Rodríguez, *Cuatrocientos Años de Policía en Buenos Aires*, 209. Whereas the 1943 decree gave the Federal Police jurisdiction only in the national territories (that is, not in the provinces), after 1944 its authority was extended to the provinces and the federal capital.

59. In my view the bureaucratic work of the police and their registration of the internal movement gives the researcher a prima facie case for suspecting an actual change in organization and/or practice. Internal reporting in police memoirs has illuminating potentialities for the study of branches such as the Special Section. Likewise, it could open ways to cross-country comparisons of policing.

60. I expand the analysis of these interventions in my doctoral dissertation. Chief of Police Arturo Bertollo admitted in an unpublished speech that for many years the police had "cooperated with the army services in national defense and with the Minister of the Interior in anti-sectarian activities." *Las policías en sus misiones de seguridad civil de la nación* (Ministerio del Interior, Policía Federal, 1950), 5–10.

61. Under the presidency of Roberto M. Ortiz, the National Constabulary (Gendarmería) was finally created, but it was severely criticized by the Capital Police for its lack of national jurisdiction and for being limited to the federal governorships. *Revista de Policía y Criminalística* (1939): 45–48. In 1938, Chief of the Investigative Division Miguel Viancarlos had introduced a project in which he proposed the coordination of police services by the federal state, but it was not approved. Bertollo, *Las policías en sus misiones de seguridad civil*, 7.

62. Local politics strongly limited the power of definition of the state. For instance, after 1912, anarchists who were fugitives from the Capital Police were protected by the local authorities of Santa Fe province, where Radicals were in connivance with anarchists. David Rock, 1975: p. 316.

63. Juan Perón, "Speech to the Federal Council of Security," in *Código de Justicias Policial*, 1952.

64. *Memoria de la Policía Federal* (Buenos Aires: Policía Federal, 1945), 407–500.

65. Perón, *Código de Justicia Policial*, 1952.

66. Comisión Nacional de Investigaciones, Libro de la Segunda Tiranía (Buenos Aires: Integración, 1958).

67. The Security Command was in charge of coordinating security, communications, and firefighters; the Political and Social Command controlled the security of the state; and the Interior Command was entrusted with extraordinary activities in the interior. Rodríguez, 1981: 212.

68. Rodríguez, *Cuatrocientos Años de Policía*, 213–16; *Memoria de la Policía Federal* (Buenos Aires: Policía Federal, 1956).

69. See Kalmanowiecki, "Military Power and Policing in Argentina."

70. Brysk, *Politics of Human Rights in Argentina*, 30–31.

71. An extensive literature exists contrasting the British and French police. See Charles Reith, *British Police and the Democratic Ideal* (Oxford: Oxford University Press, 1943); and Emsley and Weinberger, *Policing Western Europe*.

72. Donna J. Guy, *Sex and Danger in Buenos Aires: Prostitution, Family, and Nation in Argentina* (Lincoln: University of Nebraska Press, 1991).

73. *Revista de Policía y Criminalística* 9, nos. 36–39 (1945): 84–85.

10

Medellín, 1991*

Alma Guillermoprieto

The general trend that began in the late nineteenth century reflected increasing concern with the specific criminalities of blacks, women, alcoholics, wife-killers, and prostitutes. Drug dealers and gangsters certainly fit this categorizing impulse. At the same time, elite concerns about drug trafficking also revived independence-era obsessions with the more generalized criminality of lower-class men.

Mexican-born journalist Alma Guillermoprieto's 1991 report on Medellín addresses the impact of the international drug trade on Colombian society: the culture of violence produced by an illegal economy, the pervasive and ambiguous role of drug trafficking in Colombia's developing economy, and the social costs of the United States-sponsored drug war. Its international dimension makes drug trafficking a particularly thorny "crime" problem; so do its undeniable economic benefits. Thus this essay, perhaps more than any of the others, explores some of the fundamental ambiguities of criminal activity: its economic logic, its social repercussions, its political costs.

As Guillermoprieto makes clear, international concerns—the U.S. obsession with Colombian drug cartels, Colombia's need for drug dollars as foreign exchange—play a crucial catalytic role in the current dilemma. At the same time, extralegal violence has a long history in Colombia. Geography is one factor: until the early twentieth century, high mountain ranges and dense tropical forests thwarted efforts at centralized rule, encouraging local systems of social control often dominated by regional strongmen (although not all were as brutal as Pablo Escobar). To further complicate matters, for more than a hundred years after independence, Colombia suffered from extreme sectarian violence between its two principal political parties, the liberals and conservatives.

*This essay first appeared in *The New Yorker*, April 22, 1991, pp. 96–109. Reprinted from Alma Guillermoprieto, *The Heart That Bleeds: Latin America Now* (New York: Knopf, 1994), 92–118. © 1994 by Alma Guillermoprieto. Reprinted by permission of Alfred A. Knopf Inc.

The most egregious examples: the turn-of-the-century "War of a Thou-
sand Days" (1899–1902) that left 100,000 dead, and the 1948 murder of
liberal, populist President José Eliécer Gaitán that began a ten-year un-
declared "civil war" known as La Violencia, *which took between 200,000*
and 300,000 lives. In the 1960s, as liberals and conservatives reconciled
their differences in the name of national preservation, leftist insurgents
forcibly wrested sections of rural Colombia from central government con-
trol. As if that was not enough, the 1989 assassination of liberal reformist
presidential candidate Luis Carlos Galán by drug traffickers opened yet
another round of violence. Thus, a long legacy of political turmoil has
compounded the problems of a traditionally weak central government.
Not surprisingly, that government has proven unable to enforce social
order even as (and sometimes especially when) it steps up repression.
Seen in historical context, the drug war is only the latest attempt, al-
though, as Guillermoprieto suggests, it is in some ways the most serious
challenge to civil society in Colombia. Here, at least, elite anxieties about
the degenerative effects of widespread criminality may well be warranted.

"We're all going to die."
Everyone here knows that if you get shot, run over, or knifed the
place to go is the Policlínica, an emergency clinic run by the San Vicente
de Paúl Public Hospital: the surgeons and interns who staff it on weekend
nights have intensive on-the-job practice and a reputation for performing
miracles. Security is tight; there have been instances of frustrated murderers who finished off their victims in the recovery room, so now guards
at the entry gate check to see that only the wounded and their relatives or
friends go in. Standing at the gate on a recent Saturday at midnight, I
watched a man emerge unaccompanied from a taxi, with blood seeping
from a large hole in his chest. He could still walk. He needed to, because
there are no hospital orderlies to help patients in at the gate, and although
I saw five taxis screech to the entrance and deliver five severely wounded
men in less than ten minutes, not a single ambulance arrived. Metal stretch-
ers were wheeled out and operated by the victims' friends or relatives, but
the man with the chest wound was alone. "How about that?" the gatekeeper
said, watching him stagger past. "Maybe he'll survive." He was not being
cynical; he knew from experience, he told me, that on weekend nights
about ninety such men appear at the Policlínica, and between twelve and
twenty die. Another taxi pulled up, and the driver helped a hysterical
woman drag out a young man with a gunshot wound through his back and
haul him onto a stretcher. He appeared to be dead. The taxidriver matter-
of-factly mopped up a pool of blood on the back seat and drove away. The
driver of the taxi that later took me home explained that picking up
wounded passengers is part of the job. "How can we leave someone to die

on the street like that?" he asked. "Most of the time, we lose the fares, because those people are in no position to pay, but we do it anyway, out of charity."

On nights like these, one can have the impression that Medellín is about to drown in its own blood. Over the past decade, the level of violence here has risen so far above what is rationally conceivable, even in a country as violent as Colombia, that statistics make no sense: What does it mean, for example, that last year, the most violent in Medellín's history, more than three hundred police officers were killed, along with some three thousand youths between the ages of fourteen and twenty-five, or that in the first two months of this year the rate had increased? When I first came here, in mid-1989, that year was already on record as being the most violent to date; I met a judge, a woman who had become anorexic because she was receiving constant death threats, and a few weeks later I saw in the papers that she had indeed been killed. Then, there was the radical left's representative on the municipal council—a bustling, courteous man I had also interviewed—who was assassinated in his office by a young man who had walked straight past the security guards. I talked to a man who had survived six attempts on his life and was waiting for the seventh wearing a bulletproof vest, not certain he would make it. The young, highly popular governor of the *departamento* of Antioquia, of which Medellín is the capital, was murdered by a car bomb on his way to work. Things only became worse after the joint United States-Colombia offensive against the drug trade got under way, in August of 1989, and the mood of the *paisas*, as the inhabitants of Antioquia are called, swung from stunned disbelief to a kind of hip cynicism. In the offensive's fourth month, a few weeks before Christmas, the police announced that they had surrounded the most wanted of Colombia's drug traffickers, Pablo Escobar, in one of his many Antioquia country estates, and that his capture was imminent. The general assumption was that he would not be taken alive. That night, I had dinner here with some friends at a restaurant that was unusually crowded and cheerful. "I can't imagine it!" a woman in our group, a chic and lively socialite, burst out. "I can't imagine a future without Pablo Escobar. I can't understand what it's going to feel like to live without fear; but the mere possibility makes me so happy that I feel like decorating the Christmas tree with little red coffins."

That mood has now passed—swept away by an avalanche of events that did not include Escobar's capture—and has been replaced by a wave of depression and self-doubt that permeates every conversation: How is it that the *paisas*, the proud vanguard of enterprise and innovation, the architects of Colombia's industrial future, the most punctual, God-fearing, and family-bound citizens of an otherwise slapdash country, have come to this? The question has even spawned a new breed, called *violentólogos*—researchers who try to make sense of the madness that has overtaken Antioquia, and who have a hard time just keeping track of who has killed whom. The proliferation of warring groups is staggering: in addition to Escobar's brigades, which continue their attack on the government, there are drug gangs, street gangs, death squads, "militias" (left over from guerrilla groups that passed through Medellín in the mid-nineteen-eighties, now operating on their own), paramilitary squads, and extortion brigades—all of them up in arms against the police and against each other. And now that bizarre truces and deals are being worked out between the central government, in Bogotá, and the illegal traders who have made Medellín the drug capital of the world, an even more sobering question is how the city will cope with a problem that only a short while ago appeared to belong exclusively to the drug trade but currently seems beyond the very considerable abilities of even a Pablo Escobar to control.

Viewed from densely populated hills known as the northeast and northwest *comunas*, the heart of the city—its gleaming white skyscrapers and brick office buildings—seem as remote as Oz. The hillsides are as much Medellín as the bustling, cheerfully venal commercial district in the valley, but not even the citizens of the ghettoized *comunas* see it that way. The "real" Medellín has factories, travel agencies, video stores, and probably more commercial square feet of clothing boutiques than any other city its size. On the hills, the spreading network of improvised housing is mottled with tiny grocery stores, an occasional school, movie house, and, here and there, a church. Half the population of Medellín lives there—about eight hundred thousand people—in brick and concrete houses that may slant a little but are nevertheless stable, with water and electricity that the municipal government has provided to even the most outlying areas. Yet when the people who live in the *comunas* describe their neighborhoods they often say there is nothing there, because there is nothing there that counts. No wealth, no prestige, no self-respect—only a gnawing resentment of the Medellín of shopping malls and nine-to-five jobs.

This is Pablo Escobar's power base. He was born, in 1949, a little farther uphill, in the misty, densely wooded mountains that surround the Medellín valley, into a family that seems to have been the embodiment of *paisa* pride: a farmer father, and a mother who was a schoolteacher—the kind of folks who keep their farmhouses immaculately whitewashed and then deck the porch with so many pots of hanging orchid and geranium plants that the whitewash barely shows through. Of all the stories Escobar might like to tell if he is ever captured, one of the most fascinating would surely be the account of his transition from respectable farmer's son to small-time hood. Certainly he was imaginative from the first: he found a way to make a living by reselling gravestones he'd stolen from a Medellín cemetery and sanded flat. He was ambitious: in 1982, as soon as he had made enough money from drug trafficking to build up a power base, he got elected to Congress as an alternate representative on the ticket of the Liberal Party. He was also vengeful: his leap to notoriety came in 1984, when he masterminded the assassination of Justice Minister Rodrigo Lara Bonilla, who had exposed Escobar's connections with the cocaine trade and forced him out of office just months before. From that time on, Escobar operated on two fronts: he created what narcotics officials believe was the largest and most efficient individual world network for the production and delivery of cocaine, and he waged a single-minded war against anyone in Colombia who spoke out against the cocaine trade, focusing on the justice system, and on anyone who supported the extradition of traffickers to the United States, where the long arm of corruption could not spring them.

After dozens of political assassinations, and after twenty months of what must be the most determined manhunt ever mounted by the Colombian government, Escobar, although militarily weakened, remains not only at large but in control of most of his business operations—sound evidence of a vast network of loyal supporters. Escobar nurtured that support carefully—with jobs, housing, and interest-free loans for the people of the *comunas*. He built on a belief his admirers once shared with almost everyone in Colombia—that drugs were the United States' problem. He exploited the business-loving *paisas'* inability to resist a good deal; there are plenty of people here who have learned to hate him but still cannot be completely persuaded that there is anything wrong with selling merchandise—any merchandise—for which there is a market. Mostly, though, Escobar prospered and survives because through the cocaine boom and his private war he has enabled thousands of dead-end kids to make the leap from the *comunas* to the otherwise inaccessible city beyond. [Ed. note: Pablo Escobar was gunned down in Medellín on December 2, 1993, by members of the government's Search Bloc.]

Culture of Violence

Alonso Salazar, a slight, mustachioed young man who has about him an air of almost preternatural alertness, is one of the most original of the new *violentólogos*. He drifted through the faculties of veterinary and journalism schools until someone urged him to collect a series of oral histories he had been taking and turn it into a book. It is called *No Nacimos Pa' Semilla* (We Weren't Born to Bear Seed), and it is selling out all over the country, because the oral histories were provided by the *comuna* youths known, variously, as *pistolocos* (crazy guns), *los muchachos de las bandas* (gang members), and simply *sicarios* (hired assassins). Salazar started collecting the boys' stories in 1988, when the extraordinary amount of criminal activity going on in the *comunas* brought them sharply to the "real" city's attention. One series of interviews, with someone he has called Toño, was recorded as the boy was dying of gunshot wounds in a bed at the Policlínica. "He was so bad, so evil," Salazar said to me one afternoon when he and I were sitting in a dusty, garbage-strewn plaza in the northeast *comuna*. "You could almost see him salivate when he told the stories about all the people he'd killed." Still, it makes Salazar sad to think of him, because the boy came to depend on his visits, and was grateful and proud that anyone would think he was important enough to be listened to. It was the same with all the interviews. "To have their lives become a word, a line of text, thrilled them," Salazar said. "They all wanted so badly to find a place in the world."

Salazar isn't baffled anymore by the combination of vulnerability and murderousness in the kids he interviews. The first thing that happened to him when he started out, he says, was that his view of the world turned upside down. Partly, it was because the boys were so nice, so amiable, that he found he couldn't keep the concept of evil in the forefront of his mind as he worked with them, and partly it was because the stories he heard were so similar. There is, it seems, a process at work—a series of events, some known, some still mysterious—that has produced a generation of hopeless suicides, whose particular form of self-destruction happens to be murder. Salazar believes that the first crime wave was partly provoked by the massive economic crisis that hit Medellín in the mid-nineteen-seventies, when the textile factories that were the heart of the city's economy closed down or fired thousands of workers. As it happened, that was also the period when the nascent cocaine trade consolidated into several cartel-like formations, one of them headed by Pablo Escobar. What Salazar still hasn't managed to understand is why these two phenomena coincided with a runaway increase in all forms of violence. Ever since the Conservative-Liberal civil war known as La Violencia came to an end, in the late nineteen-fifties, Medellín had been relatively peaceful. "But suddenly there was a burst of kidnappings," Salazar said. "You could argue that this was the drug trade's way of accumulating working capital, but the number of rapes and homicides also shot up. It seems that the whole society began to shred then." Recent figures show the trend: in 1980, there were seven hundred and thirty violent deaths in Medellín; in 1990, there were fifty-three hundred.

The gangs put together by the traffickers went largely unnoticed in the early part of the drug era, because they were used mostly for internal business—collecting bills, eliminating stool pigeons, and so forth. It wasn't until Escobar was drummed out of Congress by Justice Minister Lara Bonilla that the *bandas* acquired a paramilitary structure and a political role. Escobar put a young man named David Ricardo Prisco in charge of Lara's murder. With four of his brothers and several cousins and close friends, he formed a gang known as the Priscos, which was Escobar's most effective terrorist squad for the next six years, which was as long as it lasted. "Thanks to that murder, the Priscos were the first band to become notorious," Salazar says. "They became the prototype of a series of highly organized bands with close links to the drug lords. Their center was the family, and the barrio, with its network of family relations and loyal friends. A *sicario* from one of the bands could earn as much as twenty million pesos"—about two hundred thousand dollars—"for a single job, buy a luxury condominium in an upper-class neighborhood, and—this is fundamental for people in this culture—provide a better life for his family. At the height of their power, the bands emulated Escobar: they helped out the community with money and public works, and were considered benefactors. In peacetime, they organized street festivals, and they often had a police escort when they rode around the neighborhood."

Since early last year, when the Medellín police underwent a thorough purge of their ranks and a complete overhaul of the high command, they have been waging war on the drug trade, and the department is now fond of providing *organigramas* that show dozens of *bandas* neatly spread out in a series of networks leading straight up to Escobar. Salazar thinks that only about thirty percent of the Medellín gangs have such formal links to the drug world, and that it's the remaining seventy percent that are at the heart of the current wave of violence. They are the *chichipatos*, or small-time hoods; the *basuqueros*, or consumers of *basuco*, a highly addictive cocaine derivative; the *punketos*, still devoted to the music of the Sex Pistols and The Clash. What Salazar calls the "countercultural gangs" don't last very long as such, nor do the individual youths who join them. They are somehow free of the middle-class aspirations that gave discipline and structure to the now extinct Priscos and their spinoffs; the Priscos made a pact with destiny which had clearly defined goals—a short life, yes, but, in exchange, a B.M.W. and a penthouse for one's mother, say. The *punketos'* minds are too frayed for such orderly planning. Maybe it has something to do with their distance from the "real" Medellín. The Priscos came from Aranjuez, a well-established working-class neighborhood just up the road from Medellín's main drag. The *desechables*, the throwaway kids, come from much farther uphill. They have only recently been translated from the strict, hardworking world of rural Antioquia that their parents fled, and they are caught between cultures. They don't want their parents' thankless lives, and, to judge from a thirty-five percent unemployment rate in the *comunas*, the city doesn't want them.

Family Dilemmas

On a narrow street in the northeast *comuna*, just uphill from a plaza in the Guadalupe barrio, the kids had gathered in large numbers the other day, sullen and fashionable in their funky haircuts, baggy Bermudas, and hightops. Virtually all the neighborhood women and a good number of unemployed and elderly men had also crowded into the street, because word had flown around the barrio that Jesus Christ was manifest and visible there. He had appeared to a bus driver, who noticed that what seemed to be a damp spot near the bottom of his bathroom door was in fact a miraculous likeness of the face imprinted on the Holy Shroud. The driver, Ricario Hernández, was sitting in his empty, rattletrap bus, honking furiously at the crowd to move aside so he could park and have lunch. He and his family had tried to keep the apparition a secret, he told me, but in a matter of hours the entire community had somehow found out, and the crowds, in their eagerness to see the face, were on the verge of knocking down the driver's front door. Almost as exciting as the miracle itself was the fact that the local media had taken note of it: when a TeleAntioquia crew showed up with a camera, people in the crowd went nearly berserk in their eagerness to be filmed. "At last!" someone in the crowd exclaimed. "They're going to show something good about us!" A young woman explained why she was so happy. "Even if it turns out to be a fake, we'll have something nice to talk about," she said of the image on the door. "All we ever get to comment on is who went crazy from too much *basuco*, or who got killed. 'So-and-So's lying in a pool of blood on the corner,' they'll say, and we all go running over and stare."

Having failed to see the miraculous bathroom, I walked back downhill with the young woman and with her rotund and lively middle-aged neighbor, whom I had met earlier and whom I'll call Doña Violeta Mejía. The women pointed out a pretty young girl who had been thrown out of her house because of her hopeless *basuco* addiction, and the corner where the son of Doña Violeta had been shot down a year ago. Doña Violeta's son, it seemed, had a bad *basuco* habit, and stole, and probably also hired himself out as a killer, to support it. Eventually, he died at the hands of former playmates in the neighborhood. Weeping, Doña Violeta said that she spends hours trying to figure out what she and her husband did wrong. "My husband would take him aside, and say, 'Talk to me as a friend,' but he would grab his head between his hands and say there was nothing to be done," she said. "In the end, he would come home so stoned, so crazy, that he would bang his head against the wall until we grabbed him and held him back. We'd tell him he was going to kill himself, but he would say that was what he wanted. He wanted to die, he'd say. He wanted to rest. There was this great anxiety inside him, and we never figured out how to get to it."

There are so many kids in the neighborhood like that, the women said. They want too much, they want lives they can't have, they have no patience, and they are seriously hooked on *basuco*. I asked the women what they thought of Pablo Escobar, and they said that he and the other traffickers had done a great deal of harm, buying kids off and turning them into murderers, and bringing *basuco* into the world. But when we reached Doña Violeta's house, and settled down in a comfortable living room, her husband, Don Jaime, who was about to set off for his noon-day shift at a plastics factory, said that the neighborhood was also much to blame. There was a woman up the hill who, ten years ago, became the first person in the neighborhood to sell *basuco*. The Mejías and other neighbors remonstrated with her, Don Jaime said, but she answered, "I have my children to bring up." She had two sons then. Now one was dead, killed in a fight, and the other was hooked on *basuco*, but she was still selling the stuff. "We *paisas* are sometimes too interested in money," Don Jaime said. And yet, he added, if he had his life to live over again he would do everything the same way. Not Doña Violeta. She had come here with her husband a quarter of a century before "from the last village on the last road in Antioquia," she said. If they had stayed in the countryside, she believes, she would still have her son. But Don Jaime used the word *fracaso*, which means a shattering failure, to refer to what would have happened to him if he had stayed on as a day laborer on the coffee fincas of southwestern Antioquia. Here he had a house with four bedrooms and real tile floors, good food, a telephone. His three youngest children seemed to be doing all right, he thought. How could he have stayed in rural Antioquia?

The Mejías went through the list of the kids in the neighborhood who had died or were on drugs. On some streets, they claimed, every household had at least one addicted son or—less frequently—daughter. They said that their nephews suffered the same uncontrollable anxiety as their son, partly caused, no doubt, by the death squads that had started operating in the neighborhood. Because the men who roamed the streets at night, with brown kerchiefs tied over their faces, were brawny and not very young, the Mejías were convinced that they were cops. The men killed *basuqueros* and petty thieves, but sometimes missed their mark. Don Jaime and Doña Violeta pointed out the bullet holes in the facade of the house next to theirs, made one evening when the masked men started shooting aimlessly up and down the street. There was no place in the entire neighborhood where one could feel safe.

Later, I chatted briefly with their surviving son, a taciturn kid named Jorge Mario who smokes a great deal of marijuana but stays away from *basuco*. It was only midmorning, but he already looked as stoned as the kids in front of the bus driver's house, who, with joints dangling from their fingers, had been waiting to see the miracle. I asked Jorge Mario what he wanted to do with his life. "I'm a bum," he answered. "What's the point of making plans if I'm not going to get anywhere anyway? All the kids around here are getting killed. We're all going to die. It's useless." Then he went out to sit on the stoop and stare down at Medellín.

"No Future"

A panoramic shot of the distant city is a recurrent motif in the work of the filmmaker Victor Gaviria, who has succeeded in presenting Medellín as if filmed through the eyes of the *pistolocos*, for whom he feels an obsessive, painful tenderness. Gaviria has dedicated most of the last five years to documenting the violent lives of these kids; his first feature film, *Rodrigo D: No Futuro*, is a fictionalized account of the lives of the punks who acted in it. (One of them was Doña Violeta's son.) In the movie, filmed in 1986, Rodrigo D tries to recover from the pain of his mother's death, fails to make it as a drummer with a punk-rock group, and remains alienated from his neighborhood friends, all of whom are living a drug-and-adrenaline high—staging holdups and playing with guns. In the end, Rodrigo throws himself from the window of one of the skyscrapers that are inescapably in view from the hills. The title role was played by Ramiro Meneses, an aspiring musician from the *comunas*. He is the only one of the cast of boys who did not have a criminal record, and the only one who has been able to make the transition to an acting career in Bogotá. All the other actors are now dead.

I had lunch the other day with Gaviria, whom I have known for some time, and asked him to talk about the boys from the *comunas*. He was in the process of preparing a Colombian version of a television documentary on the deaths of his various actors, which he had made for German television, and he was still recovering from the death of his co-scriptwriter of *Rodrigo D*, a talented twenty-one-year-old named Ramón Correa, who was not able to star in that movie because he had been arrested and sentenced to prison for armed robbery just as filming was about to start. (On being released from prison, Ramón Correa traveled with Gaviria to present *Rodrigo D* at the Cannes Film Festival, but apparently found the experience more threatening than pleasurable. He despised the food, and seemed to feel that it was his duty to pick up the wallets and watches left lying so carelessly on the beach. Back home, he tried to do some serious writing, but he never made it. He died in January, shot to death in front of his mother's house.)

Gaviria said that he was drawn to the *comunas* by the same questions that haunt all Medellín: How could this city produce a generation of murderers for hire? How could all our values go so wrong? Despite the fact that he is now in his mid-thirties, there is something wide-eyed and vulnerable about him, a kind of inner adolescence that makes him sympathetic to the *punketos*' harsh music, their morally flat view of the world, their fascination with drugs. "I fell very much in love with the lives these boys lead, and we began a dialogue that in reality was between the two cities that coexist in Medellín," he told me.

His first encounter was with a teen-ager named John Galvis, who was killed a couple of months later. "When he walked into my apartment, he said it was the first time he'd been in an apartment building for a purpose other than stealing," Gaviria recalled. "Then he talked about his love for his mother. He told us how sometimes when he was feeling upset he'd go for a little walk with her, and smoke a joint, and then he would feel better. I began to see that this was all part of the *paisas*' intense devotion to their families. I understood that the most extreme acts of terrorism had their origins in kids' inability to see their families suffer, or fail, which is what always happens in these neighborhoods—the sister starts turning tricks, the brother gets hooked on *basuco*. I spent a long time recording interviews before I knew that I had to make a movie. It was because the phenomenon came to seem so normal, so much a part of everyday life, that I felt I had to leave a record of what I'd seen."

Gaviria, who is usually full of good-natured banter and, in white sneakers, a T-shirt, and bluejeans, always looks bouncy and clean-cut, was now talking in dead earnest, brushing aside interruptions while he let his food get cold. "For the kids, who in their lives have never known the slightest power, delinquency is a way of looking for power. No one pays attention to them, no one notices their lives. They're living N.N.s"—the "No Name" that identifies paupers' graves here. "Some of them have fathers with relatively structured lives, maybe even factory or construction workers, but these men are completely defeated—they have values that are useless in Medellín. The kids fall in love with whoever has power—you know, young people like values that involve some heroic element, some ability to achieve great things. Killers can do that—the kids have seen it on television, where the heroes have guns. That's why you can't explain the *sicariato*"—the culture of the hired assassin—"as an individual pathology. It's something else. Medellín is the capital of fashion, Colombians say, and fashion is the present. Medellín is the present. You go a few miles outside Medellín and it's all the past; it's all dusty roads, and farmhouses, and they've never even heard of the Gulf War there. These kids who have no place in the world, whom nobody has ever made room for, look at least for a place in time, in the present, through fashion. It's vitally important to them to look right. When they get money from a job, they spend it immediately on something for their mothers and on clothes. Of course they're not going to have any respect for their fathers, in their shabby old backcountry suits!"

Gaviria was a poet before he taught himself to make movies, and he has paid close attention to his actors' zigzagging, hazy, humorless speech. Through their words he has come to believe that in the *pistolocos'* fragmented world their essential relationship with reality is magical. "You see it in the language," he said. "At first, they used the word *traído* to refer to the things they 'found,' or stole. *Traído*, meaning 'that which is brought,' is a term we *paisas* use to refer to the Christmas gifts that the baby Jesus leaves on the table, so they would say, 'Look at this motorcycle, or this watch—what a *traído* I found!' Then the word became its opposite: *traído* referred to an enemy, and then to a corpse. That is, *traído* refers to everything that appears in front of one, which in the end is always death." An essential part of the magic involves turning everyone into an enemy, to ward off surprises. "Once John Galvis and another boy pulled guns on my producer and me, and yelled 'Quietos!'—'Freeze!' That's another word. There's a children's game in which you point and yell 'Freeze!' and turn the others into statues. Now the kids refer to their holdup or murder victims as *quietos*. When they pulled guns on me, they were turning me into a *quieto*. You turn your potential enemies to stone, and they can't threaten you. The kids spend their days looking for enemies, spotting them, making them up. The point is to kill them before they kill you."

In the documentary for German television, Gaviria traces the swift deterioration of his actors into *basuco* addiction and, eventually, death. In the opening shots, the boys complain that times are hard, that there is no work anymore, and, bitterly, that they don't even have the money for a decent pair of bluejeans. Then, one by one, they drop away. With one notable exception, all of those who were killed died at the hands of other boys in the neighborhood—boys whose relatives they might have killed, or boys with whom they might have shared a gun or a joint or been blood brothers just days before. "I think that in the end the kids kill just to see what it's like," Gaviria said. He is now working on a script about a fifteen-year-old killer he knew, who had held a wounded friend's head in his lap in order to watch him die. "I think they want to know how their own passage from one world into another will be," he said.

The exception who did not die at the hands of his peers was a boy known as El Alacrán—The Scorpion. It seems that his death was a consequence of one of Pablo Escobar's ongoing efforts to take revenge on the state for its pursuit of him. Escobar has been severely hurt by the anti-drug offensive that started in the summer of 1989. His chief associate, the rather bloodier and more reckless Gonzalo Rodríguez Gacha, was killed in December of that year. Escobar's principal commercial subalterns have also been killed, and on the military side of his operations he has seen the Prisco band wiped out. He is said to be cornered and to have cash-flow problems, and to a large extent all this has happened because the restructured Medellín police have managed to keep him on the run. Accordingly, Escobar sent word around the *comunas* last April that he would pay more than four thousand dollars for every cop killed. El Alacrán, who told Gaviria and his crew that he had once been gang-raped by a police squad, was more than eager to take up Escobar's offer. According to what are necessarily unreliable reports, El Alacrán killed a few cops, and then, one day last October, was chased down by police in a patrol car and shot to death.

Whether the Medellín police pursuit of the drug chiefs has degenerated into a private war between cops and gangs has become an openly debated question in the last few weeks, largely as a result of a car bomb that went off here on February 16th, and the bomb's aftermath. The car bomb, the signature weapon of the drug trade, exploded outside the Medellín bullring that Saturday afternoon just as people were emerging from the ring into the improvised fair that sets up after *corridas*. Twenty-four people were killed and more than a hundred were seriously wounded. Of the dead, ten were members of the Medellín police force. After the rubble from the bomb was picked over, and the victims were identified, police officials explained what had happened: the car bomb was placed near a supporting pillar of a viaduct underpass—an area that is used as a parking lot on days when there are bullfights. Someone then phoned the police and reported signs of terrorist activity near that spot. When the police had got close enough, the car bomb was detonated by remote control.

On February 17th, police spokesmen declared that the bomb was the work of close friends of the last remaining Prisco, Conrado, in revenge for the death of his last surviving brother, Armando, during a shootout with the police in January. According to the police, Conrado was a typically evil member of the family who went by the nickname El Médico—The Doctor. The following day, Señora Leticia de Prisco announced the disappearance of her son, and when his body was found, two days later, the staff of the Metropolitan Institute of Health declared that Conrado

Prisco had been a practicing physician—a hardworking doctor, who spent his free time in volunteer work and at the staff soccer games, and had no connection that anyone knew of to the violent world of his brothers. It seemed that somewhere a mistake had been made.

It is typical of Medellín's upside-down ethical universe that the New York-based human-rights group Americas Watch has found itself having to document claims initially made by Los Extraditables, as Escobar and a group of his associates like to be called, of police torture and arbitrary execution of drug suspects, and that Los Extraditables now routinely champion the cause of human rights in their communiqués. It is also typical of the bizarre, contradictory, and confused relations between the state and the drug trade that in Bogotá the Attorney General has opened an investigation into these charges. There are several reasons for his doing so, one being that there is serious evidence that the police routinely take the law into their own hands. It is also true that Escobar is using the cause of human rights as part of a campaign to obtain status as a "politico-military organization" similar to two guerrilla groups that were able to turn in their weapons and rejoin civilian life within the last two years. To the degree that the government is considering Los Extraditables' allegations of human-rights violations, it is signaling that political status—or some satisfactory equivalent—is not impossible. But if Pablo Escobar and his Extraditables can get a hearing from the Attorney General it is mostly because they are already a political reality and a social force whose demands the establishment can no longer ignore.

"The Democratization of Pain"

Spanish is not a language that lends itself to neologisms, and they're somewhat frowned upon in Colombia, where part of the self-definition of the élite involves a commitment to guarding the purity of the language. Nevertheless, the drugs and the violence in Medellín are so far beyond the scope of the Real Academia dictionary that new words are forever cropping up: there's *basuco* from *pasta base de cocaina*, there's *pistoloco*, *violentólogo*, *paniquear* (as in the English verb "to panic"); and there's the ever-growing list words prefixed with *narco-*, among them *narcocondominio* and *narcocongresista*. Old words also come to be used in curious ways. There is, for example, the "democratization" of wealth that the trade has brought Colombia, which means the ability granted working-class people suddenly in the possession of drug money to rub it in the faces of the rich. Apologists for the drug trade often argue that the upper classes and the political establishment in Bogotá would never have opposed the drug trade if it had not enabled former punks and small-time hoods to buy property in the posh neighborhoods, and they may be right. In the nineteen-seventies, when Escobar was making his fortune, dealing cocaine was still looked upon by many as a questionable but harmless occupation, and I know society women whose mothers went on international shopping trips with Escobar's mother and thought the experience was a giggle. It wasn't until the consolidated drug trade emerged, in the mid-eighties, as an economic and paramilitary power capable of overturning the norm of doing business in Colombia that the establishment reared back in alarm. But by then the traffickers had multiplied in number and in strength. Men like the Ochoa brothers and Escobar, in Medellín, and Gilberto Rodríguez Orejuela, in the city of Cali (about two hundred miles south of Medellín), are now probably the country's most daring and successful entreprenuers. The Ochoas ran—and probably still own—state-of-the-art cattle ranches, complete with solar-heating systems and other alternative-technology innovations. Rodríguez Orejuela made handsome profits from radio stations, drugstore chains, and soccer teams he owns. Even Escobar, despite a funny greased-down hairdo and a lower-class belly, has put on airs. The 1988 bomb set by his rivals that literally blew open the luxury apartment building where he then lived revealed an apartment described as tastefully, and even soberly, furnished, stuffed with a first-rate art collection that appeared to include everything from Chinese porcelain to paintings by Fernando Botero.

At this stage, drug money has so pervaded agriculture, commerce, and real estate that, according to an estimate by Salomón Kalmanovitz, dean of the economics faculty at the Universidad Nacional, the wealth could account for as much as seven percent of the gross national product. The members of what is known as the "leading class" have always been pragmatic—that's one of the reasons Colombia has remained institutionally stable and economically healthy despite constant turmoil—and there is among them a deep-seated conviction that, however repugnant the drug traders may be, they are now too powerful to be successfully challenged. Consequently, throughout the succession of government anti-drug offensives and drug wars there has remained an undercurrent of conciliation.

In 1984, former president Alfonso López Michelsen met in Panama with Pablo Escobar and Jorge Luis Ochoa, who offered to bring their money back to Colombia and turn over their laboratories if the government proved willing to grant them an amnesty. Five years later, when world consumption of cocaine had doubled, an intermediary for the Medellín group made a new offer, this time in a series of meetings with President Virgilio Barco's private secretary, Germán Montoya. The Medellín group was again offering to get out of the business, but this time they were asking for more. This time they wanted extradition declared unconstitutional. They also wanted to make sure that the country's various guerrilla groups—which had made a practice of extorting "war taxes" on ranch land, including the very considerable holdings of the *narcotraficantes*—would be defeated. Talks between Montoya and the Medellín intermediaries ended the week after the Presidential candidate Luis Carlos Galán was assassinated and the Barco administration declared war on the drug trade. But by then there were a number of members of the establishment—like Juan Gómez Martínez, the publisher of the daily *El Colombiano* and also, at the time, the mayor of Medellín—who were willing to go on record as stating flatly that the only way to bring the violence in the country to an end was to negotiate with the traffickers and legalize the cocaine trade. People familiar with the thinking of Barco's successor, President Cesar Gaviria, say that he was convinced long before he took office last August 7 that a negotiated way out of the drug crisis was unavoidable and indispensable. One of his first acts was to issue a decree that would eliminate extradition—the principal focus of the traffickers' anti-government campaign—if they turned themselves in. In addition, the government offered a major reduction of their sentences to traffickers who took up this offer. It is Gaviria's political misfortune that Pablo Escobar decided to strengthen the Presidential resolution with a series of kidnappings of prominent Colombians which began a few weeks after Gaviria's inauguration.

Two hostages now remain in captivity: one of the heirs to Colombia's most powerful publishing family; and the sister-in-law of Luis Carlos Galán, the Presidential candidate who was murdered on the day the 1989 anti-drug offensive started. Also in the initial group of hostages were Marina Montoya, the sixty-five-year-old sister of Germán Montoya, who is now Ambassador to Canada, and forty-year-old Diana Turbay, the cherished only daughter of former President Julio César Turbay Ayala (1978–82), who is an immensely powerful man. Sometime last October, when Los Extraditables had collected ten hostages, they announced that they would like to bargain, and this time they offered much less favorable terms than any in the past. The government immediately issued a few modifications of its original extradition decree; for instance, it allowed a trafficker who may be facing serious charges in the United States to avoid extradition by confessing to only one (presumably minor) crime. Polls showed that the public supported the unacknowledged negotiations, and so did the Archbishop of Bogotá and the leftist leader and the two former Presidents—Misael Pastrana and Alfonso López Michelsen—who occasionally form a negotiating body with the drug traffickers and the guerrillas. As a sign of drug traffickers' good will, there was quiet in Medellín for a few weeks, which gave rise to a type of story that appears once or twice a year in the local press under headlines like "Medellín Resurgent."

An image that filled the television screens late in January, of former President Turbay leaning over the coffin of his dead daughter, Diana, is likely to remain with Colombians for some time. Turbay is not a popular man here, particularly among liberals and the left. During his administration, the military were given a great deal of money and free rein in their endless war against the guerrillas, and it was in those years that Amnesty International issued its first damning report on Colombia, detailing the military's systematic use of torture. I watched the television report on Diana Turbay's funeral with a leftist friend for whom loathing her father was almost a matter of principle, but the sight of the heartbroken old man muttering endearments into the coffin made my friend blink and turn away.

"It's the democratization of pain," the *violentólogo* Alonso Salazar commented later on that scene. "It used to be that only the poor of this country had to feel that kind of sorrow." It was a botched show of force by the police at a farm on the outskirts of Medellín, where Diana Turbay was being held, that enabled her captors to shoot her before their escape. In the following hours, Diana's mother, Nydia Quintero (she is divorced from Julio César Turbay), added to the national commotion by blaming President Gaviria for her daughter's death. He should have kept the police away, she said, and she went on to ask that he make peace with the drug trade as quickly as possible. That, then, was the national mood two months ago: the cocaine traffickers are too powerful to take on; let's settle with them quickly, bring them into the mainstream, and put a stop to the bloodshed.

However, when President Gaviria went on television the following week and announced that further lenient modifications of the narcodecrees were being studied and would soon be announced, the speech did not sit well. "How much did the government give in?" *Semana*, the leading newsweekly, asked. On January 30th, the day after Gaviria's speech, a communiqué from Los Extraditables announced that before Diana's unfortunate death they had ordered the execution of another hostage, and that it was probably too late to cancel the order. The body of Marina Montoya was identified on January 31st. Seventeen days later, Fortunato Gaviria, a cousin and close friend of President Gaviria, died in the course of an amateurish kidnap attempt, which appeared to have been contracted out by Escobar. When Gaviria's government minister then affirmed that the new narcodecrees would stand, quite a few people thought that the President was looking craven.

Against that charge, Gaviria's defenders affirm that the decrees are part of a strategy to continue armed attempts to stop the drug trade while offering the traffickers a bloodless way out. They point out that Jorge Luis Ochoa, Medellín's second-biggest trafficker, has surrendered, along with two of his brothers, and is peacefully awaiting trial in Medellín. They don't point out, although they could, that while Pablo Escobar may be on the run and cocaine seizures are at an all-time high, the big 1989 anti-drug offensive has hardly been a success, despite having taken the military approach to the drug problem about as far as it can go. Except for Gonzalo Rodríguez Gacha, Escobar's terrorist associate, not a single head of a drug-export ring has been caught and Rodríguez's share of the market has simply been reapportioned among a group of up-and-coming traders. United States narcotics officials believe that partly as a result of the drug war, which has been directed mostly against the traders in Medellín, a group of traders based in Cali has been able to overtake the Medellín group in terms of their share of the export market. Meanwhile, the overall production and export of cocaine from Colombia are estimated to be up slightly from what they were when the offensive began. Under the circumstances, a negotiated surrender by the drug traffickers might make sense, but a member of the diplomatic community pointed out that the government has opted for a conciliatory approach "at a stage when the judicial system doesn't seem up to the task." The roles of judge and prosecutor are combined under the country's Napoleonic Code, and those judges capable of refusing a bribe often do not have the resources to gather evidence that will stick against even the most notorious traffickers. Someone here who was closely involved with the Ochoas' surrender told me that at this stage the government has no charges against any of the brothers, and that, even with evidence provided by the United States of charges against him there, the likelihood is that Jorge Luis Ochoa will get off with a three- or four-year sentence.

As for Escobar, this person thought that he was waiting to see the results of some of the Ochoa trials before turning himself in. Opinion is divided on this. Some diplomats here think that Escobar will settle for nothing less than recognition of Los Extraditables as a politico-military organization, which could conceivably entitle him to run for Congress again in a few years. Others think that he will never put himself in a Colombian jail, where a legion of his enemies could get at him.

Lost Opportunities

No matter what happens to the founders and leaders of the cocaine trade, however, no one seems to have any idea of what to do with the gangs they are leaving behind. There doesn't seem to be any way that even Medellín's comparatively generous municipal-services structure can stretch itself to the dimensions of the crisis at hand. There aren't enough ambulances, clinics, teachers, and efficient policemen to go around, and, anyway, it's unclear at this stage whether even the most judicious efforts by law-abiding cops and enlightened social workers could bring measurable short-term relief. I talked to a man involved from the social-services point of view in the city's efforts to cope with the violence, and he went on about municipal plans to unify the various existing plans, and about joint housing-rehabilitation programs with international nongovernmental organizations, and about the redirecting of budget expenditures, until I interrupted to ask whether he had ever been on the hills, and whether, having been there, he thought that any of his proposed measures would do any good.

At that, he threw up his hands and heaved a great sigh. "You would have to change the society altogether for the problem to disappear," he said. "*Paisas* are adventurous by nature. You know, Antioquia was colonized only in the last century, and the people who came here were mostly gold miners. We're a migrant people, enterprising, and fond of wealth and risk. The tragedy was that in the nineteen-seventies, when the private-enterprise system was crashing to the ground in Antioquia, the traffickers showed up with an alternative, and in a stratified society like this one it was very appealing: the traffickers said 'You, too, can have a swimming pool, and you don't even have to work for it. Work will never make you rich.' The fundamental thing is that we can't offer better prospects. We know of a lot of companies here that fire their good workers—the ones who last—at the end of their ninth year of employment, because after ten years they have a right to half a pension. How can you convince a kid that there's a future in being a good citizen and working a steady job? I don't see any real change in the situation for this generation."

I asked this man if the city's job would be made any easier by Escobar's capture or surrender.

He looked at me in amazement. "Don't you see that part of the reason things are so bad now is precisely that Escobar is so much weaker than he used to be?" he said. "There's tremendous unemployment among the drug gangs now, and they're all fighting for the available crumbs. Also, there are all sorts of old scores that are getting settled, now that there's no one to keep the lid on things. Everybody's free-lancing; there are the death squads and the pseudo-revolutionary groups. An awful lot of teen-agers have weapons. This city is going to be in dreadful shape for the immediate future."

Self-Defense

I met a young man, about twenty-five, whom I shall call Johnny. (The English name is a favorite here.) When Johnny was ten, his father, who was an alcoholic and traveled the countryside doing odd jobs, finally settled, with his wife and their six children, in the northeast *comuna*. By the time Johnny was twelve, he had learned to contribute to the meagre family income by begging. When he was eighteen, the military press-ganged him, along with dozens of other youths, in a noonday sweep through the streets of the downtown district. Following this forcible conscription, which Johnny describes as a "waking nightmare," he served out the man-datory eighteen-month draft term, acquiring an extensive knowledge of weapons and then an honorable discharge. He returned home and found a job as a security guard for a downtown office building. An overwhelming desire to "improve my mother's life" made him single out a friendly-looking executive and sneak some time from his duty hours to wash and polish the executive's car. His hope was that the executive would notice this, be pleased, and offer him a better-paying job as bodyguard, driver, or carwasher. What actually happened was that Johnny's supervisor caught him in the act and immediately fired him.

Eventually, Johnny was able to find another job, as a messanger, but the work pained him. Above all, he says over and over, he has always wanted desperately "to do the right thing, to improve my situation, to be a *persona decente*." He wanted to furnish his mother's house with matched dining- and living-room sets, and have a job in which he was not faceless and nameless, but he couldn't see his way from here to there, from mes-senger work to being called Señor. Nevertheless, he worked steadily for almost seven years, because he had found more consuming activities, which made his daytime hours seem pale and secondary. First, he ran into one of the many guerrilla groups operating in the *comunas*, and eagerly joined its clandestine game of hide- and-seek with the military, but after several months the Army moved seriously against the neighborhood and the guer-rillas swiftly withdrew, leaving Johnny and his friends to take the heat. Johnny lay low for a while, and then, through what he calls "a pioneering innovation," he found his lifework: he founded a *grupo de autodefensa*, or death squad, and he believes that it was the first of its kind in Medellín.

What got him started was the experience of seeing his younger brother Tony wounded in the course of a *banda* holdup at the corner grocery store in his neighborhood. The *banda* kids were attacking an old man, and Tony asked them to lay off. At this, one of the boys cracked a beer bottle in half and lunged at his throat, wounding him seriously but not fatally. Johnny says that he watched the assault and felt unbearably humiliated by his own impotence, and that that emotion is what guided him to the idea of an *autodefensa*. What is more likely is that, after a lifetime of systematic humiliation and terror with no possibility of retribution, Johnny under-stood that he was finally facing an enemy he could actually take on.

Johnny has talked with reporters before, and he easily agreed to talk to me. We met in a small, crowded coffee shop downtown, and no one paid any attention to Johnny—a nondescript young man in bluejeans and a baggy T-shirt—even though he got noticeably tense, occasionally rhetorical, and at times almost giggly as he talked.

"I formed the *autodefensa* with a neighbor who had a wife and two kids and was sick of violence, too," he said. "We didn't know how the two of us would manage to defeat more than two hundred kids who would be our sworn enemies, but we agreed that it was a risk we had to take. We recruited two other boys and started out on this endless task. On my block, one out of every three families had a son or a relative who was a *banda* member. We decided that the thing to do was to clean up the block first, and spread out from there. My idea was that we had to strike terror to the heart of the community in order to be effective. We went around and borrowed black shirts and trousers from some older men around the block, and a girl we knew stitched black hoods together for us. Then, one evening, around ten o'clock, we walked up to our first chosen victim, who was sitting on a stoop drinking beer; and we did it. We executed him. Then we ran around the corner, took our hoods and shirts off, and came back to help the family take the body away."

Johnny seemed both terribly frightened and amused at this part of the story. It was, he thinks now, an act of brilliance to remain in clandestinity while the kids from different *bandas* grew paranoid and started blaming each other for the wave of murders. In the first three months, he said, the *autodefensa* eliminated some thirty "undesirables." Then the work got easier, because the undesirables started eliminating each other, and those who didn't fled the neighborhood in terror. These days, he said, his barrio is a nice place to visit. It's *tranquilo*, calm, no problem.

Was his work finished, then?

"Oh, not at all. I don't know what makes these kids so perverse, but there always seem to be a few who like the bad life. Right now, there's a little spurt of activity, and, regrettably, I think we're going to have to take measures."

Shortly after my conversation with Johnny, a communiqué was delivered to the parish priest of Barrio Santa Cruz, in the northeastern *comuna*, with the information that someone would be at the Sunday sermon to make sure that the priest read the communiqué to the congregation. (He did.) The communiqué was signed by a group calling itself the GAM, or Grupo Amable Medellín, which translates as Nice Medellín Group. It said, in part, "We alert all parents and the community in general that they should dialogue with their sons so that they will not continue smoking *basuco*, since this is harmful to their health and a bad example to growing children. . . . There will be a general cleanup, and neither sex nor religion will be respected. We will shoot anyone who does not obey this letter."

A few days later, on February 27th, a group that signs itself Robocop took credit for the recent murder of nine teen-agers, who were rounded up when they were playing soccer in the northwestern *comuna*. Because they share a common target, one might conclude that groups like Robocop, Nice Medellín, and Johnny's *autodefensa* are friendly to the police, but there is no indication that these groups are linked to the police or even to each other. In fact, when I asked Johnny if he approved of the police's alleged involvement in the killing of the Prisco brothers and other murders, he was emphatic. "Cops are murderers," he said. "They massacre everybody. I'm a Christian, and I only take human life when it's absolutely necessary. Besides, there are some very respectable *bandas*—like the Priscos were, for example. They don't attack their own communities but only work outside. We don't touch them."

After our conversation was over, we left the coffee shop together. It was the height of the afternoon rush hour and I had trouble keeping Johnny in sight—an insignificant kid from the *comunas* without even a trendy T-shirt to stand out in. But Johnny knows perfectly well that he is an important person in Medellín, and I have seen pimply kids approach him on the street to seek his help in putting together death squads of their own. He is in demand, just like the numerous guerrilla leaders in Colombia whom journalists climb over mountains to get to. He makes guerrilla-like statements, as he did to me when he told me he had never been in love. "I preferred to devote my love to my homeland," he declared, holding himself very straight. He is a person of consequence, and he will continue to be so as long as he holds life-or-death power over a sizable number of people here. It's the only power he has, a power he shares with the punk killers who are his enemies, and it's enough to keep them all going for a long time—for as long, at least, as they live.

Bibliographical Essay

Carlos A. Aguirre

The historiography of crime and criminal justice history in Latin America has not yet reached maturity, or even perhaps legitimacy within the field of Latin American studies. With few valuable exceptions, it is only in the last ten or fifteen years that the field has begun to produce substantial and steady progress. Despite generally solid traditions of legal studies in most Latin American countries, generally produced by jurists and amateur historians, there has been a surprising lack of interest among the community of scholars—historians, anthropologists, and sociologists, both in Latin America and the United States—in issues such as crime and criminal justice history. However, there are reasons to envision that the years ahead will bring about an increasing attention to issues that we consider central for understanding the history of Latin American societies.

Because the coverage of this book starts in the late colonial period, this concise bibliographical review does not include the otherwise scant literature on crime and justice in pre-Hispanic Latin America. Studies about crime in colonial Latin America concentrate on Mexico and the Andes. A major contribution is William Taylor's monograph on drinking, homicide, and rebellion in colonial Mexico (1979), where he examines a specific type of crime (homicide) and its connections with other forms of "deviant behavior." Taylor found that interpersonal violence was more likely to occur against family members and outsiders than against fellow community residents, an expression of the communal cohesiveness that he found within Mexican villages. Two solid doctoral dissertations deal with crime in colonial Mexico City (Scardaville, 1977; Haslip, 1980), while MacLachlan (1974) analyzes the operation of the Tribunal de la Acordada, one of the most salient institutions of penal repression in New Spain. Sexually related offenses are examined by Penyak (1993) and Stern (1995), the latter within a more ambitious study of gender relations in late colonial Mexico. Several studies on bigamy, adultery, rape, and abduction in colonial Mexico also touch on related issues (see, for example, Boyer, 1995).

In the case of colonial Peru, Ward Stavig has long studied the history of crime and violence within the indigenous communities of the Cusco region (Stavig, 1986, 1990, 1991, 1995). Stavig underplays the role of crime in the strategies of resistance by Andean communities against the colonial state, stressing the divisions generated by unlawful behavior. Flores Galindo (1984) depicts crime in late colonial Lima as a major contributor to the generalized situation of anomic violence in the city, also discarding notions of "social crime" among urban plebeians.

The advent of independent nations in the early nineteenth century was bound to effect changes in the nature and patterns of crime as well as in crime repression policies, though continuities with the colonial past also were inevitable. Patricia Aufderheide (1976), for example, stresses continuity in penal practices in Brazil after independence, a process intimately linked to the maintenance of slavery as the central feature of Brazilian society. Studies about bandit gangs and their political significance before, during, and after the age of independence have illuminated many of the connections between crime and politics, especially in Mexico and Peru (Archer, 1982; Taylor, 1982; Hünefeldt, 1979; Walker, 1990). The intricate connections between the construction of new independent states and attitudes toward law and order have also been explored, especially for Argentina and Brazil. Szuchman (1984) and Slatta and Robinson (1990) studied crime and social disorder in Buenos Aires during the early nineteenth century. Slatta (1980) also reviews rural crime in the Buenos Aires province. In Brazil, studies concentrate on the connections among crime, repression, and slavery. Holloway (1993) highlights the role of the police in the control of slaves in Rio de Janeiro, Huggins (1985) studies crime in rural Pernambuco from a *dependentista* perspective, and Pereira Machado (1987) studies crimes committed by slaves in rural São Paulo.

The years between 1870 and 1930 have become, not surprisingly, the focus of intense scholarly attention. This is the period in which new discourses about crime and punishment were adopted in the region—particularly positivist criminology and penology—and various innovations in crime control policies were introduced such as new penal codes, modern penitentiaries and reformatories, systems of classification, and scientific study of the criminal population. This was also a period of increasing urbanization, immigration, capitalist development, and industrialization, all of which impacted on patterns of urban and rural criminality. The development of criminology as a scientific discipline has been analyzed by Buffington (2000) and Piccato (1995) for Mexico, Salvatore (1992), Ruibal (1993), Caimari (1997), and Salessi (1995) for Argentina, Salvatore (1996) for Brazil, and Poole (1990) and Aguirre (1996) for Peru. An earlier regional synthesis is offered by Rosa del Olmo (1981). Ana María Goetschel (1992) produced a valuable study of the connections between ideologies of state and discourses about criminality in nineteenth-century Ecuador.

Positivist criminology informed various attempts at reforming penal institutions in the region. Laurence Rohlfes (1983) analyzes penal and police reforms in Porfirian Mexico. Several articles in the volume edited by Salvatore and Aguirre (1996), as well as other contributions (Buffington, 1996; Cruz, 1989 and 1992; Cavieres, 1995; Picó, 1994), analyze the connections between new medico-legal discourses about crime and society and attempts to reform carceral institutions. Studies of specific penal institutions add to our understanding of both incarceration policies and the making of criminal subcultures. A fascinating monograph is the ethnography of the Lurigancho Prison in Lima written by Pérez Guadalupe (1994). Although prisons for women were less numerous and of less concern for reformers and authorities, studies of female carceral institutions are indispensable for understanding the connections between crime and punishment and a variety of discourses and practices (Caimari, 1997; Guy, 1997; Pearson, 1993; Rivera-Garza, 1995; Zárate, 1996).

Two classical themes in the European historiography of crime have received continuous attention in the context of Latin American societies: the relationship between crime and urbanization on the one hand, and the almost universal phenomenon of rural banditry on the other. A number of articles published by Lyman Johnson and Julia Blackwelder (1982, 1984 and Blackwelder, 1990) study the connection between levels of urbanization and crime for the case of Buenos Aires, using a mostly quantitative methodology. Urban crime, as a manifestation of various forms of social and cultural conflict, also has received scholarly attention (Fausto, 1984; Gudmundson, 1978; Silvestrini, 1980; Sánchez León and Del Mastro, 1993). Rural banditry has received considerably more study. Singelman (1975), Chandler (1978), and Lewin (1979) analyze the political implications of rural banditry in Brazil. In 1982, Paul Vanderwood published his superb study of rural banditry and policing in Porfirian Mexico (2d edition, 1992). The volume, edited by Slatta (1987), offers a showcase of the "varieties" of rural banditry in Latin America, while Aguirre and Walker (1990) edited a similar volume focusing on Peru and Bolivia. Rosalie Schwartz and Louis Pérez published valuable studies of political and social banditry in Cuba (Schwartz, 1989; Perez, 1989). Lewis Taylor (1986) has studied political banditry in Hualgayoc, Peru, during a period of growing state intrusion and capitalist development. Most of this literature was inspired by (and established a critical dialogue with) the Hobsbawmian notion of "social banditry." In an insightful essay, Gilbert Joseph (1990) calls for the integration of banditry within the larger field of rural conflict and resistance, thus trying to overcome the somehow sterile dichotomy between "social" and "common" banditry.

Sexually related offenses have continued to receive scholarly attention. Although not always technically a "crime," studies about prostitution are becoming numerous and offer a fascinating angle to approach the social, political, economic, and cultural construction of "deviance." Donna Guy (1991) studies prostitution in Buenos Aires during a period of accelerated social change; Sandra Graham (1991) analyzes prostitution in nineteenth-century Rio de Janeiro as part of the variety of alternatives that black women used to overcome poverty and deprivation; and David McCreery (1987) examines the lives of Guatemalan prostitutes at the turn of the century. Both Katherine Bliss (1996) and Cristina Rivera-Garza (1995) have produced important studies of prostitution in Mexico City during the revolutionary period. William French (1992) also has studied prostitution and other sexually related offenses in his social/cultural histories of Chihuahua, Mexico. Scholars have noted other links between gender and criminality. Kristin Ruggiero (1992) has studied infanticide in late-nineteenth-century Buenos Aires and Susan Besse (1989) crimes of passion in early-twentieth-century Brazil. The Brazilian discourse on female criminality has been studied by Sueann Caulfield (1993) and Martha de Abreu Esteves (1993), and Buffington (1997) has explored conflicting constructions of criminality and homosexual "deviance" in Mexican prisons.

The multiple ramifications of the alcohol and drug problems are of interest for an analysis of crime in Latin America. Piccato (1997) explores elite concerns about the degenerative effects of alcoholism in Porfirian Mexico, and Buffington (1994) analyzes its effects on U.S.-Mexico relations during Prohibition. Alonso Salazar (1992) offers a vivid portrait of drug-related youth violence in Medellín, Colombia. The legal, cultural, and social dimensions of the drug problem are analyzed in the volume edited by William Walker (1996). A historical and cultural account of the coca problem in Peru has been written by Gagliano (1994), and connections between the illegal drug traffic and political subversion in Peru are studied by Tarazona-Sevillano (1990).

Studies about the police are still few in number, and most concentrate on the twentieth century. Kalmanowiecki (1996) offers an insightful reconstruction of the history of Argentine police. For Brazil, Marcos Luiz Bretas (1994) has studied policing in Rio de Janeiro during the early decades of the twentieth century, while Elizabeth Cancelli (1993) analyzes Brazilian police during the age of Vargas. Martha K. Huggins (1991) has edited an important volume on vigilantism and extralegal violence, and

Paul Chevigny (1995) focuses on police violence in Latin America within a comparative framework.

Scholarly attention on these topics is gaining momentum, but there is still a great deal to do in the development of studies about crime and criminal justice history. Several geographical areas and periods are much unrepresented. Some topics—rural banditry or positivist criminology—have received considerable attention, while others—the making of criminal subcultures— are just beginning to be explored (Aguirre, 1996; Bliss, 1996; Piccato, 1997). We only hope that this volume will encourage further research and study on the criminal justice history of Latin America.

References

Aguirre, Carlos. "Criminology and Prison Reform in Lima, Peru, 1860–1930." Ph.D. diss., University of Minnesota, 1996.

Aguirre, Carlos, and Charles Walker, eds. *Bandoleros, abigeos y montoneros: Criminalidad y violencia en el Perú, siglos XVIII–XX*. Lima: Instituto de Apoyo Agrario, 1990.

Archer, Christon. "Banditry and Revolution in New Spain, 1790–1821." *Bibliotheca Americana* 1, no. 2 (November 1982): 59–90.

Aufderheide, Patricia. "Order and Violence: Social Deviance and Social Control in Brazil, 1780–1840." Ph.D. diss., University of Minnesota, 1976.

Besse, Susan K. "Crimes of Passion: The Campaign against Wife-Killing in Brazil, 1910–1940." *Journal of Social History* 22, no. 4 (Summer 1989): 653–66.

Blackwelder, Julia. "Urbanization, Crime, and Policing: Buenos Aires, 1870–1914." In *The Problem of Order in Changing Societies: Essays on Crime and Policing in Argentina and Uruguay, 1750–1940*, edited by Lyman L. Johnson, 65–88. Albuquerque: University of New Mexico Press, 1990.

Blackwelder, Julia, and Lyman Johnson. "Estadística criminal y acción policial en Buenos Aires, 1887–1914." *Desarrollo Económico* (April–June 1984): 109–22.

———. "Changing Criminal Patterns in Buenos Aires, 1890–1914." *Journal of Latin American Studies* (November 1982): 359–80.

Bliss, Katherine. "Prostitution, Revolution and Social Reform in Mexico City, 1918–1940." Ph.D. diss., University of Chicago, 1996.

Boyer, Richard. *Lives of the Bigamists: Marriage, Family, and Community in Colonial Mexico*. Albuquerque: University of New Mexico Press, 1995.

Bretas, Marcos Luiz. "You Can't! The Daily Exercise of Police Authority in Rio de Janeiro, 1907–1930." Ph.D. diss., Open University, Great Britain, 1994.

Buffington, Robert. *Criminal and Citizen in Modern Mexico*. Lincoln: University of Nebraska Press, 2000.

———. "Los Jotos: Contested Visions of Homosexuality in Modern Mexico." In *Sex and Sexuality in Latin America*, edited by Daniel Balderston and Donna J. Guy, 118–32. New York: New York University Press, 1997.

———. "Prohibition in the Borderlands." *Pacific Historical Review* 43, no. 1 (February 1994): 19–38.

———. "Revolutionary Reform: Capitalist Development, Prison Reform, and Executive Power in Mexico." In *The Birth of the Penitentiary in Latin America*, edited by Ricardo Salvatore and Carlos Aguirre, 169–93. Austin: University of Texas Press, 1996.

Caimari, Lila. "Positivist Criminology and the Classification of Prisoners in Early Twentieth-Century Argentina." Paper submitted to the 20th International Congress of LASA, Guadalajara, April 17–19, 1997.

———. "Whose Prisoners Are These? Church, State and Patronatos and Rehabilitation of Female Criminals (Buenos Aires, 1890–1970)." *The Americas* (October 1997): 184–208.

Cancelli, Elizabeth. *O mundo da violencia: A policia da era Vargas*. Brasilia: Editora Universidade de Brasilia, 1993.

Caulfield, Sueann. "Getting into Trouble: Dishonest Women, Modern Girls, and Women-Men in the Conceptual Language of Vida Policial, 1925–1927." *Signs* 19, no. 1 (1993): 146–76.

———, and Martha de Abreu Esteves. "Fifty Years of Virginity in Rio de Janeiro: Sexual Politics and Gender Roles in Juridical and Popular Discourse, 1890–1940." *Luso-Brazilian Review* 30, no. 1 (1993): 47–74.

Cavieres, Eduardo. "Aislar el cuerpo y sanar el alma: El régimen penitenciario chileno, 1843–1928." *Ibero-Amerikanisches Archiv* 21, nos. 3–4 (1995).

Chandler, Billy. *The Bandit King: Lampiao of Brazil*. College Station: Texas A&M Press, 1978.

Chevigny, Paul. *Edge of the Knife: Police Violence in the Americas*. New York: New Press, 1995.

Cruz Barrera, Nydia. "Los encierros de los ángeles: Las prisiones pobladas en el siglo XIX." In *Espacio y perfiles: Historia regional mexicana del siglo XIX*, edited by Carlos Contreras, 223–42. Puebla: Centro de Investigaciones Históricas y Sociales de la Universidad Autónoma de Puebla, 1989.

Del Olmo, Rosa. *América Latina y su criminología*. Mexico City: Siglo XXI Editores, 1981.

Fausto, Boris. *Crime e Cotidiano: A criminalidade em São Paulo (1880–1924)*. São Paulo: Editora Brasiliense, 1984.

Flores Galindo, Alberto. *Aristocracia y plebe: Lima, 1760–1830*. Lima: Mosca Azul Editores, 1984.

French, William E. "Prostitutes and Guardian Angels: Women, Work, and the Family in Porfirian Mexico." *Hispanic American Historical Review* 72, no. 4 (November 1992): 529–54.

Gagliano, Joseph. *Coca Prohibition in Peru: The Historical Debates.* Tucson: University of Arizona Press, 1994.

Goetschel, Ana María. "El discurso sobre la delincuencia y la constitución del estado ecuatoriano en el siglo XIX (powerboats Garciano y Liberal)." Master's thesis, FLACKS, Quito, 1992.

Graham, Sandra. "Slavery's Impasse: Slave Prostitutes, Small-Time Mistresses, and the Brazilian Law of 1871." *Comparative Studies in Society and History* 33 (October 1991): 669–94.

Gudmundson, Lowell. *Aspectos socioeconómicos del delito en Costa Rica, 1725–1850.* Heredia: Universidad Nacional, 1978.

Guy, Donna J. "Girls in Prison: The Role of the Buenos Aires Casa Correctional de Mujeres as an Institution for Child Rescue, 1890–1940." Paper presented at the Yale University conference on "The Contested Terrains of Law, Justice and Repression in Latin American History," 1997.

———. *Sex and Danger in Buenos Aires: Prostitution, Family, and Nation in Argentina.* Lincoln: University of Nebraska Press, 1991.

Haslip, Gabriel. "Crime and the Administration of Justice in Colonial Mexico City, 1696–1810." Ph.D. diss., Columbia University, 1980.

Holloway, Thomas. *Policing Rio de Janeiro: Repression and Resistance in a 19th-Century City.* Stanford: Stanford University Press, 1993.

Huggins, Martha K. *From Slavery to Vagrancy in Brazil: Crime and Social Control in the Third World.* New Brunswick: Rutgers University Press, 1985.

———, ed. *Vigilantism and the State in Modern Latin America: Essays on Extralegal Violence.* New York: Praeger, 1991.

Hünefeldt, Christine. "Cimarrones, bandoleros, milicianos: 1821." *Histórica* 3, no. 2 (1979): 71–88.

Johnson, Lyman L., ed. *The Problem of Order in Changing Societies: Essays on Crime and Policing in Argentina and Uruguay, 1750–1940.* Albuquerque: University of New Mexico Press, 1990.

Joseph, Gilbert. "On the Trail of Latin American Bandits: A Reexamination of Peasant Resistance." *Latin American Research Review* 26, no. 1 (1990): 7–54.

Kalmanowiecki, Laura. "Military Power and Policing in Argentina." Ph.D. diss., New School for Social Research, 1996.

Lewin, Linda. "The Oligarchical Limitations of Social Banditry in Brazil." *Past and Present* 82 (1979): 116–46.

MacLachlan, Colin. *Criminal Justice in Eighteenth-Century Mexico: A Study of the Tribunal of the Acordada.* Berkeley: University of California Press, 1974.

McCreery, David. " 'This Life of Misery and Shame': Prostitution in Guatemala City, 1880–1920." *Journal of Latin American Studies* 18 (1987): 333–53.

Pearson, Jennifer. "Centro Femenil: A Women's Prison in Mexico." *Social Justice* 20, nos. 3–4 (1993): 85–128.

Penyak, Lee M. "Criminal Sexuality in Central Mexico, 1750–1850." Ph.D. diss., University of Connecticut, 1993.

Pereira Machado, Maria H. *Crime e escravidao: Trabalho, luta e resistencia nas lavouras paulistas, 1830–1888*. São Paulo: Editora Brasiliense, 1987.

Pérez, Louis. *Lords of the Mountain: Social Banditry and Peasant Protest in Cuba, 1878–1918*. Pittsburgh: University of Pittsburgh Press, 1989.

Pérez Guadalupe, José Luis. *Faites y atorrantes: Una etnografía del penal de Lurigancho*. Lima: Centro de Investigaciones Teológicas, 1994.

Piccato, Pablo. "Criminals in Mexico City, 1900–1931: A Cultural History." Ph.D. diss., University of Texas at Austin, 1997.

———. "La experiencia penal en la ciudad de México: Cambios y permanencias tras la revolución." *La experiencia institucional en la ciudad de México, 1821–1929*. Edited by Carlos Illades. Universidad Autónoma Metropolitana-El Colegio de Michoacán, forthcoming.

———. "El Paso de Venus por el disco del Sol: Criminality and Alcoholism in the Late Porfiriato." *Mexican Studies/Estudios Mexicanos* 11, no. 2 (Summer 1995): 203–42.

Picó, Fernando. *El día menos pensado*. Río Piedras: Editorial Huracán, 1994.

Poole, Deborah. "Ciencia, peligrosidad y represión en la criminología indigenista peruana." *Bandoleros, abigeos y montoneros*. Edited by Carlos Aguirre and Charles Walker. Lima: Instituto de Apoyo Agrario, 1990.

Rivera-Garza, Cristina. "The Masters of the Streets: Bodies, Power, and Modernity in Mexico, 1867–1930." Ph.D. diss., University of Houston, 1995.

Rohlfes, Laurence. "Police and Penal Reform in Mexico City, 1876–1911: A Study of Order and Progress in Porfirian Mexico." Ph.D. diss., Tulane University, 1983.

Ruggiero, Kristin. "Honor, Maternity, and the Disciplining of Women: Infanticide in Late Nineteenth-Century Buenos Aires." *Hispanic American Historical Review* 72, no. 3 (August 1992): 353–73.

Ruibal, Beatriz. *Ideología del control social: Buenos Aires, 1880–1920*. Buenos Aires: Centro Editor de América Latina, 1993.

Salazar, Alonso. *Born to Die in Medellín*. London: Latin American Bureau, 1992.

Salessi, Jorge. *Médicos, maleantes y maricas: Higiene, criminologá y homosexualidad en la construcción de la nación argentina (Buenos Aires, 1871–1914)*. Rosario: B. Viterbo Editora, 1995.

Salvatore, Ricardo. "Criminology, Prison Reform, and the Buenos Aires Working Class." *Journal of Interdisciplinary History* 23, no. 2 (1992): 279–99.

———. "Penitentiaries, Visions of Class, and Export Economies: Brazil and Argentina Compared." *The Birth of the Penitentiary in Latin*

America, edited by Ricardo Salvatore and Carlos Aguirre. Austin: University of Texas Press, 1996.

————, and Carlos Aguirre, eds. *The Birth of the Penitentiary in Latin America: Essays on Criminology, Prison Reform, and Social Control, 1830–1940*. Austin: University of Texas Press, 1996.

Sánchez León, Abelardo, and Marco Del Mastro. *En el juego de la vida: Ser delincuente en Lima*. Lima: Desco, 1993.

Scardaville, Michael. "Crime and the Urban Poor: Mexico City in the Late Colonial Period." Ph.D. diss., University of Florida, 1977.

Schwartz, Rosalie. *Lawless Liberators: Political Banditry and Cuban Independence*. Durham: Duke University Press, 1989.

Silvestrini, Blanca. *Violencia y criminalidad en Puerto Rico, 1898–1973: Apuntes para un estudio de historia social*. Río Piedras: Editorial Universitaria, 1980.

Singelman, Peter. "Political Structure and Social Banditry in Northeastern Brazil." *Journal of Latin American Studies* 7, no. 1 (1975): 59–83.

Slatta, Richard W. "Rural Criminality and Social Control in Nineteenth-Century Buenos Aires Province." *Hispanic American Historical Review* 60, no. 3 (1980): 450–72.

————, ed. *Bandidos: The Varieties of Latin American Banditry*. New York: Greenwood Press, 1987.

————, and Karla Robinson. "Continuities in Crime and Punishment: Buenos Aires, 1820–1850." *The Problem of Order in Changing Societies*, edited by Lyman L. Johnson, 19–46. Albuquerque: University of New Mexico Press, 1990.

Stavig, Ward. *Amor y violencia sexual: Valores indígenas en la sociedad colonial*. Lima: Instituto de Estudios Peruanos, 1995.

————. "The Indian Peoples of Rural Cusco in the Era of Thupa Amaro." Ph.D. diss., University of California, Davis, 1991.

————. "Ladrones, cuatreros y salteadores: Indios criminales en el Cusco rural a fines de la colonia." *Bandoleros, abigeos y montoneros*, edited by Carlos Aguirre and Charles Walker, 69–104. Lima: Instituto de Apoyo Agrario, 1990.

————. "Violencia cotidiana de los naturales de Quispicanchis y Canas y Canchis en el siglo XVIII." *Revista Andina* 3, no. 2 (1986): 451–68.

Stern, Steve. *The Secret History of Gender: Women, Men, and Power in Late Colonial Mexico*. Chapel Hill: University of North Carolina Press, 1995.

Szuchman, Mark. "Disorder and Social Control in Buenos Aires, 1810–1860." *Journal of Interdisciplinary History* 15, no. 1 (1984): 83–110.

Tarazona-Sevillano, Gabriela. *Sendero Luminoso and the Threat of Narco-Terrorism*. New York: Praeger, 1990.

Taylor, Lewis. *Bandits and Politics in Peru: Landlord and Peasant Violence in Hualgayoc, 1900–1930*. Cambridge: Centre for Latin American Studies, 1986.

Taylor, William. "Bandit Gangs in Late Colonial Times: Rural Jalisco, Mexico, 1794–1821." *Bibliotheca Americana* 1, no. 2 (November 1982): 29–58.

———. *Drinking, Homicide, and Rebellion in Colonial Mexican Villages.* Stanford: Stanford University Press, 1979.

Vanderwood, Paul. *Disorder and Progress: Bandits, Police, and Mexican Development.* 2d ed. Wilmington, DE: Scholarly Resources, 1992.

Walker, Charles. "Montoneros, bandoleros, malhechores: Criminalidad y política en las primeras décadas republicanas." *Bandoleros, abigeos y montoneros,* edited by Carlos Aguirre and Charles Walker, 105–36. Lima: Instituto de Apoyo Agrario, 1990.

Walker, William, ed. *Drugs in the Western Hemisphere: An Odyssey of Cultures in Conflict.* Wilmington, DE: Scholarly Resources, 1996.

Zárate, María Soledad. "Vicious Women, Virtuous Women: The Female Delinquent and the Santiago de Chile Correctional House, 1860–1900." *The Birth of the Penitentiary in Latin America,* edited by Ricardo Salvatore and Carlos Aguirre, 78–100. Austin: University of Texas Press, 1996.

Selected Filmography

Films on the history of crime and criminality in Latin America for English-speaking audiences—in English, dubbed, or subtitled—are few but, for some fairly selective topics at least, extraordinarily rich. Of special note is a trio of great films on juvenile criminality. Spanish surrealist director Luis Buñuel, exiled to Mexico by the Fascist regime of Francisco Franco, won the 1951 Cannes Film Festival Award for best picture for *Los Olvidados* (usually and unfortunately translated as The Young and the Damned), his devastating portrayal of street children in mid-twentieth-century Mexico City. In *Los Olvidados*, Buñuel explores the corrosive and criminalizing effects of modernization on Mexican family life. Noteworthy are his vivid urban landscapes and telling juxtaposition of bad parents and benevolent state: an abusive, amoral mother and a sympathetic Lázaro Cárdenas lookalike in the guise of a trusting reformatory director. Brazilian director Hector Babenco's *Pixote* (1981) with its relentless urban squalor—São Paulo in this case—and grim prison scenes is every bit as devastating as *Los Olvidados*. To reinforce *Pixote*'s naturalistic tone, Babenco uses real street children in several roles. His lead, Fernando Ramos da Silva, ultimately returned to the streets and a "life of crime" before his 1987 death at the hands of Brazilian police. The subtitle of Victor Gavira's depiction of juvenile criminals in Medellín, *Rodrigo D: No Futuro* (1988), could serve for all three films. His interview with Alma Guillermoprieto (see Chapter 10) conveys his deep sense of despair at the ongoing alienation, criminalization, and destruction of Latin America's children. Also noteworthy are Clemente de la Cerda's *I Am a Delinquent* (1976), based on the autobiographical account of a Venezuelan youth's descent into a "culture of criminality," and Sandra Wernek's documentary on the murder of Brazilian street children, "A guerra dos meninos" (Children's War, 1991).

Two excellent films by Argentine directors dealing at least tangentially with criminality during the Rosas period (see Chapter 4) are María Luisa Bemberg's *Camila* (1984) and Hector Olivera's *El Muerto* (Dead Man, 1975). In *Camila*—a true story of forbidden love between an upper-class socialite and a Jesuit priest executed for "crimes" against the fatherland—Bemberg explores the repressive paternalism of state, church, and father in Argentina's age of caudillos. Olivera's *El Muerto*, based on a short story by Jorge Luis Borges, tells the tale of a young man who is forced to flee to the Uruguayan countryside after killing a rival in a knife fight in Buenos Aires. The "hero" joins a gang of smugglers, attempts to usurp his *patrón*, and is ruthlessly executed. Although neither film relates directly to the issues raised in Salvatore's essay (*El Muerto*, however, does illustrate the stereotypical view of the violent countryside that Salvatore rejects), both underscore the socially constructed nature of criminality in the newly emerging Latin American nations.

The theme of rural violence also appears in two important films from Brazilian Cinema Novo director Glauber Rocha: *Black God, White Devil* (1964) and *Antonio das Mortes* (1968). Graphically realistic and politicizing Cinema Novo style, both films take as their backdrop Brazil's impoverished *sertão* (backlands). The first portrays the criminalization of a poor peasant from preacher to bandit; the second, the adventures of a bounty hunter of bandits. True to their Marxist roots, both films portray crime as the natural by-product of the dehumanizing effects of rural poverty, social inequality, and political repression.

The link between social conditions and criminality is a recurring theme in Latin American cinema. Of special interest are Chilean director Miguel Littin's *The Jackal of Nahueltoro* (1969), which explores the underlying social causes of a famous 1963 murder; *Alias, La Gringa* (1991), a Peruvian film that uses the escapades of the picaresque "La Gringa" as a window into politics; and *Secuestro* (The Kidnapping, 1993), Colombian director Camila Motta's wrenching portrayal of the "business" of kidnapping and its human costs.

State-sponsored violence, the theme of Laura Kalmanowiecki's essay, has also inspired some great films. Two of the most important— Hector Olivera's *La Noche de los Lápices* (Night of the Pencils) and Hector Babenco's *Lúcio Flávio*—are not yet available in English. However, excellent choices remain. Greek director Constantine Costa-Gavras's *Missing* (1982), the true story of an American father searching for his missing son, exposes the complicity of the U.S. government in the overthrow of Chile's elected Marxist president Salvador Allende and the systematic brutality of Augusto Pinochet's bureaucratic authoritarian regime. *La Historia Oficial* (The Official Story) by Argentine director Luis Puenzo won the 1985 Academy Award for best foreign film for its heartrending story of a mother who discovers that her adopted daughter is the child of a *desaparecida* (a young woman "disappeared" by Argentina's ruling military junta in the 1970s) and her husband is a torturer. Another Academy Award winner (best actor for William Hurt), Hector Babenco's *Kiss of the Spiderwoman* (1985), explores the complex nature of socially constructed deviance in a prison saga of two men: effeminate window dresser Molina and macho revolutionary Valentín. Polish director Roman Polanski's film version of Chilean playwright Ariel Dorfman's *Death and the Maiden* (1994) explores the psychological consequences of persecution and torture generated by the criminalization of political deviance.

For better or worse, Latin American cinema's sleazy crime dramas are not usually exported for English-speaking audiences. There are, however, some entertaining films that toy with the ragged edges of B-movie sleaze. Brazilian director Bruno Barreto's *El Amor Bandido* (Bandit Love, 1979) examines the amoral lives of a young Rio stripper and her boyfriend, a serial killer of taxi drivers, as they are pursued by the girl's none-too-moral policeman father. In a more cheerful vein is Mexican-American director Robert Rodríguez's surprise debut film *El Mariachi* (1992), in which Rodríguez, who shot the film for seven thousand dollars in fourteen days, brilliantly captures the lawless aspects of life—drug smuggling and corrupt police—on the U.S.-Mexico border. Last but not least, Chilean director Gustavo Graef Marino's *Johnny Cien Pesos* (1993) provides a tragicomic interpretation of the newly democratic Chilean state's efforts to deal with ordinary crime—armed robbery, in this case—in the hothouse environment produced by a sensationalist media and paranoid criminals. The links between criminality and gender inequalities are given a sensational twist in Solvieg Hoogeseijn's *Macu: The Policeman's Wife* (1987), the film representation of a real-life sensational murder of a child-bride by her policeman husband in contemporary Venezuela.

The generally forgettable stream of North American action adventures centered on the drug-trafficking activities of pony-tailed Colombians clearly demonstrates the negative stereotyping of Latin Americans and is too numerous to list here. A personal favorite is still Brian de Palma's *Scarface* (1983) with Al Pacino as a hustling *marielito* and screenplay by Oliver Stone. For a more serious view see the PBS 1995 documentary on Pablo Escobar, "The Godfather of Cocaine."

This list is of course incomplete. Those interested in other films in English, Spanish, and Portuguese should consult Ronald Schwartz, *Latin American Films, 1932–1994* (Jefferson, NC: McFarland and Company, 1997), and Julianne Burton, *The New Latin American Cinema: An Annotated Bibliography of Sources in English, Spanish and Portuguese* (New York: Smyrna Press, 1983). Both works include detailed plot synopses. For analyses of Latin American films see E. Bradford Burns, *Latin American Cinema: Film and History* (Los Angeles: UCLA Latin American Center, University of California Press, 1975); John King, *Magical Reels: A History of Cinema in Latin America* (London: Verso, 1990); John King et al., eds., *Mediating Two Worlds: Cinematic Encounters in the Americas* (London: British Film Institute, 1993); and Zuzana M. Pick, *The New*

Latin American Cinema: A Continental Project (Austin: University of Texas Press, 1993). A good up-to-date filmography is *A Guide to Latin American, Caribbean, and U.S. Latino-Made Film and Video* (Lanham, MD: Scarecrow Press, 1997).